THE MILITARY ATTACHÉ

THE
MILITARY
ATTACHÉ

ALFRED VAGTS

PRINCETON, NEW JERSEY

PRINCETON UNIVERSITY PRESS

1967

CONTENTS

v

CONTENTS

THE MILITARY ATTACHÉ

INTRODUCTION

Writing about service attachés—their history and, at least by implication, their sociology—must almost inevitably result in historical injustice. For it is largely by their indiscretions that they are known to the world. Not their achievements but their failures are celebrated, whatever form the celebration may take: documentary publications, memoirs, news items emanating from the police, courts of justice, or other sources— "revelations" and "exposures" which focus a pitiless glare of publicity on a group most eager to shun it.

For as long as service attachés have existed as a recognized category—less than 150 years—they have been under standing or specific orders to observe, judge, and report on foreign military events and economy, organizations, developments, personalities and materiel, perhaps military thought as well. Operating against odds, only too often in periods of tension, they must exercise discretion in all their procedures: they must refrain from spying or other conspiratorial activities, and contacts likely to disturb regular, "harmonious," peace-conducive diplomatic relations between states. Only the utmost discretion can make tolerable and congruous the presence of military men in embassies which were intended to house men devoted to the maintenance of peace. If the attachés disregard such orders in their zeal to ferret out the maximum information about the host land's forces and equipment, and are too often obsessed by a sort of "materielism" (weapons, fortifications, etc.) to the neglect of such factors as morale, economy, and other war potentials, they may betray themselves. If their activities are discovered, or even suspected, they will be sent home, there to be silenced by the diplomatic wing of the double authority under which the service attaché seems to act, orders to the contrary notwithstanding.

Hence they are better known by their irregularities than

* A selected bibliography of books and documents, for which short references are used in the notes, appears at the end of the book.

their regularities—only one considerable file of attaché reports has ever been examined by a historian as far as is publicly known[1]—while the sheer statistical fact remains that the scandalous termination of their tours of duty *is* the exception. The *regular* service attaché has had less publicity, has made considerably less history than the agent who attracts the unpleased attention of his superiors and contemporaries, or of historians.

Another *caveat* without which this book should not be read or evaluated: owing to the available documentation, the activities and inclinations of the Prusso-German armed forces attachés are better known than are those of other powers. One might well conclude that they—together with their Tsarist counterparts, about whom there is much less documentation—were the most militaristic, the most antagonistic to the civilian supremacy which is taken for granted in most other countries. Many, if not the majority, of the German attachés came from the Great General Staff or the Admiralty Staff, and they carried into the Reich's outposts the fight that went on in Berlin, around the Emperor, against the Foreign Office and civilian supremacy.

Service attachés have nearly always been chosen on the basis of superior qualifications, and only occasionally for extraneous reasons (to reward a political favorite, or to exile an officer who had become too "awkward" to keep at home). Consequently they form an elite, one to be measured in permillages rather than percentages: in 1948, each of the three branches of the U.S. armed forces had stationed abroad about three such attachés for every 1000 commissioned officers of their authorized strength. Merely in statistical terms, that amounts to a high degree of selectivity indeed. Their exceptional character is further enhanced by the position they have held and, perhaps to a lesser degree now, still hold in that important but ambiguous zone between diplomacy and defense.

To what use have these picked officers been put? Appointed

---

[1] This has been done by Georges Castellan in *Le réarmement clandestin du Reich, 1930-1935*, which is based on the archives of the Second Bureau of the French General Staff, including the attaché reports from Berlin and some other capitals for these years; they are very numerous, reaching an average of three to four per diem.

to see and report on everything of military relevance, they have not escaped the trend toward specialization:[2] obviously in the last 150 years they have had to shift their attention from the cavalry to nuclear weapons and long-range missiles. From a larger point of view, the attachés were originally intended for a versatility that might prepare them for posts such as commander or chief of staff, qualified by intimate knowledge of at least one foreign country, its forces and its leaders, but relatively few of them have actually been raised to such positions. Instead, attachés returning from foreign capitals have been shunted into intelligence and liaison work—an indication of the increasing value attached to the peacetime knowledge of home forces, tactics, weapons, and the techniques of command as compared with the high wartime importance which Clausewitz ascribed to "intelligence about the enemy."

Another outcome of specialization became a definite weakness in the attachés: the service egotism which determined their judgment and which might become utterly misleading to those entrusted with national defense. Not only were they nearly always more warlike in their outlook than the ambassadors,[3] they were also inclined to see war and peace, national strength and weakness, in terms of "service patriotism": unless the attaché's army or navy received a larger budget, his country would be in danger of attack by a determined enemy. During the British discussions of 1907-1908 about the danger of a German landing, much feared by Sir John French and other generals and writers agitating in favor of larger territorial forces, the British military attachés on the continent shared this fear, for which they had to furnish

---

[2] Though a ready writer of reports, and later of memoirs, the service attaché, considering his opportunities, has made relatively small contributions to technical military literature. Among the exceptions might be mentioned Friedrich von Bernhardi, not so much for his *Germany and the Next War* (London, New York and Toronto 1914), translated from *Deutschland und der nächste Krieg* (Berlin 1912), but for works such as *Vom heutigen Kriege* (Berlin 1910).

[3] During the Bosnian crisis of 1908-1909, the alarms of Isvolski, the Russian foreign minister, were traceable to the reports made by the Russian military attaché in Vienna, who was so pessimistic regarding the preservation of peace that the British ambassador in Vienna had to try repeatedly to calm him. *British Documents on the Origins of the War*, V, 771.

reasons in their reports. The naval attachés were less alarmist, in keeping with the British Navy's confidence that such a threat could be met if the Navy's strength were kept up. The German military attaché in London, agreeing with his ambassador, thought the threat of an Anglo-German armed conflict remote, while the naval attachés depicted it as imminent,[4] in accordance with Tirpitz' determination to keep the naval arms race hot. To meet this danger of overspecialization, the Wehrmacht in the mid-1930's introduced the *Wehrmacht-attaché*, appointing the most suitable of the three attachés in a foreign capital, not only to report on military strength but also to judge his own country's all-round interest in the host land's war potential. The specialist might not have seen the . forest for the trees.

If only for the purpose of best using the attachés' services, it was and is imperative to keep them out of politics, though interest and the intimate observation of diplomatic intercourse often makes such activity tempting. Not all the home authorities have succeeded in this necessary endeavor, or have even aspired to do so; sometimes they have preferred, like Waldersee or Tirpitz, to pit the attachés against the civilian authorities. The historical record can but demonstrate that such "politicking" has proved one of the worst corrupters of military men, lowering their professional judgment and their highest usefulness to the military establishment of a nation or to its general political direction. The country's directors—normally civilian—are aware of the attaché's striving "to make themselves independent of any political control"—as was so often attempted in the German Second Reich—but they must bear in mind that, as an exponent of civilian supremacy emphasized, "the observations of these military attachés are of immediate significance for the direction of political as well as military affairs."[5] Thus Holstein, essentially the director of German diplomacy between 1890 and 1906 and the person most acutely aware of the need for unification of civilian and military diplomacy in the Reich of William II, justified the work of the attachés. Only unification, he felt, and the result-

4 George W. F. Hallgarten, *Imperialismus vor 1914*, 2 vols. (Munich 1951), II, 59.
5 Rich and Fisher, I, 31.

ing use of military observation and military reports by the political directors, can result in overcoming either departmentalism or the over- or undervaluation of military considerations.

Even this will not guarantee the highest usefulness of attaché reports—they may not be appreciated, believed, or even read by the home authorities. Hitler extended his contempt for the professional diplomats, that "defeatists' club," to the service attachés (unless they happened to be Party-tested). He paid little attention to their reports on the obvious shortcomings of the Italian Army, believing instead that Fascism was giving it a new strength and overcoming weaknesses in materiel; he gave practically no heed to the warnings of the attaché stationed in Moscow, General Köstring, about the war industrial strength of the Soviet Republic or the stability of its political system.[6] And when at last the warnings of the attachés made it clear in Berlin that German rearmament before 1939 was making more and more enemies, Blomberg, the Reich war minister, shrugged it off: "Then it is just 'many enemies, much honor.' "[7]

"Unwelcome" reports will always be considered unbelievable by the home offices. When the Japanese military attaché in Berlin reported on June 16, 1941, that still more war was imminent, though the exact date remained uncertain, he was not believed in Tokyo.[8] On the other hand, "welcome" reports, confirming preconceived notions of the home offices, war ministries, general staffs, and foreign offices, will be least discounted. When a naval attaché in Copenhagen in 1913 reported the conclusion (which never took place) of a German-Swedish naval convention, it was readily believed at the Quai d'Orsay. "The news has nothing in it which surprises," noted Paléologue, the political director, who always relied strongly on attaché reports and believed that Sweden had

[6] Heinz Guderian, *Panzer Leader*, transl. Constantine Fitzgibbon (New York 1952), p. 151.

[7] Moriz Faber du Faur, *Macht und Ohnmacht. Erinnerungen eines alten Offiziers* (Stuttgart 1953), pp. 195ff.; Geyr, *The Critical Years*, generally.

[8] William L. Langer and S. Everett Gleason, *The Undeclared War, 1940-1941* (New York 1953), p. 626.

slipped entirely into the Pan-German orbit.[9] When the State Department had written off Formosa in 1949 and its fall to Communism seemed imminent, Admiral Charles Maynard Cooke (who later testified in favor of a "high level civilian advisory group on intelligence to evaluate information on which U.S. policy is to be based," something like the CIA) learned that one of the assistant military attachés in the Far East, Captain J. R. Manning, had wished to report facts which did not fit in with what was apparently desired by the State Department representatives on the spot. He therefore made direct reports to the War Department, "whereupon he was summarily detached from his duty as assistant military attaché" and transferred.[10]

General staffs as recipients of intelligence can at times present as closed a mind as any diplomatic office. The German Army General Staff between 1933 and 1939 paid relatively little attention to the reports of its attachés, who seemed to be stationed in foreign capitals for the purpose of defending German military prestige abroad rather than to gather information. Instead the General Staff relied largely on the intelligence reports of the *Abwehr* under Admiral Canaris' direction, with the result that it "groped in the dark and believed that it could not beat France but Russia instead."[11] Responsibility was at least equally divided between General Staff and service attachés when North Africa as the landing shore for American forces remained unexplored until 1940 at the earliest. Washington "had not rated Africa high on its list of vital interests, and our military and naval attachés had given it only casual attention." In an attempt to make up for this neglect a U.S. naval attaché was then stationed at Tangier, who though a mere "retread," proved very efficient in providing the latest information.[12] Without proper, unified arrangement for the gathering and evaluation of *all relevant* information the best attaché reporting must remain without value.

[9] Georges Maurice Paléologue, *Au Quai d'Orsay, à la veille de la tourmente: journal de 1913-1914* (Paris 1947), pp. 21, 104.

[10] *The New York Times*, November 12, 1960.

[11] Faber du Faur, pp. 190ff.

[12] Robert Murphy, *Diplomat among Warriors* (New York 1964), pp. 70, 92.

I. HISTORICAL OUTLINE

CHAPTER 1

FORERUNNERS AND BEGINNINGS

Observation of the armed forces of a foreign country, their readiness or unreadiness for war, and the country's war power in general, has usually, and certainly originally, been among the foremost tasks of ambassadors and other diplomats. It is this sector of their business that earned them the epithet "spies," "honorable spies" as they were called by Commynes and Sir Henry Wotton, both of whom spoke from personal experience.[1] "Embassadors are nothing but Publick Spies," wrote the Spaniard Diego de Saavedra Fajardo in his *Idea de un principe politico Christiano* (1640), "and without prejudice to the Law of God, or that of Nations, may endeavor, by bribes and presents, to corrupt the fidelity of ministers . . . and to sift out what ill contrivances are in agitation against their Prince."[2]

Under simple conditions the ambassador was able, actually or presumably, to do the necessary spying himself, but when military and naval developments came to demand greater expertise, governments either sent out military men as ambassadors or provided the civilian ambassador with expert assistance, the "spy of the spy," so to speak, the military, naval or air attaché. Only the nomenclature dates from the nineteenth century, the functions, many of them, are much older. "He, like a privileged spy, whom nothing can discredit" (Donne), may be detected in writings of late antiquity when soldiers became for the first time literary, or when it was first believed that war could be learned, in part at least, from books. Frontinus (A.D. 40-103) includes the spy's services among the *Stratagems* of his collection, which was designed for

<hr />

[1] Logan Pearsall Smith, *The Life and Letters of Sir Henry Wotton*, 2 vols. (Oxford 1907), I, 110.

[2] From English translation of *The Royal Politician* (London 1700), II, 222f.

the instruction of the Roman officer. He relates how Caius Lelius, sent by Scipio into the camp of Syphax under the pretense of an embassy, took along several army officers to do some expert spying, disguised as his domestics; when one of them was on the verge of being detected, the ambassador coolly caned him, to make everyone believe that he was only a slave.[3]

Medieval and even later warfare was on the whole too uncomplicated, too devoid of military division of labor and planning to necessitate special reconnaissance missions, though one of the monkish writers of the Fulda Annals suspected that the ambassadors sent by the Hungarians to King Arnulf in 900 were actually spies who were to reconnoiter the roads into the Reich.[4] Machiavelli in his *Arte della guerra* (Book 6) writes of "ambassadors, accompanied by expert officers disguised as valets, using the occasion to view the enemy's army and to examine its strong and feeble parts," but this is perhaps more likely to have been gathered from ancient literature than from contemporary experience. Actually, the inclusion of the expert military observer in diplomatic missions remained a rare thing for nearly two centuries after Machiavelli.

Such an observer reappeared in the wars of coalition—wars conducted by allies—in the seventeenth and eighteenth centuries, as liaison officer with allied armies. His duty was to concert the armies' movements in more detail than the ambassadors might have arranged, to give advice to the allied general, to report on the use made of money subsidies by the recipient, or to represent the ambassador who might not be able to leave the capital.

Progress in the conduct of wars of coalition since Bouvines (1214) had not been impressive, and the subsidies—"moneys paid to one potentate by another for the purpose of entertaining the war," to use an early eighteenth-century definition[5] —were not always used in a rational manner. The providers

---

[3] *Strategematicon*, Book I, ch. 1.

[4] "Missos illorum sub dolo ad Bavarias pacem optando, regionem illam ad explorandum transmiserunt," *Annales Fuldenses*, A.D. 900.

[5] Johannes Hübner, *Reales Staats-, Zeitungs- und Conversations-Lexicon*, 4th ed. (Leipzig 1709), p. 1579.

4

of subsidies, Richelieu for one, did not suffer gladly the uncontrolled and wasteful spending of the money which
France's northern ally Sweden received over many years.
Richelieu, whom many credit with the introduction of the
permanent legation as a means of uninterrupted observation
and diplomatic competition, had a military emissary in the
camp of the Swedish marshal Gustav Horn during part of the
Thirty Years' War, and under his successor a French lieutenant
general was detached to follow the warlike Charles X Gus-
tavus in his campaigns in Prussia, Pomerania, Poland and
other Baltic provinces. When this diplomatic camp follower
died, his mission was taken over by the Chevalier J. Terlon,
who participated in the spectacular march across the frozen
Belts early in 1658, and who contributed a good account of it
to military historiography.[6]

While the War of the Spanish Succession proved fairly successful as a war conducted by allies, thanks to the close and
sincere cooperation of Marlborough and Prince Eugene, the
later wars of coalition of the eighteenth century, particularly
the Seven Years' War, often showed the armies' inability to
work together; they lagged behind the diplomacy of their
sovereigns, who added military missions to the diplomatic ones
in each other's capitals. In order to obtain a modicum of unity
in warfare, "to follow the operations of the allied army
and, in case of need, to aid it with their counsel," France sent
several officers to the Russian and Swedish armies, either taken
from the retinue of the ambassador or dispatched from Paris
expressly for the purpose. Austria also had an emissary with the
army of Apraxin; together with his French colleague, he
complained bitterly about the Russian general's unwarranted
retreat eastward after the successful battle of Gross-Jägerndorf
(1757).[7] While these men seem to have preserved diplomatic
decorum in their complaints, this was not the case with the
French emissary in the Swedish camp in Pomerania in 1761-
1762; according to Danish reports he was "a man of *esprit*,
and one says that he enjoys a high reputation in the military

[6] Beauvais, p. 7; Vagts, *Landing Operations*, pp. 58-59.
[7] *Recueil des instructions données aux ambassadeurs de France*, IX
(Russie II), 61, 101, 103.

field; he seems to be in need of that in order that people may forgive him his altogether too great facility of talking and, above all, his talking about himself."[8]

The most outstanding and satisfactory of these military liaison agents during the Seven Years' War was Brigadier General Marc-René Marquis de Montalembert (1714-1800), a military writer of considerable originality and distinction. He was first sent, in October 1756, to the Swedish army, which was operating not very successfully in Pomerania at the time, with orders "of employing himself particularly with the ways and means whereby the union of our forces with those of Sweden could be rendered more useful as well as more glorious to the two nations."[9] He served for two campaigns with the Swedes and for three more with the Russians, who were equally in need of recent information on progress in the field of fortification, which he represented.

When Montalembert departed for St. Petersburg, he received two sets of instructions, one from the Duc de Choiseul, foreign minister, and one from the Duc de Belle-Isle, secretary of war, a reminder of his double allegiance. Belle-Isle almost went out of his way to stress subordination to the ambassador, "who will present him to the Empress in order to inform her of the purpose of his mission; and he will take from him his instructions about the conduct to observe while serving with the army from the moment said ambassador will judge it appropriate to send him there." Whatever independence later ministries of war or general staffs might have claimed for *their* attachés, the original subordination to the embassy chief could not have been more fully conceded.[10]

The instructions which Montalembert received from the foreign ministry emphasized "the interest which the King takes in the success of Her Majesty the Empress and which makes him wish to have a general officer with the army of that Princess which is to act in Pomerania, in order to be witness of its operations, to make himself useful to it as far as that de-

---

[8] Aage Friis, ed., *Bernstorffske Papirer* (Copenhagen 1904) I, 455.

[9] *Recueil*, IX, 104.

[10] Fleury de Saint-Charles, "Un attaché militaire français à l'armée russe (1759): Le Marquis de Montalembert," *Revue d'histoire diplomatique* (1903), pp. 265ff.

pends on him and render account of the happy events which one can promise oneself from its activity. . . ." Provided with letters of introduction from the ambassador to the Russian commander Fermor, whose confidence he is to seek, "he will inform himself regularly about the strength of the Russian army, about what he can learn relative to plans of that general, his operations, the movements of the Prussian army opposed to him and generally about all that might occur relative to the military subject." Montalembert was provided with a cipher to enable him to correspond with the secretary of war as well as with the French representatives with the Swedish and Austrian armies, and his arrangements with the latter enabled him to overcome some, at least, of the conflicts which divided Frederick's enemies: his services to the much-hampered coalition were considerable. He lasted three campaigns with Fermor, whom he persuaded in 1760, when Berlin lay open to him, not to turn back but boldly to march on and occupy the Prussian capital—if only for a few days, and with other Russian army commanders. He did not return to France until 1761.[11] He kept his, often low, opinion of the Allies to himself until sixteen years later, when he published his correspondence for the years 1757-1761.[12] The book provoked scandal and smirking among the neutrals; they read that the Marquis had considered himself "as preceptor on the part of the French given to the armies of Sweden and Russia. He seems very authentic. . . . Several Swedes will be furious about it. They could not have been better depicted and characterized." That was the opinion of the Danish ambassador at Paris, who had been assured by a Danish general that "the portraits are of a striking verity and resemblance."[13]

Missions such as Montalembert's give definite indications of a certain amount of independence on the part of military agents abroad; indeed in his particular case, it could hardly have been otherwise. But the strict directive as to his sub-

[11] *Recueil*, IX, 105ff.

[12] *Correspondance de M. le marquis de Montalembert étant employé par le Roi de France à l'armée suédoise . . . pendant les campagnes de 1757, 1758, 1759, 1760 et 1761*, 3 vols. (London 1777).

[13] Friis, III, 533.

ordination to the ambassadors in Stockholm and St. Petersburg, who represented the French foreign office, left no doubt of the respective positions of the ministries of foreign affairs and of war. The two had long fought for the lion's share in the conduct of foreign affairs, including diplomatic reporting, which presumably covered worthwhile military information, but the foreign ministry had now reached a position that allowed it to speak of the "primacy of foreign policy." This had certainly not been the case during the reign of Louis XIV, when constant conflict arose over the tendency of Louvois, the secretary of state for war, to maintain independent agents abroad who reported not only on military but also on political affairs; Torcy, the foreign secretary, often insisted that the severe setbacks suffered by France in the later years of the Ludovican reign were mainly due to the low esteem which his own ministry had enjoyed throughout that reign as compared with the Ministry of War or even the Superintendent of Buildings.[14]

By the end of the *ancien régime* the supremacy of the foreign ministry and with it that of the ambassador seemed definitely established. Sometimes his personnel included officers or former officers especially well informed and able to observe and judge on military affairs—among such men were the later "Citizen" Genêt, who had been an officer of Dragoons and was something like a military attaché in St. Petersburg (1779),[15] and Count Axel Fersen, the Swedish friend of Marie Antoinette and engineer of the flight of the royal family to Varennes. Talented assistants did not in the least impair the standing of the ambassador, however, whose position was rather similar to that of the master manufacturer, the *Fabrikherr*, in early industrial organization. To the outside world

[14] Camille Georges Picavet, *La diplomatie française au temps de Louis XIV* (Paris 1930), pp. 187, 42ff.; Gaëtan de Flassan, *Histoire générale et raisonnée de la diplomatie française, depuis la fondation de la monarchie jusqu'à la fin du règne de Louis XVI*, 2nd ed., 7 vols. (Paris 1811), IV, 404.

[15] *Recueil*, IX, 479. Genêt's first predecessor in America took along a sort of military attaché who would enable him to judge and discuss plans and operations of the War of Independence. Henri Doniol, *Histoire de la participation de la France à l'établissement des Etats-Unis*, 5 vols. (Paris 1886-1892), III, 189.

the ambassador represented the enterprise and was responsible for it, whatever may have been the inside arrangements for a division of labor.

The Revolutionary and Napoleonic eras set back the predominance of the "civils" in France, and to a certain extent elsewhere as well—although Talleyrand did obtain from the Directory a decree excluding soldiers from serving as ambassadors unless they were provided with a diplomatic character. Napoleon, besides using generals as ambassadors in the interest of his continual war schemes, made spying the exclusive occupation for part of the personnel of some French legations. In 1806 a captain was appointed Second Secretary of the Vienna Embassy with the special order that "he keep strict account of the strength of the Austrian regiments and their location." This information, gathered, organized and kept up-to-date by a card-index system, was to be reported every month to the General Staff of the *Grande Armée* and to the foreign ministry; to this task the captain-secretary was to dedicate himself completely "so that no battalion was to be moved without his knowing about it."[16] In all but name this captain was one of the first true modern military attachés: his paramount duty was *constant* systematic observation of the potential enemy, and in the mounting military competition of the nineteenth century such an attaché became an indispensable instrument. Tasks other than statements of strength were entrusted to still another officer-secretary of the Vienna embassy when, on Napoleon's orders, he was sent early in 1807 to Widdin on the lower Danube to gather information about military movements in the Balkans.[17] And, in anticipation of the war with Prussia in 1806, the Emperor attached some of his best younger officers to the Berlin embassy to report on the movements and the assembly of the Prussian Army;[18] it may well have been in reaction to their presence that the hotblooded Prussian guards sharpened their swords on the doorsills of the French embassy building.

[16] Beauvais, p. 10; Napoleon to Berthier, March 3, 1806. *Correspondance de Napoleon Ier*, 32 vols. (Paris 1858-1870), no. 9919.
[17] Auguste Boppe, *La mission de l'adjutant-commandant Mériage à Widdin* (Paris 1886); Pierre Bertrand, *Lettres inédites de Talleyrand à Napoleon* (Paris 1889), p. 350.
[18] Beauvais, p. 11.

9

Napoleon was not the only general, perhaps not even the first, to think of making army officers members of an embassy and of the intelligence service at the same time. Massenbach, the chief of staff of the loser at Jena, had proposed as early as 1795 and 1800 that Prussia "ought to attach to our legations in Petersburg, Vienna, Paris, London, etc., officers who are destined to the higher command in the army and who during their stay at these courts may make it their business to study the characters of those who might be put in the future at the head of hostile or allied armies. Only in this way shall we prepare in an appropriate fashion for war."[19] Archduke Charles, Napoleon's most formidable enemy among the Austrian generals, seems to have thought of joining officers to the Austrian legations, but the civilian authorities were not receptive to the idea. In fact Cobenzl, State Chancellor and foreign minister, was rather shocked to learn in 1804 that the War Department maintained secret agents in Milan and London who were in communication with Dumouriez, a man currently employed by the British to devise measures against French landing projects.[20] The Vienna bureaucracy was still anxious to reserve civilian supremacy in all matters of foreign relations. And when Schwarzenberg was appointed ambassador to Paris in 1809 and received a military aide as member of the embassy staff, the *Staatskanzlei* obtained the ruling from the Emperor that "all the military employed in the diplomacy would no longer draw salary from the army pay office, but would henceforth receive their pay from the *Geheime Hof- und Staatskanzlei*," like the rest of the diplomats.[21] Thus, at least to the extent that the purse exercises control, the officer on diplomatic duty was brought under civilian rule.

This control was further stressed in the Austrian "Instruction for an Officer of the General Quartermaster Staff Attached to a Legation Abroad" of 1810. Drafted by Radetzky, later Field Marshal, this paper laid down the principle that such a mission had two supreme purposes: to obtain for

[19] Vagts, *Militarism*, p. 179; Gerhard Ritter, *Staatskunst und Kriegshandwerk: Das Problem des "Militarismus" in Deutschland*, 3 vols. (Munich, 1954-), I, 210f.
[20] August Fournier, *Gentz und Cobenzl* (Vienna 1880), p. 122.
[21] Beauvais, p. 12.

the State correct and detailed military information about the country of residence and to educate the officer in question so that he would become useful in future dealings with such a foreign State. The officer was to give the ambassador the strictest account of all the subjects mentioned below, whether civilian or military. Above all, in order that the Imperial service should be best promoted, he was to be completely guided in his political behavior at the foreign court by views with which the ambassador would provide him. The observations of such a general staff officer were to cover essentially the following subjects:

(1) Exact and detailed knowledge of the forces of the foreign State, not only the numerical strength of the various arms and their changes from time to time, but also the quality of the troops, their morale, training and military address, their manner of marching, maneuvering, camping and fighting, their food supply, recruiting and interior administration; and, in particular, information about their leaders and other military chiefs, whose character and intellectual qualities were to be given to the last detail.

It cannot be too difficult to obtain the necessary data on the strength of the troops and other arrangements, for which purpose the chief of legation will know how to lighten the labor of the officer attached to him. He might be enabled to obtain such data in an unobjectionable indirect manner through the nearest neighbors of the country in which he is stationed, thus proving himself worthy of commendation; only it must be emphasized again that in this respect as in his behavior generally he must observe the greatest wisdom in the choice of his means in order to avoid altogether the impression of being a spy and thus compromising the Imperial service.

(2) Indications and measures pointing to a war, near or distant, call for the closest possible attention and observation. This includes giving continued attention to the newspapers, to other prints and public papers in the State of residence, to the forming of depots, the making defensible of fortresses and other military points, to arsenals and pro-

11

visions for war, concentration of troops in camps or close quarters, and generally to all similar preparations which are important for the profound judging of the relations of the two States.

Under the guise of sociability the experienced officer will know how to initiate military and other contacts which will enable him to make useful and interesting observations without being detected; quite often a good connoisseur of men and an adroit observer, through confidential relationships with carefully selected individuals, will more easily obtain the knowledge of a state secret than in another manner which might expose him in the hateful role of a spy. The greatest caution is enjoined upon the officer in question since he is certain of being always observed by the secret police of the foreign State. But if he goes to work with discretion, he may easily succeed in establishing connections within the foreign State from which he himself and his Government may in future obtain desirable information.

(3) The definite and prompt knowledge of truly warlike movements, their direction and strength, is a main object of this officer's observations, as well as the closest possible survey of operations in a war between the country of his residence and a third State. To achieve this, he should endeavor to have confidants, at points where several important roads converge, who are fit to report either on the marches of the troops or on the war operations themselves. Should personal presence in the theater of war be of supreme usefulness, either the ambassador himself ought to go, or he should obtain permission for the officer attached to him to participate in the campaign.

A diary is to be kept about this and about all other important military occurrences in the State under observation; the diary is to be submitted either periodically as a contribution to military history or, in the case of important and momentous incidents, without loss of time—all this in order to complement the news obtained by the General Staff's own information service and through the *Geheime Hof- und Staatskanzlei*.

(4) A description of the country of residence based on military considerations is to be submitted, including the whole country's offensive and defensive aspects, its important military positions and posts and the most promising method of making war on it. The necessary materials must be collected without undue haste, on discreet voyages, and gathered into a whole later.

(5) The attached officer must observe and report on all the military, scientific, police and educational institutions in the country of residence so that anything worthy of imitation, as well as other useful inventions, can be transplanted to our own country should this be considered necessary; hence the need of submitting the relevant literary works, including military almanacs, army lists, decrees about improvements and the arrangement of the military budget, textbooks used in military establishments, valuable new maps and plans, publications on geography and statistics.

The officer's education, his modest language and the pretense that he is concerning himself with these things merely for his own information, will obtain him full access everywhere; and in all such cases, as well as when payment of bribes may be required, he will apply to his chief who will be able to provide him with the necessary funds.

If, now, this officer of the embassy proceeds with wisdom and modesty, which cannot be recommended too much, and always keeps the All-Highest interest before his eyes, and endeavors in his language and actions as well as by the strictest prudence in his correspondence to avoid all that is compromising, he will find the ways and means to be useful to the military administration by becoming acquainted and connected with persons whose influence, knowledge and service should prove useful in case of the outbreak of war, and on other occasions.

In addition, confidence is placed in every officer who is employed on such service: he will know how to judge with wisdom in all cases not specifically mentioned here, and all his steps will be in keeping with the views and directions of the ambassador.[22]

These early standing instructions for Austrian officers—attachés in all but name—emphasize not only most of the tasks imposed upon the modern service attaché, but also the confidence placed in his knowledge and judgment, in his behavior in foreign surroundings, in the discretion which enables him to preserve the honorable character of his always suspect mission—hence the usual *agrément* for service attachés, not required for any other personnel except mission chiefs.[23] And they stress, again and again, the admonition that the ambassador, whether military or civilian, is his superior while he is employed as part of the embassy personnel. In all basic features, these were or became the rules laid down for the service attachés of most of the great military and naval powers of the nineteenth and twentieth centuries, with the exception that the Austrian and a few other military authorities subsequently obtained the emancipation of the military attaché from ambassadorial control.

[22] Condensed from *Denkschriften militärisch-politischen Inhalts aus dem handschriftlichen Nachlass des K. K. österreichischen Feldmarschalls Grafen Radetzky* (Stuttgart and Augsburg 1858), pp. 40ff.

[23] Potiemkine, III, 806. The Foreign Office in July 1963 refused to accept a new air attaché the Soviet Government had wanted to assign to London. *The New York Times*, July 6, 1963.

CHAPTER 2

THE NINETEENTH CENTURY

In certain respects the military attaché of the nineteenth century is part of the military progress instituted by Napoleon, and adopted by those who overthrew him even while they rejected his militarism. Thenceforth the military sector of diplomatic reporting took on a more expert character, and military competition called for specific information on foreign armies. The all-civilian embassies and legations also observed and reported on military affairs, dispatching an attaché or secretary to the local scene if necessary—as young Robert Morier went to explore the Austrian military frontier (*Militärgrenze*) in 1856, "in order to obtain hints for the proposed military colonies in the Cape"[1]—but some powers also attached special officers to their embassies after the close of the Wars of Liberation.

General von Grolman, Prussia's first Chief of the Great General Staff, pointed to this fact and precedent in a memorandum of 1816 to the War Minister, who was then and for over fifty years to come the Chief of Staff's superior. Grolman suggested that Prussia must not be backward, but must follow the lead of other nations. The War Minister and Hardenberg, the State Chancellor, agreed, and six appointments were made immediately, the officers holding the rank of major or captain. The institution as such did not develop at once, however, owing to imperative Prussian economies rather than to any opposition on the part of the civilian governors. Grolman had assured them that "the purpose of the assignment . . . was precise knowledge of the States from a purely military standpoint. Their purpose is altogether non-political and they are to avoid any and all meddling in politics and they must,

---

[1] Rosslyn Wemyss, ed., *Memoirs and Letters of Sir Robert Morier*, 2 vols. (London 1911), I, 145ff.

above all, take care to observe utmost caution and discretion in their conduct."[2] The vow of abstinence from politics could not have been more explicit and, as far as Grolman himself was concerned, more sincere.

Another attempt to add officers to the Prussian legations failed a few years later: in 1824, the Inspector General of Artillery Prince Augustus of Prussia submitted to the war and foreign ministers a "suggestion as to the appointment of officers to the legations being of military importance," since the legations as then constituted were only rarely able to furnish complete information about military institutions and resources. Of late, France, Russia, Austria and Britain had rather often placed officers with their legations, something that Napoleon had already found useful; indeed, had the latter kept such an officer in Berlin early in 1813, he would have known of the Prussian preparations for war which took place right under the eyes of the French legation. The next appropriations for the Great General Staff provided for six such officers, but there were only two actual appointments: one for St. Petersburg and the other for the Frankfurt Bundestag. The foreign minister proved unreceptive: the appointments would stir up distrust in the foreign capitals; he himself had to avoid everything "which would hurt in even the slightest manner the trust and uprightness underlying the up to now happily preserved ties of alliance and friendships."[3] He would not have anything like the proposed military emissaries disturb the good climate of the Holy Alliance.

What the military in France scornfully called "the halt in the mud" after 1815, the denial of military progress as part of reactionary tendencies, was not born of the soldiers' desires for a long rest but was largely imposed upon them by civilians, once more in the ascendant. The reorganizer of the French army after Waterloo, Gouvion St. Cyr, attempted to salvage for the Bourbon army some of the organizational advances made under Napoleon, including permission for officers to be

2 E. von Conrady, *Leben und Wirken des Generals Carl von Grolman*, 3 vols. (Berlin 1894-1896), III, 29f.
3 Meisner, *Militärattachés*, p. 10.

stationed with the embassies and legations for prolonged periods "in order to reconnoiter and study the state of the military arts among the various powers by comparing it with the state of the same art as existing in France." What St. Cyr wanted was far more modest than Napoleon's *service de renseignement*, but his colleague at the foreign ministry, the Marquis Dessolle, who had once been a general, was afraid that such a proposal would appear far too Napoleonic, and would compromise the pacific character of French missions abroad. "Europe, hardly recovered yet from the fright of all it had to suffer from the military and adventurous spirit of France, would see only with a keen sense of uneasiness anything that might remind it of that epoch"; besides, this innovation could hardly fail "to be interpreted as an instrument used by the French Government to keep itself informed about the military state of the foreign powers" (1819).[4]

Clearly, it was the inclusion of a regular military component in the diplomatic agencies abroad, and the consequent alarms and "dangers of war" as reported by military experts, that Restoration diplomacy wanted to avoid. But it put no obstacles in the way of the military, usually general staff officers, going abroad to study foreign military institutions and progress. This seemed less upsetting to peace than permanent stationing. The relations of such traveling officers with their country's embassies varied greatly, but usually included introduction to the military authorities of the land visited, and other facilities to make such missions successful. This diplomatic protection at times proved more hindrance than help: one French officer said in 1829, after a mission which had tied him to the apron strings of the Vienna embassy, that "his quality as diplomatic agent had kept him from observing as much detail as a simple traveler could have done."[5]

Considering the relative rarity of wars immediately after 1815 the neutrals were always eager to participate in such campaigns as did occur. Opportunities arose with the Austrian intervention in Naples in 1821, the French intervention in Spain in 1823, the Russo-Turkish War of 1828 and the

[4] Beauvais, p. 14.   [5] Beauvais, p. 15.

French expeditions to Algiers. Europe itself was kept at peace by the diplomacies, but there were still wars to watch along the frontiers of civilization, in Africa, in the Caucasus and elsewhere. Permission to follow the operations was sometimes applied for with the polite remark that one wanted one's own officers to participate in "a chivalrous expedition" such as the conquest of Algiers, where "the Russian uniform ought to be perceived side by side with the French"; it was usually granted with the assurance that such an emissary "would meet with the most amicable reception and the most desirable facilities."[6] One of the few denials of admission on record occurred when the Prussian Military Plenipotentiary Count Münster applied for permission to follow the Russian Army in the Crimean War. The Western Allies were far more ready to admit Prussian and other neutral observers to their camps; "the headquarters of Maréchal de Saint-Arnaud took on the aspect of a small military congress,"[7] where one could see an unpreparedness, a waste and improvisation, nearly equal to what the Russians were trying to hide from even the friendliest observer. Prussian reports on the state of the Russian Army, however, as seen from St. Petersburg, became generally known when they were stolen by an agent in the pay of the French legation in Berlin.

Occasionally, but only occasionally, a military officer was attached to the legations abroad for somewhat prolonged periods, but he was not called "attaché," a term first applied to civilian members and as such not in English usage before 1835. On the whole, however, the diplomacy of the Restoration period preferred to do without such assistants, or would maintain that their services proved of little help. The July Revolution, which at first threatened to have military complications, marked a certain change in that resistance "on account of the change in the war constitution in France." Prussia in 1830 for the first time posted a captain as "military expert" (*Militär-Sachverständiger*) with her Paris legation, her first true military attaché, though as yet without the

[6] Beauvais, p. 16; Gustave Gautherot, *La conquête d'Alger 1830* (Paris 1929), p. 29.

[7] Beauvais, p. 23.

18

title,[8] and France herself decided in 1833, as part of the reorganization of her general staff corps, that members of that body "might be put at the disposition of the Ministry of Foreign Affairs in order to be attached to embassies and be employed on diplomatic missions." During the later 1830's some four members of that corps, usually with the rank of captain—the rank most military attachés carried for a long time to come—were detached from the army and admitted to the French foreign service. They sometimes worked at the Quai d'Orsay (for the military evaluation of incoming reports, one wonders?) and sometimes abroad.

This dual allegiance, reminiscent of feudal struggles between political and military authorities, plagued service attachés for the next hundred years. In spite of all original admonitions to obey their temporary superiors, issued with or without a mental reservation on the part of the military authorities to the officers assigned to embassies and legations, the attachés' strongest loyalties remained with the services from which they came and to which the great majority of them returned. The Prussian military attaché for Vienna during the Crimean War, Prince Kraft zu Hohenlohe, was the first to be chosen from the corps of general staff officers and trained in its systematic ways of assembling and evaluating information. Before he left Berlin, he was told by the Chief of the General Staff that he could not demand any direct communications from officers assigned to legations; these reports would reach him by way of the Foreign Office and the War Ministry. In the War Ministry he was informed that he was formally assigned to the minister plenipotentiary and must consider him his superior in all questions of official correspondence, but that the War Ministry deemed it desirable that the officers serving in legations kept altogether independent in all essentials. The minister, however, should read all his reports before they went off. As for the rest—"in Austria one finds out everything if one knows how to court the ladies." During his tour of duty Hohenlohe carefully avoided all occasions that might have led to a clarification of his status under

---

[8] Meisner, *Militärattachés*, p. 10.

the minister plenipotentiary, and addressed his reports "To the Royal Ministries of Foreign Affairs and of War."[9]

Both addressees were inclined to claim control over him and his colleagues. In an interdepartmental agreement of the early 1850's, never fully observed, if observable, it was provided that service attachés should "limit themselves to military-technical questions" in their reports, and avoid reaching over into the political field. The war minister pointed out, however, that seemingly technical questions often had political implications and that this should not prevent the attaché from making his report on such a question—hence the understanding that the legation head was to see all reports and pass them on, with or without his own observations. Still later, apparently after 1869, correspondence in "purely military-technical questions" between the attaché and the War Ministry or the General Staff was freed of this supervision and allowed to go direct.[10] The diplomatic-military conflict, lightly foreshadowed in these years, received part of its acumination from that dogmatism, that sense of superiority which scientism, even non-Comteism, is apt to introduce into politics. It was around 1860 that general staff organization, and notably its intelligence services, in Prussia and somewhat later in France, underwent its scientific "management" organization.[11] When the military men compared their efficient, scientific ways of operating with the muddled processes of diplomacy, they easily developed a sense of superiority which the military victories of 1864, 1866 and 1870-1871 would swell into a veritable General Staff *hubris*—at least in Germany.

From a fairly early time the Prussian military attachés, hardly ever restrained by what they soon realized was their true permanent superior, the Chief of the General Staff, became the Staff's eager servitors. But this was a challenge to civilian supremacy, which constitutionally rested in the

9 Prince Kraft zu Hohenlohe-Ingelfingen, *Aus meinem Leben* (Berlin 1879), I, 242ff., 254, 339. For Hohenlohe's activity in Vienna see Gordon A. Craig, *Political Science Quarterly*, LXIV (1949), 67.

10 H. O. Meisner, ed., "Aus Berichten des pariser Militärattachés Freiherrn von Hoiningen gen. Huene an den Grafen Waldersee (1888-1891)," *Berliner Monatshefte*, XV (1937), 959.

11 For the French side see Castellan, p. 16.

Prime Minister, later the Chancellor, and it became necessary, again and again, to insist on diplomatic control over the attaché in uniform. As early as 1854, the Prussian Minister of War could inform the Chief of Staff that an officer such as the military attaché in Paris must be considered as temporarily in the diplomatic service, subordinate to the local head of legation; that he was not allowed to explore independent political relationships; that his reports and the instructions given him must pass through the local minister's hands; and that his reports must be restricted to military subjects, with political subjects included only insofar as they were closely connected with military ones.

Even for those days of less acute arms competition these rules implied a rather unhurried routing of military information; it came first to the war minister, and to the Prussian soldier-kings who proved rather eager to read such reports; it took weeks to reach the Chief of Staff, Moltke, who consequently ordered at least one attaché in 1876 to send copies or extracts of his reports directly. Thereafter it was ordered that reports of a "purely military technical" nature were to be addressed to the attaché's "direct military superior" (orders of 1869 and 1875).

Who was he? The Minister of War or the Chief of Staff? Moltke, carried away by the prestige his office had gained in three successful wars, thought it was he, but the King-Emperor would neither confirm nor deny this view (1876). And Bismarck also left the "question of competency" alone when he had to concern himself with the attaché problem, usually in connection with some espionage case, a business he decreed must be left exclusively "to socially lower ranking persons" (1877). The problem of the attachés' "direct superior" was reopened when Waldersee, as Quartermaster-General and Moltke's successor-designate, took over the direction of the Great General Staff (1882). With Bismarck's somewhat careless approval he managed the removal of a strongly constitutionally-minded war minister who had stood "between the King and his Chief of Staff," and the Chief thus became one more soldier "in immediate relationship" to the War Lord, whom these officials in uniform encircled and tried to remove from the Chancellor's civilian control and influence. Only belatedly did the Bismarcks become aware of the effects of Waldersee's scheming, and of his office habits, including direct dealings with the attachés abroad, the full effect of which was not apparent until after the accession of the new emperor in 1888.

By the summer of 1889 the Foreign Office, as the supreme political office which would ultimately have to bear the juridical and political consequences, began to reassert a measure of control over the attachés. Intelligence problems? "Military directives which might have to be excluded from this, will, as a rule, not at all be suitable for written procedures and official responsibility for them will therefore not be provable." While it may be an open question how far this rule went in washing diplomats' hands of the dirty business of military espionage, no doubt can remain as to the Chancellor's insistence on being "master in the (diplomatic) house." He even made the attachés report to him on so-called purely military affairs, when critical diplomatic situations seemed to require it, as in 1887-1888.

Final assertion by the Chancellor of absolute control over the service attachés, as far as this seemed attainable by a "general instruction," remained in abeyance; Bismarck was now in the final stages of a struggle with Waldersee (since 1888 Chief of the General Staff) for control of the giddy young Emperor, and this was clearly not the hour to insist on civilian supremacy. His successor, however, General Count von Caprivi, knew from previous experience at least as well as Bismarck how much or how little importance so-called military secrets could possess. He was stirred into action by yet another espionage affair and strongly backed up by the "permanents" in the Foreign Office, who were fully aware of Waldersee's private diplomacy through "his" attachés. Caprivi successfully claimed—successful not least because of the estrangement between the Emperor and the Chief of Staff, who had dared openly to criticize a maneuver exercise led by the War Lord—that the service attachés

as regards their activity abroad are placed under the mission chief . . . whose organs they are. . . . An independent role they shall never want to play. . . . If they are in a position to make political observations, they will have to advise the mission chiefs of these.[12] . . . The latter are entitled, on their own initiative, to give orders of a military nature to the service attachés.[13] . . . If and when the attachés are offered information about the foreign army or navy which derive from a sordid source, they may accept those following approval by the mission chief. To go out after such information on their own initiative, however, is prohibited. The attachés in the fulfilment of their duties, must not be misguided into taking steps which, if they should become known, might endanger the reputation of the German officers. . . . They have to report, as often as it seems advisable to them, to the Chancellor on the military observations made by them. These "military reports" have to be submitted to the mission chief before dispatch, to be marked by the latter with a "Read." As a matter of principle, they are to be kept free from all political matter and commentary unless they be inseparably connected with the military content. . . .[14]

In arguing with either the Emperor or the War Minister Waldersee emphasized that such instructions would be tantamount to a degradation of the officers' estate, would not incite them to greater exertion, and would stop up valuable sources of information about political conditions. The order obliging the attachés to execute official orders of their mission chiefs meant delivering them "mercilessly to the whims of diplomats. . . . It could only be termed measureless insolence on the part of a chargé d'affaires to take it upon himself to give a military attaché orders about his conduct." All these arguments, including the assertion about "the notorious mental superiority" of the military over the diplomats, or the remark that the idea of mission chiefs giving orders of a military nature to attachés belonged in the field

[12] Waldersee's marginal observations on the draft of the "general instruction": "They are therefore degraded to the rank of reporters."
[13] Waldersee: "That would turn into a nice nonsense!"
[14] Waldersee: "Aha! But what does that inseparably mean? . . . Who decides about the concept inseparableness?"

of comics, were addressed to the worst militaristic traits in the young Emperor. Only the final break between the Emperor and the Chief of Staff, who was abruptly removed (January 1891) from the post whence he had once hoped to move into the Chancellery, kept these appeals from finding more fertile ground and further holding up the "General Instruction for the Officers Stationed with Missions Abroad" which went out on December 11, 1890.[15]

With no apparent cooperation by the several foreign offices, the number of military attachés as part of the foreign services, noted by the *Almanac de Gotha* from 1839 on, grew slowly from the 1830's through the 1850's. It still did not achieve full permanence, but it did acquire greater public visibility. Some years before Wellington's death in 1852 the corps of military attachés in London, and perhaps elsewhere too, had become an exhibition of international panache—a popular colored British print showed the Iron Duke in Hyde Park on the Queen's birthday, mounted on a black charger, with the foreign military attachés following on horseback.[16] As perhaps the first of the powers to take the step to permanence, France started the regular stationing of such an attaché at her Berlin legation in 1851. Austria did not follow suit until early in 1859 when "the first of the species," as his ambassador noted, arrived in Paris on the very eve of the Italian War, too late to be very helpful.[17] Nomenclature remained unstandardized for several decades: some powers called them military agents, others military secretaries, *addetti militari, agregados militares*; the Prussians did not always restrict the term military plenipotentiary, *Militärbevollmächtigter*, to the officer stationed with the Tsar. This term, which the Austrians also used for certain of their military representatives abroad until the late 1890's, was a misnomer from beginning to end

[15] For the above see Gerhard Ritter, *Die deutschen Militaer-Attachés und das Auswaertige Amt. Aus den verbrannten Akten des Grossen Generalstabs* (Heidelberg 1960).

[16] C. T. Courtney Lewis, *The Story of Picture Printing in England during the Nineteenth Century* (London n.d. [1928]), p. 329.

[17] Joseph Alexander von Hübner, *Neun Jahre der Erinnerungen* (Berlin 1904), II, 149.

insofar as the officers were almost never possessed of full powers to negotiate.[18]

The same title was applied to the military representatives of the member states at the Bundestag in Frankfurt and, after 1866, to the military representatives of the larger German federal states, Bavaria, Baden—only for a time—Württemberg and Saxony, who were stationed at Berlin, the capital of the North German Confederacy and the Reich; this followed the signing of the military conventions of 1866 and 1867 whereby the losers of the war of 1866 had submitted to the military hegemony of Prussia. The plenipotentiaries were accredited to the King of Prussia, who in turn maintained their counterparts—later only attachés—in the capitals of the several States; they were originally intended to elaborate in detail the provisions of the military conventions.[19] Later, they came to assure the essential unity of the diverse armies in the Second Reich, in which some "States' rights" sentiments and arrangements survived to the last. They provided diplomatic channels for the transmission of information and proposals between the Berlin top military offices and the war ministries of

[18] Eduard von Wertheimer, *Graf Julius Andrassy, sein Leben und seine Zeit*, 3 vols. (Stuttgart 1910-1913), III, 269. The incumbent of the Berlin office at the time of the change wrote: "With a little hair splitting one might have discovered a *capitis diminutio* for the holder of the old title. Military plenipotentiary sounded perhaps more sonorous and perhaps also more magnificent than military attaché. But the latter term was certainly the one more suitable for the position. To a plenipotentiary belonged after all a full power providing the incumbent with definite rights. This, however, in the nature of the job, could not be the case." Stürgkh, p. 167. This nomenclature never did go altogether out of usage. During World War I, German GHQ included not only *Militärbevollmächtigte* of Bavaria, Württemberg and Saxony, but also, considerably more "empowered," for purposes of liaison, such plenipotentiaries from Austria, Turkey and Bulgaria, while the Reich had a "German general with full powers" in the Austrian GHQ and military plenipotentiaries in Constantinople, Sofia and, after the Treaty of Brest Litovsk, in Moscow. Hermann Cron, *Geschichte der deutschen Heere im Weltkriege 1914-1918* (Berlin 1937), p. 6.

[19] Meisner, *Militärattachés*, pp. 43ff., for details. For the "military Anschluss" of Baden, where the Prussian plenipotentiary became the war minister in 1868, see Hermann Oncken, ed., *Grossherzog Friedrich I von Baden und die deutsche Politik von 1854-1871* (Stuttgart 1927), II, 35, 40ff., 67ff., 113f.

the smaller states. Whenever military questions came before the *Bundesrat*, they represented the military side of "states' rights," in addition to *ad hoc* military plenipotentiaries of the still smaller states. They were not subordinates of the ministers plenipotentiary of their countries in Berlin but corresponded directly with the war ministers of their home governments, without diplomatic control, although their standing instruction was to remain in "continued contact with the Royal legation," and minister and military plenipotentiary were to exchange information "whenever this is of importance for the full unified representation of Bavarian interest."[20]

The military progress that these men observed was achieved in spite of the general disinclination of the diplomacies to promote such advances—the introduction of the breech-loading gun and rifle, of rifled cannon, steam navies and ironclads, of army reorganizations as in Prussia. The urgent desire of the military and naval authorities to keep a close watch on such developments, as they occurred abroad, grew insistent enough to demand the permanent stationing of military and naval attachés in the foreign capitals. The resistance of the diplomats had grown weaker, at least to the same extent that the power ratio had altered within many of the great nations and their governing strata after 1848, when the military as the makers of civil[21] and foreign conflicts were gaining over the diplomats as peacemakers. In France the regime of Napoleon III depended most heavily on the support of the army—therefore it was most open to the army's demands, including that for permanent military attachés.

The year 1860 witnessed a veritable blossoming—of "fleurs du mal," some would insist. In January 1860 the Emperor agreed to the appointment of a major from the general staff as military attaché in London; two more officers were sent in the

---

[20] For some of the activities of these plenipotentiaries see Karl Demeter, ed., "Politische Berichte Ludwigs Freiherrn von Gebsattels, bayerischen Militärbevollmächtigen in Berlin, 1905-1911," *Preussische Jahrbücher*, 231 (1933), 24ff.

[21] In October 1852 the Austrian Police Minister, General Kempen, demanded that general staff officers be assigned to various Austrian legations in the German capitals "in order to obtain for my own department organs that are totally wanting there." Josef Karl Mayr, ed., *Das Tagebuch des Polizeiministers Kempen* (Vienna 1930), p. 266.

same capacity to St. Petersburg and Vienna, and there already was one in Berlin. In April, in recognition of the fact that "it would be useful and to the good of the service to place near the ambassador of France in London a higher ranking naval officer, in the quality of military attaché," the Emperor appointed a frigate captain, probably the first naval attaché. The navy had heretofore proved rather less curious about its competitors than was the sister service, or else had used other channels of inquiry.

The French ambassador in London, whose position these two officers were to strengthen, was not overjoyed at this double appointment, as the firstcomer of the two promptly reported to the War Ministry. He expressed doubt as to whether his mission would prove at all successful, considering the "ill will" of the ambassador; he also feared that the British Government might take umbrage, not having been asked for its prior *agrément*. Apparently, however, the British merely reacted by sending a naval captain as second military attaché to Paris, where Colonel Claremont, a fixture of the Second Empire, had been attaché for some years.[22] He knew "France and the French Army like a Frenchman" and his reports were often handed on to Berlin.[23] The French example of 1860 was followed more or less closely by the great powers and to a certain extent by the minor ones, though sometimes only over the opposition of the foreign office at home.

Britain for years and almost desperately had tried to keep aloof from such continental developments. The Crimean War, however, had brought her into long-shunned entanglements such as sending liaison officers, so-called Commissars of the Queen, to allied headquarters at Paris, Turin and Constantinople, and to the French contingent in the Orient. The results of the war gave her no great desire to continue these ties, and military attachés, perhaps to wind up affairs, survived

[22] Beauvais, pp. 24f.
[23] Oncken, *Rheinpolitik*, III, 372; II, 545, 552, 576f. While Cobden in 1859 was attempting to get his Anglo-French *entente cordiale* started, Palmerston was panicked by Claremont's reports that Napoleon was assembling a large number of flat-bottomed boats for an invasion of Britain. Herbert C. F. Bell, *Lord Palmerston* (London and New York 1938), II, 245, 458.

only at Paris and Turin. They were called by this name from 1857 on, and appeared in the list of diplomatic personnel (but in the Army list only from 1874 on) : an indication of the claims of the Foreign Office over such officers, who addressed their reports to Downing Street. The Turin attaché, rather than the Paris one, clearly was thinking in the spirit of contemporary British diplomacy with its vague hopes for disarmament when he reported (in 1860) : "The more an international system is put to work, the aim of which is to take secretiveness away from military secrets, the greater the guarantee for peace. And one might add that if one supposes that an unevenness results to the various nations as to the benefits resulting from this system, the advantage would accrue to the less military nations and to those who have the least tendency of disturbing the peace of Europe."[24]

The Duke of Cambridge, commander-in-chief of the British Army, which was not in the van of progress at the time, was greatly impressed by the perfection of Prussia's military reorganization even before it had been demonstrated on any battlefield, and wanted to station a military attaché in Berlin for at least half a year to observe that progress in detail. He proposed this to Lord John Russell in May 1860, but nothing was done. In March 1864 the Duke returned to the attack and raised the whole problem of military attachés, to be sent to Berlin, Vienna and St. Petersburg. Considering the highly technical character of recent military developments, he pointed out, the ambassadors, however earnestly trying to submit reliable military information, could no longer cope with its complexity and were apt to overlook important matters: "In the present disturbed state of Europe, when military operations and preparations are going on in so many States, I think it really would be of the greatest importance that we should have military attachés at all our principal missions, such as Berlin, Vienna, Copenhagen, St. Petersburg, etc. Indeed, I think it would be well to extend the system even to America. I do not ask for Commissioners; these would be ob-

24 Lothar W. Hilbert, "L'origine du service des attachés militaires en Grande-Bretagne," *Revue d'histoire diplomatique*, LXXVII (1961), 155ff., also *Journal of the Society of Army History* (December 1959).

jectionable very likely. . . . I would take care to select officers of not too high rank so as not to attract any particular attention."[25] This time the Foreign Office relented, probably shaken if not shamed by the outcome of its policies on the question of the Duchies, and the appointments to the three capitals were made in April 1864.

Eventually such officers were stationed in Paris, Berlin, Turin, St. Petersburg, Vienna and Frankfurt (until 1866), plus two naval attachés in Paris and Washington. And by 1874, whether it be cause or consequence, the British Army felt itself finally involved in the military competition rampant in Europe: a major, who taught history at Woolwich and was sent to the continental capitals to study attachédom, wrote: "There is nothing new or contrary to the British mind in the idea of studying such and such characters and such and such statistics which would seem necessary to be known in order to make good and solid plans for the case of an eventual war."[26]

Prussia's military successes of 1864 and 1866 combined with the increase in technical complexity in the military field to diminish severely the former importance of the diplomats, and of their reports covering military subjects—and incidentally what control they might have thus exercised over the military. Previously, all military information that the foreign ministry had gathered through diplomatic channels had been turned over to the war minister, who passed on to the chief of staff what he thought to be of strategic importance. Nor were the reports of the military attachés addressed to the general staff; they traveled by way of the legation head and the foreign minister to the war ministry, which again decided what in them was of a strategic nature and therefore was to be communicated to the general staff.[27] While Bismarck was strong enough to prevent changes in the channeling of reports, even he could not make his ambassadors report on what might too easily appear matters of "purely military interest"—of

[25] Col. Willoughby Verner, *The Military Life of H.R.H. George, Duke of Cambridge*, 2 vols. (London 1905), I, 322, 361f.
[26] Hilbert, p. 160.
[27] Gerhard Ritter, *Lebendige Vergangenheit* (Leipzig 1944), p. 111.

which they knew nothing, or not enough to find grace in the eyes of the haughty military.[28]

Bismarck was not altogether satisfied with the services rendered by the Prussian military attachés in his work of unifying Germany through three wars. When the attaché in Paris, Lieutenant Colonel von Loë, came to GHQ in Bohemia in the summer of 1866, uncalled, and lingered there, the Chancellor censured him sharply: "As Military Attaché in Paris you are my subordinate, and it is as your superior that I am issuing this reprimand, because you absented yourself from your post where you were urgently needed." For a long time Bismarck resented the fact that Loë had not informed him more correctly about the true state of French military unreadiness, and had done so only after his return to Paris, and after Bismarck had concluded peace with Austria and the other enemies on terms that might have been more favorable had he been more thoroughly briefed. But Napoleon III had been served no better by his attaché in Berlin, Major Count Clermont-Tonnerre, who had strengthened French beliefs in Austrian superiority, notably by his observations during the War of 1864 when Prussian and Austrian troops fought side by side in Schleswig. The Austrians had shown so much more dash than the Prussians—incidentally incurring needless casualties—that Clermont-Tonnerre and his superiors were quite misled.[29]

The military expert stationed abroad regularly and permanently had come to stay by the early 1870's, so much so indeed that he began to be noticed by military literature and political science. Wilhelm Rüstow, an ardent military democrat and Garibaldi's chief of staff in 1860, who wrote prolifically from the neutral base of Switzerland after his flight from the Prussian Army, apparently did not think highly in the early 1870's of this new feature of military organization. Possibly he was

[28] By the end of Bismarck's chancellorship the Reich had military attachés in Paris, Vienna, St. Petersburg (from 1891 on, before that the military plenipotentiary had functioned as such), Rome, London, Brussels (from 1872), Bern (from 1875), Madrid (from 1883, due to a suggestion from the Wilhelmstrasse) and Bucharest (from 1888). Meisner, *Militärattachés*, pp. 17ff.
[29] Rich and Fisher, I, 27ff.

too provoked, as a democrat, by the roster of noble names usually filling these posts, both then and later, but in any case he proceeded to set right popular misconceptions about the attachés. Many people at the time believed that "military attachés ought to be nothing but *salon* officers, representative figures, having nothing serious to see for themselves but rather designed to cover up the actions of other officers charged in a secret manner, or officially, with temporary missions." This, Rüstow pointed out, was quite erroneous, for officers sent on short-term missions could never fulfill the role of military attaché. "For, in order to see things well, one has to work on them continually; if that is not done, many details escape one and one loses sight of the whole."[30]

Lorenz von Stein, writing of the attaché in his *Lehre vom Heerwesen* (*System of Military Institutions*, 1872), the one nineteenth-century classic in its field, made the attaché the special servant of what he called "military statistics," an institution of the highest importance for every army. "Only when contemplating it, one must not think merely of the assembling of data, for true statistics must elevate itself beyond statistics of forces which find their expression in numbers. The institution without which the latter task would be fundamentally worthless, is that of the military attachés (*Militär-bevollmächtigte*) of the legations; they are even more the statisticians of the spirit than of the facts of the foreign army in question. These statistics must not remain restricted to the simple facts which refer directly to the military institution; they will be the better the more they extend into the statistics of the material, and in particular the economic, condition of the army and its warlike activity."[31] The demand for such statistics presumes a character that most statistics must have in order to be truly useful, permanence, which as we have seen the office of military attaché had now attained.[32]

---

[30] The first edition of Wilhelm Rüstow's *Feldherrnkunst des 19. Jahrhunderts*, of 1857, does not deal with the military attaché, who appears in the third edition of 1878. On this is based the French translation *L'art militaire au XIXᵉ siècle* (Paris 1881). The quotation is from the latter, II, 111.

[31] P. 199.

[32] From 1860 on or shortly afterwards 27 offices of military attachés

Others were more skeptical as to the usefulness, or the relative rank and importance, of the military attaché. An early (and rare) opponent of the militarism which kept Europe forever disunited, the German publicist Constantin Frantz, also an opponent of Bismarck, asked in 1882: "Does it not characterize our conditions that now to the great embassies are added everywhere so-called military plenipotentiaries who are to observe the military institutions and the military potential of the country in question? To be informed about them, seems so important that a special expert is appointed. Maybe so; but I ask: why are there not also civilian plenipotentiaries who would have to observe and report on the progress of legislation, the development of culture and national economy?"[33]

Between 1870 and 1914 more military and naval attachés were added to the personnel of embassies and legations and, occasionally, to that of a consulate—France in the process of gradually extending control over Tunis saw need for the services of a military attaché on the staff of the consul-general in that country. The small military and naval powers sent attachés to the great powers, the developers of military progress, but they sent only a few to each other unless strategic neighborhood considerations demanded it. The great powers had attachés in the capitals of the lesser nations, sometimes to exercise control, as exemplified by the Russian military attaché in Montenegro.

Service attachés were stationed in even the most sensitive spots of imperialist competition; there was no longer any hesitation, such as older statesmen such as Bismarck had felt. In 1875 it was proposed that a German military attaché be added to the Constantinople embassy, but Bismarck vetoed the idea: he did not want to arouse Russian suspicions that

---

remained permanently filled. France, in search of the causes of her defeat in 1870-1871, and of the means of her future *revanche*, after the end of the war added eight more military attachés to the five already abroad; a second attaché was added to the Berlin and Vienna embassies. By 1914 the French total had risen to 24. Beauvais, pp. 30f., 49.

[33] *Die Weltpolitik unter besonderer Bezugnahme auf Deutschland* (Chemnitz 1882), III, 25.

Germany might have an active interest in the Straits problem; should military information be required, an officer might be appointed secretary to the embassy. He kept down the number of German instructors serving the Sultan, and knew how to make their activities acceptable to the suspicious Russians— they thought them vastly preferable to English and French instructors at the Bosphorus. But gradually, after Bismarck's fall, Constantinople became the fulcrum of the imperialist competition waged by agents of the general staffs, of finance capital or of armament firms.[34]

The entry of the United States into this military and naval competition dates in a way from a law passed by the Congress on September 22, 1888, authorizing the appointment of military and naval attachés to diplomatic missions abroad. The first five appointments, to Berlin, Vienna, Paris, London and St. Petersburg, were made in 1889, and others to Rome (1890), Brussels (1892), Madrid (1893), Japan and Mexico (1894) followed. During the war with Spain the number of such attachés was raised to sixteen, to obtain information about the enemy which the utterly neglected and unprepared Washington intelligence service did not possess, and also information about any military measures of the neutrals.

Promptly after the end of the war in 1898 the number of attachés was again fixed at ten[35] by Washington, as another expression of Congress' determination to keep the military establishment under control. Still later, when pressure was again applied by the services, more attachés were sent abroad, particularly to the Latin-American capitals, to serve the Pan-American idea as the armed services understood it. Not all the legation heads wanted them on their staffs: in 1903 the United States Minister to Brazil, Thompson, assured his German colleague in Petropolis that "as long as he could stop it, no military attaché would come to his legation." William II's marginal comment on this piece of civilian courage, "he will scarcely succeed in that," proved true—obviously the Em-

[34] For details see George W. F. Hallgarten, *Imperialismus vor 1914*, 2 vols., 2nd ed. (Munich 1963), I, 225f., 231; II, 373ff., 551ff., etc.

[35] Beauvais, p. 33. During the Anglo-German-Italian intervention in Venezuela of 1903 Washington stationed a naval attaché in that country for eight months.

peror knew the force of service pressure better than did the American politician turned diplomat.[36]

By the outbreak of war in 1914 or shortly thereafter, the United States had as many attachés abroad as did Russia, 23 military—7 of them in Latin America—and 8 naval—3 of them in Latin America. None of the powers had more. By that time the total number of service attachés in the world had risen to 305, of whom 214 were military and 85 naval attachés.[37] Germany, with 25 attachés abroad—17 military plus 8 naval—and 30 foreign officers accredited at Berlin, was the foremost "receiving" nation, with France next in line; Great Britain, as the first naval power, had the largest number of naval attachés accredited to her. This was not merely a compliment to power, it signified the areas where military science and military inquiry could hope to learn most.

Thus, by 1914, the service attaché had become a regular feature of the majority of embassies and legations, respected and still more suspected by diplomats, both of his own country and in the country of his post. He was the most exposed and advanced agent of military competition; his work called for a maximum of discretion and tact, and for that chivalry among warriors which the arms race made harder to afford with each generation,[38] especially before, during, and after wars. The reestablishment of diplomatic relations between ex-enemies is always a delicate affair. Should, for instance, the new postwar embassies at once include service attachés or would their prompt reappearance prove too reminiscent of the late clash at arms? The Austrians conquered in 1866 deemed it more tactful to wait until the middle of 1869 before they again sent a military attaché to Berlin, while the same post at Florence, the capital of the minor ex-enemy, had been filled since 1867.[39] It signified a progress in brutality when Bismarck in 1871 made the prewar military attaché in Paris, Count

[36] Report of German Minister von Treutler, Petropolis, October 23, 1903, with Emperor's marginal note. *Archives of Auswärtiges Amt.*

[37] Beauvais, pp. 44ff.; Meisner, *Militärattachés*, pp. 36ff.

[38] For the friendship of German Fieldmarshal von Loë, Prussian military attaché in Paris (1863-1866), and General Marquis de Gallifet see Schlözer, pp. 25ff.

[39] Beauvais, p. 28.

Waldersee, the postwar chargé d'affaires who reopened the embassy, or when in 1919 the Allies denied Germany the right to send service attachés abroad while they themselves—at least some of them, as well as many neutrals such as Spain[40]—kept or restationed such attachés in Berlin almost at once. A different sort of occasion was put to use by the three United States attachés in Lima in 1962, when they met socially with leaders of the Peruvian armed forces ten days after a military junta had overthrown a civilian regime and the United States had suspended all formal relations. The meeting preceded the eventual recognition of the new regime by Washington.[41]

In regard to the appointment of attachés the army proved practically everywhere the senior service. At first, the military attaché reported on naval affairs as well, notably so and longest among the smaller naval powers, but specialization gradually increased. When the stationing of a naval officer with the Prussian Embassy in Paris was considered as early as 1869, the plan failed "due to the numerous claims on the strength of the personnel." In 1894 William II gave orders that henceforth the second military attaché in that capital was to be a naval man, but the naval authorities were less than completely satisfied. They argued that, because of French distrust of all Germans, naval officers in such a disguise were unlikely to learn more about naval things than an army officer who, in this respect, would be considered "innocent"; should such an appointment be due to a suggestion from the French themselves, an exchange of naval attachés would still not be in the best German interest. The main source of data about the French Navy was the French press, whereas the French would find but little naval information in the German press.

"The French are therefore forced, more than we are, to obtain information in other ways. After the capture last year of two of their naval officers attempting secret espionage, has blocked their ways somewhat, they will want to obtain infor-

[40] For the Spanish military attaché in Berlin, from 1913 to the mid-1920's, Col. Don Luiz Ruiz de Valdivia, see *The Rebel Prince. Memoirs of Prince Louis Ferdinand of Prussia* (Chicago 1952), p. 55 and passim.
[41] *The New York Times*, July 29, 1962.

mation in a more legal way by means of the naval attaché. Since the German is not as hostile to the French as vice versa, the attaché would not have to apply caution as great as we would have to in Paris. Hence, it appears unquestionable that an agile French naval attaché will succeed in learning here in Berlin and in the naval ports much that is useful." This argument on the part of the naval command did not prevail: a Cabinet order of November 19, 1894, appointed the first naval attaché for Paris, Lieutenant Commander Siegel, later naval expert at the First Hague Conference.[42]

The Austrian Navy was worth little in the power scales before 1914, and no German naval attaché was placed in Vienna until 1911. The post was taken care of before that time, if at all, by the naval attaché in Rome, who had first been appointed in 1891—an act of belated reciprocity, for the eager Italians had his counterpart in Berlin as early as 1889.[43] In London the Germans had kept a military attaché ever since 1869; he was a naval man from 1882 on. Schlieffen, the Chief of Staff, severed this "personal union" in 1898, and from then on there were to be both a naval and a military attaché. A German naval attaché for "the Northern empires" (Russia, Sweden-Norway, Denmark) was stationed in St. Petersburg in 1886. As for the United States, the originally quite "friendly" naval relations between Berlin and Washington led to the appointment, which had been under consideration in Berlin since 1869, of a German "attaché for naval affairs" in 1873. The first incumbent was Corvette Captain von Eisendecher, later minister in the same capital. When he was appointed minister resident in Tokyo in 1875, the Washington office remained vacant until the eve of the Spanish-American War.[44]

[42] Meisner, *Militärattachés*, pp. 11f.
[43] *Ibid.*, pp. 13f.   [44] *Ibid.*, pp. 16f., 19, 21f.

CHAPTER 3

THE FIRST WORLD WAR

The immediate responsibility for the First World War and the resolution to go to war in August 1914 lay with the European governments—all of them believed they would win. But ambassadors and service attachés bear some remote responsibility for the diplomatic and military confidence built up over the years from their reports and advice. In July 1914 these men proved more conforming, more subordinate to their home offices, than at many another time. No ambassador, no service attaché of any European power advised against war; they all believed in victory.

The war uses to which the powers put their attachés now returning from abroad, or older ex-attachés, were relatively unimportant. Almost no nation considered attaché service as qualifying an officer for high command; there was little left of the early expectation that an officer previously stationed in a potential enemy country might have learned to know the future enemy commander, his strength and his weaknesses. One of the worst failures, before 1914, was the loser of Tsushima, Rozhestvenski, who was given a field command after many years as naval attaché in London.

Two exceptions to this rule were General Grierson, who was to command one of the army corps of the BEF in 1914, but died before his corps was fully assembled,[1] and General Pershing, who had been detached from a post in the Philippines and sent to Tokyo in order to follow the Japanese Army to Manchuria as a military attaché. Several ex-attachés eventually served as chiefs of staff: Payton C. March, United States Army

---

[1] As expressed in the obituary style, Grierson had "an understanding of *la grande guerre* and an intimate knowledge of the German army that made his premature death an incalculable loss to the British cause." *Encyclopaedia Britannica*, XIIIth ed. (London and New York 1926), Suppl. II, 294.

Chief of Staff, and one-time attaché and observer on the Japanese side in the war of 1904-1905; Pellé, Joffre's chief of staff, who had been military attaché in Berlin 1909-1912; and Count von der Schulenburg, German military attaché in London from 1902 to 1906, and during the war chief of staff of the army group nominally headed by the Crown Prince—a group, incidentally, which never actually faced British forces. From his insight into the ultimate relative strengths of the opposing sides, Schulenburg—and under his influence the Crown Prince—at a relatively early date came to the conclusion that "we must strive for an understanding," and no longer for a "victory peace," which was the only thinkable outcome of the war for Ludendorff and so many other German generals. "But there was no way of standing up against 'the dictator,'" Ludendorff. He was a soldier singularly ignorant of foreign countries and their strength,[2] and heedless of political considerations—no matter who raised them—in connection with command decisions, which must remain "purely military."[3]

The greatest usefulness of the former military attaché in time of war, if unacceptable for high command, is in assembling and evaluating information about the country in which he recently resided,[4] or in services of liaison with friendly or allied powers.[5] Such considerations of usefulness must necessarily overrule all personal desires for a field com-

[2] Wolfgang Foerster, *Generaloberst Ludwig Beck. Sein Kampf gegen den Krieg* (Munich 1953), pp. 17, 154. Beck, who served on the same staff, never forgot this schooling in "defeatism," as the Hitlerites would call it, hence his opposition to Hitler's wars and to Hitler as another Ludendorff, another war-maker with no "terminating facilities."

[3] For the suggestions made by the military attaché in The Hague, which were to be taken into consideration in the undertaking of the German offensive in the spring of 1918 and which were designed to make peace just a little more possible, see *The Memoirs of Prince Max of Baden*, transl. by W. M. Calder and C.W.H. Sutton, 2 vols. (New York 1928), I, 268f.

[4] Widenmann, former naval attaché in London, was head of the Intelligence division in the Reichsmarineamt in 1915-1916. Alfred von Tirpitz, *Politische Dokumente*, vol. II, *Deutsche Ohnmachtspolitik im Weltkrieg* (Stuttgart 1926), 631.

[5] For the role of the German military attachés in liaison work see Ernst von Wrisberg, *Wehr und Waffen 1914-1918* (Leipzig 1922), pp. 173ff., 187, 208. The German military attaché in Turkey received such full powers that his title was changed to *Militärbevollmächtiger*.

mand. When the French military attaché in St. Petersburg in 1914, General Marquis de Laguiche, found himself as liaison officer at Russian GHQ, together with his British colleague, Colonel (soon General) Knox, and time lay heavy on their hands, the Frenchman was in despair: "To think that I, at the end of 38 years of service, after having dreamed of *la revanche* so much, must remain here when the hour had struck!" He found it small compensation that he could be of considerable assistance to the Russians, with his excellent knowledge of the armies of both Germany and Austria, countries in which he had served as attaché.[6]

Colonel Huguet, who had been French military attaché in London for a number of years before 1914, was made head of the French mission attached to the British Army which provided liaison not only between Joffre and General French, but also between the BEF and the French civil authorities and civilian population.[7] "He was very suave and friendly, professing the greatest admiration for England and all things English," but he seems to have soured on the insufficiencies of British support during August 1914, which no one should have foreseen better than he. A French major, who had been attaché in Brussels, "was therefore obviously the right man for liaison with the Belgians" when, after violation of their neutrality, they decided to throw in their lot with the Western allies.[8] And the paragon liaison officer during the First World War (André Maurois' writings on the fictitious Colonel Bramble notwithstanding) was Lieutenant Spears of the British Army, who at the start of the war had just begun a term of duty with a French regiment.

American military attachés in the countries of the "Associates," from whom they had received favors before 1917 and had been allowed to observe the latest manifestations of war on any available front, were kept under the diplomatic aegis when the United States entered the war. Wilson and Secretary of War Baker thought it advisable to exempt them "and others

[6] Knox, I, 41, 46.

[7] Charles Julien Huguet subsequently wrote *L'Intervention militaire britannique en 1914* (Paris 1928).

[8] Brig. Gen. Edward Louis Spears, *Liaison 1914* (London 1930), p. 87.

of the Army who may be on duty with our several embassies"
from Pershing's otherwise all-inclusive command over the land
forces in Europe.[9] This arrangement seemed to promise their
greatest possible usefulness and best diplomatic behavior, and
also to ensure diplomatic supremacy. Some high defense officials thought this was carried too far, Franklin D. Roosevelt
for one, at the time Assistant Secretary of the Navy. His eagerness during a trip to the theater of war to get as close as possible to the Western front, even under fire (thus gaining the
prestige of a combatant—he applied for membership in the
American Legion on the strength of this "participation" in
hostilities) was thwarted by a naval attaché's attempt to detour
him around the fighting zone. Roosevelt "persecuted the
poor man for months afterwards."[10]

When Germany was conquered, many an attaché who had
formerly served in that country was employed on the Commission charged with supervision of the execution of the
Armistice conditions. One of the American members was
Colonel Samuel G. Shartle, before and after 1914 the United
States military attaché in Berlin. At the same time General von
Winterfeldt, military attaché in Paris before 1914, was one of
the signers of the Armistice convention and the leading military member of the German Armistice Commission. "He
proved to be a cool-headed spokesman for the German
mission, always courteous but persistent in presenting the German view," according to Colonel Shartle. "In the 'spats' between him and General Nudant [the French head of the
Armistice Commission] he always carried off the honors, because he never lost his head."[11]

The home authorities do not always find the best uses for the
returning attaché. When Captain Boy-Ed came home to Berlin
from Washington he seemed to some of his Navy colleagues

[9] Frederick Palmer, *Newton D. Baker, America at War*, 2 vols. (New
York 1931), I, 171. For the war services of one American attaché see Mott,
pp. 190ff. in particular.

[10] James MacGregor, *Roosevelt: The Lion and the Fox* (New York 1956),
pp. 65, 80.

[11] Col. Samuel G. Shartle, *Spa, Versailles, Munich* (Philadelphia 1941),
pp. 40, 48, and passim.

"altogether Yankee," telling everyone that America would certainly declare war on Germany unless she compromised in the Lusitania case. As a representative of Tirpitz in GHQ reported to that "father of the lie" (February 7, 1916) : Boy-Ed would not himself find the war with America fatal, "but the enemies of U-boat warfare use him as a star witness against this warfare. Herr von Müller [Chief of the Naval Cabinet and Tirpitz' enemy] has now appointed Boy-Ed who never served on the Admiralty Staff before and has no idea of its war work, the representative of the Admiralty Staff at GHQ! Commentary superfluous. But I still hope 'to straighten him out' in due time. . . . For the time being a wild scramble about U-boat warfare is on."[12] This logomachia was to be decided far above the head of Boy-Ed, largely by "the Navy" which, as the American naval attaché in Berlin was told by a German naval officer, would do whatever it considered right regardless of what the Wilhelmstrasse were doing.[13] The advice about American war potential of the other German service attaché booted home from Washington, von Papen, was equally unavailing; he told Hindenburg and the Chancellor: "Unless your Excellencies succeed in keeping America out of the coalition of our enemies, you have lost the war; about that there can be no doubt."[14]

Professional pessimism about preserving the peace had made probably the majority of service attachés foresee the coming of the World War, but scarcely any of them foretold correctly the shape it might take or even the opening moves of the enemy. Some of the more active or more realistic preparers of war, men like Henry Wilson, had been dissatisfied before 1914 with the working methods of some of the attachés. When Wilson, shortly after his appointment as Director of Military Operations of the Imperial General Staff in 1910, came to inspect the office of the British military attaché in Paris, he found it backward. "There is much that I will change here, and, I suppose, in the other military attachés.

---

[12] Tirpitz, *Deutsche Ohnmachtspolitik*, p. 471.
[13] *Ibid.*, p. 407.
[14] Ernst Fränkel in *Jahrbuch für Amerikastudien*, V (1960), 117.

They appear to me to be dealing with details and with peace, and not with war."[15] But the better judgment was not always in an influential position.

The French military attaché in Berlin until 1914, Colonel Serret, later killed in command of *Chasseurs alpins* in the Vosges, expressed himself as certain that the Germans would not only violate Belgian neutrality—which was generally expected by the Paris and London general staffs—but would form a wide arc with their very strong right wing. The French general staff thought this impossible: because of the Russian threat, Germany would not have the forces necessary for such a gigantic maneuver.[16] Serret had foreseen correctly, but he was blamed by others for having overlooked the contemplated use by the Germans of their reserve divisions at the very outset of the war.[17] (This raises the question: was the great strength of the right wing at all thinkable without the initial use of reserve divisions?)

Major General Knox, British military attaché at St. Petersburg in 1914, spoke for the entire group when he admitted in December 1915 to Kitchener, who had himself expected a prolonged war at an early time, that "military attachés had erred in good company in imagining that the great war would be a short war, and one that would not therefore tax the internal structure of the various countries." In other words, they had shared the opinion, formulated by Schlieffen and others, of the ruling military society of which they were an integral part. Kitchener, with the future of war in mind, thought certain changes necessary in the outlook and reporting of the attachés; they would have to take into consideration aspects of economic warfare and the enemy's economic war potential: "In the future military attachés would have to report on the manufacturing capabilities of the countries they are accredited to, instead of as in the past, merely on the army and its organization and training."[18] The improvised offices for economic warfare in London and Washington after the outbreak of the Second World War, as compared with the systematic preparation of economic warfare in the Berlin Mili-

---

15 Callwell, I, 86. 16 Spears, p. 41.
17 Pertinax, I, 25. 18 Knox, p. 364.

tary Economics and Armaments Office, and the paucity of materials available for these offices in the attaché reports, was to testify how little this demand had been heeded.

Those attachés of the belligerents who remained at their posts, or were newly sent out,[19] tried to support the war endeavor of the homeland in both legitimate and illegitimate ways. The activities of Germany's service attachés in Washington, Captain Franz von Papen and Lieutenant-Captain Boy-Ed, who instigated and financed sabotage against American industries producing for Germany's enemies, became so flagrant—or so opportune for a showdown—that late in 1915 the American Government demanded their recall.[20]

Respect for neutrality[21] was not much greater among the Entente attachés. The French military attaché at The Hague, General Boucabeille, together with German deserters and former Russian police agents, organized a paper called "Le Kempf" (sic) which was "in reality an agency for deserting and revolutionary propaganda." This his home Government was willing to tolerate. But when that same inventive attaché proceeded to the Banque de France to find out whether and how it was possible to manufacture false German banknotes, which he said he might need in his operations inside Ger-

---

[19] A new German attaché for Persia, a country whose neutrality no belligerent respected, organized a guerrilla force of Persian volunteers, operating against British banks and Entente consuls. For details see *Wissen und Wehr* (1926), pp. 180ff.

[20] *Papers Relating to the Foreign Relations of the United States: The Lansing Papers, 1914-1920* (Washington 1939), I, 75ff.; for a criticism of American government policy see C. Hartley Grattan, *Why We fought* (New York 1929), pp. 100ff. On Papen see also Franz von Rintelen, *The Dark Invader—Wartime Reminiscences of a German Naval Intelligence Officer* (London 1933), Horst P. Falcke, *Vor dem Eintritt Amerikas in den Weltkrieg* (Dresden 1928), and Papen's *Memoirs*.

[21] For the violations of Spanish neutrality by the German military attaché, Major Kalle, and Secretary of Legation Stohrer, later Hitler's ambassador to France, both of whom were expelled at the end of the First World War, see *Neue Weltbühne* (Paris), December 22, 1938. Several of the Japanese military attachés during the Russo-Japanese War established contacts with and financed the activities of various enemies of Tsardom, the Finns, the Poles, and the Socialists, including Lenin. *Documents diplomatiques français*, II. ser., X, 706f., and Stefan T. Possony, *Lenin: The Compulsive Revolutionary* (Chicago 1964), pp. 78ff., for much detail.

many, Clemenceau, either because he thought such capitalist convictions as the sanctity of money must be preserved even in war, or because he feared the scandal in case of detection, told this *hurluberlu*, this hare-brained person, as he called him, to keep quiet.[22]

The neutrals in that war and their attachés did not always remain neutral, but favored one side or the other, or themselves, as they thought best. Tension grew high between Turkey and Greece and nearly led to the severance of diplomatic relations, when in December 1914 the Turks threatened to execute a Greek sailor who had been in the pay of the Greek naval attaché and had been sentenced for espionage. German diplomacy tried to mediate by suggesting that the sailor be freed and the attaché, whom the Russian minister in Athens called "active and well-informed," and one to whom "among many other things we owe the greatest part of the information about the activities and movements of the Turkish fleet," be recalled by his Government. Venizelos categorically declined this proposal, which would have robbed the Entente of a valuable source of information, and instead declared himself ready to close the legation and recall the whole personnel.[23]

It was in no small measure the doings of the French service attachés in Athens that made the story of the intervention of the Allies in Greece in 1915-1916 so infinitely complicated, if not almost criminal. The naval attaché, Frigate Captain de Rocquefeuil, acted on the authority of the Paris Marine Ministry, to whom he reported directly as part of wartime intelligence work, rather than to the civilian diplomatic offices directed by Briand. In vain did the French minister in Athens complain that "the conditions under which the intelligence service is functioning give him absolute independence, and I cannot prevent its chief—the local naval attaché—from telegraphing what he pleases to the minister on whom he depends directly." The attaché and the Venizelists were both

[22] Raymond Poincaré, *Au Service de la France—Neuf années de souvenirs* (Paris 1926-1933), X, 276ff., 335.

[23] *Die internationalen Beziehungen im Zeitalter des Imperialismus* (USSR), II. Reihe, Bd. VI, 568.

eager to push Greece out of the neutrality which the King tried to maintain, but their conspiracy reached criminal heights when a gang, hired by the attaché, staged an incident. They penetrated the French legation grounds and fired shots which appeared to be aimed at the ministers of the Entente assembled in the legation at the time. The secret of this incident, which forced the hand of both the London and Paris governments, was bared almost before Briand's slow-moving civilian diplomacy had removed the King and brought Greece into the war on the Allied side.[24]

The most responsible part of the neutral attaché's duty was to judge the strength of the forces under his observation, their movements in relation to his own country and their chances of final victory. Did the latter warrant joining one side rather than the other? The Bulgarian attaché at Petrograd came home in mid-January 1915 to report orally on the state of the Russian army. Much to the satisfaction of King Ferdinand and the prime minister he expressed his conviction that the want of equipment of all kinds would prevent the Russians from taking the offensive. The Austrian legation in Sofia was informed of these conclusions and duly reported to Vienna, but the report was stolen somewhere en route and ended up in Russia. Sasonov gave himself the malicious pleasure of reading it in the original German to the Bulgarian minister in Petrograd, and the minister immediately wired his Government that the attaché must be recalled in order to avoid the worst kind of incidents.[25]

The belligerents employed a few of their former attachés to seek peace, or at least an armistice with the countries in which they had served. General von Winterfeldt, German military attaché in Paris until 1913 (where a severe automobile accident during maneuvers had earned him many expressions of sympathy, then called chivalrous) was made a member of the Armistice Commission, while the prewar Austro-Hungarian military attaché to Bucharest, General Staff

[24] Georges Boussenot, "Le drame du 1er décembre 1916," *Revue d'histoire de la guerre mondiale* (January 1938); Georges Suarez, *Briand Sa vie—son oeuvre*, 6 vols. (Paris 1938-1952), III, 446ff.

[25] *Die internationalen Beziehungen*, Bd. VII, 35f.

Colonel Randa, was employed by Emperor Karl and Count Czernin to save thrones, including the Austrian, in eastern Europe. At the opening of peace negotiations with Rumania in 1918 the Germans thought of sweeping Ferdinand from the throne, but Karl and Czernin opposed this threat to legitimacy since it might backfire on the Double Monarchy. While the allied headquarters were still negotiating about military measures to make Rumania more peace-minded, Randa traveled secretly to Iassy with orders from Karl to talk Ferdinand into a receptive mood; Hapsburg would guarantee this Hohenzollern at least his throne, for the monarchs of all countries must unite for the protection of legitimacy (and against Ludendorff). While the Germans were not informed of this step, Rumania learned at least that the Central Powers did not agree on every point.[26]

Another Balkan dynasty, the Petrovic, proved completely unsalvageable by any military attaché or other agency. During the second half of 1915 King Nikita of Montenegro sent word to the Austrians that he would like to negotiate through the former military attaché at Cetinje, Colonel Hubka, but the war situation improved so much for the Entente and for Nikita himself by the time Hubka had been brought over from the Italian front that the meeting was as unproductive as Nikita's later attempts to come to a separate peace with Austria.[27]

The military attachés of the Western powers at Petrograd had tried their best to boost the morale of the Tsarist armies. Immediately after the First Revolution of 1917 it seemed that it might be possible to keep Kerenski's Russia in the war; a British officer (Cromie?) wrote from Cronstadt that it was the Russian policy "to coax the people into a summer offensive in the hope that peace will then slip into the background. I am not hopeful. Everyone is clear that Russia is sick of the war." The British military attaché, General Knox, "the plain-spoken officer who not only saw things as they were, but reported and recorded them without gloss to his superiors,"

---

[26] August von Cramon, *Unser österreichisch-ungarische Bundesgenosse im Weltkriege* (Berlin 1920), p. 143.

[27] *Die Weltbühne* (Berlin), September 6, 1927, p. 369.

was, according to Lloyd George, more "at the head of Russian affairs at this time" than was the ambassador. Knox was an Ulsterman, and later a diehard MP; he was very early considered a reactionary with Tsarist sympathies, whom President Wilson would not allow to cross the United States on his way to head the intervention forces in Siberia. At first Knox was not without hope: "The heart of the people was sound, but force was required, and force could have been assembled if the Government had contained a single man of will." But after the failure of the Kerenski offensive in July 1917, he feared that the Socialists "would prefer a class war rather than a national war, and to the mass of soldiers this appeals as being not so dangerous. . . . Tseretelli and others think they can run both wars simultaneously. . . . This is impossible."

Late in August 1917 General Knox returned to England to inform the War Cabinet about the Russian situation, leaving to other attachés and liaison officers the task of keeping the Bolshevists in the war, and of maintaining relations not only with officers of the old Army but also with the new incumbents of the Petrograd offices, including Trotsky.[28] When the latter was left without an answer to his "insolent communications" to the ambassadors, who would not recognize the "pretended government" of the Soviets, he chose the attachés to receive the next messages—about the intended negotiations with the Germans which were to bring about a general, and not a separate, armistice. The attachés protested against the violation of the terms of the Treaty of September 5, 1914, which bound Russia not to make a separate peace, and the military attaché of the United States, not a party to that treaty, protested "categorically and energetically against any separate armistice which may be made by Russia." He came to realize only later that "the time for protests and threats addressed to the Soviet authority is over, if it ever existed." These protests were addressed to the Stavka, to whom Allied recognition was transferred in the hope that the Russian Supreme Command would "hold the Russian Army at the front facing a common enemy." The intended boost to morale failed com-

---

[28] For the above see *War Memoirs of David Lloyd George*, 6 vols. (London 1933-1936), III, 466; V, 80, 82, 98; VI, 176f.

pletely. The Stavka circulated the Allied declaration to the Army, and hints as to Allied action against the Soviet Government, but Trotsky protested such efforts as "forcing by threats the Russian Army and the Russian people to continue the war in execution of the treaties concluded by the Tsar"— treaties which they would not honor. He warned the Allied military missions that his government "cannot permit Allied diplomatic and military agents to interfere in the internal affairs of our country and attempt to incite civil war."

The last pro-Allied commander-in-chief was murdered, and the attachés began casting around for "well-disposed" Russian military leaders to organize and lead White armies.[29] Some of them, like Captain Sadoul of the French military mission and Colonel Ruggles (USA), negotiated with Trotsky from March to May 1918 about a reorganization of the Russian Army with the help of Allied military missions, instructors and materiel;[30] others, like the British naval attaché, Captain Cromie, continued contacts with the emerging White opposition. A series of political murders during the summer of 1918 turned the suspicions of the Bolshevists against the Allied diplomats, and a mob, searching for "proof" of conspiracy, tried to break into the British Embassy in Petrograd. They were met by Cromie, and they murdered him outside the Embassy. Inside, the military attaché was burning incriminating papers, according to the version given out by the Cheka, who took him away and imprisoned him in the Peter and Paul Fortress—in retaliation Litvinov and his staff were put under "preventive arrest" in London.[31] Revolutions are no respecters of immunities, diplomatic ones included, in the defense of which some service attachés preferred to die.

[29] *Lloyd George*, V, 106ff., 123f.; John W. Wheeler-Bennett, *The Forgotten Peace, Brest-Litovsk March 1918* (New York 1939), pp. 72ff., 143.
[30] Louis Fischer, *Soviets in World Affairs* (London and New York 1930), pp. 62, 96, 98 and passim; *Papers Relating to the Foreign Relations of the United States: The Lansing Papers: Russia*, passim.
[31] Nicholas Wreden, *The Unmaking of a Russian* (New York 1935), pp. 175ff.; for the conspiratorial doings of the French military attaché see Fischer, p. 118.

CHAPTER 4

BETWEEN THE WARS

Deeds and misdeeds of the military attachés on the losing side gave rise to the prohibition, in the various peace treaties of 1919 (Versailles, art. 179, Saint-Germain, art. 158, etc.) , against the Central Powers sending abroad in future any "military, naval or aeronautical mission." The abolition of military attachés in the interest of peace had been advocated before, usually by Socialists and pacifists, but not the one-sided measure which was now to be executed. When the articles of peace were signed, both sides clearly understood that this prohibition covered the whole institution of attachés. It was to form part of the thorough disarmament of the Central Powers, which Lord Bertie, former British ambassador to Paris, thought an excellent idea, "but who," he said, "are the persons to supervise and control German proceedings in such matters? Military attachés would not be of any account and would be deified,"[1] something which Bertie clearly thought they did not in the least deserve. Actually, the victors did not entrust this supervisory mission to the attachés, who were sent back to the capitals of the losing side almost at once,[2] but to international control commissions (functioning until January 31, 1930) .

Not until "normalcy" had returned to postwar international relations were military attachés again used for international control or fact-finding purposes, functions which had occasionally been assigned to them or proposed for them before.[3] When a serious incident occurred on the Bulgarian-Greek border in October 1925, and was brought before the Council of the League of Nations, it was settled by the use of attachés. The Council ordered the troops involved to stop all

[1] Francis Leveson Bertie, 1st viscount, *The Diary of Lord Bertie of Thame, 1914-1918*, 2 vols. (New York 1924), II, 320 (March 20, 1919).
[2] Among the latter was the later Admiral Halsey; see William F. Halsey and Joseph Bryan, *Admiral Halsey's Story* (New York 1947), pp. 48f.
[3] See, for instance, *Grosse Politik*, XVIII, 5524ff., 5579.

hostilities and retire at once to their own soil, under threat of sanctions, and asked the British, French and Italian Governments to order some of their officers stationed nearby to proceed there at once and report directly to the Council about the observance of its orders. The officers nearest the scene—and also most "neutral," i.e. not residing in either Sofia or Athens —were the military attachés of the three powers in Belgrade. They appeared promptly, notified the local commanders of the Council's decisions, supervised the orderly retreat of the invading Greek troops, and the advance of the Bulgarian troops to the frontier, without any new incident. They reported to the Council their intention to extend "their investigations to ascertain a number of military and material facts which should be cleared up before those who have participated in the incident should leave the region and before the bad season made access to the points where the facts had occurred and notably a detailed inquiry into the original incident altogether too difficult." The Council did not make full use of their offer, but when a special commission of inquiry was subsequently sent to the locality, it called upon the officers for cooperation.[4] When another dangerous situation arose in 1927, the Council, having found that attachés could serve the cause of peace quite satisfactorily, employed them once more. A school and language conflict between Lithuania and Poland had led to the massing of troops on both sides of the frontier and, considering the inflamed state of mind, worse was feared. British and French military attachés were sent immediately, and succeeded in calming those on the spot as well as those in the Western capitals.[5]

The satisfactory work of these groups of attachés as fact-finders, as *commissions de constatation* ascertaining the details of an incident of a military nature, inspired various Geneva proposals of 1931-1932 for the reduction and limitation of armaments and the prevention of war; they envisaged the employment of military, naval and air attachés as members of fact-finding commissions, together with other diplomatic

---

[4] *Journal officiel de la Société des Nations*, VII (1926), 194ff.; Beauvais, pp. 189ff.

[5] Beauvais, p. 191.

personnel.[6] While these proposals came to nothing, they nevertheless showed a certain readiness on the part of the peace-loving nations to turn the exponents of the armaments race into contributors to peace.

Demoniac schemers like Hitler and Ribbentrop turned this feeling to the advantage of German rearmament in the Peace Plan of the German Government of March 31, 1936. They proposed that a commission, composed of representatives of Great Britain and Italy, as guarantors of the Locarno Pact, and a third, neutral and disinterested power, should be made guarantors of the assurances made by the German, Belgian and French Governments that they would not reinforce their troops in the vicinity of the Rhine frontiers in the four months remaining before the signing of non-aggression pacts. This commission would make the necessary investigation with the help of British and Italian military attachés.[7] Czechoslovakia also wished to give the service attaché a new kind of employment when, at the end of 1936, there were violent accusations in the German press that she had sold herself to Soviet Russia, had built subterranean airdromes for the use of Soviet planes, and had allowed hundreds of Soviet officers to stay in her territory and prepare the promised military assistance. The Prague Government proposed to Britain that she order her representatives in the country, notably the military attaché, to ascertain the truth about these accusations. The British accepted, but the German Government, to whom a similar invitation had been extended, brushed it off.[8]

International fact-finding bodies, in a case of conflict, can function only if all participants want the facts to be put on record. This was not in the least the intention of four out of the five participants in the Non-Intervention Committee set up in London during the Spanish Civil War, near the end of 1936. It was composed of the ambassadors of the great powers

[6] For details see Beauvais, pp. 191ff. A British military attaché was on the spot to observe and characterize as "pure invention" the incident in September 1931 on which the Japanese based their case for aggression in Manchuria. Potiemkine, III, 438f.

[7] Beauvais, p. 194.   [8] Beauvais, p. 194.

and a Foreign Office representative, with sub-committees of service attachés who were to find ways to stop the flow of volunteers and other help to the parties in that war. But since no side, with the possible exception of the British, honestly wanted to put an end to this traffic and possibly keep the war from spreading, the work of the committees and sub-committees amounted to nothing but a "political swindle high on horseback," according to the German military attaché who participated in the discussions.[9]

In the meantime, the network of service attachés among both greater and lesser powers had been extensively rebuilt, accompanied by ever more extensive paperwork.[10] As soon as the Interallied Military Control Commission had ended its supervisory work in Germany (January 3, 1927), after Locarno, ascertaining infractions of the military treaty terms right up to the end, French (after February 1927), British, Italian and Belgian service attachés took up its fault-finding labors. They watched the regrowth of German military strength, reporting in the greatest detail on military organization and reorganization, on industry and manpower, on rearmament inside and, to a much lesser degree, outside the Weimar Republic, on military thought, on the new chiefs and chiefs of staff, on mobilization preparation, schooling, and much else that was prohibited under the terms of the Versailles Treaty.[11]

The secret they were least able to penetrate was that of the ties established between Reichswehr and Red Army, though it was obvious enough that the Reichswehr was eager to avert not so much another war as another war on two fronts. With this thought in mind Germany tried to divide the French and British and to get on near-alliance terms with the

[9] Geyr, passim; for the participation of the Berlin military attachés in the drawing of the Czech frontiers after Munich see *Documents on German Foreign Policy*, Ser. D, IV, 2f., 9, 22, etc.

[10] When Waldersee (his *Denkwürdigkeiten*, I, 67) was attaché in Paris in 1870, he wrote on the average one report every fortnight. The French military attaché or attachés in Berlin in 1927 and later sent three or four reports per diem. Castellan, passim.

[11] For the reports of the French military attachés to 1935 see Castellan, in the great detail; for the less detailed reports of the British attachés see *Documents on British Foreign Policy*, IInd ser., I, 598ff.; II, 182ff., 515ff.; IV, 254.

Red Army; this would neutralize their common enemy, Poland, which was a part of France's second military and diplomatic front. Only the specter of Hitler, and the unwillingness of Poland to form a second front in the East together with Russia and Czechoslovakia, brought about a first rapprochement between Moscow and Paris, marked most clearly by the arrival of the first postwar French military attaché in Moscow, two months after seizure of power by the Nazis. He was received with promises by the Red Army chiefs. Voroshilov, after he had obtained Stalin's permission to attend a dinner at the French Embassy and meet the attaché, told him he would see more and more of the Red Army, but "gradually, to the degree that our relations become more amicable, something that can be attained only if the military attaché is not the only French officer to take an interest in our Army and enter into contacts with it. . . . Why don't you send us technicians who can help us to construct submarines, torpedo boats, or even cruisers? Our Navy needs them very much; we have much work to do to get it under way again."[12]

Tukhashevski, who directed the work of arming and equipping the Red Army at the time, indicated a certain readiness to let French war industries take over the role of the Germans as the provider of military and industrial progress,[13] but French professional desire for implementation and reciprocity remained limited. Admiral Darlan, virtual leader of the French Navy well before 1939, was even unwilling to have a French naval attaché go to Moscow, lest a Soviet naval representative, who might revolutionize the French sailors, come to Paris.[14] On the other hand, in 1933 American service attachés were once more stationed in Russia.

The Reichswehr had never gladly suffered the suppression of attachés, had considered it "unfortunate" that their activity had to be terminated on April 1, 1919, as the biographer of Seeckt, himself a general, noted.[15] It had treated this *dimi-*

---

[12] Castellan, pp. 490f.

[13] *Ibid.*

[14] Sir Lewis Namier, *In the Nazi Era* (London 1952), p. 170.

[15] General Friedrich von Rabenau, ed., *Hans von Seeckt. Aus seinem Leben, 1918-1936* (Leipzig 1940), p. 214; for the Berlin *interna* about service attachés after 1919 see Meisner, *Militärattachés*, pp. 37ff.

nutio capitis as of relatively minor importance—there were other more serious restrictions in the Peace Treaty to be over-come or evaded—still, it had rankled. Some of the military perhaps remembered—as some of the civilian diplomats did —Falkenhayn's proposal during the war that after the victory the civilian ambassadors should be dismissed and replaced by military attachés.[16]

The suspension of attaché duty did not mean that the study of foreign armies and their progress had been neglected in Berlin, or even in Germany's posts abroad; much to the regret of the Reichswehr, however, such reporting was as a rule left to younger members of the staffs who often did nothing but subscribe to clipping bureaus.[17] The Reichswehr's knowledge of foreign armies was for a time restricted to material from such sources and to military literature, some information was even imparted to persons in the confidence of the Bendlerstrasse through the medium of *Wehrgedanken des Auslandes* ("Military Thought Abroad," a periodical published privately by the Reichswehr Ministry from 1924 on). It showed again and again how deeply the foreign press was interested in questions of defense while Germany and her press remained ultra-pacifist.

Relations between the Reichswehr and the foreign military attachés in Berlin were in part harmonious, at least among the Anglo-American attachés and the neutrals; the British and Swedish attachés both showed strong "understanding for the satisfaction" which Guderian and other generals felt when Hitler reintroduced conscription in March 1935.[18] The British thought some of the disarmament restrictions imposed by the Versailles Treaty almost too preposterous for a modern army to submit to, and they could not hide from their superiors their admiration for such veterans and paramilitary organizations as the Stahlhelmbund. While they were noting at least some of the infractions of the disarmament paragraphs, they had to concede that sometimes this information

16 Monts, p. 180.   17 Geyr, passim.
18 Heinz Guderian, *Panzer Leader,* transl. Constantine Fitzgibbon (New York 1952), p. 35.

was gained in a manner "which made it impossible for a charge to be made against Germany of breach of treaty." The French attachés, considering their Government's determined clinging to one-sided disarmament, could never listen receptively to the appeals of Reichswehr generals to grant Germany "equality of status" as the first condition of a "just and honorable Franco-German understanding out of which sincere friendship might develop." Such an appeal was directed by the German chief of staff to the French attaché departing near the end of 1930, and after that, according to the British view, "relations between the French and German armies grew steadily worse." A French ex-attaché, General Tournès, published a series of "offensive and inaccurate" newspaper articles—offensive to the Reichswehr officers, who naturally made things difficult for his successor. "A still more tactless and unfortunate incident" occurred in April 1931, when the French assistant military attaché and two members of the French intelligence service were arrested for photographing some military installations.[19] The attaché was recalled.

The intended one-sided prohibition of service attachés could not last, the genus proved irrepressible. The Treaty of Lausanne, which replaced the imposed and unratified Treaty of Sèvres which had included the prohibition, did not repeat it, and Turkey again maintained attachés in capitals such as Athens, Bucharest, Paris, Rome and Sofia, after 1923. The Reichswehr, supported but feebly by the Wilhelmstrasse, worked in vain for a long time to obtain the *agrément* of the Versailles Treaty powers to the renewed stationing abroad of German service attachés. Seeckt's successor, General Heye, personally made the attempt in Washington when he went to

[19] The above is based on reports of the British military attaché in Berlin for 1931 and the Memorandum of the Chief of the Imperial General Staff on the military situation in Germany, January 1930. *Documents on British Foreign Policy*, IInd ser., I, 598ff. and III, 515ff. The British attaché in December 1931 was ready to admit that there was much to be said in favor of German *Wehrgeist* as a defense against Bolshevism. "Most decent Britons, were they Germans today, would be Stahlhelmers." *Ibid.*, II, app. IV.

America in the autumn of 1927, again in vain.[20] Other defeated nations proceeded more boldly: Hungary in 1927 and Bulgaria in 1930 sent military attachés to Paris and Berlin, Paris and Rome, respectively, where they were not rebuffed. In doing so, they seem to have acted in keeping with an interpretation of the Conference of Ambassadors, the organ for supervising the execution of the "suburban" treaties: in 1926 the Conference obtained an opinion of jurists that Art. 179 of the Versailles Treaty, and the corresponding articles in the others, merely forbade Germany and the other defeated nations to send "military missions of instruction" abroad, such as the Liman von Sanders mission of 1913-1914. The emphasis was shifted to the preamble of the various treaties: they provided that "official relations" between the defeated and the victorious Allied and Associated powers "would be resumed as soon as these treaties would come into force." And did not "official relations," to be called complete, include the exchange of service attachés? Whether out of pride[21] or for other reasons—perhaps to nourish the resentment over having no German attachés abroad, a major grievance of German militarists against the powers of Versailles—the Reichswehr or the Wilhelmstrasse preferred for a time not to make use of this reconciliatory interpretation. Only after the Five Power agreement on the "equality of rights of armaments" of December 11, 1932, did the Reich Government resolve to appoint such attachés again to a restricted, but soon increased, number of its embassies and legations. Their acceptance by the Powers was taken by the Germans as a sign of incipient approval or sufferance of German rearmament.[22] While their appointment took place during General von Schleicher's Chancellorship, they began their activity on April 1, 1933 (anniversary of the suppression of their predecessors?), after the Nazis had come to power. At that time military

[20] This was told the author at the time by a member of the German embassy in Washington. See also *Die Weltbühne* (Berlin), October 18, 1927.

[21] As the quasi-official *Handbuch der neuzeitlichen Wehrwissenschaften*, 3 vols. in 4, Hermann Franke, ed. (Berlin and Leipzig 1936), I, 510, put it: "After the World War Germany gave up sending military attachés abroad. . . ."

[22] Statement of the defense for von Leeb. *Trials of War Criminals*, X, 170f.

attachés were sent to Paris, London (whence Brussels and The Hague were also served), Rome, Warsaw, Moscow and Washington and, a little later, to Prague, Vienna and Tokyo. Naval attachés, some of whom had worked before 1933 "under disguise,"[23] as part of the clandestine rebuilding of the Navy, were stationed, then or later, in London, Paris, Rome, Stockholm, Tokyo and Washington. Austria followed the German example a year later.

Mindful of the experiences with service attachés under Bismarck and William II, the Wilhelmstrasse had insisted that these officers would have nothing to do with espionage, were to employ no agents of their own, and must submit their reports to the mission head for his information and counter-signature, and where necessary for his remarks and counter-statement. The reception which some of them found was distinctly chilly. When Ambassador von Hoesch in London heard that once again service attachés were to be sent out, he said: "Now what are they for? Politicking, I suppose."[24]

These German attachés as a rule were of comparatively high rank, which gave them precedence right below the ambassador or minister, and one of them in each embassy, the *Wehrmachtattaché*, was to report on the host country's military and war power as a whole, in addition to his specific field. They had qualified for their posts in various ways. The military attaché for Paris, Colonel, later Lieutenant General, Kühlenthal, had directed the department of "Foreign Armies" (*Fremde Heere*) in the Reichswehr Ministry, which had kept tabs on armies abroad since 1928; in Rome, Major, later Lieutenant General, Fischer, had been chief of the counter-espionage department in the same Ministry,[25] and there is reason to assume that from Rome he directed German espionage against France. Colonel, later General, Köstring had been in Moscow since 1931 as the Reichswehr's "unofficial" representative; once his status had been made official he freely imparted his own estimates of Soviet military weak-

23 *Trial of the Major War Criminals*, II, 329.
24 Geyr, *Erinnerungen*, p. 15.
25 Berthold Jacob, *Das neue deutsche Heer und seine Führer* (Paris 1936), p. 87.

nesses and isolation from military progress to his British colleague, who did not consider him a violent Nazi supporter. Köstring told the Britisher in May 1938 that but for the purge in the Red Army, which was temporarily out of action, the Germans would not now be in Vienna.[26] The foremost military engineer of the *Anschluss* was the military attaché in Vienna, Lieutenant Colonel, very soon Lieutenant General, Muff, who had been recalled to duty from retirement and a university professorship of military science, practically the first one in the Weimar Republic.[27] He soon got on the nerves of the Wilhelmstrasse diplomats for his "purely political reports," dealing with things not falling "within his competence. Why does General Muff expatiate so much on political questions?"[28]

According to his nominal superior, von Papen, Muff "maintained good relations with the Austrian army circles which were inclined towards National Socialism, but had no contact with the far more worthy part of Austria."[29] It has been maintained that the Nazis intended to have him assassinated in Vienna in order to provoke the Reichsheer, which might be moved by *ésprit de corps* to avenge his murder on Austria.[30] After his early warnings (August 1933 and January 1934) that from a military point of view Nazi intervention could not succeed, considering the loyalty of the Austrian Army and the weakness of the Austrian S.A., his activities culminated in the March days of the *Anschluss* when he delivered an ultimatum from Goering. His "inclination towards the Party," as von Papen put it, as well as his record in Austria, earned him rapid promotion from Hitler, with whom he spent days at a time in Berchtesgaden.[31]

[26] *Documents on British Foreign Policy*, IIIrd ser., I, 418ff. For Köstring see now Hermann Teske, ed., *General Ernst Köstring. Der militärische Mittler zwischen dem Deutschen Reich und der Sowjetunion, 1921-1941* (Frankfurt 1966).

[27] Castellan, p. 422.

[28] *Documents on German Foreign Policy*, Ser. C, III, 376.

[29] U.S. Chief of Counsel for the Prosecution of Axis Criminality, *Nazi Conspiracy and Aggression*, 8 vols. (Washington 1946), Supplement, 2 vols. (Washington 1947-1948), Suppl. A, 449.

[30] Martin Fuchs, *Showdown in Austria* (New York 1939), p. 174.

[31] *Nazi Conspiracy and Aggression*, IV, 314; *Documents on German*

The *Drang nach Osten,* resumed by the Nazis, was served by attachés in various other places. Those stationed in Moscow, soon and sincerely regretted the rupture of the old ties between Reichswehr and Red Army,[32] while the first military attaché sent to Poland, with whom temporary friendship was being sought, was received by Pilsudski with "soldierlike candour," including the confession that he, the Marshal, "was opposed in principle to the institution of military attachés. For what purpose were 14 military attachés needed in a state like Poland," so unequivocally allied with France? On account of all that "Germany had done against Poland in the last few years . . . the Polish public looked with distrust at a German military attaché," and the Marshal himself had been opposed to the appointment although he had nothing against the first incumbent, of whom he had received only the best possible information and whom he assured of a hospitable welcome in Poland. "Only direct relations with the troops were not admissible."[33]

The successful candidate for London knew languages, a knowledge that according to him had become rare in the German Army since Moltke; he also knew horses. The military and air attaché for Ankara, Athens and Teheran, Colonel Hans Rohde, was a prolific writer on Near Eastern questions, somewhat in the Haushofer style of "geopolitics," during the First World War and the period of temporary German disinterest in that region after 1918. The naval attaché for London, Rear Admiral Erwin Wassner, had commanded the first German warship to visit New York harbor since 1912, and in November 1932 was the first Reich naval officer to place a wreath on the Arlington tomb of the Unknown Soldier; the successful performance of these gestures contributed to qualify him for the London post. There he played a considerable role in the negotiation of the Anglo-German

---

Foreign Policy, Ser. C, I, 165; II, 437; III, 255ff., 342, 373ff.; Ser. D, I, 300, 584ff.; Ernst Heinrich, Freiherr von Weizsäcker, *Memoirs,* transl. John Andrews (London 1951), p. 122; Papen, p. 427.

[32] *Documents on German Foreign Policy,* Ser. C, I, 609, 819ff., 856ff.
[33] *Ibid.,* I, 401ff.

naval pact of 1935, the first act to recognize that Germany was again a participant with equal status in the world's naval armaments competition.[34] The military attaché in Washington, General von Boetticher, almost the only attaché whose reports Hitler praised—and misinterpreted—was a specialist on the history of the American Civil War.[35] Colonel Ott in Tokyo had been an aide of General von Schleicher, who had been assassinated by the Nazis. He was a pupil from the school of Colonel Nicolai, director of German intelligence during the First World War—the school had been reactivated under Hitler. Ott found himself promptly on intimate terms with his Japanese counterpart, Colonel Oshima, soon to become Japan's military attaché in Berlin; both men were intriguing their way up to the top of their respective embassies —spies as ambassadors.[36] From 1935 on, with war drawing closer, the German service attachés were called home annually for consultation. Some of the leaders listened willingly to their oral reporting, including warnings that Britain would fight should Germany provoke a war; others, including Hitler, listening unwillingly or not at all.[37]

If the Bolshevists, heirs to a few of the military thoughts of Socialism, had early in their regime considered doing away with service attachés altogether, such a notion remained foreign to the various Fascisms. For their foreign as well as their military policies such attachés were indispensable. At the very beginning of Fascism's bombastic appearance in the international arena, with its brutal assertion of the nationalist ego over all diplomatic considerations, occurred the incident involving the Italian military attaché in Athens, Colonel Perrone di San Martino. On August 27, 1923, the very day that

[34] For more details see obituary in *The New York Times*, August 25, 1937.

[35] On von Boetticher's good relations with the Washington General Staff and their common antipathy to Red Spain see *Documents on German Foreign Policy*, Ser. D, III, 304. He knew better than to distribute Nazi pamphlets among American officers for whom they were designed. *Nazi Conspiracy and Aggression*, Suppl. A, p. 577. See also General Gerhard L. Weinberg in *American Historical Review*, LXIX (1946), 1012.

[36] *Neue Weltbühne* (Paris), February 9, 1939.

[37] Beauvais, p. 74; Geyr, passim; Moriz Faber du Faur, *Macht und Ohnmacht. Erinnerungen eines alten Offiziers* (Stuttgart 1953).

the Italian Tellini mission was murdered on Greek soil, though perhaps not by Greek nationals—murder which led to the bombardment and temporary occupation of Corfu— Perrone split the head of an innocent Greek merchant who had, in the Italian officer's hearing, loudly ordered a dish of macaroni. The Italian was offended and, without further inquiry, proceeded to defend his own and his country's honor.[38] Having qualified by this brutal aggressiveness for a fact-finding mission, Colonel Perrone was named by the Italian ultimatum of August 29 as his country's representative "under whose cooperation" the Greek authorities were to make a very strict inquiry in the neighborhood of the massacre. The ultimatum made the Greek Government "absolutely responsible for the personal safety of Colonel Perrone" whose task, to be completed within five days, it must facilitate in every way.[39] Greece appealed to the League of Nations, Mussolini to the guns; one of the few humiliations Greece was spared was the service of Perrone as fact-finder.[40]

The Italian and German service attachés were cogs essential for the smooth working of the Berlin-Rome Axis, including the joint intervention in Spain.[41] As far as Berlin was concerned it had been initiated through Colonel Beigbeder, long the Spanish military attaché in Berlin, and later Commissioner in Spanish Morocco. He and Franco appealed to the Reich Government early in the military uprising through "their friend" General Kühlenthal, German military attaché in Paris, for transport planes to fly from North Africa to Spain. Prominent members of the Spanish Nationalist Com-

---

[38] Beauvais, p. 142.

[39] For text of the ultimatum see *Europäische Gespräche* I (1923), 314.

[40] Fascist Italy sought in Greece, the lesser power, an outlet for her inferiority complexes. When in 1939 the Greek military attaché in Budapest had uttered some negative remarks on the military qualities of the Italian forces, Ciano threatened to break off relations with Athens. The break, or worse, was averted by the prompt recall of the talker. Gordon A. Craig and Felix Gilbert, eds., *The Diplomats 1919-1939* (Princeton 1953), p. 523.

[41] The German military attaché in Belgrade submitted the offer of a White Russian general heading a legion of 1500 men who were willing to serve Franco. This offer was handed on to Franco by Berlin. *Trial of the Major War Criminals*, XXVIII, 346ff.

mittee set up in Paris were the service attachés who had resigned from the service of the Republic. "Since these are
friends of our own military and naval attachés, connection is
established," wrote the German ambassador from Paris, less
than two weeks after the start of the rebellion, and he designated the naval attaché of the embassy to serve as "unofficial
liaison who meets with his former Spanish colleague but, of
course, only at constantly changing neutral places, using all
possible precautions, in order to avoid compromising a
member of the embassy."[42] Beigbeder, originally deeply impressed by the might of the German military machine but
later appalled by the bills the Germans presented for services
rendered, was made foreign minister by Franco. He eventually
became openly anti-Hitler and pro-British, believing in spite
of the disasters of 1940 in the ultimate victory of the Anglo-
Saxon powers, and Hitler decreed that "as Beigbeder had
sold himself to Sir Samuel Hoare [the British ambassador] he
must go." Franco dismissed him in October 1940.[43]

In spite of the prohibitions under which the defeated
nations had labored and which had helped to reduce the
number of service attachés, their total increased considerably after 1918. The new nations such as Poland, Czechoslovakia and others made ample use of the institution—or
misuse, as some have charged against the later Colonel
Beck[44]—in order to keep informed of the progress achieved
by their greater allies and to take care of the details of military
alliances, where such existed. The older military powers
reciprocated, to keep themselves informed about the military

---

[42] *Documents on German Foreign Policy*, Ser. D, III, 4, 7, 24, 154, etc.
[43] Sir Samuel Hoare, *Complacent Dictator* (New York 1947), p. 55 and
passim.
[44] According to the official Russian *Histoire de la diplomatie* (Potiemkine, III, 608), which hardly mentions another service attaché in its
2,000 pages, the French General Staff in 1923 found out that certain
information referring to its own army which had been given only to the
representatives of allied armies, including the Polish, had come into
German possession. The following year Beck, the Polish attaché, was
forced to leave France in connection with this scandal, at the demand
of Foch himself. When early in 1932 Poland sought the *agrément* for
Beck as ambassador and the French denied it, Pilsudski, out of spite,
made Beck foreign minister.

62

potential of the new nations or their *non-valeur*, as in the case of India, where Japan soon dispatched attachés, and Ireland.

Soviet Russia had welcomed back the last Tsarist military attaché in Paris, Count Ignatiev, and for years afterward he was a teacher of tactics in her military schools. Early in 1922 Russia decided, as part of the reorganization of her diplomatic service, that service attachés, even under a new title, were still worth having, and that the mission chiefs should have "military and naval agents" at their disposal. A set of rules, of November 12, 1923, regulated the appointment and the place in the diplomatic mission of such attachés, as they were soon called again; military attachés for Germany, China and Italy, and naval attachés for Great Britain and Finland were promptly appointed.[45]

Some attachés were suspected of having instigated or furthered local Communist putsches even as late as 1929, but on the whole they, like the civilian diplomats, were excused from such tasks in the service of world revolution; they were thus enabled to dedicate themselves to more strictly military observation and the study of military progress abroad. The Red Army stationed some of its best heads and higher ranking officers, including later army corps commanders, in the various capitals, especially Berlin, where they sent officers like Kork and Putna (1929-1931). The latter also served in London later. These men became victims of the xenophobic purge of 1937,[46] although to those Westerners who had official or social contacts with them they had seemed "completely and utterly loyal" to their masters.[47]

Service attachés from nations who had recognized the Soviet Government were received in Moscow. A German officer, assisted at the outset of his labors by a pre-1914 German attaché in St. Petersburg, was the first to arrive, though he was not called military attaché again until 1933. He, rather than the ambassador or any other civilian, was the liaison

[45] Beauvais, p. 38.
[46] For the suspicious doings of Kork and his recall from Berlin in 1929 see Castellan, pp. 479ff. Putna and Feldman were Poles and Blücher not a full Russian either.
[47] *The Memoirs of General Lord Ismay* (New York 1960), pp. 225f.

officer between Reichswehr and Red Army.[48] At first these foreigners were allowed relative freedom of movement and intercourse, including contacts with members of the Red Army. When a group of attachés visited an artillery regiment in Rjasan early in 1930, exuberance or vodka led to some curious confessions on the hosts' part. One Red Army officer boasted of the strict and efficient political control over their men, thanks to the commissar arrangement which the foreign officers abominated above all other Russian innovations: "Our political service is admirable; foreign armies know nothing of the kind and thus are wanting one of the most decisive factors in war; we shall transmit the Red bacillus to you." The Polish member of the group was treated with particular attention, and was sent off with the Russians' parting assurance: "See you again, and that will be soon!"[49] By the time of the purges Stalinist xenophobia had put an end to all such fraternization, and had restricted the movements of foreigners, considered as potential spies, inside the USSR— the attachés, indeed, were limited almost to their own company. Among themselves they discussed the military effects of the purges, of which they could see only the negative side; most of them agreed that "the fighting efficiency of the Red Army had been adversely affected" for at least two to three years to come, both by the purges, which had taken no less that 65 per cent of the higher ranks since June 1937, and by the reintroduction of the political commissars.[50] Russian intervention in European affairs in favor of the *status quo* powers seemed to the majority of the military observers in Moscow, with the possible exception of the American, more than doubtful: they would fight only if the USSR were attacked; for the rest, they would grasp at any pretext to evade their obligations to France and Czechoslovakia. The French and Czech military attachés talked with their doubting British colleague in April 1938, at the time of the first crisis over

[48] Julius Epstein in *Der Monat* (Berlin), November 1948, p. 49; Gordon A. Craig, *The Politics of the Prussian Army: 1640-1945* (New York 1955), p. 411.
[49] Herbette, p. 165.
[50] *Foreign Relations of the United States: The Soviet Union, 1933-1939*, pp. 519ff.

Czechoslovakia, as if Russian intervention in favor of the Czechs were a foregone conclusion; the Frenchman was convinced that Paris would have "to speak very strongly to Poland and force her back to the side of France," force her if necessary to remove Colonel Beck, the foreign minister, and "allow Soviet troops to pass through Poland to Czechoslovakia."[51] But Polish opposition to Russian troops on Polish soil, even if only in transit, remained adamant, then as later.

It was only natural that military personnel prepared the way for the "strange alliance" struck between the United States and the Soviet Union—it was based on military considerations and reasoning, something of late often forgotten. As early as February 1933 the Russian military attaché in Tokyo sought out his American counterpart and told him, while also imparting some recent intelligence on Japanese forces and intentions, how much "it was to the interest of both the United States and the USSR to come to some friendly understanding."[52] And Ambassador Bullitt, immediately upon his first arrival in Moscow in December 1933, after American recognition, found War Commissar Voroshilov, who considered a Japanese attack on the Soviet Union imminent, "especially anxious to have a full equipment of American military, naval and air attachés in Moscow," preferably men who spoke Russian and would give the Russians expert advice on the latest progress in aviation. "He made it clear that, if our Government desires, our military and naval men can have a relationship of the utmost intimacy with the military authorities of the Soviet Government."

These military hopes materialized as little as had others. Several American service attachés were withdrawn early in 1935 as a gesture; Washington told them to let Voroshilov know how Litvinov had put unnecessary obstacles in the way of Soviet-American friendship. Not all the attachés believed

---

[51] *Documents on British Foreign Policy*, IIIrd ser., I, 161, 172f., 418ff., 303ff.

[52] Tokyo, February 23, transmitted to State Department by War Department, March 21. *Foreign Relations of the United States: The Soviet Union*, p. 3.

that their departure best served American interest; the military attaché, Lieutenant Colonel Faymonville, pointed out that, however unpleasant relations had become with other Moscow offices, the contacts established with the Red Army offered possibilities of breaking through the front of obstruction; that from a strictly military view the attachés ought to stay and continue to observe what was then the world's largest army and largest air force, with officers among whom they were intimately and favorably known. But Washington in its bitterness and disappointment could not be dissuaded: nearly all service attachés had to leave. Voroshilov, whom the American soldiers called "our outstanding friend," was chagrined; he did not hide his dissatisfaction with the Foreign Commissariat and its tactics, which were denying him the chance to learn more about American planes and their production. Only Faymonville, a Soviet military attaché and a Soviet naval attaché remained in their respective posts, and Bullitt suggested in August 1935 that their recall and dismissal be postponed until Russia took "further offensive steps." "As the Military and Naval Attachés are not in the direct diplomatic line and as the Red Army representatives are unquestionably on a higher plane as human beings than other Soviet citizens, and as Voroshilov (for his own purposes to be sure) desires genuinely friendly relations with the United States, I consider that this step may be held in abeyance."

The purges of 1937-1938 in the military sector and the reinstallation of political commissars in the Red forces brought a considerable drop in Russia's "alliance value" as estimated by practically all foreign attachés in Moscow, with the possible exception of Colonel Faymonville. He in turn strengthened Ambassador Davis in his sometimes fantastic, though from a military standpoint imperative, convictions about Russia's strength. Davis displayed a trustfulness, a judgment, that would have deserved greater praise had it been restricted to the military field.[53]

A few of the smaller nations, notably Denmark, Ecuador and the Netherlands, abolished the post of service attaché,

[53] *Ibid.*, pp. 58f., 171, 173f., 177, 182f., 247f., 519, 597, 600f. For Faymonville's career see obituary in *The New York Times*, March 31, 1962.

as a sign of their earnest intention to disarm—or of their
conclusion that they could carry no weight in the arms competition and the maintenance of attachés amounted to *faux
frais*. With the new stepping-up of arms competition, however, in the early 1930's, the Netherlands reestablished the
posts at London, Berlin, Paris and Brussels. By 1936 only the
following minor powers were, permanently or temporarily,
without service attachés accredited abroad: Albania, Afghanistan, Denmark, the British Dominions, the Central
American Republics (with the exception of Cuba and the
Dominican Republic), Egypt, Ireland, Liberia, Switzerland
and Siam.

The number of attachés was further increased by the introduction of the air attaché, a result of the increasing importance
of the air arm and the highly technical nature of this force,
its manufacturing and its maintenance. France was the first to
appoint these new attachés (under a decree of December 11,
1920), and by 1936 the powers had no less that 46 of them on
duty. While some of the smaller countries—and some of the
great ones in minor posts—combined the functions of military
or naval attaché with that of air attaché, many of them, with
the United States forming an exception for a prolonged
period, thought it necessary to maintain specialists at least in
the capitals of the foremost air powers. As a rule, they were
selected by and from the armed services and "charged with
missions, put at the disposal of ambassadors and minister
plenipotentiaries in order to study all the questions which
fall within their specialty." (French decree of December 11,
1920). In France they were originally under the jurisdiction
of the sub-secretariat of aeronautics in the Ministry of Public
Works, the office through which the French tried to develop
air power, and hence assumed a character not unlike that of
commercial attachés. Their original instructions were "on the
one hand to make researches, gather and communicate" to the
sub-secretariat "all information relative to the technical
development and the civilian and commercial use of aviation
and aerostats" in the countries where they were stationed,
"and on the other hand be of aid to the expansion abroad of
French aeronautical industry." In this instruction the old sub

rosa orders for military and naval attachés (to aid their national armament industries in competition abroad) were for once frankly stated; with the importance of the new technology in war preparation the old inhibition against officers acting openly as salesmen went out the window, and Napoleon's spiteful dictum on the British, "Sono mercanti," became true of at least certain groups of officers. But whatever their affiliation, all these original French aeronautical attachés were air force officers, with the exception of the civilian official stationed in Germany, which under the Versailles Treaty (art. 108) was not supposed to have any aviation of a military character. When an Air Ministry (*Ministère de l'air*) was created in 1928 the air attachés came under its jurisdiction, and thus remained part of the military-civilian twilight zone which would be an essential part of total war and its preparation.[54]

Foreign air attachés were stationed in Germany years before the Luftwaffe officially existed. The Nazis preferred to start their rearmament in the air gradually, under the guise of a civilian-looking *Reichsluftfahrtministerium*. Only in March 1935 was it announced to the foreign air attachés that henceforth the aviators in that Ministry would be "soldiers," soldiers like the air attachés themselves with the exception of M. Poincaré, the French air attaché who was a civilian but was soon afterward replaced by an officer-aviator.[55] Thus the future Luftwaffe was announced as officially in existence and allowed to grow like a mushroom.

By 1936 the total number of service attachés had risen from some 30 at the outbreak of the war of 1870-1871, and some 300 on the eve of the First World War, to over 450; it continued to increase rather than decrease in the remaining years of peace. In 1936 the greatest number of such *milites missi* came from France (50), with Great Britain (38), the United States (34), and Italy (30) next in order; Germany and Russia each maintained 24 attachés in foreign capitals. These numbers may be taken as a measure of the watchfulness of the victorious

[54] Beauvais, pp. 40ff.
[55] Report of the British air attaché at Berlin to British ambassador, March 9, 1935. *Trial of the Major War Criminals*, XXXIX, 45f.

nations over the rearming of the world, or of uncertainty over the value of military alliances or isolation. The number of attachés *received* by the great and small powers, however, while also indicative of this deep concern, reveals certain convictions on the part of the military chiefs about those centers of military competition where something new might be learned. France's military reputation was still high in 1936 and she received the largest number of service attachés of all kinds, 48; ominously enough, Germany was a fairly close second with 42, followed by Great Britain (38), Italy (25), the United States (22), Russia (21) and Japan (20). The relatively large number of stationings in Rome expressed the usual over-estimation of the military value and importance of Italy.[56] In addition, several armies, including the British from April 1935, and the American from July 1938, resumed some "old-time military courtesies" by arranging for the exchange of officers between the German Army and their own for purposes of instruction.[57]

So numerous (and self-contained?) had service attachés become in the 1930's that they formed a corps within the diplomatic corps of various capitals. In London, they had their *doyen*[58] and elsewhere "the attaché group" was given a "bear leader" by the host country, an officer to give or to deny them information, to guide or if necessary misguide them.[59] During the Wehrmacht crisis of 1938 set off by the dismissal of the anti-war Army Chief of Staff, Beck, "the foreign attachés were shown maneuvers in East Prussia in order to keep them away from the center of the Reich."[60] "Privately" given information would sometimes go rather far: during the Czech crisis of 1938 the British military attaché, though hardly any other

---

[56] For the data on which the above is based, see Beauvais, pp. 44ff.

[57] *The New York Times*, April 24, 1935, and July 11, 1938. For details of the British-German exchange of officers, "definitely unpolitical youths" who were "to get drunk together," see Geyr, *Erinnerungen*, pp. 69ff.

[58] Geyr, *Erinnerungen*, p. 18.

[59] For the false information handed out in Berlin on March 11, 1938, the day of the *Anschluss*, see *Documents on British Foreign Policy*, IIIrd ser., I, 9f., 167. For the relations of the French military attaché with the Reichswehr Ministry section for foreign attachés see Castellan, pp. 440f. and passim.

[60] Siegfried Westphal, *Heer in Fesseln* (Bonn 1950), p. 75.

attaché at this time, was given unmistakable hints as to the existence of an "underground opposition to the Party" among Wehrmacht men, especially the General Staff, which before Munich was hinting at the desirability of a clear British stand against any "direct action" on Hitler's part. Without such help the Army would have to bow to Hitler and to the Party extremists such as Himmler, who might be given supreme command if the Army's opposition should become too obvious. "The Army was not yet in a position to stand up to the Party and go into open opposition. It might never succeed in being able to do this." The recipient of these confidences doubted that any outside attempt "to interfere with Germany's domestic politics during Hitler's lifetime" could be successful; instead it would "most assuredly lead to exactly what we all wish to avoid"—full Nazi control over the Wehrmacht, and war.[61] This attitude must have generated some of the earliest rebuffs to the German opposition to Hitler and its hopes for outside help.

Not only was there a quantitative increase in service attachés, but over the years they had also risen in rank: generally speaking from captain or lieutenant during the nineteenth century (the U.S. naval attachés of the 1890's were mostly lieutenants), to colonel and major general or even lieutenant general after the First World War. It marked the increasing importance of defense questions in the business of diplomacy as well as the services' tendency to ensure their own representatives on the diplomatic team sufficient rank in relation to the rest of the legation personnel.

Whether any of these observers became fully or early aware of the potentialities and intentions of the Wehrmacht and its master, may seem as much open to doubt as the effect on the home authorities of the warnings that some of them sent home. The first American ambassador to Hitler, William E. Dodd, found the four military members of his staff—three of them with German names, chosen presumably on account of their knowledge of the language—poorly equipped for their task. "Army and Navy attachés here, and I think all over

[61] British Documents on the Origins of the War, IIIrd ser., II, 42ff., 65ff., 126f., 148.

Europe, are utterly unequal to their supposed functions. They simply have never received good training, except in drill and tactics.[62] They may know a little formal history, but they do not grasp the social and economic problems in countries to which they are accredited. Nor are they clever enough to spy on German military performances. Spying is really what governments expect in such fields." At the same time, Dodd, as a historian, found that the German military attaché in Washington, General von Boetticher, knew the American Civil War "as no American attaché here knows German war history." The Ambassador considered his first military aide, Colonel Wuest, a diligent and watchful man, "but the military appeal is strong and he instinctively approves of the [German] army drills and demonstrations—contradictory as these are to the interests of the United States"; also Wuest seems to have suffered from the weakness of many of his colleagues, allowing excitability to follow on periods of complacency in the surveillance of the foreign power in question. In October 1934 the Colonel, who had been driving around the Reich for days, came to the ambassador. "He was excited. 'War is imminent, preparations everywhere,' but he was not specific and I had little time to listen."[63]

This deafness when an attaché really had something worthwhile to report on Germany's rearmament was also too often adopted by Roosevelt, according to some of his critics. They maintain that he kept from the Congress the warnings which at least one United States military attaché in Berlin addressed to his superiors, after the shape of things to come, from the Third Reich and particularly from the Luftwaffe, had grown considerably more discernible. In order to penetrate its secrets a little better, this officer, Major Truman Smith, managed in 1936 to make Goering invite Charles A. Lindbergh for an inspection of the new air power, its installations and pro-

[62] This goes with the opinion of the first German postwar military attaché in London, Geyr (*Erinnerungen*, p. 14): "Compared with other Western European armies language knowledge was probably least demanded in the German army, whereas tactics as the supposed *arcanum* of victory was madly cultivated and appreciated."

[63] W. E. Dodd, Jr., and Martha Dodd, eds., *Ambassador Dodd's Diary* (New York 1941), particularly pp. 149, 151f., 181, 202.

71

duction lines. Lindbergh's estimates were readily accepted by the "appeasers" but disbelieved by others, including British Intelligence and many in Washington who would not accept his later low opinion of Russian air power either. Smith himself, an early observer of the Nazi movement, the rise of which he foresaw even better than later followers of Hitler like "Putzi" Hanfstaengl,[64] kept up friendly relations with Lindbergh even after the latter had become an "America Firster" and *persona non grata* in Washington. Smith kept on warning the War Department, reporting in November 1937 that "Germany is once more a world power in the air. . . . The outstanding growth of German air power from a zero level to its present status in a brief four years must be considered one of the most important world events of our time. . . . It forces the foreigner—even the American who is accustomed to think in big terms—to pause, ponder, and wonder as to the future."[65]

But Roosevelt, unimpressed, according to his Congressional critics, withheld the document in question from the proper Committees and thereby brought about a cut of $40,000,000 in the War Department appropriations for 1938, and perhaps also in subsequent years before Pearl Harbor, thus contributing to America's unpreparedness.[66] Others were more willing to listen to such warning voices, Winston Churchill for one, to whom, though he was not in office at the time, the French estimate of the size of the Luftwaffe as of mid-1938 was communicated by the French military attaché in London on orders of his Government. Churchill thanked the latter "for

[64] Ernst Franz Sedgwick Hanfstaengl, *Hitler. The Missing Years* (London 1957), pp. 31f.

[65] Published as "An American Estimate of the German Air Force" in *Airpower Historian* (April 1963).

[66] *The New York Times*, March 12, 1939, and October 25, 1944. For Smith's observations and activities in Berlin see Gen. Albert C. Wedemeyer, *Wedemeyer Reports* (New York 1958), pp. 6of., who calls it Smith's "most effective intelligence exploit" to have instigated the German invitation to Col. Lindbergh to come and see for himself the growth of the Luftwaffe—this in the expectation which proved true that the Germans would not let the colonel see more than other foreigners; also see Kenneth S. Davis, *The Hero, Charles A. Lindbergh and the American Dream* (Garden City 1959), pp. 374, 408.

the invaluable information" which he would "use only with the greatest discretion, and in our common interest."[67]

The French seem to have been informed fairly accurately about the Luftwaffe and its progress, but more because of an inspection trip by an expert than because of their attaché on the spot. Moreover, their military attaché, General Didelet, had left the General Staff in the dark about the Panzer divisions and their true value. Pertinax, the Paris journalist with the most intimate contacts in army circles, indicates that "there would be much to say about the negligence with which the French military attachés for Berlin were chosen during the twelve years preceding the conflict. Neither the predecessor of Didelet nor his aide spoke German. Had Weygand, who appointed them, forgotten the disastrous repercussions as far as our operations of August 1914 were concerned of the reports of Colonel Serret, military attaché during the years to 1914, concerning the non-participation of the German reserve divisions in the opening operations?"[68] According to the same witness, the overconfidence of the French army leaders in their own forces, which had sunk to a low during the period of one year of military service, rose again once the two-year term had been reintroduced in the spring of 1935, and was imparted to the German and Italian military attachés in Paris —but not to the American, Colonel Fuller, who remained skeptical.[69] The reports of the Axis attachés may well have induced caution on the part of the Wehrmacht chiefs with regard to advances into the Rhineland, Austria and Czechoslovakia, which Hitler ordered over their hesitations.[70]

The warnings of the military attaché in London, Colonel Geyr von Schweppenburg, had been so alarming—the Colonel had even offered his diplomatic services to avert war during the remilitarization of the Rhineland—that Hitler, recovering from his own panic, demanded that Geyr be censured. This the compliant Blomberg proceeded to do, while

---

[67] June 6, 1938. *The Second World War. The Gathering Storm* (Boston 1948), p. 265.
[68] Pertinax, I, 23.   [69] *Ibid.*, I, 29.
[70] For these reports and their effect in Berlin see *The Von Hassel Diaries*, p. 90.

General Beck, Chief of Staff of the Wehrmacht, defended the right of the officers of his staff to express their views freely.[71] Two years later Hitler was so confident of his own might and of the timidity of the appeasers that he went over to the offensive. Some weeks before Munich a large-scale naval demonstration, to which the foreign attachés were invited, showed them, if they did not already know, how much of the German Navy had been rebuilt; these sea maneuvers, followed by land exercises showing tanks in action and other up-to-date equipment, were designed as a demonstration to foreign observers of what might be expected by Czechoslovakia should she and her allies resist Germany's demands.[72] This and other Hitlerian bluffing proved successful enough: the British military attachés in Berlin and Prague in 1938 were very pessimistic, far more so than the German General Staff, as to Czech ability to resist a German attack.[73] And other attachés' eve-of-the-war judgments were far from infallible: when the later Lord Wavell examined the French military arrangements and doctrines of the mid-1930's, he found them "extremely rigid and archaic, smacking of the static warfare of 1916. . . . The great efficiency of the French General Staff had been somewhat loudly vaunted by successive British military attachés."[74]

[71] Geyr, *The Critical Years*, passim.

[72] Potiemkine, III, 649.

[73] John W. Wheeler-Bennett, *Munich: Prologue to Tragedy* (New York 1948), p. 152.

[74] Maj. Gen. R. J. Collins, *Lord Wavell* (London 1948), pp. 151f.

CHAPTER 5

THE SECOND WORLD WAR

The number of service attachés continued to grow: in 1939 there were no less than nine American attachés in Berlin, and nine each in London and Paris, and they were more widely dispersed—there was an American military attaché even in Afghanistan, said to have been "the first American diplomat" in that country.[1] More officers of the technical branches were employed on such duty; shortly after the outbreak of the war in 1939 there were more field artillery officers among American attachés than officers of any other arm.[2]

Apparently the reports of these numerous officers about the preparations for the Second World War were of much the same nature as those before 1914: war was bound to come,[3] sooner or later.[4] Specific information abounded, such as the report of the American military attaché in Rome of mid-August 1934 that the Italian General Staff had plans ready for the conquest and occupation of Ethiopia.[5] But accurate forecasting of the totality of war, rather than its foreseeable political configuration,[6] seems to have been lacking, and hence too

[1] Gordon Enders, *Foreign Devil* (New York 1942).

[2] *Field Artillery Journal* (September-October 1940), p. 364.

[3] Ambassador Joseph C. Grew, *Ten Years in Japan, 1932-1942* (New York 1944), p. 98, noted on September 7, 1933: "One of our assistant military attachés says that he and his colleagues consider war—between Japan and Russia—absolutely inevitable and predict it for the spring of 1935, although some believe it may come much sooner."

[4] Among the several voices warning of the German attack on Russia in 1941 was that of the Soviet military attaché in Berlin. But Stalin would not believe him, a neglect that was included in the long list of his sins and errors compiled by his successors in 1956. *The New Leader* (New York), April 16, 1956.

[5] *The Memoirs of Cordell Hull*, 2 vols. (New York 1948), I, 418.

[6] A number of officers of the anti-Axis grouping, American, English, French and Polish, assembled in Lisbon in the summer of 1938, agreed that preventive war against the Reich was advisable, considering German war preparations. The U.S. naval attaché, Commander John Allyn Gade, whom the Pole considered a confidant and personal friend of Roose-

often the data required for the war's successful conduct was also lacking. Sentiment in favor of war was definitely limited, in at least some service attachés, as well as on the general staffs from which most of them came. A German military attaché, coming to Berlin in February 1939, found the traditional eve-of-war sentiment reversed: "The gallant blades sit clearly in the Foreign Office and the diplomats in the Reich War Ministry; it was here that they fought for keeping the peace—because the means of making the war were absent."[7]

Some attaché reports, indeed, proved highly misleading. In March 1938 and again in May, the Czechs complained that Germany was starting military moves against them, but they were at once assured to the contrary by the German military attaché in Prague. When the British press took up the accusation, and the British military attaché in Berlin did not correct it, Ambassador Sir Nevile Henderson was ordered by his government to talk with the Wilhelmstrasse. On May 22, after considerable delay, Henderson dispatched two of his attachés on automobile trips through Saxony and Silesia to find out whether large-scale German troop movements in the direction of Czechoslovakia were really under way. Neither of these emissaries, about whom the Germans knew at once, nor other foreign attachés including the French, could discover any such "dangerous" movements or any "single mobilized man," much to the satisfaction of the Germans and the mortification of some of the great powers. They felt misled by the Czechs' anxiety, and their ambassadors claimed that false rumors had been spread by Czechoslovakia "for the express purpose of serving as a pretext for planned partial Czech mobilization" (Henderson).[8]

---

velt, and who was wealthy and very unfriendly to Germany, told the rest: "As far as ideas go, we are completely on the side of the democracies. At present, they are studying in America the possibilities for immediate help to England and France; they are convinced that help must not come only after a year [sic] when the first American soldiers actively intervened, as happened in the World War, but that within seven to ten days after the start of the war one thousand planes must be sent." Drittes Weissbuch der Deutschen Regierung, *Polnische Dokumente zur Vorgeschichte des Krieges* (Basel 1939), p. 13.

[7] Vagts, *Militarism*, p. 451.

[8] Nevile Henderson, *Failure of a Mission* (New York 1940), passim;

The Germans resolved, during the Czech crisis, to give no information about military measures in future to foreign attachés.[9] When they actually started mobilization in 1939, they again kept the attachés from observing troop movements and restricted them to Berlin. The immobilizing of these officers in their greatest hour became common practice: in 1938 the Czechs threw a cordon of police around the German Legation in Prague, making the military attaché complain to Berlin that no more military information of any kind could be obtained.[10] It was carried to the greatest lengths in Russia, and even in free America Secretary Hull, on March 5, 1941, asked the Italian ambassador, Prince Colonna, to keep him informed of all movements of his service attachés outside Washington; some of them were suspected of sabotage intentions.[11]

But the attachés, whether free to move around or pinned down in the capital, proved no more successful as forecasters than, let us say, during the Balkan War, when most of them were surprised by the defeat of the Turks.[12] In Brussels, where the division of opinion of military attachés and chiefs of mission with regard to the German threat to Belgian and Dutch neutrality is documented, the majority pronounced against a German attack—it seemed either impossible or improbable. Only three mission chiefs, following the advice of their attachés, believed that it would take place and in the summer of 1940. Among them was the American ambassador. He was relying on the judgment of his military attaché, Colonel Brown, who had held from the outset that the attack on the two Netherlands was inevitable, thereby, as the ambassador came to testify, "greatly influencing Embassy appraisals and reporting."[13]

Documents on German Foreign Policy, Ser. D, II, 169, 175, 295f., 330, 341, 349f., 407, 416, 449.

[9] Ibid., p. 690.   [10] Ibid., p. 976.

[11] The New York Times, April 3, 1941.

[12] See for example Grosse Politik, XXXIII, 12332.

[13] Field Artillery Journal (September-October 1940), p. 366. In the Reich Embassy in Rome, ambassador and naval attaché disagreed in April 1940, the former assuming Italy's entry into the war, the latter,

The two governments in the Low Countries did not agree. Neither they nor most of their representatives abroad would listen to the warnings of an impending German invasion which they received from the anti-Hitler opposition inside Germany. The Belgian minister in a neutral capital discounted such reports: informers must be traitors and he did not believe that traitors could exist in or near the German command. The Dutch military attaché in Berlin received a similar warning from the same source less than twelve hours before the attack on his country—again disbelief at home.[14] The Netherlanders had not really taken to heart the fate of Denmark and Norway, whose military attachés in Berlin had been similarly warned by the opposition to Hitler, and even by Admiral Canaris, chief of counterespionage. Both attachés remained firmly convinced that the Germans were unable to undertake overseas operations.[15]

That the attaché is a political animal whose views may color his professional reports may already be suspected—and the evidence will accumulate. In April 1939 the acting U.S. military attaché in Berlin reported at length that unless Germany could bend Poland to her will through negotiations, she would attack within the next 30 days. "The present situation when viewed in the light of an active war which Germany is now in the process of waging becomes clearer. It is an economic war in which Germany is fighting for her very existence. Germany must have markets for her goods or die, and Germany will not die." Roosevelt and Hopkins, at least according to their biographer, deduced nothing about the character of the coming war from this report; instead they took it as proof "that the military attaché was not only attending to his job of observing the Wehrmacht and the Luftwaffe; he was

---

presumably on the strength of his knowledge of the Italian Navy, concluding that she would stay out. *Hassell Diaries*, p. 135.

[14] Hans Bernd Gisevius, *To the Bitter End* (Boston 1947), pp. 454f.; Görlitz, p. 530; *Vierteljahrshefte für Zeitgeschichte*, VIII (1960), 17ff.

[15] Görlitz, p. 528. The Swedish military attaché in Berlin hinted during the first days of April that the northern countries were expecting a German attack on them. *Hassell Diaries*, p. 131.

also listening faithfully to Goebbels' propaganda and reflecting it in his official reports."[16]

Conservative sympathies made some American observers ascribe a conservative character to the last changes in the Japanese Government before Pearl Harbor, though actually when General Tojo became premier the last truly conservative hopes were gone. But the U.S. military attaché in Tokyo, Colonel Cresswell, reported: "Since the make-up of the new Cabinet appears to be essentially conservative in character, the resignation of the old Cabinet is not regarded as indicating any drastic change in Japan's policy in the immediate future, at least. . . . While General Tojo is first of all a thoroughgoing Japanese, with the national ambitions and welfare inherent in his make-up, he is believed to have a breadth of vision which would seem to preclude the possibility of his taking extreme radical actions."[17] And there is more testimony from the American side as to the common error of conservatives, both military and civilian, in approximating Fascism and conservatism, and in regarding aggressive moves of the Axis partners as defensive in nature.[18]

The functions, activities and opportunities of the service attachés during the Second World War, as far as we now know, were in many respects, probably in most, the same as those from 1914 to 1918. The neutrals were again anxious to learn about war in its new character and to discover the intentions of the belligerents. They also wished to observe

[16] Robert E. Sherwood, *Roosevelt and Hopkins* (New York 1948), p. 116. Was it the same officer who spontaneously congratulated the German High Command at the close of the Polish campaign on its success when he was fully aware that it was Hitler who had the deciding voice in this campaign? *Trials of War Criminals*, X, 712f.

[17] Sherwood, p. 419.

[18] When the Japanese moved into French Indo-China after the ultimatum to the Vichy Government of July 12, 1941, the Military Intelligence Estimate, prepared by the G-2 section of the U.S. War Department, stated that this movement "while opportunistic in conception, was also strategically defensive in character and designed primarily to prevent British and American influence from shutting off supplies of rubber, tin and rice from Thailand and Indo-China which are badly needed by Japan." Memorandum for the Chief of Staff, July 17, 1941. *Pearl Harbor Hearings*, unnumbered.

79

other neutrals, such as Russia, and sometimes they had the opportunity: in November 1940 the High Command showed parts of the Red Army to the foreign attachés, both neutral and belligerent, after an interim of half a year during which Timoshenko, the new Commissar for Defense, had undertaken certain reforms.[19]

The number of neutral attachés was increased still more; the United States had over 60 of them abroad in 1940 as against 34 in 1936. An American military attaché opened shop in Turkey where none had been stationed since the First World War, and in the beginning of 1940 the United States Navy filled five new attaché posts including one at Batavia, Dutch East Indies, one of the first such posts outside a capital.[20] The United States Legation in Cairo was complemented by military, naval and air attachés, whereupon the Japanese Government at the beginning of 1941 asked permission to station one of its military attachés there also—the Japanese had not sent one to Cairo before. The Egyptians were somewhat hesitant. They probably feared Japanese spying on behalf of the other Axis powers[21]—an activity they carried on from every imaginable vantage point, even landlocked Berne, where they maintained a naval attaché during the Second World War.[22]

Wartime spying became so much the work of service attachés that spies and attachés grew to be almost indistinguishable, a development probably not in the best interest of diplomacy as an institution. The Americans sent to their Vichy embassy an assistant naval attaché who "did not know which end of a boat went first." He was actually a secret OSS agent, as the Ambassador learned eventually, "a very good spy—capable and discreet," but not so good as to prevent the Nazis from suspecting him of espionage.[23]

The ancient opportunity of following the belligerents'

---

[19] Associated Press dispatch from Moscow, November 3, 1940.
[20] Associated Press dispatch from Washington, May 29, 1940.
[21] *The New York Times*, January 18, 1941.
[22] Toshikazu Kase, *Journey to the "Missouri"* (New Haven 1950), p. 222.
[23] William D. Leahy, *I Was There* (New York 1950), p. 22.

armies to the battlefield was denied the neutrals' attachés[24] even more firmly and completely than during the First World War. When it is said that an American attaché stationed at Berlin at the outbreak of the war "served as an observer with the German armies and saw campaigns in Poland, the Low Countries, Denmark and Norway,"[25] this meant little more than that he participated in guided tours on which the Wehrmacht took the neutral attachés once the battle was over. The British, however, who were expecting the Americans to become their "associates" as in the First World War, and at an earlier time, allowed American officers a share of their experience. In a way, they groomed Brigadier General Sherman Miles for his job during a tour of duty as military attaché in London from August 1939 on; he became Chief of the U.S. Army's Intelligence Division in the spring of 1940. The British and French air forces seem to have imparted some secrets of technology and production to American air attachés stationed in their capitals.[26] The Japanese were quite eager to teach the Germans the experience they had gained earlier in the field of landing operations[27] but, since the landing in England was never undertaken, there seemed little use in accepting that kind of information.

The Russians, not at all anxious to enter the war themselves, confirmed their initial neutrality agreement with the Nazi Germans not only with an exchange of considerable amounts of war materials but also with a show of friendship between Red Army and Wehrmacht, almost to the end. When the Japanese foreign minister, Matsuoka, ended his 1941

[24] On September 7, 1939, General Marshall gave directives to "start at once to examine into the details of the tactics and techniques of the arms as employed by the belligerents. To do this we should send to our military attachés, or with missions which we may send, a list of specific questions regarding which we desire detailed information." Watson, p. 47. At the recommendation of the U.S. naval attaché in London, who had advance approval from the Admiralty, naval officers were assigned to British fleet units as observers. *Ibid.*, p. 106.

[25] Obituary of Col. W. Hohenthal, *The New York Times*, February 9, 1949.

[26] Associated Press dispatch from Washington, May 29, 1940.

[27] *Trial of the Major War Criminals*, XXXV, 103.

tour of the West in Moscow, Stalin told his guest that he was "a convinced adherent of the Axis and an opponent of England and America." And Stalin himself appeared with great ostentation for a farewell ceremony at the Moscow station on April 12; he threw his arm around the shoulder of the German ambassador and said, "We must remain friends and you must do everything you can to that end." Then he turned to Colonel Krebs, the acting German military attaché, after making sure that he was a German: "We will remain friends with you—in any event!" (auf jeden Fall). It was a performance intended to be seen by everyone, particularly by the Moscow diplomatic corps.[28] It was also a last allusion, on the eve of the German attack on Russia, to the strange intimacies that had tied together the two armies at various times.

In these two armies, probably most of the time, there had been spying. "Case Barbarossa," the German plan for the attack on Russia, at least in regard to "judgment of leader personalities, among whom only Timoshenko is outstanding," was based on data supplied by General Köstring, the military attaché in Moscow.[29] Neither Köstring nor his *adlatus* Krebs were able to provide the planners of the war against Russia with reliable data on Russian strength, though Köstring warned repeatedly against dangerous underestimates.[30] Once war had broken out, he and other officers with experience in Russia were employed, not unsuccessfully, to recruit Russian prisoners of war for service with the Wehrmacht, a policy which but for the insane occupation measures of the Nazis could have been made infinitely more successful.[31]

A fairly close repetition of the Boy-Ed episode of the First World War occurred, or was staged, on April 2, 1941, when the State Department requested the then neutral Italian Government to withdraw its naval attaché in Washington, Admiral Alberto Lais. The request stated that "various facts and circumstances," which remained unspecified, had come

---

[28] *Nazi-Soviet Relations, 1939-1941*, pp. 324, 326.
[29] *Trial of the Major War Criminals*, XXVI, 392.
[30] Görlitz, p. 546.
[31] For some details see *New Leader* (New York), January 28, 1950.

to the attention of the United States Government connecting Lais "with the commission by certain persons of acts in violation of the laws of the United States"; these circumstances made him "no longer agreeable to this Government." It was generally assumed at the time, and Hull maintained, that Lais was preparing sabotage measures in the event that the United States sequestered Italian merchant ships in American ports. In his own defense Secretary Hull declared, in a public statement, that "some governments today involved in lawless activities, do not hesitate to resent activities of foreign representatives and governments which are within the range of legality." The Italian Government, however, insisted that Lais' activities in Washington "were always strictly confined to the legitimate range of his functions which he carried out in the most praiseworthy manner," but that on the contrary the doings of the assistant military attaché of the American embassy in Rome, William C. Bentley, were not so confined, and that this made him no longer acceptable. Bentley, they said, had engaged in "activities which certainly surpassed his functions and which even transgressed his duties as guest in a country at war." This was quite obviously retaliation— retaliation in kind was beyond the power of the Italian Government, which could only point out the United States' eagerness to obtain Axis shipping, and denounce her methods as "deeds of plunder against merchant ships that do not belong to them." While the State and War Departments promptly cleared Bentley "of any personal or official blame for the position in which he is placed," the Italians insisted that they considered him *persona non grata* for "precise and specific reasons" which, like the American ones, remained unpublished.[32] The American case against Lais was not half as good as that against Boy-Ed.

Again as in the First World War a number of military attachés of the belligerents, and of the neutrals who would later become belligerents, were made liaison officers in the countries where they had previously served, in the interest of a unified war effort.[33] When the United States sent Briga-

[32] *The New York Times*, April 4, 12, 22, 1941; Hull, *Memoirs*, p. 927.
[33] For the liaison services of the French military attaché in London, Gen.

dier General John Macgruder as the head of a military mission to China in 1941 under the Lend-Lease Act, it was explained that his long previous experience in China, where he had served twice as military attaché, would enable him to work "on familiar ground among people he knows well and to whom he is well known." The later choice of General Joseph W. Stilwell for a commanding post with Chinese troops was again due to his former attaché service in China. Stilwell himself thought his former humble position might disqualify rather than assist him: "They remember me as a small-fry colonel that they kicked around. They saw me on foot in the mud, consorting with coolies, riding soldier trains."[34]

Whether or not such liaison men had had previous experience, there was friction, distrust, misunderstanding among the coalition partners on each side, due to diversity of national interests, temperaments and strategical outlook. Subordinate personnel, chafing under uncongenial and irksome liaison conditions, had to be kept in line or removed by the higher ranking men, who were determined not to have the coalition effort impeded by wrangling and misunderstanding.

Some intra-coalition conflicts were so violent that they became known even to the enemy. The Siamese Prime Minister told the Americans, after the Japanese move into Indo-China in July 1941, that the German military attaché in Bangkok had warned him against "going too far" with Japan, "because you cannot trust Japan; Germany would settle with Japan after she had won the war in Europe." To the Intelligence Division in the American War Department this piece of information, though it concerned only relatively subordinate personnel, seemed portentous and of a highly divisive character. Judicious use of it, such as placing it in the hands of the Japanese ambassador, might help to dissolve the Axis. "Any action on our part which will make Japan an even more reluctant Axis partner weakens our potential

---

Lelong, from May 1939 on, see Auswärtiges Amt, *Les documents secrets de l'Etat-Major Général français* (Berlin 1941), passim (German White Book).

[34] Theodore H. White, ed., *The Stilwell Papers* (New York 1948), p. 19.

enemies, enhances our own prestige and authority and materially and favorably affects our national defense." It does not seem to be known whether the advice from Intelligence was followed—that the Secretary of War urge the Secretary of State to inform the Japanese ambassador—in any case, it could not be made very convincing as expressing German suspicion of Japan in the higher echelons.[35]

As for Russia, her distrust of partners who had apparently changed their old roles as enemies in class warfare, but only temporarily, threatened to turn into a xenophobia which was readier to accept outside assistance than to admit that it was a help. Russia proved loath even to furnish information for which the Allies' representatives were eager—perhaps without greatly needing it, perhaps only out of long-established attaché routine—but information which they thought was the least due them in return for Lend-Lease goods.[36] Contrary to the customs of earlier wars of coalition, the Russians kept even the friendliest observers from seeing the realities of totalitarian warfare. It is not clear from the available record whether this exclusion from all-important information furnishes the explanation for the startling difference in opinion, in 1941, about the Russian fighting strength and power of resistance, between the U.S. military attaché in Moscow, Major Yeaton, and his predecessor, Colonel Faymonville. The unconventional Hopkins sent Faymonville, whose judgment and impartiality about Russia many in Washington had doubted, back to Moscow as representative of Lend-Lease. While Yeaton in October 1941 foresaw the near end of Russian resistance, Faymonville remained convinced of their staying power, and Hopkins trusted him rather than Yeaton.

[35] Memorandum for the Chief of Staff, signed Sherman Miles, Acting Assistant Chief of Staff, G-2, July 30, 1941. *Pearl Harbor Hearings*, Exh. 33.

[36] War Secretary Stimson told the Russian ambassador, who was requesting more war goods to help the common cause: "I have no eyes to see the things you tell me. You have taken my eyes and until I get my eyes back, I cannot take the responsibility of recommending giving away our weapons." Said the Russian: "You mean your Attaché should be allowed to go to the front?" Stimson: "I mean just that." That was a poser for the Russian, Stimson thought. Henry L. Stimson and McGeorge Bundy, *On Active Service* (New York 1948), p. 526.

It could not be expected, he told Hull from his own brief Moscow experience, that any military attaché "could get any reasonable expression of opinion from commuters or the general public which would be worthwhile." This seems to mean that these were the only possible sources of information for an attaché in Moscow at that time.[37]

Military missions fared no better. "The Russians remained inclined to view and treat the military mission in much the same manner as the former attachés, even though it was instructed, and seemingly conformed, to orders given at its departure by General Marshall, not to go after information and thus endanger, through irritating the highly suspicious Russians, the more important operational cooperation." Such was the conclusion drawn by the head of the American Military Mission to Moscow from 1943 to 1945, Major General John R. Deane, about the "strange alliance" which he tried valiantly to serve.[38]

On the Axis side German-Japanese cooperation seemed firmly established when the former military attaché and ambassador to Berlin, General Oshima, was for a second time made ambassador to Hitler at the end of 1940. One of his earliest tasks at Berlin would be, he stated publicly, "collaboration with the Germans in appointing joint military commissions as part of the alliance's machinery."[39] But this organization was never set up, nor was Oshima able, much sound military reasoning notwithstanding, to persuade his Government to make Russia its first enemy, rather than the United States.

The vast distance between Tokyo and Berlin presented traffic, transportation and communications problems which became even worse after the outbreak of war between Russia and Germany. Not all Germans and Japanese of military age residing in the two allied countries could be sent home for military service. Therefore, to give the Germans in Tokyo some basic training, the German military attaché began to

[37] Sherwood, *Roosevelt and Hopkins*, pp. 327, 395f.
[38] Gen. John R. Deane, *The Strange Alliance* (New York 1947), pp. 46f.; Watson, p. 329.
[39] *The New York Times*, December 20, 1940.

drill them once a week in the autumn of 1941, thereby starting a rumor that "the Germans intend to form a *Freikorps* to fight with the Japanese Army in the event of Japan entering the war."[40] The Japanese in Germany must have provided for something similar, for Japanese fighting with the Wehrmacht were made prisoners in Normandy in the summer of 1944.

On the Berlin-Rome Axis, activities of military attachés were endangered by resentment and treachery on the part of the weaker ally. After the close of the Polish campaign the Italian attaché in Berlin reported on German plans for the invasion of Belgium and the Netherlands, and the Duce, who "now for the first time desires German defeat," told Ciano secretly to inform the diplomatic representatives of the threatened countries (December 26, 1939). In part, this was a result of the incipient Italian dislike of the Germans, noted as early as the autumn of 1939. Rintelen, military attaché in Rome, and probably swelled by the recent victory over Poland, on one occasion "arrived unexpectedly among the Italian troops and began to ask indiscreet questions with the air of one who is making an inspection of the front. This was resented by our soldiers, especially by the officers."[41] The Italians, suffering from a military inferiority complex, worked off their resentment on the unfortunate Greeks: Mussolini raged about their military attaché in Belgrade, who was said to have expressed himself disparagingly about the Italian Army. Prime Minister Metaxas hastened to use the most flattering terms, and recalled the officer. Although completely exonerated, he was put on half-pay to please the Duce.[42]

Many of the attachés of the belligerents were recalled to duties in the field or at home, sometimes, at least, on posts where their previously acquired knowledge seemed most serviceable. The former British naval attaché in Paris, Commander Holland, chosen to deliver the British ultimatum to

[40] Grew, *Ten Years in Japan*, p. 464.
[41] Hugh Gibson, ed., *The Ciano Diaries, 1939-1943* (New York 1946), pp. 169f., 183.
[42] Greece, Office of Information, *The Greek White Book, Diplomatic Documents Relating to Italy's Aggression against Greece* (London 1942), no. 45.

the French naval forces at Mers-el Kebir in July 1940, pleaded in vain with the French admiral to join Britain in the fight against Hitler. On at least one occasion this change from attaché duties to fighting was interfered with by the government of the country of residence: on the day of the German attack on Yugoslavia in 1941 the Nazi Government ordered the military attaché of that country to be put in a concentration camp.[43] And on another occasion the change was extremely rapid: the German air attaché in Oslo, and the naval attaché who had played an active role as intermediary between the traitor Quisling and Reich authorities before the invasion,[44] donned their uniforms and took command of units of the landing force. It was said that Norwegian patriots, infuriated by this breach of neutrality, later shot the sailor to death,[45] while the airman was killed in the attempt to capture the Norwegian King.[46] One service attaché, male, was freed for front duty when the United States War Department in April 1944 appointed Major Florence C. Jepson, of the WACs, assistant military attaché in London,[47] the first woman to hold such a post.

The military record of one-time service attachés, as far as we have been able to follow it, does not seem to include any outstanding generalship. None of the German attachés who had served in the great capitals reached high rank of renown, with the exception of Colonel Krebs, the assistant military attaché in Moscow whom Stalin had so ostentatiously singled out in 1941 on the eve of the "Barbarossa" enterprise, and who received the hollow distinction of becoming the last German Army Chief of Staff. He had served as chief of staff of one of the army groups on the Eastern front where a large-scale Russian offensive achieved a breakthrough in June 1944

[43] *Trial of the Major War Criminals*, XXXIX, 275ff.

[44] *Ibid.*, XXXV, 404.

[45] *The New York Times*, April 18, 1940, report from Moscow. As far as we have been able to verify the story, this poetic justice did not take place and the attaché survived the war. For his activities during the invasion see Anthony K. Martienssen, *Hitler and his Admirals* (New York 1949), pp. 57f.

[46] T. Kingston Derry, *The Campaign in Norway* (London 1952), p. 38.

[47] *The New York Times*, April 21, 1944.

(Krebs was luckily absent at the time, participating in a National Socialist indoctrination course according to an order of July 29, 1944, that each general staff officer should henceforth be something like a National Socialist "leader officer"). He was made Chief of Staff in March 1945 when the military outlook had become hopeless, and proved so much a Hitlerite, "a smooth serving type," that he stayed with the Führer until his very last days. Then Krebs vanished, according to some reports ending his life in Russian captivity, or, more likely, by suicide. He had failed to obtain from Zhukov, whom he seems to have known in Moscow, better armistice terms than that unconditional surrender on which the East had agreed with the West.[48]

On the side of the "democratic" powers Stilwell, whose organizing abilities much surpassed his diplomatic gifts, bogged down in the mud of Chinese mandarinism—he would always be remembered as a mere attaché and not allowed "enough face" to put himself over. This, with inertia and corruption, plus the inter-service quarrel with General Chennault, who stood higher in the favor of the White House than did Stilwell, made all American help ineffective. Stilwell was preceded, if his mission was not actually inspired, by the activities of the British military attaché in Chungking, Major General L. E. Dennys, who had emerged as chief of a military mission sponsoring guerrilla and RAF activities.[49]

American-British coalition warfare after Pearl Harbor was prepared by such men as Captain Alan Goodrich Kirk, "naval attaché and naval attaché for air" in London (1939-1941), and Brigadier General Raymond Eliot Lee, from 1940 on military attaché in London, who even under the onslaught of the Blitz remained confident that the Luftwaffe would ultimately fail.[50] His colleague in Cairo, Colonel Bonners F. Fellers, on

[48] H. R. Trevor-Roper, *The Last Days of Hitler* (New York 1947), pp. 110, 209f., 215; Görlitz, pp. 637, 670, 700ff.; *Der Monat* (January 1951), p. 441.

[49] Charles F. Romanus and Riley Sunderland, *Stilwell's Mission to China* (Washington 1953), p. 28 and passim.

[50] *The New York Times*, April 8, 1958.

the other hand, was very skeptical of the British ability to hold Egypt and the Suez Canal against Rommel's attacks.[51]

Among the top commanders of the war Eisenhower was one of the few who had served a short tour of duty abroad as military attaché, an experience which seems hard to evaluate as far as its military side is concerned; the sentimental effect of a service sojourn in Paris seems more obvious.[52] As far as the gaining of diplomatic experience went, it would have helped to prepare him for the exercise of those talents which are indispensable in the commander of a vast coalition force. Another commander's apprenticeship included attaché duties: the later Marshal Vasili I. Chuikov was serving as military attaché in China at the time of the German invasion of Russia in 1941. He was recalled to serve as a kind of high-command trouble-shooter, to help block Hitler's thrust in the direction of the Caucasus and then to turn it back at Stalingrad. His successful defense there set off his career, and he reached the high point of Supreme Commander of Soviet Land Forces by the early 1960's. Perhaps his early attaché reporting was stirring in him when he wrote *Battle for Stalingrad*, the first publication of a top-ranking Soviet commander to provide a full-length battle narrative from the command's point of view—the first, at any rate, to be made accessible to the West.[53]

On the losing side, the Italians were inclined to make chiefs of staff out of military attachés, which may be considered a sign that under Fascism, if not also later, politics rather than service with troops provided the necessary qualifications. Pariani, Army Chief of Staff (1937-1939), had formerly been attaché in Tirana and instructor of the satellite Albanian Army; Marras, Italy's post-1945 Chief of Staff, had been military attaché in Berlin more than once since 1938, and so had

[51] Maurice Matloff and Edwin M. Snell, *Strategic Planning for Coalition Warfare, 1941-1942, 1943-1944* (Washington 1953-1959), pp. 246, 297. Fellers is the author of *Wings of Peace* (Chicago 1953). After 1945 he participated in ultranationalist, isolationist agitation.

[52] Lieut. General Lewis H. Brereton (*The Brereton Diaries*, New York 1946, pp. 341f.) served as an air attaché in Paris from 1919 to 1923, "a seventh heaven to a young aviator who thought the whole world his oyster."

[53] *The Battle for Stalingrad*, Introduction by Hanson W. Baldwin (New York 1962).

Roatta, Chief of Staff at the time of Italy's entry into the war in 1940 and again during the collapse of 1943. The Nazi Germans, rather than the military, distrusted him, and Hitler in his table talk called him "a rat," "a sneaking spy," part of "the aristocratic Mafia" that was thwarting the Duce's best intentions, "the Fouché of the Fascist revolution, a completely characterless spy." The Führer considered it almost treasonable that Roatta had staged the attack on France along the Alpine frontier, where it proved unduly costly, rather than from the Upper Rhine as the Germans had planned or strongly suggested. In August 1943, when Badoglio was negotiating Italy's capitulation and desertion from the Axis, he offered the Germans the choice of one of these three men as ambassador to Berlin—a sign of his earnest intention to stick to the "Steel Pact" to the last.[54]

In general, however, examples make it evident that the military powers continued to consider attaché duties no part of an officer's best qualification for high command. Instead, such experience prepared for less outstanding, though still indispensable, positions in the field of liaison[55] and intelligence[56]—if attachés formed an elite, it was one that would not often rise to the top of the military hierarchy.

This negative conclusion can only be strengthened by Russian procedure. As far as is known, few of the Russian commanders of the Second World War had served abroad. Putna was the one general whose qualifications for command or chief of staff duty had included four terms as attaché, in Berlin, Tokyo and Helsinki in the 1920's, and in London in

[54] Felix Gilbert, ed., *Hitler Directs His War* (New York 1950), pp. 29ff.; *Hitler's Secret Conversations, 1941-1944* (New York 1953), p. 254; Franz von Rintelen, *The Dark Invader, Wartime Reminiscences of a German Naval Intelligence Officer* (London 1933), passim. For Roatta's own version see his *Otto milioni di baionette. L'esercito italiano in guerra dal 1940 al 1943* (Milan 1946).

[55] "General John R. Deane, our military attaché in Moscow in October 1944 who was representing the U.S. Chiefs of Staff. . . ." Edward R. Stettinius, *Roosevelt and the Russians* (New York 1949), p. 91.

[56] Canaris, head of the German Abwehr, had been naval attaché in Spain during World War I. "The very taciturn, very remarkable Col. Marujama," as his German colleague as military attaché in the mid-1930's calls him, became head of Japan's intelligence service. Geyr, *Erinnerungen*, p. 18.

the 1930's, with a term as chief of staff of Blücher's Far
Eastern Army in between. He became a victim of the Moscow purges of 1937. Foreigners as different as the French and
the Germans had thought of him as "one of the most capable
heads" of the Red Army, "an astounding man" who was
frank enough to tell foreigners that "Bolshevism was not of
Russian origin but the invention of a German Jew." Such
heretical views may have contributed to his downfall and
execution, but publicly it was explained that Putna, of Polish
origin, was guilty of having lived on intimate terms with a
German officer while on active duty in London.[57] The great
"patriotic war" was to be led by none but true, if untraveled,
Russians.

[57] French Embassy Report from Moscow, March 21, 1928. Herbette,
p. 76; Geyr, *Erinnerungen*, pp. 17ff.; Castellan, pp. 479ff., 484ff.

AFTER 1945

When the armistice with Japan had been signed, the Japanese military attaché in Stockholm, Major General Makato Onodera, declared in a press interview that now, after "this sporting match mingled with heroism," the Allies should shake hands with his country as one would after a tennis match. He did recognize, however, that the atomic bomb had revolutionized warfare, "no longer leaving room for chivalry."[1] There was, indeed, chivalry neither in the treatment of the defeated nor, after a short pause, in the relations, diplomatic and military, of those who had been temporarily united against the Axis. Return to concepts and practices of class warfare in the international sphere, the moratorium on which had always been more strictly observed on the capitalist side, and the threat which the Russians discovered in the one-sided possession of the atomic bomb, promptly started a new cycle of military competition.

Military, rather than naval and air, attachés were soon observable among the foremost reconnaissance forces in this clash between East and West, but hardly anything became known about the attachés' liaison and kindred services within the two great military blocs.[2] "Foresightedly," which in politics so often means preparing the dangers of the future

---

[1] United Press dispatch from Stockholm, August 11, 1945.

[2] Recognition of the East German "People's Republic" included the stationing of military attachés in East Berlin by the "satellites." Among these was the Czech Col. Jaroslav J. Sustar, who had masterminded the assassination of Heydrich, of Himmler's S.S., at Lidice in 1941. When his country fell under Communist control, he defected to the West. *Newsweek*, April 16, 1956. The East German regime stationed a military attaché as far away as Peiping, where he was assured by the Deputy Premier and Defense Minister, Marshal Peng Teh-huai, that an "imperialist" attack on East Germany would be regarded as an "attack on the whole Socialist camp" and that China would give her "all-out support." *The New York Times*, March 2, 1959.

as well as preparing to meet them, the United States War Department wanted to have highly skilled "military diplomats" ready for the problems of peace and of renewed arms competition. From July 1945 on they had been grooming officers of the rank of colonel and lieutenant colonel in regional courses, for subsequent service as military attachés in specific regions. One course for Europe was given, with 30 participants, and one each for Inter-America and the Far East, where there was still a war of considerable dimensions and worse consequences to observe.[3]

At no time of their half-secret, half-open history have service attachés so often, so bluntly and so officially been called spies as after 1945—to view them as such was part of the psychotic aspect of the cold war. When the wartime spying at Ottawa, which had never before been an important station for attachés, was revealed—executed by the Russian military mission under the direction of the military attaché, Colonel Zabotin—it set off a series of plainly retaliatory charges and measures by the Communist-controlled governments against attachés of the Western powers. The Russians seem to have hoped that publication would be suppressed.

Russia began the series of what might be called non-amenities by denying Canadian representatives the usual privilege of visiting military establishments, whereupon Canada retaliated in January 1948 by excluding Russian attachés from visiting her training bases as the other seven countries represented in Ottawa had been invited to do.[4] And as if on a signal from Moscow, in the autumn of 1947, Russia and practically all the satellite countries accused attachés of Great Britain and the United States, with France to follow, of spying against their host countries, of having been caught in the act, and of having been in contact with conspirators against the existing regimes. Military and other tribunals "uncovered" the criminal procedures implicating the officers, and invariably the satellite governments and their Moscow

[3] As to other Washington intelligence training programs for service attachés see J. W. Masland and L. I. Radway, *Soldiers and Scholars* (Princeton 1957), p. 388.

[4] Associated Press dispatch from Ottawa, July 19, 1948.

masters asked the American and British Governments for the recall of these discredited attachés, "to be effected in the shortest possible time" because their presence could no longer be considered desirable. The Western countries acceded to such requests, in keeping with usual international practice. In the course of such a conflict with Rumania, however, the United States Government rejected "as ridiculous and entirely contrary to fact the grounds upon which the Rumanian Government presumes to base its request for their recall," and in obvious retaliation and in the absence of suitable service attachés demanded the recall of two Rumanian civilian diplomats as no longer *persona non grata* in Washington.[5]

The Polish Communist Government, which considered the American Embassy in Warsaw a highly active supporter of the underground opposition in 1945-1947, did not go as far as declaring the assistant U.S. military attaché, Lieutenant Colonel Frank Jessic, *persona non grata*, but it complained about him constantly, and charged him with entertaining contacts with the opposition, or with having insulted the President of the Polish Republic. It resented the Colonel's activity and constant travel, which went far beyond the Poles' idea "of what a military attaché in this country ought to do. Its idea roughly is that an attaché should participate in parties in full dress as a decoration to his ambassador and accept gratefully an occasional Polish invitation to watch a parade or visit an artillery maneuver. Any activity beyond that is considered superfluous and dangerous even though it consists only in the attempt to gather information that the War Department and the press in the United States willingly supply to foreign missions."[6] After some six months of continued diplomatic representations the War Department recalled the energetic colonel in April 1948, well ahead of a case pending before a Polish military tribunal, which was to expose the "treasonable" relations between the underground and various members of the British and American embassies.

[5] American-Rumanian exchange of notes, of December 7 and 10, 1948. *The New York Times*, December 12, 1948.

[6] *The New York Times*, April 12, 1948, report of its Warsaw correspondent.

The new diplomacy, Moscow-Byzantine style, went further: it assumed the right to decide how much personnel foreign missions actually needed. While there was an obvious inflation of service attachés everywhere, and not only in Warsaw,[7] diplomatic amenities had heretofore forbidden such infringement of the right of sending and maintaining as much personnel as the sending government thought appropriate. In March 1950, however, the Polish Government requested the United States Embassy—though no other—to reduce its staff of service attachés, eight officers plus eleven non-commissioned personnel. This followed a precedent set earlier in the year by Hungary, where the Communist Government had requested Britain to cut her legation personnel because "it greatly exceeded their prewar numbers."[8]

There was great competition among the satellites to imitate the Russian example or to follow its slightest hints. They had had more prolonged and more intimate contacts with the West than had Moscow, but it was now demanded that they cut off all channels through which their military personnel (not as a rule among those who had delivered their countries into the Moscow orbit) might be influenced by the West and its representatives.

The activities of attachés in countries behind the Iron Curtain were kept within ever narrower bounds by almost complete severance of personal relationships with the civilian and military population, restrictions as to travel,[9] which

[7] Not long before its fall the Chinese Nationalist Government closed its 50 military attaché offices throughout the world in order to meet the demand for officers at the front. *The New York Times*, August 14, 1949.

[8] *The New York Times*, March 19, 1950. The Moscow Government, in May 1960, turned down an American request for the accreditation of three additional service attachés, pointing out that there were already four military attachés stationed in the country. *Ibid.*, May 20, 1960.

[9] On September 30, 1948, the Soviet Government imposed a ban on travel for foreign diplomatic personnel, limiting their movements in the main to a radius of 50 kms. from Moscow; for movements beyond this region the foreign ministry or the armed forces ministry had to be notified beforehand. This restriction went considerably beyond an earlier ban, imposed May 16, 1941, and never revoked, on the eve of the war with Germany. *The New York Times*, October 5, 1948. Rumania aped the master's voice by ordering foreign diplomats to stay out of two-thirds of her territory, including a belt 30 miles wide along the frontiers. Associated Press dispatch from Bucharest, April 29, 1949.

satellite nations like Hungary were able to impose on diplomatic personnel once the provisions of the peace treaties guaranteeing this freedom to enforcement officers had lapsed, and by constant and close surveillance by the Communist police. The police, indeed, were accused by the State Department, in connection with a Moscow espionage case and in language shorn of diplomatic amenities, of having arranged "a plant, in good American language" against an American naval attaché.[10] The United States Secretary of Defense stated in his *Report* for the first half of 1950 that Army intelligence was now "severely hampered by two factors: a reduction in Military Attaché personnel and the forced reduction of our diplomatic missions in the Eastern European countries under communist domination."[11] What could attachés still learn? Taking their superior knowledge for granted, the British War Office in September 1948 assembled the military attachés from all over the world for a week's conference in London, in the presence of Field Marshal Montgomery, just returned from the United States. It was stated that this was merely resuming "a normal peace time procedure," but the outside world took it for granted that the attachés from behind the iron curtain would have "the most eagerly awaited reports."[12] None of the information submitted at the conference, needless to say, has been made public.

Such meetings normal or not, could only sharpen mutual activity, suspicion and vigilance. In May 1954 two Soviet assistant air attachés were accused by the British Government of having tried to obtain data on British jets by bribing workers in aircraft factories; their further presence in Britain was declared undesirable. Four days later, in obvious reprisal, an assistant British military attaché, on leave from Moscow at the time, was declared *persona non grata* by the Russians on charges of "general espionage," Both sides recalled the accused but denied the charges; on both sides, it might be

10 *The New York Times*, August 16, 1948.
11 Department of Defense, *Semiannual Report of the Secretary of Defense*, January 1 to June 30, 1950 (Washington 1950), p. 75.
12 *The New York Times*, September 15, 1948.

observed, it was assistant attachés, usually the ones entrusted with espionage, who were accused and sacrificed.[13]

In the spring of 1951, a Communist agent in West Germany came into temporary possession of, and photocopied, the very compromising diary of the U.S. military attaché in Moscow, Major General Robert W. Grow. It was published in East Germany and revealed many of the worst features of a poorly qualified service attaché: advocacy of a preventive war against the host land, notes on "contacts," on talks with other service attachés, on air war targets inside Russia, and on his dislike of his nominal superior, the ambassador (a disqualification for either intelligence work or diplomatic behavior). These indications of a misassignment reflected on his Washington superiors and their methods of selecting officers for such exposed posts as Moscow. A hurried recall and a court-martial could only confirm the damage done to the American side in the cold war.[14] It provided a "first" in the history of the service attaché, the first case of public punishment for poor services rendered.

As if to illustrate the dubious character of the 1955 let-up in the cold war, the diplomatic amenity resumed by the Russians did not extend to the service attachés. In 1953 the United States Government had demanded the recall of three Russians, an assistant naval attaché, a second secretary to the Soviet Delegation to the United Nations, and an assistant air attaché alleged to have been spying; the Kremlin in turn expelled two American service attachés who were charged with attempts at espionage and other activity "incompatible with their diplomatic status." This series of recriminatory actions was resumed by the Russians in the summer of 1955, when

---

[13] *Ibid.*, May 14, 1954.

[14] For a discussion of the Grow case see Hanson W. Baldwin in *The New York Times*, April 13 and 18, and June 6, 1952, and Demaree Bess in *Saturday Evening Post*, September 27, 1952. Excerpts from the diary are to be found in Richard Squires, *Auf dem Kriegspfad. Aufzeichnungen eines englischen Offiziers* (East Berlin 1951). Charged with improperly recording classified military information in private records and failing to safeguard it properly, Grow was given a reprimand and relieved of holding command for six months by a court-martial in July 1952, a judgment upheld by the Court of Military Appeals in 1953. *The New York Times*, April 19, June 6 and July 19, 1952, and July 18, 1953.

Soviets easily outmaneuvered the US in the propaganda war

they demanded and obtained the withdrawal of three American assistant military attachés. The change in the diplomatic atmosphere was merely marked by a somewhat unusual discretion on both sides in handling the case.[15] Only a little earlier, the NATO camp had expelled two Russian air attachés from London. As the House of Commons was told: one of them "had been detected in a blatant attempt to suborn a serving officer of Her Majesty's forces," unsuccessfully, while the other had made "at least attempts to recruit agents" (Minister of State Selwyn Lloyd, May 17, 1955).

In Switzerland and Sweden, both trying hard to stay neutral in the espionage-ridden cold war, spy rings connected with citizens of two satellite countries, including in both cases the Czech military attaché, were detected by the authorities; they demanded that the legation members involved leave on account of activities "which are incompatible with diplomatic usage."[16] The Iranian Government complained in February 1956 that the Soviet Union had stepped up its espionage since Iran's accession to the pro-Western Bagdad Pact of 1955. They expelled the Russian assistant military attaché, after they had caught him with an Iranian Air Force officer who was handing over documents pertaining to air force installations.[17]

Did the uncounted but ever larger number of service attachés and assistant attachés[18] become subject to Parkinson's Law? At least one protest against attaché inflation was voiced by a retiring United States ambassador, Ellis O. Briggs, who told the Senate that in the late 1950's in Athens (not a focus of the cold war) he had some 70 sailors, soldiers and airmen attached to the embassy on his hands. "Had I been able to deploy them for three hours every morning in full-dress uniform, playing leapfrog across the Acropolis, that would have

---

[15] *The New York Times*, June 18, 1955.

[16] *Ibid.*, December 23, 1954, and March 15, 1955.

[17] *Ibid.*, March 2, 1956.

[18] On May 1, 1948, the U.S. Army and Air Force had 640 members (258 officers, 55 non-commissioned officers and 327 enlisted men) on military and air attaché duty in 59 countries, while the U.S. Navy, as of January 1, 1948, kept 120 officers on attaché duty in 43 countries. *The Army Almanac* (Washington 1950), p. 4.

made as much sense as most of the attaché duties they solemnly declared they were engaged in." When Briggs was ambassador in Prague, he had obtained State Department approval for a reduction of his personnel from 80 to 40, in the interest of efficiency and economy, but he ran into the determined resistance of the other Washington agencies represented in Prague, who declared their attachés indispensable. The reduction would never have been achieved if the Czech Government had not declared all but 13 Americans *persona non grata* for having spied or conspired.[19]

Every nation was eager to employ service attachés, except Germany and Japan: ten years after the close of hostilities they had not again stationed such attachés abroad, and seemed hesitant about it. But under American prompting, it would appear, by 1955 they were on the verge of doing so once more. The Bonn Government was invited in May 1955 to send a military attaché to Washington soon, preferably a young man and not an old general, in order to speed coordination between the American and the—hardly even existing —German forces.[20] And Japan's civilian governors announced in September 1955 that they would station members of their "self-defense" units with the principal embassies abroad, that a beginning would be made by placing an officer in Washington, but that there would be a marked difference from the pre-1945 order of things: these military observers would be civilianized, they would be secretaries rather than officers. They began to arrive by the end of 1956.[21] Obviously, neither Germany nor Japan were in a hurry to re-create service attachés in their old splendor and independence, not to mention their insolence and insubordination. Since then, little

---

[19] *Time*, July 5, 1963. The problems brought on by proliferation continue: in December 1964 Defense Secretary McNamara announced that he had designated one attaché in each embassy as senior defense attaché, "the senior representative of the Department of Defense at the embassy at which he is stationed." This officer would report to him through the Joint Chiefs of Staff, thus "to increase the efficiency of our attaché work at the embassies in which they serve." *The New York Times*, December 13, 1964.

[20] *Die Zeit* (Hamburg), May 19, 1955.

[21] *The New York Times*, September 13, 1955, February 18, 1957.

by which to judge their activities has become known, but one wonders whether they are not again up to the old tricks of the trade. It is reported for instance that the West German Defense Minister, Franz Joseph Strauss, a very ambitious man who aspired to succeed Adenauer, used the *bundesdeutschen* attachés to provide him with analyses of the foreign political situation, and to provide the NATO allies with materials for the build-up of Herr Strauss.[22] He went further, in fact beyond what under cold war conditions seemed permissible, in a feud with the news magazine *Der Spiegel*, which he maintained had committed treason by printing articles on the state of German rearmament. He gave the military attaché in Madrid direct telephonic orders, without troubling the Foreign Office, to have the Spanish police (who proved very accommodating, assuming that this was an Interpol request) arrest and extradite a *Der Spiegel* writer who was vacationing in Spain at the time. Partly because of this action, and because of lying about it, Strauss had to quit the Bonn political scene and forego the immediate chance, at least, of succeeding *Der Alte.*

A new flowering of the evils of attachédom, quite like old times, arose in the Near East. Not only were one-time military attachés among the most active politicians of the Pan-Arab movement at home, but they exerted themselves in its favor abroad, especially the Egyptian attachés after Nasser's coming to power. The officer stationed in Libya organized the "Front for the Struggle of the Libyan People," which was to put up "resistance to the oppressive Imperialists," the Anglo-Saxons of course, with their air bases on which the country's economy largely depended. After the Anglo-French attack on Suez he stepped up his work, the Front blew up a pipeline and threw bombs, provided by the Egyptian, who was at last besought to leave by the Libyan Government. He would not go, barricaded himself in the embassy, threw leaflets into the street and brandished a machine-gun—to no avail, no demonstrators showed up, only police. At last the colonel was

22 *Der Spiegel* (Hamburg), April 26, 1961.

persuaded to leave, in November 1956, and he was followed by an exodus of other Egyptian emissaries, including Libya's attorney-general and some 400 schoolteachers.[23]

In the countries where Nasser's leadership was less completely acknowledged, his military attachés, going well "beyond their normal duties," organized Fedayeen raids from Jordan into Israel, stirred up agitation against the monarchical powers in Ethiopia, Jordan, Saudi Arabia or the Christian-Arab state of Lebanon, where an attaché's car loaded with explosives was stopped on more than one occasion. Saudi Arabia and Jordan openly accused these attachés of plotting the murder of "official personalities," including, it was hinted, the heads of state. Civilian control by diplomats went by the board, as these and other discoveries emphasized "the dominant role played by military attachés, representatives of Egypt's military regime, in Egyptian embassies."[24]

Soviet and satellite military attachés showed their hands at least occasionally, arranging for the arm supplies to Egypt and, still more, to Syria, a country at times practically run by ex-attachés such as Lieutenant Colonel Abdel Hamid Serraj. He was attaché in Paris in 1953-1954, and was later chief of his country's intelligence service; he accused American diplomatic personnel, including the military attaché, Colonel Robert W. Malloy, of having conspired with Syrians, among them the military attaché in Rome, for the overthrow of the existing regime.[25] The "Red colonel's" sway over Syrian affairs, which a rightist group tried in vain to shake in the spring of 1957 when they proposed to exile Serraj to Cairo as attaché,[26] went so far at last that the remaining civilians were forced to seek union with Egypt under a Nasser who seemed considerably less Red-dictated than did Serraj. Nasser rather promptly promoted him and others, then unseated them once unification had been perfected. This was too much for "the faithful dog to Nasser," as Egyptians called Serraj be-

[23] *Time*, December 9, 1956.
[24] For details see *The New York Times*, May 4 and 12, June 11, 1957; *Die Weltwoche* (Zurich), July 26, 1957.
[25] *The New York Times*, March 22, 1957.
[26] *Ibid.*, December 11, 1956, and August 15, 1957.

hind his back, and he was one of the engineers of the September 1961 putsch, which weakened the UAR once more.[27]

Apparently a majority of Syrian officers favored Pan-Arabism, but there were enough who opposed it to succeed in a new military coup after some seventeen months of harsh Egyptian overlordship. Syria again became independent, and General Abdel Karim Zahreddin, leader of the coup, headed the government. He was quickly confronted by three major and untold minor pro-Nasser counter-coups, but he managed to hold on until March 1963, when Colonel el Hariri, suspected of heading yet another conspiracy, was ordered to leave the country and go to Jordan as military attaché. Instead, el Hariri appeared at the head of an armored column, took over Damascus and put the anti-Nasser Baathist party into power. Pro-Nasser officers were pensioned off en masse or sent abroad on training missions or as military attachés, including soon enough Colonel el Hariri himself to whom this purging, hurtful to Pan-Arabism, seemed to go too far. In July 1963, the Government in Damascus announced that it had been in touch with various foreign governments to find one to whom he would be acceptable as military attaché—such a post having become a kind of honorable exile for politically restless officers. The Government flew him to Paris, whence he was to proceed to the idyllic post of Vienna. The new strong man was Major General Amin el Hafez, whose earlier career included attaché duties in Moscow and Buenos Aires. He put down yet another pro-Nasser putsch and then proved inconsiderate enough to line up some 30 participants, mostly officers, before firing squads, instead of sending them abroad as attachés, a liquidation which Nasser found highly unsporting.[28]

Not all service attachés could bring themselves to serve the new mid-Eastern and similar regimes, with the novel require-

[27] *Ibid.*, September 29, 1961.

[28] The above is based on news reports from the Near East, notably those in *The New York Times*, May 5, July 9 and 28, 1963; *Time*, March 15, 1963. As the result of a still later military coup in Syria, in February 1966, no less than eight officers of the losing military faction were posted abroad as military attachés. *The New York Times*, March 12, 1966. The same honorable exile was decreed for some officers on the losing side in the Dominican upheavals of 1965-1966. *Ibid.*, January 27, 1966.

ments demanded of their agents abroad; some preferred to follow the example of the Russian soldiers and diplomats who had earlier sought and obtained asylum in the West (Kravchenko, Gouzenko, Petrov, etc.). Lieutenant General Izydor R. Modelski, sent as Polish military attaché to Washington in 1946 to direct a spy system for the Communist bloc, broke with the Warsaw government in 1948, and received asylum in the United States. He told the House Committee on Un-American Activities in detail how Communist espionage, with its center in the Russian embassy, was being run.[29] The Gomulka regime in Poland lost not only two renegade military agents in Paris and Tokyo, but also Colonel Pawel Monat, military attaché in Washington until 1958, and later in charge of coordinating the work of Polish military attachés in all the foreign capitals. Monat applied for American asylum in the summer of 1959; in Poland he was subsequently sentenced to death, in absentia, for desertion.[30] At almost the same time the military attaché of the Czech Embassy in Washington, Lieutenant Colonel Frantisek Tisler, quit and obtained political asylum.[31]

And a number of Cuban service attachés, for the most part original partisans of the Castro Revolution, resigned or fled their posts, the majority to seek asylum in the United States. The naval attaché in Washington, Lieutenant Commander Miguel F. G. Pons Goizueta, was denounced by the new Cuban Government as a thief and traitor, suborned by foreign, that is American, interests, "which are trying to destroy the Cuban revolution."[32] Another Cuban naval attaché, Lieutenant Commander Jaime Varela Canosa, sought refuge in the United States, to him still "a brother American country," in March 1960, charging Communist influence in his own country.[33] He was followed in April 1960 by the air attaché in

---

[29] See obituary in *The New York Times*, September 28, 1963.

[30] *The New York Times*, November 23 and 24, 1959; June 20, 1960. Monat subsequently wrote his spy memoirs (with John Dille), *Spy in the U.S.* (New York 1962).

[31] *The New York Times*, November 5, 1959.

[32] *Ibid.*, March 20, 1960; *Time*, March 28, 1960.

[33] *The New York Times*, March 26, 1960.

Mexico, Captain Manuel Villafama Martinez, who had been chief of Castro's air force for a short time and who also declared that the ideals of the Revolution were being betrayed; in evidence, he submitted details of Cuban activities abroad.[34]

Cuba, however, was only a minor and new participant in the cold war, which broke out afresh after the shooting down of a CIA plane over Russian territory on May Day, 1960: accusations of espionage activities by the service and other attachés on either side were the inevitable result. President Eisenhower explained the incident as a result of "specific activities," of which "the normal, the regular visible agencies of our Government are unaware which stay clear of operational involvement in specific detailed activities. . . . We do not use our Army, Navy and Air Force for this purpose, first to avoid any possibility of the use of force in connection with these activities, and second, because our military forces, for obvious reasons, cannot be given latitude under broad directives, but must be kept under strict control in every detail."[35] After this restatement of diplomatic usage or parlance, a United States memorandum submitted to the United Nations gave a detailed account of espionage activities on the part of Russian diplomatic personnel, service attachés and others, stationed in Washington as well as near UN headquarters.[36]

The anti-spy campaign engendered in Russia in connection with the Powers trial in the late summer of 1960 would not have been complete without accusations against American service attachés. In August 1960, the U.S. air attaché, Colonel Edwin M. Kirton, was recalled for activities "incompatible with his diplomatic status," according to the USSR, and also for having "acted in an offensive manner to Soviet citizens." At the same time his assistant was given "a stern warning," and three months later his recall was requested as well.[37] This expulsion was in obvious retaliation for the ouster nineteen days earlier of a third secretary of the Soviet Embassy in

[34] *Ibid.*, April 13, 1960.
[35] Press conference, May 11, 1960.
[36] Text in *The New York Times*, May 25, 1960.
[37] *Ibid.*, August 11 and November 22, 1960.

Washington, for having bought aerial photographs of strategic target areas in the United States.[38] He was the thirteenth Soviet diplomat to be expelled in ten years.

In Moscow the tourist season was enlivened by the anti-spy campaign. *Izvestia*, for a change, rather than the Foreign Office, accused the American "military air attaché," Colonel David Windsor, of having had a "secret meeting" with an American oil expert, member of a delegation which had inspected Russian oil installations; the oil man was said to have misused the occasion to do some spying, including photographing of strategic installations.[39] But the front in the cold war was not limited to Russia; the American Government at about the same time expelled the Hungarian military attaché, Colonel Karoly Laszlo, after repeatedly warning him on his activities in gathering information. Hungary retaliated by demanding the departure of the U.S. military attaché, Colonel Carl W. Miller, who had been in the country less than a month; since nothing could be held against him as yet, the ouster was explained as "on account of the activities pursued by the military personnel of the U.S. Legation in Budapest"[40]—the cold war did not favor the continuance of diplomatic amenities. In the autumn of 1962 *Pravda* described an assistant U.S. naval attaché, asked to leave Moscow, as having "roamed our land like a wolf and dictated espionage information in a whisper into a tape recorder hidden under his clothes"; he was detected "red-handed," however, by the vigilance of two Soviet patriots. The charge came a few days after the United States had requested the departure of two members of the Soviet mission at the United Nations, for having bought defense secrets from an American sailor who was subsequently sent to prison for a prolonged term.[41] And Czech President Antonin Novotny told a Polish-Czechoslovak rally in September 1963: "The military attachés and some other workers of the Western capitalist states are now constantly working overtime because they

38 *Ibid.*, August 11 and 14, 1960.
39 *Ibid.*, September 18, 1960.
40 *Ibid.*, August 14, 1960.
41 *Ibid.*, October 7, 1962.

are combing the [Czech] republic left and right looking for Soviet troops and rocket bases."[42]

Where the cold war became temporarily hotter, as in Laos in 1960-1961, military attachés were encountered in and above the loosely-drawn battle lines. Flying in an unarmed American plane to watch Soviet air drops to the Pathet Laos rebels, an American assistant military attaché, Major Armand Riser, was shot at, either from the ground or from Russian planes. His machine was hit, but was able to return to its base.[43] Three months later another plane with eight Americans aboard, among them another assistant military attaché, Major Lawrence Bailey, was less fortunate. It was shot down, and men and plane declared missing.[44]

"Peaceful coexistence" deteriorated markedly when late in September 1964 some fifteen agents forcibly entered the hotel rooms of one British and three American service attachés traveling through Siberia on an authorized trip. Contrary to the usual observance of diplomatic immunity, the officers were detained and searched, and some of their belongings confiscated, including notebooks, cameras and films which, as the Russians afterwards proclaimed, betrayed spying intentions. While this could hardly be denied, the violation of internationally accepted practices, including those laid down in the 1960 Vienna Convention on Diplomatic Relations, of which the USSR was a signatory, was a serious matter in the annals of diplomacy, endangering as it did a fresh attempt at the codification of behavior. The United States and Great Britain strongly protested and apparently the Russians gave no answer. While they termed the activities of the officers "impermissible" and not in keeping with "the strict observance of the standards and rules of behavior of accredited diplomatic representatives," they kept silent on the point of immunity, and in fact allowed the three to return to Moscow, though severely restricting their movements. The "settlement" of this particular incident came nearly three months later: the two Western powers recalled the four men involved and expelled an equal number of Russian attachés, accusing them

---

[42] *Ibid.*, October 1, 1963. [43] *Ibid.*, December 9, 1960.
[44] *Ibid.*, March 28, 1961.

of "activities incompatible with their diplomatic status." The State Department indicated that their transgression had been minor, and under different circumstances would have been overlooked.[45]

Thus "incidents" involving attachés, rather than the regular performance of their duties, provided news, and reflected the ups and downs of the cold war—but it was always the Russians who set the thermostats. At one time, in 1961, they would show foreign attachés tactical exercises involving a motorized unit supposedly operating on a nuclear battlefield, the first time since 1936 that such officers had been invited to watch a ground maneuver.[46] In two cases in February 1964, however, American attachés attracted hostile Russian mobs which seemed to them to be inspired by the authorities, or possibly by reading about spies. The Kremlin promptly clamped a travel ban on the attachés involved, and included some Britishers and others, in order to call attention to the East-West front. These restrictions met prompt retaliation by the Western powers, including a travel ban for the ten Russian service attachés in Washington—three each for the army and air force and four for the navy—to last as long as did the Moscow ban. Measured by the standards that had evolved in the cold war, these measures were considered "unusually mild."[47] And even a far more lurid incident elicited only a mild protest by the State Department, the disclosure that during a visit to Odessa one British and three American attachés had been drugged so that their rooms could be searched.[48]

It is, naturally, far too early to evaluate the truly military performances of service attachés during the cold war, although visible marks of recognition have already been awarded to a few of them. The U.S. naval attaché in Cuba when Fidel Castro came to power, Captain C. R. Clark, later posted to Madrid, was decorated in July 1964 for first suggesting the

---

[45] *Ibid.*, October 6-8 and December 15, 1964.

[46] *Ibid.*, August 18, 1961.

[47] *Ibid.*, April 11, 1964.

[48] *Ibid.*, May 8, 1964. The Russians denied this, alleged that the officers had been "dead drunk" at the time, and were among the eight attachés caught in the act of spying during the preceding twelve months.

presence of hidden Russian missiles on the island, and advancing the theory by which their presence was subsequently established. He "gathered and brilliantly analyzed available intelligence information."[49] The most outstanding ex-attaché is General Charles Louis Marcel Alleret (Class of 1907), chairman of the French Chiefs of Staff since July 1962. After the Second World War he spent a year as military attaché in Moscow (1945-1946), whence he is said to have returned "with a strong respect for Soviet military power." His rise to eminence began with De Gaulle's return to power in 1958; both generals had the same concept of atomic war as it should be conducted by the West—a massive nuclear retaliation in answer to a major Soviet aggression, rather than the expressed American preference for a flexible reaction.[50]

[49] *The New York Times*, July 10, 1964.
[50] *Ibid.*, July 30, 1964.

CHAPTER 7

THE SERVICE ATTACHÉ AND "SOCIETY"

Like the diplomats, the pre-1914 service attachés belonged, by birth or through other qualifications, to what is usually and deceptively called "society," or the "governing classes" of the Western world. Actually, as it proved, these classes were governing certain forces in their midst or below them so little, so ineffectually, that within one generation they witnessed the downfall of the regimes with the conservation of which they had been identified and entrusted.

Owing to the prevailing systems of qualifications for military and diplomatic service in most European countries, and to a certain extent in the United States, attachés were well-to-do, if not rich, at least up to 1914.[1] In general, they belonged to a plutocracy which neither recognized nor fought its basic foes, imperialism,[2] chauvinism, militarism, navalism; instead they saw enemies almost exclusively in Socialism, Communism and pacifism.

[1] The American *beau ideal* of the military attaché as of 1940 has been described as follows: He must have special preparation for his service. If he has served in more than one branch of the army, it will be to his advantage. Initiative, intelligence, force, judgment, common sense, cooperation are required of him, as well as knowledge of languages. Private fortune is desirable, but less and less so. The job is "less and less a social cynosure and more and more a 'he-man,' 'go-getter' job. A certain amount of social 'going-about' and entertainment is necessary, of course." Major Lowell M. Riley, "Duty as Military Attaché," *Field Artillery Journal* (September-October 1940).

[2] In February-March 1900, the German military attaché in London, von Lüttwitz, of Kapp Putsch fame, was the guest in South Africa of Cecil Rhodes who, "in long talks and on horseback rides," favored Anglo-German cooperation "not only in African affairs but in other questions of Weltpolitik as well." In London Rhodes had suggested leaving Germany "a free hand in Asia Minor and possibly in Mesopotamia as well. The world was so much filled with dying nations which had hardly a right to existence any more, that there was plenty of room for the expansion of our two healthy nations." Report from Bloomfontein, March 17, 1900. *Archives of Auswärtiges Amt.*

110

Obviously the socially most acceptable and adroit officer was not necessarily the best possible observer and judge. Not only was he often the *arrivé* type, a man who had already acquired, by birth or wealth, his place in the world, and hence worked less hard, but his wealth kept other officers, professionally better qualified, from the position he held. The Intelligence Section in the British War Office recognized this situation early in the century: "the amount of information procurable by a military attaché was largely governed by the amount of money he could spend in entertaining those from whom he might hope to procure it." The Intelligence directors also observed that attachés, whose selection did not depend solely or even mainly on the War Office, were chosen for money or other "insufficient reasons," such as being society favorites, or having an attractive wife or a friend in the Foreign Office; they therefore proposed to obtain higher salaries in places where living costs were high for their own superior (though more impecunious) choices, but found that these were "facts which left the Treasury mind unmoved."[3] Before 1914 the vast majority of German low-ranking officers, whose emoluments, however, were higher than those of all diplomatic personnel below the ambassador,[4] and many French officers, had to rely on financial support from their families.[5] This was especially true of attachés on duty in foreign capitals where many sons or sons-in-law of the rich were serving, such as Speck von Sternburg or Papen in Washington, or the later Major General Sir John Marriott, Commander of the Guards Division (1945-1947), who in 1920 married a daughter of financier Otto H. Kahn.[6]

While American Army and Navy officers were and are the best paid of any, the financial requirements of service on a foreign post were beyond the means of the 60 per cent or more who had no income beyond their pay. In order to hold

[3] Field-Marshal Sir William Robertson, *From Private to Field-Marshal* (Boston and New York 1921), p. 131.

[4] Meisner, *Militärattachés*, p. 49.

[5] Up to 1900, no French officer obtained the marriage permit unless his wife could show a dowry of at least 1200 francs. Raoul Girardet, *La société militaire dans la France contemporaine* (Paris 1953), p. 258.

[6] *The New York Times*, October 25, 1960.

"the most prized of all details, that of military attaché at one of the U.S. legations, . . . officers who accept such posts generally have outside incomes of their own or such as are derived from their family connections."[7] The military attaché in St. Petersburg in 1905, Major Stephen Slocum, was "notable in the service as being the proud nephew of one of the chief heirs of Mrs. Russell Sage, who was supposed to gild his career beyond the dreams of avarice."[8]

The older bureaucratic systems, if they cared sufficiently, were able to help out an officer whom they considered exceptionally well suited for an expensive foreign post, by drawing on secret funds. As the dispenser of such funds Bismarck asked the military attaché in St. Petersburg, Count Yorck, who wanted to be transferred because he was too poor to afford a decent marriage and household in that post, how much he would need for the purpose; when told, Bismarck granted the required extra pay at once (1889).[9] Such grants remained outside all budgetary control: when around 1910 the anti-Navy Reich Treasury reduced the emoluments of the naval attaché in London, where living costs were exceedingly high, in the hope of curtailing his activities, Tirpitz made good the difference from secret funds at his disposal.[10]

The shift of fortunes after world wars and world revolutions had an equalizing effect: officers, whether at home or abroad, were now living on a strictly salaried basis, and the armed forces attachés thus became more than ever professionals of the professionals. In fact, until the Second World War there were only a few military attachés who were non-professionals. Two of them were historians: Theodor von Bernhardi, a civilian with vast military knowledge who had never even served in an army, was an intimate of Moltke and was made military attaché by Bismarck for the purpose of observing the disappointing military performance of the Italians in the 1860's; and the late Harold Temperley served for a time as

[7] Hanson Baldwin in *The New York Times*, April 13, 1952.

[8] Post Wheeler and Hallie Erminie Rives, *Dome of Many-Coloured Glass* (Garden City 1955), p. 300.

[9] Wilhelm Friedrich, *Maximilian Graf Yorck von Wartenburg* (Berlin 1941), p. 21.

[10] Widenmann, p. 65.

military attaché in Belgrade as a Balkan expert. Hamilton Fish Armstrong, for many years editor of the New York magazine *Foreign Affairs*, had also been a U.S. military attaché for a time.

Technical proficiency apart, including linguistic ability and usually staff experience, service attachés of the European countries, before 1914 at least, qualified by belonging to the so-called best families and best regiments, which is to say the Guards where such existed, as in Britain, Germany and Russia. The three pre-1914 empires employed bearers of noble names as military attachés as much as in the rest of their diplomatic corps and even more than in their armies generally, though this was not true with regard to their navies.[11] Among the military attachés sent out from Berlin, to mention only those of the higher nobility, were Prince Kraft zu Hohenlohe-Ingelfingen and Count von der Groeben, in Vienna in the 1850's and 1860's, and Count Waldersee in Paris in 1870; among those of the newly founded Reich were a younger brother of Chancellor Bülow, two Counts Posadowsky, Counts Wedel, Dohna-Schlobitten, von Hülsen-Haeseler, Yorck von Wartenburg, von Bredow, von der Schulenburg, and the ubiquitous von Papen, who had served as a page at the Imperial Court, in the 1st Regiment of Guard Uhlans and afterward in the Great General Staff. An occasional non-noble, however, often proved aggressive and bellicose. France of the Third Republic, with all her egalitarianism, also made considerable use of noblemen as attachés in capitals such as Vienna, St. Petersburg, and Berlin, in all three of which a Marquis de la Guiche was attaché before and after 1914; in Berlin a Prince de Polignac, married to a Princess Croy, served as military attaché (1872-1876),[12] a Baron de Grancy and a

---

[11] Still, there were these noble names among the pre-1914 naval attachés: Vicomte de Faramond de Lafayolle (Berlin), German Captain von Fischer-Lossainen (St. Petersburg), Austrian Corvette Captain Prince Johann Liechtenstein (Rome), French Captain Mercier de Lostande (London) and his successor Frigate Captain Comte de Saint-Saine.

[12] Bismarck, greatly suspicious of petticoat government, ascribed some of the hostility shown abroad to his "war in sight" policy of 1875, which seemed designed to start a preventive war against France, to accusations spread by Polignac and his wife, who had been admitted to the intimacy of the German Empress (no friend of the Chancellor), and "through

Vicomte de Faramond as naval attachés. It was to such noblemen that William II made his confidences, to such a man (it was a Major de la Tour du Pin) that Count Andrassy, on the day that he signed the alliance with Germany, and ended French hopes of making Austria-Hungary an ally for the day of *revanche,* said "it was altogether too ridiculous to live under a republic if one is the oldest monarchy in Europe" (as France was).[13] Tsarist Russia had a Prince Wittgenstein and a Baron Fredericks (not Russian names) and a Prince Trubetzkoi as military attachés in Paris, a Prince Engalitchev and a Prince Dolgoruki as military and naval attachés respectively in Berlin, between 1870 and 1914.[14] Another Dolgoruki was military plenipotentiary in Berlin during the 1880's. He was a friend of good German-Russian relations, which he feared were endangered by the unfortunately large number of army officers who delivered anti-German speeches, "had democratic leanings and had lost their sense of discipline."[15] The Austrian military attaché in Berlin from 1882 to 1895 was Baron von Steininger; he was followed by a Count Stürgkh. Italy made use of her nobility too: a Marchese Gualterio, a Conte di Robilant and a Conte Candiani were naval attachés in Berlin and London, and the Contes di Trombi and Baratieri in Constantinople (1896) and Paris (1901) respectively. Lord Edward Gleichen, of a branch of the old German Hohenlohe family that had moved to England in Victorian times, served as military attaché in the Berlin of William II and the Washington of Theodore Roosevelt. And Roosevelt's sister married a U.S. naval attaché, Commander William S. Cowles, who served in London in the 1890's.[16]

---

whose agency rumors and accusations of various sorts have found their way hither and yon." *Grosse Politik,* I, 180.

[13] Daniel Halévy, *La République des ducs* (Paris 1937), p. 312. For the titled officer in the French Army, on the increase particularly in the 1870's, see Girardet, *La société militaire,* p. 186.

[14] Wittgenstein was the brother-in-law of Prince Hohenlohe, later third Reich chancellor. Alexander von Hohenlohe, *Aus meinem Leben* (Frankfurt 1925), pp. 255f.

[15] To Waldersee. The latter's *Denkwürdigkeiten,* I, 227.

[16] Lilian Rixey, *Bamie: Theodore Roosevelt's Sister* (New York 1963).

For obvious reasons, attaché posts were much coveted. As an Austrian count and former attaché explained: a military attaché "already [holds] in his younger years an exceptional position, draws a high salary, enjoys great independence and freedom, in short a plethora of pleasant things which were the more enticing since they formed the opposite to what a normal career at home offered the officer."[17] Giving such posts to titled and well-connected officers was another indication of the favoritism which helped their advancement, gave them greater longevity of service, and a better chance to pass the dangerous "major's corner" where so many careers foundered.

Service attachés could expect a welcome to the good society of foreign capitals, the society of military-minded monarchs, courts, great houses, fashionable clubs, even business circles,[18] milieus where they could exercise those social talents which had been among the criteria for their selection.[19] In the upper crust of democratic Washington, the German military attaché in the 1890's, later first secretary and ambassador in the same capital, Speck von Sternburg, was well liked by the aristocratic set of coming men, Theodore Roosevelt, whose influence later helped him to get the coveted embassy, Henry Adams and John Hay, whose horses he was allowed to train.[20] A later holder of Sternburg's post, Franz von Papen, found himself in 1913 drawn into a "continual social whirl," meeting celebrities present and future, including young Franklin

[17] Stürgkh, p. 99.

[18] During the Luxemburg crisis of 1867, the Prussian military attaché in Paris knew when General Fleury, a mainstay of Bonapartism and a speculator, was bearish or bullish, and could thus judge the outlook for peace or war. Otto Graf zu Stolberg-Wernigerode, *Robert Heinrich Graf von der Goltz* (Oldenburg and Berlin 1941), p. 263. For Waldersee's information from Paris bankers and brokers on the eve of the war of 1870—since "most of the higher officers and officials in Paris speculated, there was naturally no state secret for the financial bigwigs"—see his *Denkwürdigkeiten*, I, 76f.

[19] Such talents obviously played a role in the choice of T. Bentley Mott for attaché posts in Paris and St. Petersburg. See his *Twenty Years as a Military Attaché*, passim. In Paris he lived in the best American society, rather than the French.

[20] Harold Dean Cater, ed., *Henry Adams and his Friends* (Boston 1947), p. 192.

115

D. Roosevelt, in clubs and elsewhere. Since he always had a taste for work, he felt somewhat out of place, as he put it,[21] until he could take up his absorbing war work of sabotage.

Only in a society that took armies and navies and war for granted, and, like Schlieffen—with his plan for a short war, the only one that a capitalist economy could endure—expected war to be over rapidly, without greatly upsetting the *status quo*,[22] could such hospitality remain unsuspecting. Gossip and other indiscretions gathered in such surroundings could serve as pieces in a puzzle for the attachés: Viennese society gossip, together with other bits of information gathered from the press or through agents, enabled the Prussian military attaché during the Crimean War to put together with great accuracy the Austrian order of battle.[23] On the other hand, one of his successors, serving on the eve of the war of 1866, fell so far victim to the charm of Viennese society or the sense of superiority which it radiated, that knowledge of Austrian war preparations was sadly deficient in Berlin.[24] Non-military "liaisons" in such society might furnish military information: in October 1941 Ciano made a note in his diaries about an American-born Marchesa, suspected of espionage and of being the mistress of the U.S. military attaché in Rome.[25]

The male society of fashionable clubs in the various capitals, those "schools of coarse good-fellowship and noise" (Cowper), many of which were open to foreign attachés in pre-1914 St. Petersburg, London, Washington, Paris—there was relatively little club life in which foreigners could participate in Berlin—might furnish scraps of an informative nature to military ears. During the last days of peace in July 1870 the Prussian military attaché in Paris, Count Waldersee,

---

21 Papen, p. 15.

22 When the Prussian ambassadress left Paris in July 1870, the French foreign minister told her: "After some pistol shots along the frontier, all will be over and one shakes hands." Waldersee, *Denkwürdigkeiten*, I, 81.

23 Gordon A. Craig in *Political Science Quarterly*, LXIV (1949), 67.

24 Waldersee, *Denkwürdigkeiten*, I, 24.

25 Gaudens Megaro in *American Historical Review*, LIV (1949), 132, noting the absence of this entry from the American version of the *Ciano Diaries*.

116

assembled various hints as to French intentions from the *Cercle impérial*, a club including British attachés with whom he was on good terms, who told him that several French generals had demanded to start the war with non-mobilized troops—as they so nearly did. He also gathered information at his own club, the *Cercle de l'Union*, which he frequented as long as possible and until the French members began to make ugly faces at all Germans.[26]

In London, the capital which had the most club life before 1914 and even after 1918, the foreign service attachés were accepted as honorary members by the various service clubs. They joined in the hope of learning more than they would give away. As one of Tirpitz' aides explained: "Since I could soon observe how useful this daily intercourse was, I joined this habit. Above all other things, one could always meet naval officers working in the Admiralty, in the nearby United Services Senior Club, and find occasion for unofficial talks. . . . There I picked up many a useful piece of information."[27]

Some, at least, of the participants must have taken for granted that a certain amount of spying and counterspying took place in such club life, but they were only occasionally upset by the detection, actual or presumed, of such ungentlemanly behavior. In pre-1914 St. Petersburg the Yacht Club was one of the

> haunts of the diplomats. . . . Sumptuous dinners naturally predisposed the members—bigwigs all of them—to candid conversations. On one occasion, a determined effort to overhear these conversations was made by none other than the German naval attaché specially attached to the "person" of Nicholas II, Admiral [recte: Captain] von Hintze. Staying behind after the diplomats' meal, he secreted himself behind a screen. Unfortunately for him, a waiter knocked the screen over by accident and there before the eyes of the diners was exposed the titled representative of a "friendly"

26 Waldersee, *Denkwürdigkeiten*, I, 76ff.
27 Widenmann, pp. 37, 46ff.

Power. It is related that this spy, caught red-handed, was not even embarrassed.[28]

Another sector of the male society of ante bellum warriors, the officers' regimental messes and casinos, could afford to be less suspicious of such guests and hence more careless, more bibulous, because its members knew fewer worthwhile secrets. It was perhaps only of some sociological significance for the spread of political ideas in Tsarist Russia that in the 1880's officers of the St. Petersburg Chevalier Guards and other regiments, when in their cups, told the visiting Prussian military attaché that Constantinople and Prague "had to be the goals of Russian policy"; this, it seemed to the guest, was "the outcome of years of Panslavist propaganda in muddled heads."[29]

The common base of relations among officers of the various national forces was a concept of honor and gentlemanly behavior that was to prevail between, and to a more limited extent even during, wars. It was vague enough as to what was permissible and what disallowed, and would vary from person to person even more widely than within each national group, where courts of honor and other institutions and convictions served as regulators. It made possible doing ungentlemanly things, such as spying, in a gentlemanly manner. Owing either to its vagueness or to the diplomatic talents and careful selection of the officers employed abroad, international affairs of honor implicating attachés remained rare, much rarer than might have been expected.[30]

Service attachés were so well received in society, and appeared so personable or "dashing," that a number of them contracted foreign marriages. Bismarck and others had so

[28] Ignatiev, pp. 96f. Who would vouch for the historicity of the tale, significant as it may be for the views that members of the diplomatic-military pre-1914 society took of one another?

[29] *Grosse Politik*, III, 617 (1884).

[30] After the sinking of the "Maine" in 1898, the Spanish military attaché in Washington sent challenges for a duel to the U.S. Consul General in Havana, General Fitzhugh Lee, and Admiral Sigsbee, both addressees well chosen as far as their war-mindedness was concerned. He believed that this settlement would satisfy the honor of both the United States and Spain and thus avert war. Vagts, *Deutschland und die Vereinigten Staaten*, p. xvii.

severely frowned upon such ties as contrary to the national interest that they often had to be compensated or over-compensated for by hypernationalism on the part of the male contractant. Three years after the close of his attaché service Waldersee, the second German Chief of Staff and the second to marry an Anglo-Saxon, took as wife an American heiress whose fortune allowed him to finance the behind-the-scenes politics which he hoped would bring him the Reich chancellorship. Speck von Sternburg married an American whose sister became the wife of a French naval attaché in Berlin, Vicomte de Faramond. Count Yorck von Wartenburg, military attaché in St. Petersburg in the 1880's and 90's, married a Russian divorcée and soon found himself excluded from most of that capital's society, a circumstance that did not diminish his already strong Russophobia. Contrary to many expectations, in an age of nationalism such ties did little or nothing to further what is euphemistically called a better understanding between the countries concerned.[31] Among Germany's bitterest enemies in Edwardian England were Lord Edward Gleichen, who had numerous relatives in Germany, and Sir Eyre Crowe of the Foreign Office. Crowe's German mother was the stepsister of Admiral von Holtzendorff, and his brother-in-law was the German naval attaché in Paris at the turn of the century.[32] And the fact that von Papen, who married into money and "a completely cosmopolitan family," could still maintain after two World Wars, in which he had served as military attaché and as Hitler's ambassador, that these "predominantly internationalist sentiments were in due course

[31] It is hard to say what other effects international marriages of service attachés might have had, as in the case of General Fagalde, after 1918 French military attaché in London for a number of years, "married to an American and very well known in London Society," close to Churchill and other British politicians. Paul Reynaud, *In the Thick of the Fight* (New York 1955), p. 364.

[32] Dawson, p. 281; Widenmann, p. 36. The most extreme case of the foreign-married hypernationalist was Lieut. Cmdr. Count E. von Reventlow, a Pan-German, Big Navy man, anti-Semite, Hitlerite, who took the ban on foreign marriages for officers so seriously that he quit the naval service after having married a Frenchwoman, and then began his publicistic career. Johannes Fischart, *Das alte und das neue System* (Berlin 1919), p. 219.

119

transmitted to me,"[33] can only be explained by a feudality of sentiment that did not know it was out-of-date.

European nobility in the century after 1814 assisted in that pseudo-reconciliation which was becoming necessary after wars. The majority of the "great ambassadors" of the European powers were noblemen, so were their attachés, and gentlemen always preferred to deal with gentlemen. The first ambassador to Berlin from the Third French Republic after the peace of 1871 was the Vicomte de Gontaut-Biron. He announced in his first meeting with Bismarck that the personnel of his embassy would presently be completed by two military attachés (instead of one, as before), Prince Louis de Polignac and Comte de la Ferronnays, for whom he hoped to have the Chancellor's good will. He was relieved to meet no objection to this doubling of military observers.[34] Was the obviously intended higher efficiency of the attaché office, the intention to discover the secret of German military success, sweetened by the fact that noblemen filled these posts? At any rate, it seemed to somewhat assuage bourgeois worry about the costly and dangerous arms competition; the infusion of nobility endowed the whole profession of arms with glamor at the very time that technology brought greater perfection and greater deadliness to the equipment of war. Thus the doyen of the foreign military attachés in Paris, Baron Fredericks, a Russian with a Germanic name and title, could offer a toast at the close of the French autumn maneuvers of 1891: "Our presence here is proof of the solidarity which unites all of us in the pursuit of the beautiful profession of arms."[35]

This supranational solidarity among military professionals helped to form a common front against the governing (or at least financially dominant) bourgeoisie. In a conversation which took place between Sarajevo and the outbreak of war, the German military attaché in Paris, Major von

[33] His *Memoirs*, p. 9.
[34] Otto, Fürst von Bismarck, *Die gesammelten Werke*, 15 vols. in 19 (Berlin 1924-1935), VIII, 25.
[35] A. Hamon, *Psychologie du militaire professionnel* (Paris 1895), p. 25; Charles de Freycinet, *Souvenirs, 1878-1893*, 9th ed. (Paris 1914), p. 471.

Klüber, was the sympathetic recipient of the confidences of his opposite number, Colonel Dupont, head of the Foreign Armies section in the French War Ministry, sub-section: Germany. The colonel complained that he had several times, but always in vain, insisted in discussions with superiors that the French Army was backward; that the French field-gun actually compared unfavorably with the corresponding German gun; that the French infantry rifle was inferior to the German; that instruction in the French Army suffered from want of training grounds; that the fortresses were also in poor shape but that this did not greatly matter since France was resolved to undertake a strategic offensive. The report to Berlin ended: "This remark is of particular interest."[36]

In a few cases this brotherhood-in-arms would survive the outbreak of wars. On the day of the fall of Lemberg in September 1914 the Russian naval attaché in Constantinople— "very loquacious, since years my friend"—told his Austrian military colleague that this "was a Pyrrhic victory. Russian casualties were tremendous and the whole of Western Russia one large hospital; the Russians had neither expected such an obstinate resistance nor such battle efficiency on the part of the Austro-Hungarian Army."[37] But after 1918, little of this nobility of sentiment survived, or in some countries, few of its original bearers. There were attempts to revive it, to put international military understanding on a different, masculine basis such as that of veterans' organizations or of sports,[38] but the effect was to be slight.

By this time European nobility itself preserved practically nothing of the supranational solidarity of group interest which the monarchs and statesmen of the Holy Alliance had hoped to reestablish after the Napoleonic Wars, though there was still some group sentiment stressing the virtues of war. Bismarck had killed most of it in Germany, and hated to

[36] *Revue de l'Histoire de la Guerre mondiale,* XIII (1935), 259.

[37] Von Pomiankowski, *Der Zusammenbruch des ottomanischen Reiches* (Vienna 1927), p. 61.

[38] The most glowing description of the Nazi regime the author ever encountered in the USA was from an American military attaché who had witnessed the Berlin Olympic Games as arranged by the Nazis, and was inclined to extend his praise to most of the rest of Nazi organizing.

detect survivals in the diplomats serving under him, who came so largely from the nobility—the old one of birth, the newer one of money, or the amalgamation of the two. Conservatively thinking diplomats after 1871, including Bismarck, might look backward and draw some of the ethos of their profession from the contemplation of a peace that was worth preserving. But service attachés, in equally exposed positions of observation in foreign capitals, could only look forward to war, as dictated by the noblest ancient sentiments and for the furtherance of the best national interest.[39] That the latter would only too often coincide with the service interest could not be better illustrated than by the activities of the German Navy since the turn of the century, which brought its non-noble or neo-noble officers, including the attachés, into disastrous conflicts with the diplomats, both in Berlin and in the foreign capitals. Service interest and service ambition sharpened such conflicts, which reached their greatest acumination when the ambassador was of the type of a *grand seigneur* and the officer of the poorer and lower nobility or not noble at all. While this conflict is best documented for Germany, it was hardly less prevalent in Russia, particularly among the Pan-Slavists, and to some extent in Austria.

The rise of Bolshevism and the far from chivalrous relations between winners and losers after 1918 hindered, or made impossible, the regrowth of an international society where warriors could meet unofficially and to a certain extent sympathetically, between wars. The meetings between military warriors out for revenge, such as Seeckt and his aides, and the class warriors such as Radek and other Bolshevists were largely clandestine to start with,[40] but gradually acquired a public character in social meetings. For a time,

[39] Before leaving Berlin for his new post in Paris at the time of the Boulanger agitation, Military Attaché von Huene was received by the Crown Prince. The audience left him "deeply depressed." The Prince had spoken almost with fear of a war with France, had not spoken too nicely about our own Army and beseeched Huene not to send alarming reports but rather mild ones, such as those of Ambassador Count Münster. Waldersee, *Denkwürdigkeiten*, I, 305.

[40] For some details see Wipert von Blücher, *Deutschlands Weg nach Rapallo* (Wiesbaden 1951); also Helm Speidel, "Reichswehr und Rote Armee," *Vierteljahrshefte für Zeitgeschichte*, I (1953), 9ff.

until the 1937-1938 purges, the Soviet Government allowed German-Russian gatherings and even an occasional meeting between Red Army officers and foreign military attachés, in regimental messes where the hope for Red imperialism had temporarily replaced the great Pan-Slavist expectations of yore.[41] According to a 1932 French secret service report from Berlin, "German influence had penetrated deeply into the ranks of the Red Army whose cadres are pro-German to the point that they would not hesitate to take their *mot d'ordre* from Berlin in case of domestic troubles."[42] Even the suspicion of such pro-German attitudes was more than Stalin would suffer, and he ordered *nettoyages* along the home fronts which were partly explained to the public by the victims' guilty intercourse with foreigners. After that, the iron curtain slammed down in Moscow.

With the restratification of fortunes and the vastly different composition of governments and governing circles, with the growth of secretiveness, of nationalism either on the defensive or aggressively expansive, the society of the Western capitals which military foreigners could frequent was severely reduced after 1918. There was some, very slow, unfreezing after Locarno, even among ex-enemies: when the German Chief of Staff, General Beck, visited Pétain in 1937, the Frenchman expressed his joy that he had been able to shake his ex-enemy's hand, "though only 20 years and not two hours after the end of the strife as had been customary earlier, in more chivalrous times."[43]

Attachés "went into society" again in the foreign capitals; some occasions were organized for them, others were not of a "state" character. In Berlin they could again pick up fragments of information, even concerning such tabooed topics as Reichswehr-Red Army relations or Reichswehr-Nazi relations as viewed by the military chiefs and their "reactionary" wives. When the French attachés participated in the social life of Berlin, they were given to understand that social relations on equal terms must ultimately imply that "equality

41 Herbette, p. 165.
42 Castellan, p. 484.
43 Ludwig Beck, *Studien*, Hans Speidel, ed. (Stuttgart 1954), p. 297.

of armaments" which the French were so slow in conceding. Conclusions of military significance were drawn from the attendance of certain officers on certain occasions: the presence of the foremost ballistics experts of the Reichswehr at a reception given by the Italian military attaché in 1931 confirmed for the French attaché the "hypothesis that continued relations exist between the German and Italian armies regarding the manufacture of war materiel." Or again, the presence of a dozen Reichswehr officers at the house of the Polish military attaché in December 1933, where few had been seen before, indicated to his French colleague that "the German-Polish Pact was beginning to bear fruit." "Two receptions," following closely upon one another in 1931, gave the French military attaché in Berlin much to think about: first a dinner given for him and his assistant by the Reichswehr commander where the French were particularly pampered and toasted, "a meeting that one might call amiable and almost familiar" but where all the talk was of hunting or military anecdotes; the other, a "five to seven" at the house of the Soviet military attaché, General Putna, with some 150 persons assembled under the portrait of Lenin. "From the beginning, one dominant note, *Feldgrau*. Whereas at all other similar receptions Reichswehr Ministry uniforms amount to only two or three, with civilian black and ladies' toilettes forming the background of the picture, here the proportion is in reverse. One sees nothing around the table but generals, colonels, majors and captains and their families."[44] Thus far, at least, Reichswehr-Red Army relations came out into the open.

With Nazism, a new freeze set in. The open anti-Axis stand taken by the Roosevelt Administration led to a near-break in diplomatic relations and a more complete one in social intercourse between American and German diplomats; the latter was broken off by order of Ribbentrop early in 1939, after which the Americans and Germans treated each other like outcasts. The Germans in Washington, after the outbreak of

[44] The above is based on Castellan, pp. 425f., 432, 435, 456, 464, 474, 482 and passim.

the war, were "completely boycotted by so-called good society and the greater part of the Diplomatic Corps that is neutral." At the same time, the armed forces attachés in Washington continued "to carry on regular social intercourse with all branches of the American armed services and in that way were frequently in social contact with members of the State Department," even exchanging certain confidences with the General Staff. Since this non-intercourse policy had started in Berlin, it had to be called off there; after weighing the inconveniences involved, this was done in the autumn of 1939.[45]

At least a reminder of the old preference for titled officers as German service attachés survived under the Nazi vulgarians, who nourished until 1944 the hope of amalgamating the old nobility with the new one of the racially superior and ideologically fanatical. Among the titled attachés of the Third Reich were Freiherr Geyr von Schweppenburg in London, von Faber du Faur in Belgrade, and von Boetticher in Washington, of whom Hitler thought highly.[46] Von Rintelen in Rome lasted longest of all although, according to reports reaching Goebbels, he was "quite black" in politics, interested in Church questions, managed receptions of German soldiers by the Pope, and surrounded himself "with only clerical or aristocratic elements." Goebbels gathered data intended to turn the Führer against him and effect a recall, but von Rintelen lasted as long as Mussolini did.[47]

The aristocratic LaRochefoucauld said, about society in the restricted sense of the term, that men would not live together long were they not each other's dupes, but society continues to exist, nationally and internationally, in spite of all truly democratic desires and democratic contempt. Since 1914, however, international society is more State-affected, its occasions are more "State affairs" than ever,[48] and with

[45] *Documents on German Foreign Policy*, Ser. D, VIII, 159f., 331.

[46] *Hitler's Secret Conversations, 1941-1944* (New York 1953), pp. 396f., December 16, 1942.

[47] Louis P. Lochner, ed., *The Goebbels Diaries* (New York 1948), p. 246; December 16, 1942.

[48] For years before 1956, the State Department tried to obtain from Congress the granting of larger funds as "representative allowances"

the rise of Bolshevism and the declaration of class war the duping has become more barefaced. When toasts to Soviet-American-British friendship were drunk in Moscow after the forming of the alliance of 1941, it was "amazing" to the head of the United States Military Mission to the USSR, General Deane, "how these toasts went down past the tongues in the cheeks."[49] Both parties to this make-believe, the one by intention, the other by necessary imitation, are in effect class warriors,[50] in a state of constant belligerency that formulas like coexistence cannot veil for long—coexistence is tantamount to an armistice declared by one side only, the Red side, in the expectation that the other will accede and adhere to it. The "social" meetings during such intermissions, parties and banquets that are the very reverse of the old German saying, *Bei Tische scheiden sich die Klassen* (at table, classes separate), are in the logic of class warfare mere pauses on the road to the end of capitalism. Such an attitude, in a way, makes all participants armed forces attachés, and those among them who bear this title officially are merely better trained for spying, for which purpose they "move" in "society."

That service attachés also moved in the lowest society of the host countries, or in the border zone where high and low intermix, and that sooner or later they were suspected of being "on the spy" in doing so, was revealed in the Profumo scandal of 1962-1963. A Soviet naval attaché stationed in London and the Secretary of State for War in the Macmillan cabinet, John Profumo, had not only met at receptions in the

---

which would enable embassies and consulates to entertain better, "because it is on the social occasions that you make far more progress, as a rule, than merely handing formal notes and the like" (Secretary Dulles), and "are perhaps getting information highly valuable to the United States." *The New York Times*, March 24, 1956.

[49] U.S. Department of State, *The Conferences at Malta and Yalta, 1945* (Washington 1945), p. 448.

[50] A British military attaché, who served in Moscow after 1945, would "never forget that fanatical Communists regard themselves as being *already at war* with the non-Communist world. . . . Any trick is regarded by them as permissible tactics in such a war—e.g. adoption of an apparent attitude of reconciliation and international goodwill." Hilton, p. 194.

Soviet embassy but also on the Cliveden estate of Viscount Astor, where both encountered a prostitute whose favors they enjoyed at nearly the same time. This aroused public suspicion that a breach of security rather than of morals had occurred. The judicious report of Lord Denning, one of the highest ranking judges in the kingdom, laid these suspicions to rest, but it also brought out that the Russian attaché, in addition to carrying out his customary duties in Britain since 1960, "was also a Russian intelligence officer" who had been entrusted with "a new role in Russian technique. It was to divide the United Kingdom from the United States" by various means such as continually propagating the Kremlin's standpoint among those whom he met in London society high and low—particularly during the Cuban crisis of 1962— in the hope of undermining American confidence in the integrity and discretion of ministers or in the security service.[51]

[51] *The New York Times*, September 26, 1963.

CHAPTER 8

THE SERVICE ATTACHÉ
AS POLITICO

*It is always dangerous for soldiers or
airmen to play at politics. Winston
Churchill, The Gathering Storm.*

The paradox in the existence of the service attaché derives
from the conflict between the original expectation and instruction, usually vague,[1] that he serve as a non-political technical expert, and his subsequent evolution into a politician
of sorts. Abroad, indeed, he is doubly foreign, serving among
civilians in his own embassy, and serving in another nation.
The friend-foe relations of the politicized attaché typically
develop in such a way that the agent of the home forces becomes an active foe of the country of residence, if this country happens to be an actual or potential enemy. He may also
become a foe of the civilians in his own embassy, even of the
whole foreign service of his country; the diplomats, he may
assume, misunderstand the foreign country in question and
arrange the relations with it badly, a condemnation which
he may even extend to diplomacy as an institution. Again, he
may turn into a friend of the country of residence, if the latter is an actual or potential ally.[2]

[1] "The field of duty of a military attaché in Austria-Hungary was not
circumscribed by any binding instructions. . . . In Vienna before my
departure I received in the intelligence department (*Evidenzbüro*) of
the General Staff some vague directions. I learned most from the reports
of my predecessors. If the latter were matter of fact and also detailed
and if the author did not go wrong in his prognostications, people at
home were satisfied and the officer went far in his career." Giesl, p. 19.

[2] According to the reports of his Austrian colleague the Russian military attaché at Belgrade before and during the Balkan Wars. Col.
Artamonov, was a "Pan-Slav of the extreme kind, who is rather smiled
upon on the part of the diplomatic corps on account of his exaggerated
'admiration' for the Serbs. He has a far from unimportant influence in
the Serbian War Ministry and in the officer corps. As I am told confidentially, he is attempting to undermine the respect for the Austrian

Though sent only to observe and report, the attaché is often tempted to political judgments and, as a further step, to political activity. This may culminate in the attaché's ambition to become an ambassador himself, if possible in lieu of his superior—after all, a few of his colleagues received such promotion, men like Ignatiev, the warmaker at Constantinople and peacemaker at San Stefano, or Speck von Sternburg in Washington. And a British military attaché serving under Morier in St. Petersburg (1888-1891), Colonel Gerard, "had always felt that he himself was the man for the post," and that he was better qualified than at least one of the men chosen as Morier's successors.[3] More than one attaché has felt this way.

Disregard of the injunction against political activity[4] will almost invariably endanger or disrupt the unity of direction and the systematic division of labor within the diplomatic team to which the attaché belongs. Situations may also arise where he must use diplomacy in order to avoid what he has been instructed to avoid, and restrict himself to mere listening and reporting. Occasionally, however, he may be specifically instructed by the diplomatic authority to receive political confidences and advances and to answer them on the basis of definite instructions.

Criticism by an attaché of his own country's diplomacy can also undermine the work of the diplomatic team; it is at once resented as "too political" by the civilian diplomats and provides a basis for complaint. As an example: Tirpitz' naval attaché in London in March 1912 made a report which

---

Army and is particularly deprecating the state of our artillery equipment and the national difficulties inside the Army." *Oesterreich-Ungarns Aussenpolitik*, V, 5852.

3 Waters, *"Secret and Confidential,"* pp. 158f.; for similar aspirations see *Grosse Politik*, XXV, 8814; XXVI, 9315, 9504, as regards the former Russian military attaché in Berlin, Prince Engalitchev, who wanted to return there as ambassador, to the horror of German diplomacy. For more details on this metamorphosis see below pp. 176ff.

4 When Papen (his *Memoirs*, p. 15) arrived in the Washington embassy in 1913, he was promptly warned by Count Bernstorff "that it was no part of the military attaché's duty to make political reports," and that he had caused the recall of Papen's predecessor for failure to stick to this rule.

the ambassador and the Wilhelmstrasse greatly resented. The report, they said, "breathed hatefulness and distrust of England which . . . are not justified and which in case the naval attaché should express this to outsiders could provoke an unnecessary complication of our relations with England." The Secretary of State for Foreign Affairs, von Kiderlen, long bent on curbing the attachés, submitted to the Kaiser that when this officer spoke of "English maneuvers" as a consequence of "Germany's hesitations" he "took the liberty of passing judgment, to which he is not entitled and which is improper, on a *political* action directed by Your Majesty Himself." The protest was only partly successful. The pro-Navy Emperor decided that the attaché's report was of the essence, restriction to technical naval questions was impossible, and that in this respect the reports of the attaché had been invaluable. "On the other hand, His Majesty saw in the incriminating remark on 'Germany's hesitations' an impermissible criticism of the Reich's policy." The attaché was to be so informed—not by Kiderlen, however, who had asked for the assignment, but by the Chief of the Naval Cabinet, the Navy's personnel office.[5]

A passion for politics may lead the observer-officer to neglect his true office duties. A civilian colleague called the German military attaché in St. Petersburg in the late 1870's, Major von Lignitz, "one of the most ambitious climbers I have ever met," after he heard from the Great General Staff that "Lignitz bothers his head only with high policy and hence neglects military details which are for us the main thing; we should like to send a better observer to Russia; unfortunately, the Foreign Office cannot do without him on account of his political talents." And in the Wilhelmstrasse they said: "If only Lignitz would leave his clumsy hands off politics! But for the General Staff he is indispensable on the Neva." Ambassador Schweinitz found him a particularly difficult subordinate. During the period of increasing Germanophobia in Russia he was himself extremely careful in his statements on military movements and measures, press

[5] *Grosse Politik*, XXXI, 11413-11414.

stories and salon gossip, in order to keep mutual distrust at a minimum, but Lignitz reported on these things with alacrity. Whenever the ambassador could not induce the attaché to change his reports, he accompanied them with long explanations of his own which were not always considered successful in Berlin. An observer of this dissension, who rightly considered himself a faithful servant of Bismarck, realized here "for the first time what damage over-zealous military attachés, who mix in politics, can do. . . . Later, when the old Emperor and Bismarck were no longer at the tiller of state, such dangers often made themselves felt."[6]

An attaché's penchant for politics may also prove dangerous to his technical abilities, it may dim the eye that "is born to behold and ordered to watch." Political sympathy or antipathy can be dangerously misleading. Various American,[7] French,[8] and apparently also British attachés viewed the Fascism in Italy, Germany and Japan as essentially conservative in nature and aims, rather than revolutionary, and thus misjudged the ability, readiness and determination of the Axis powers to undertake war.[9]

A well-integrated service attaché will know or learn the limitations imposed on him. In a discussion of the startling Russian maneuver situation of 1910—"Germany and Sweden are at war with Russia"—the military plenipotentiary at St. Petersburg, Captain von Hintze, proceeded to deal at length with the political conditions which had produced that portentous order. But suddenly he reminded himself of the limitations imposed upon his office: "However, politics are not

[6] Arthur von Brauer, *Im Dienste Bismarcks* (Berlin 1936), pp. 53f.

[7] Robert E. Sherwood, *Roosevelt and Hopkins* (New York 1948), p. 419.

[8] According to Pertinax (I, 18) the Italian Army of the 1930's was widely overestimated in Paris, due to "the reports of General Parisot, military attaché in Rome, dazzled by the honors with which the Fascist regime surrounded the military chieftains."

[9] The U.S. naval attaché in Rome in 1936 was favorably "impressed with the moral and spiritual preparations of the men and officers of the Italian Navy," when its material readiness was actually notoriously low. And a U.S. military attaché in Berlin in September 1939 thought almost as highly of the Polish ability to resist the German onslaught as did the Poles themselves. Charles C. Tansill, *Back Door to War: The Roosevelt Foreign Policy, 1933-1941* (Chicago 1952), pp. 252, 554.

within my province,"[10] thus exhibiting a self-control beyond the power of many men. In general, the service attachés of the democracies have obeyed the injunction to keep out of politics distinctly better than did those of the three former empires (clear records for the later periods are wanting).

Attachés may overrate the hostile elements in the country to which they are assigned, and underrate its friendly intentions, thus overlooking opportunities to work for peace, whether present or future. During the period after Fashoda, the personnel of the French embassy in London was quite divided over the question of British bellicosity. Paul Cambon thought the majority of the British people not hostile, "but we are up against a certain number of extremely keen [meaning: bellicose] politicians. Will they succeed in carrying their nation along with them? . . . Our military and naval attachés are doing their utmost to warn me against optimistic influences. According to them the English are only waiting for the first excuse to pounce upon us, relying on our blunders, on the indiscretions of our Press, on some further incidents in the colonies: they are ready, and they are satisfied that we are not, and that they will never find a better opportunity. . . . Both these officers, whose experiences I cannot ignore, express the same opinion in the plainest and most emphatic terms."[11] Cambon had been in London only a few months and the attachés much longer, but he lived to see the founding of the Entente.

The evidence of diplomatic history tends to make pessimism the typical attitude of the service attaché—on the general basis of the soldier's "existence for war" as against the diplomat's supposed "existence for peace."[12] There have

[10] *Grosse Politik*, XXVII, 551.

[11] Alfred Coville and Harold Temperley, eds., *Studies in Anglo-French History* (Cambridge 1935), p. 152.

[12] Within the German embassy in London in 1912 there was strong difference of opinion as to the binding character of the Anglo-French military understandings. The soldier was convinced that since 1911 an offensive and defensive alliance had clearly existed, whereas the diplomat insisted that though England had been resolved to assist France in the Agadir crisis, with arms, and might again decide to do so, she still kept a free hand and would decide from case to case what to do. Both were in a sense right, the civilian echoing the conviction of the English civilian

been notable exceptions, however, where the attaché, on the basis of strictly military observations rather than professional bellicosity, was able to contradict the more bellicose convictions of his superiors. Both the German military attaché and the German ambassador in Paris, during the "War in sight" crisis of 1875, believed less in the danger of impending war than did Bismarck himself.[13] And in 1894 Major Waters, the first British military attaché allowed to travel in Russian Turkestan, told both London and the Government of India, which was periodically worried about war with Russia over Central Asia, that on the basis of his observations on the spot there was "no good reason for their anxiety."[14]

Before 1918

During the early days of the military attaché the diplomats and the governments in general do not seem to have paid much attention to these neophytes' observations and reports, or else they would use them regardless of their original functions or possible consequences. An outstanding example is the reaction to the reports of the French military attaché in Berlin, Colonel Baron Stoffel, before 1870-1871. After having served in Napoleon's immediate entourage, Stoffel was sent to the Bohemian theater of war late in July 1866 as an observer, and then as attaché to the Prussian capital. He warned the Emperor and his government about Germany's increasing military superiority, owing to the better organization of the Great General Staff and its systematic preparation for war, though even he, an artilleryman, seems to have overlooked the specific threat arising from the improvements in the German artillery. In his reports he tried conscientiously to keep within the limits of his "purely military function"

---

politicians like Edward Grey, and the soldier those of General Henry Wilson, etc. For William II this "all amounts to the same. The diplomat admits the fact unwillingly—since they don't like to hear it in the foreign office—the military man draws the conclusion resolutely and gives the child the right name since the effect is the same practically." *Grosse Politik*, XXXI, 11552.

[13] *Ibid.*, I, 171. [14] Waters, pp. iv, 82, 110ff.

and to abstain from political judgments. But Napoleon himself asked for an opinion on the chances of a war with Prussia, and Stoffel ventured to say that the war seemed to him inevitable and at the mercy of an incident. Prussia, he said, had no intention of attacking France, she in no way wished the war and would do all that lay in her power to avoid it; but Prussia was clear-sighted enough to realize that the war would certainly come, and therefore she was making every effort not to be caught unprepared. France did not have the same foresight.[15] In certain respects, Bismarck, who liked to flatter Stoffel and received him in the intimacy of his estate at Varzin, could have wished for nothing better than the French reaction: Benedetti, Stoffel's immediate superior in Berlin, considered him "too Prussian" and wanted him recalled.[16] Napoleon and his military entourage tired of this Cassandra in uniform, after an early interest in his reports; they considered his information somber and probably excessive, and they preferred "to suspect his judgment instead of accusing themselves of negligence; in the military bureaus they told one another: Stoffel is a Prussomaniac whom Bismarck has fascinated." In the end, the war minister, Marshal Leboeuf, withheld Stoffel's warnings from his colleagues in the cabinet. When the war came, Stoffel embraced the vague French reasons and aims, and told everyone in Berlin who cared to hear, including the representatives of the South German states, that "the war was the consequence of Prussia's preponderance since 1866 and that as against this preponderance France needed security of her frontiers which only the possession of German territory as far as the Rhine could furnish. Nothing but the possession of the Rhine could secure the peace between the two nations. The nationality principle of Emperor Napoleon would no longer find application."[17]

Stoffel's reports were published immediately after the fall

[15] Report of August 12, 1869. Lieut. Col. Baron Stoffel, *Rapports militaires écrits de Berlin, 1866-1870*, 3rd ed. (Paris 1871), p. 301.

[16] Émile Ollivier, *L'Empire libéral*, 18 vols. (Paris 1895-1918), XI, 339f.; XII, 326ff.

[17] Report of Bavarian minister at Berlin to Ludwig II, July 18, 1870. Oncken, *Rheinpolitik*, III, 459.

of the Empire, and established his reputation as a prophet, the only person who had foretold the disaster and had warned against unpreparedness.[18] The reports procured their author no military career under the Third Republic, but they greatly contributed to the creditability and prestige of the military attaché. As a Red Army general and former Tsarist military attaché summed it up: "More and more attention came to be paid to the reports of such 'military agents' and their predictions often proved more sound than those of the regular diplomats" (Ignatiev).

Stoffel's case also indicated that a modicum of literary ability,[19] which had sometimes helped to make an officer into an attaché, could also help make him a politico in uniform, employing his pen. Friedrich von Bernhardi, of the third generation of a writing family, began his ominous political activity while military attaché at Berne (1891-1894), with an anonymous brochure entitled *Videant consules* (1892), dealing with a future war. He considered it as unavoidable and necessary then as he did in 1912, when he published *Germany and the Next War*.[20] His contemporary Count Yorck von Wartenburg, who had been employed for a time, like Bernhardi, in the war history section of the Great General Staff, was removed from the post of military attaché in St. Petersburg (1885-1893) at the request of his ambassador, General von Werder, because he had antagonized too many people.[21] In 1897 Yorck wrote a militaristic world history, *Weltge-*

18 Ollivier, XIV, 99; Pierre de la Gorce, *Histoire du Second Empire*, 7 vols. (Paris 1908-1911), VI, 130. Later, when he had retired, Stoffel wrote a much discussed pamphlet, *De la possibilité d'une future alliance franco-allemande* (Paris 1890), in which he warned against a Russian hegemony over Europe as a result of the then beginning Franco-Russian alliance. He expressed the hope that Germany would retrocede Alsace-Lorraine as the price for an alliance of all the West against Russia. See *Documents diplomatiques français*, Ist ser., VIII, 61.

19 There are numerous memoirs of attachés and other writings authored by them, including even a comedy written by the German military attaché in Paris, von Winterfeld, and staged in Berlin in the spring of 1914 by amateurs of high society. Eckart von Naso, *Ich liebe das Leben* (Hamburg 1953), pp. 328ff.

20 Friedrich von Bernhardi, *Denkwürdigkeiten aus meinem Leben* (Berlin 1927), p. 146.

21 *Ibid.*, p. 154. For Yorck see the biography by Wilhelm Friedrich, *Maximilian Graf Yorck von Wartenburg* (Berlin 1941).

schichte in Umrissen, which made still more enemies for the German Army. In this somewhat *funeste* category, if category it is, also belongs Colonel Charles à Court Repington (1858-1925), one-time British military attaché in Brussels and The Hague (1900-1902); after his military career had "ended abruptly through domestic causes," he turned to journalism and eventually became the military correspondent of *The Times.*

But this perhaps alarming development of the service attaché into a political pamphleteer or journalist was late. There had been little or no early warning of it, and the attaché seemed a safe, if irregular, agent to be employed by the directors of foreign affairs as an occasional channel for diplomatic reporting, instructions or commissions. Various foreign offices and royalty itself proceeded to make use of attachés, regardless of ambassadorial hierarchy and other service regulations. The Prussian and Russian military plenipotentiaries were not the only soldiers to carry on negotiations between those monarchs who had retained some absolutism— in spite of constitutional limitations which they and the officers endeavored to avoid in military and foreign affairs for as long as possible.

The Italian attaché in Paris (to 1870), Count Vimercati, was the tool of Victor Emmanuel during the Franco-Austrian-Italian alliance negotiations more than of the constitutional ministers at Florence, who were incompletely informed about what went on. Vimercati had lived in Paris since the coup d'état, had relatives there, and had been in the French civil service for a time. He had been on intimate terms with Rouher and Prince Napoleon, Victor Emmanuel's son-in-law and Italy's advocate in Paris, and he was in the confidence of the two monarchs; but he was on bad terms with the minister plenipotentiary Nigra, who repeatedly tried to have him recalled. Bismarck had kept an eye on him for some time, and allowed the Prussian military attaché, von Loë, to enter into relations with him soon after the conclusion of the Italian-Prussian war alliance of 1866 against Austria. Vimercati promptly made himself the mouthpiece of Napoleon, with the proposition that Prussia obtain the

Emperor's approval for her designs for "all of Germany" by ceding him the left bank of the Rhine, just as Italy had paid the price of Nice-Savoy. Bismarck turned a deaf ear to this proposal for a French Rhine, and to similar ideas which followed. During the later triangular negotiations for the alliance against the too successful Bismarck, the Austrian negotiator found Vimercati "shrewd where that is necessary without appearing so, altogether made for the role of hyphen which he has played to the satisfaction of those who have employed him. . . . He wishes for the war and does not make a secret of it. Like his King, he thinks that the Italian Army ought to seize the first moment in order to make forgotten the sad role it played in the last campaign." The triple alliance was not ready when war came in July 1870, largely because of the immodesty of Italian desires; Vimercati in the end included such demands as a rectification of the Isonzo line at the expense of Austria.[22]

The channels of Bismarck's diplomacy, at least before 1871, were anything but conventional on occasions that seemed to call for formality. He used the still new category of military attachés where it seemed useful, at least for diplomatic reporting, although he was usually loath to allow the military to encroach on what he considered the diplomatic preserve. In one case, Bismarck chose a strange procedure in order to steer between the Scylla of an unsuitable but unremovable legation head and the Charybdis of military *hubris*: he sent Theodor von Bernhardi, who had never served in the army but was a military writer of whom Moltke thought highly, as military plenipotentiary to Florence on the eve of the war of 1866. This civilian military attaché had a caustic tongue and sharp eye, resented by the blundering Italians who had expected a regular Prussian officer. Bernhardi's reports on the military sector were to complement those of the regularly accredited minister Count Usedom; the latter was considered inefficient and out of sympathy with Bismarck's diplomacy, but he could not be removed because Berlin royalty favored him. Bismarck was satisfied with Bernhardi's activities and

22 Oncken, *Rheinpolitik*, III, 181ff., 189f., 194f.; Ollivier, *L'Empire libéral*, XV, 452.

reporting, and sent him again to Italy in 1867 for reliable information about the true value of the Italian army in an alliance. Usedom's reports, he told Bernhardi, were "unreliable and good for nothing." But he could not bring the King to replace him and could not himself order any of Usedom's secretaries to submit special reports, so there remained no channel but that of the military plenipotentiary, "who had an autonomous position, independent of the minister." The two top military authorities, Roon and Moltke, had proposed Bernhardi for this mission and the Chancellor was only too glad to comply. Bernhardi was to send not only reports of a military nature addressed to Moltke, which Bismarck would also see, but political ones, in the form of private letters addressed to a foreign office official. After this mission Bernhardi was similarly employed in Spain in connection with the Hohenzollern candidature.[23] Only after the founding of the Reich in 1871 and the trend toward conservatism in the purposes and methods of Bismarck's diplomacy did the Chancellor begin to find fault with Bernhardi's services.[24]

Bismarck employed another military attaché on diplomatic business, Baron von Loë in Paris, the recipient of the first indication of Napoleon's demand for the left bank of the Rhine. On his own initiative, Loë traveled posthaste to the Bohemian theater of war at the time of the battle of Sadowa, thinking that his advice on the military strength and intentions of an intervening France would be needed and welcome. As one of his friends, von Schweinitz, also a former attaché, pictured his dilemma: "Heavy responsibility rested on him—as the Paris military attaché he knew, and he alone, how to judge the condition and the power of the French army, on the strength of which resolutions of the greatest consequence were to be formed." Bismarck censured Loë for leaving the Paris post, but Schweinitz thought the criticism unjustified; in fact, Loë should have been called to GHQ

---

[23] *Aus dem Leben Theodor von Bernhardi's*, 9 vols. (Leipzig 1893-1906), VII, 57, 162, 286f., 319f., 377; Germain Bapst, *Le maréchal Canrobert: Souvenirs d'un siècle*, 6 vols. (Paris 1898-1919), IV, 40f.; Meisner, *Militärattachés*, pp. 14f.

[24] Moritz Busch, *Bismarck. Some Secret Pages of his History*, 2 vols. (London 1898), I, 493 (January 25, 1871).

to transmit up-to-date information on the French army, and then he should have returned at once to Paris.[25] A Prussian Crown Council, which doubtless considered Loë's reports, discussed and declined the French demands for compensation submitted by Ambassador Benedetti, and Loë was sent back to Paris to announce the decision which the King said made war inevitable. "It is hard for me," he said to Loë, "to impose upon my people at once a second war, one at least as bloody as the first one, which has called for such heavy sacrifices—but I cannot do otherwise." Loë reassured the monarch about France—in spite of her warlike intentions she was not Prussia's military equal at the time. This was also Moltke's view, and on August 8, the day Loë departed for Paris, he submitted his opinion that two fronts were feasible, provided Italy stayed in the war and the rest of Germany joined the Prussian cause. Loë fulfilled his mission, openly declaring to one of the French generals, rather than directly to the Emperor, "You know as well as I that France is too badly prepared for a war. She is short of artillery, trains, horses. That is the consequence of Mexico."[26]

As long as Bismarck went on fighting his various wars he continued to use some of the Prussian military attachés for his own purposes. When Loë's second successor, Count Waldersee, was sent to Paris in February 1870, on the eve of the war with France which had been the Count's "passionate desire for years" and which he had studied thoroughly, Bismarck warned him against "hasty judgments such as his predecessor had often passed" and gave him good advice on how to get along with the ambassador. "He is no swallow catcher, but a good and thoroughly honest man; beg him to let you read the dispatches; he will gladly do it; and I should rather like you to have knowledge of them."[27] This is clearly the way an elder statesman would instruct a bright young official in whose discretion he had confidence, and the Chancellor continued in the same vein when he appointed Wal-

[25] Schweinitz, *Denkwürdigkeiten*, I, 234.

[26] Arnold Oskar Meyer, *Bismarck. Der Mensch und der Staatsmann* (Leipzig 1944), pp. 326f., 330, but see above, p. 30.

[27] Waldersee, *Denkwürdigkeiten*, I, 49f.

dersee the first chargé d'affaires in Paris upon the resumption of diplomatic relations with France in 1871.

England, where military influence was assiduously kept out of diplomacy and out of the Cabinet—no soldier of active status was a member of the Cabinet between Wellington and Kitchener—the *homo novus* in the foreign service, the military attaché, nevertheless came to play a diplomatic role. One of the "three most violent men in Europe," all of whom were in the Constantinople diplomatic corps on the eve of the Crimean War and pushing toward conflict, was Colonel Rose, the British military attaché.[28] The dangerous character of such attachés, even under a constitutional monarch like Victoria with her inclination toward absolutism, was also demonstrated during the Eastern crisis of 1877 (though not in public). Victoria and Disraeli, behind the back of the Foreign Secretary, "in a clearly unconstitutional manner" (Seton Watson) and in fact disloyally, entrusted Colonel Wellesley with a mission to the Tsar. He was British military attaché in St. Petersburg and at the Russian GHQ, where war was temporarily halted in the summer of 1877, and his mission was "to be considered secret and on no account to be mentioned at the Foreign Office." Wellesley had had two interviews with the Queen, and believed that she "certainly looked forward to the possibility of war," and numerous conversations with Disraeli; on the strength of this he was to tell Alexander that if Russia should undertake a second campaign against the Turks, England would not be able to remain neutral and "would take her part as a belligerent." Furthermore, he was to assure the Russians that the reported dissensions in the Cabinet did not actually exist, and that Bismarck, rather than England or Disraeli, was responsible for driving Russia into this disastrous war. The Russians knew better on all points and were merely moved to resume the fighting and try to finish it before winter, thus lessening the chances of British intervention, which Disraeli wanted but the Cabinet majority did not. The campaign proved so exhausting for the Russians that Wellesley wrote to Disraeli,

[28] *American Historical Review*, LXII (1947), 41.

suggesting that the most favorable moment had come for Britain to step in and undertake the "inevitable" war with the Tsar. Disraeli, who put great trust in the Colonel, "whose reports appear always to have been accurate," was inclined to consider this advice sound, but Salisbury, in spite of this "most interesting and disquieting letter," believed Russia far from utterly exhausted and the Turk of no possible help to England. "I see therefore no reason for agreeing with Wellesley that this is a good moment for seeking to bring on the inevitable collision with Russia, if it be inevitable" (December 26, 1877).

Wellesley went home for consultation in February 1878, when Russia was practically in Constantinople; he continued to advocate war, and said that England need not fear it even without allies. "The Baltic and the Black Sea both blockaded, Russia would never know where the military attack would take place, whether in Central Asia, or the Euxine, or any other part, and she would have to keep her armies in exhaustive restlessness."[29] The war was postponed, however, like so many others presented as "inevitable" by military attachés. And Colonel Wellesley proved elastic enough to bear "very conciliatory assurances on the part of his government" when he returned to St. Petersburg in April 1878,[30] after Salisbury went to the Foreign Office.

Bismarck, in his complicated alliance and reinsurance arrangements, at first met little resistance, either overt or secret, from the personnel of the armies concerned. France remained enemy number one to the Germans, and to the others an undesirable, because weak, ally. While France and her officers kept alive their desire for *revanche*, little such sentiment survived in the Austro-Hungarian army. Archduke Albrecht, the victor of Custozza, inspector-general of the army and its

---

[29] The above is based on William F. Monypenny and George E. Buckle, *The Life of Benjamin Disraeli, Earl of Beaconsfield*, 2 vols. (New York 1929), II, 971, 1045ff., 1083, 1118; Lady Gwendolen Cecil, *Life of Robert, Marquis of Salisbury*, 4 vols. (London 1921-1932), II, 169f.; Robert W. Seton-Watson, *Britain in Europe, 1789-1914* (Cambridge 1937), pp. 527f.; Arthur Ponsonby, *Henry Ponsonby. Queen Victoria's Private Secretary* (New York 1943), pp. 164f.

[30] *Documents diplomatiques français*, Ist ser., II, 330.

designated commander-in-chief in case of war, was for a time the center of military groups which contemplated *Anschluss* with Russia. Their boldest spokesman was the military attaché at St. Petersburg, Colonel Count Bechtoldsheim, who had made a name for himself as the leader of a brilliant cavalry attack at Custozza. Like most of the German officers who had gone into Austrian service, he was strongly against Bismarck's politics. Bechtoldsheim returned to Vienna in 1878, after serving as observer with the Russian Army in the Balkans, in order to warn the general staff against a war with Russia,[31] and to urge them instead to come to terms with her, after the Treaty of San Stefano, rather than with Germany or with both empires at the same time. Conservative officers acclaimed his argument that in case of a war with Russia, Bismarck would cold-bloodedly leave Austria in the lurch in order to maintain traditional Prusso-Russian friendship. But Andrassy, a Hungarian and an advocate of the German alliance, won out when Francis Joseph approved his suggested diplomacy. The Emperor was ready to recall Bechtoldsheim from St. Petersburg, where he was acting like an agent of Gortchakov and was openly hostile to the Germans. But Andrassy advised against it as likely to attract too much attention, and Bechtoldsheim remained at his post, admonished by the ambassador to control his tongue.[32] Archduke Albrecht, by 1879 at the latest, came to the conclusion that "Austria's salvation for the future rested on the closest possible *Anschluss* with Germany,"[33] and that was the end of Germanophobia in the Austrian Army.

The most active undermining of Bismarck's *status quo* system during the 1880's came from the military. Russian

[31] His counterpart was played by the Austrian military attaché in Constantinople, Major zur Helle (1831-1917). He had assured his Turkish friends that his own country would enter the Russo-Turkish War on their side. When the Dual Monarchy remained neutral, the major thought that he ought to retire from his country's service. He assumed a Turkish name and served as a simple private in the Turkish army, but was soon made a colonel and still later pasha and chief of the intelligence service. Giesl, pp. 44f.

[32] Eduard von Wertheimer, *Graf Julius Andrassy, sein Leben und seine Zeit*, 3 vols. (Stuttgart 1910-1913), III, 77ff.; Glaise-Horstenau, p. 199.

[33] *Grosse Politik*, III, 455, 458.

officers, Pan-Slavist and pro-French (men like Skobelev, who turned a military credit earned in the field into political capital), attacked the understanding with Germany and Austria, and what was left of Prussian and Russian inter-army harmony went to pieces. The German military attaché, Major von Lignitz, on one occasion lost his equanimity and called out to Russian officers: "If it is war you want, we can wish for nothing better, and we are ready,"[34] while the Russian military attaché in Paris, Baron Fredericks, delivered a speech practically endorsing *revanche* at the unveiling of a French war monument. After watching a military review in France in 1888, he turned to a French politician with the challenge: "Avec une pareille armée, qu'attendez-vous donc? Faites un pas en avant et nous vous ouvrirons les bras."[35]

Gestures like these encouraged French hopes for the Russian alliance, and the French embassy at St. Petersburg tried to promote it in every possible way. One of the military attachés, who had been stationed there for years and was thoroughly familiar with the Russian language, collected valuable information in quarters where other personnel could not easily penetrate; he "entertained especially close personal relations, of which he prided himself, with Katkov," the foremost Pan-Slav publicist of the day.[36] Towards the end of the 1880's the French military attachés "were delighted to signal from St. Petersburg, in their correspondence with the Rue Saint-Dominique, the daily increasing interest which Alexander III showed toward all that touches us and the definite marks of sympathy and confidence of which our army is the object on the part of officers and particularly on the part of the Russian great general-staff."[37]

The diplomats of the Central Powers observed that these reckless anarchic Russian tendencies, "whims" as some German diplomat called them, were no longer firmly controlled from above with steady conservative intent; they indicated an anarchism emanating from the right, which finally reached the point "of pursuing the policy of communism under the

34 Toutain, p. 23.
35 *Grosse Politik*, VI, 1199; VII, 1510.
36 Toutain, pp. 169f.   37 *Ibid.*, p. 181.

national flag," as the Austrian military attaché in St. Petersburg somewhat ambiguously called it.[38] They appeared to be a real military threat directed against both Germany and Austria, when accompanied by a constant increase in the Russian troops garrisoned in Western border zones, but the Russians termed these shifts "purely administrative."[39] It was one of the disadvantages of Bismarck's reinsurance arrangement that he could not easily call such Russian movements by their right name or point out to the Russians their possible dangerous consequences—among "friendly powers" it is understood that such military measures are never of an inimical nature.

In view of these Russian concentrations, the military in Berlin and Vienna increasingly persuaded themselves that Bismarck's diplomatic arrangements with Russia were dishonest and a pretense. And when Alexander III visited Berlin in October 1889 and Bismarck, rather than the young Emperor, succeeded once more in gaining his confidence, Waldersee, now chief of staff, wished that the meeting had not taken place, "for I fear we allow ourselves once more to be misled into believing that something could still be arranged with Russia."[40] Waldersee himself had concluded some time ago that war between the Central Powers and a Russian-French alliance was inevitable and should be sought rather than avoided, and his most important attachés, Count Yorck in St. Petersburg and Deines in Vienna, agreed with him. They were "rejoicing that I counsel action," wrote Waldersee,[41] who had encouraged their political reporting over the years, both as quartermaster-general and as Moltke's understudy.

If Bismarck noted political comments in official correspondence—there were private letters besides—he would rebuke the writer for reaching out beyond his assigned sphere. The most incorrigible transgressor was Major von Deines, who served first in Madrid, later in Vienna (1885-1893), and still later as tutor of the last Crown Prince. He was a favorite

[38] *Grosse Politik*, VI, 1153.   [39] *Ibid.*, VI, 1150.
[40] Waldersee, *Denkwürdigkeiten*, II, 70.
[41] *Ibid.*, I, 338.

with Waldersee, and a friend of Chancellor von Bülow, to whom he confessed that "he did not like the diplomats at all, because he thought them either treacherous or flabby." When Deines embroidered a report from Madrid with well-meaning advice, Bismarck termed it "political rather than military." "Since I have the responsibility for political advice which is being submitted to the Emperor and for the resolutions which the Emperor consequently forms, I shall not submit the letter in all-highest quarters because I do not agree with the opinions evolved in it." The ambassador in Madrid was instructed to deliver a lecture to the attaché on the limitations of his office.[42]

The experience, though painful, taught the politically-minded Deines nothing. He was transferred to Vienna, where he "busybodied around among the archdukes"—according to his civilian colleague, Secretary Count Monts. At first he was not curbed by the ambassador, who would not believe Monts' warnings that Waldersee was taking a direct hand in Austro-German relations and was using Deines as an agent, that the latter's ideas "had not grown on the barren field of the attaché's rather confined mind," but were Waldersee's own.[43] The ambassador only became suspicious when, contrary to Bismarck's peaceful policy in the crisis of 1887, Deines' talk encouraged Austrian hopes for a warlike settlement with Russia, and in a conversation with Francis Joseph he advised seeking for a winter campaign as the war-opening most favorable to Austria. In the Chancellor's opinion such talk was in itself conducive to war and also encroached on the political sphere. He sent the attaché a stinging rebuke, and another to the ambassador who had not called him to order.

> Your *Hochwohlgeboren* thus encroach directly upon the sphere in which I alone am entitled and called upon to counsel the policy of H.M. the Emperor, and above all in the most important question that can be put up to the policy of the German Empire: whether or not we shall involve Austria, and following it, Germany voluntarily and consciously in a war of aggression against Russia, a war

[42] Witzleben, pp. 149f.   [43] Monts, p. 173.

which would have as its immediate consequence the defensive war with France, that is to say, the greatest of all wars possible now on two fronts. Even if we make it victorious on both fronts, it would have for us no acceptable prize of victory and no success foreseeable at the outset except the permanent spreading of the French sentiment of revanche to the Russian nation. . . . If I submit to you briefly these considerations which are guiding me in the political counseling of H.M. the Emperor, it is not done for the purpose of convincing you of their justness, but rather in order to spare myself the undesirable necessity of begging H.M. to break off the official relations which the Foreign Office entertains with your *Hochwohlgeboren*. The foreign policy of H.M. is not under advisement from the General Staff but is counseled by myself alone, and you are not empowered, without my definite instructions, to attempt to exert an influence of high consequence on political circles in Vienna and on their resolutions.

This thunderbolt from Friedrichsruh had its effect for the rest of Bismarck's chancellorship; one wonders, however, why he did not force the attaché's recall. Deines gave a formal "promise to work henceforth only in accordance with your Serenity's instructions," and old Moltke himself admitted to the Wilhelmstrasse that Deines had been "carried too far by military zeal."[44]

Under the new Emperor, Bismarck's authority over the service attachés was greatly endangered. Waldersee persuaded William that it was highly inadvisable to keep these officers under the Chancellor; they were much superior to the professional diplomats, and their reports were also superior, because of independence—the diplomats wrote only what Bismarck wanted to hear. A monarch must hear a variety of opinions in order to govern more safely—one version of *divide et impera*. Waldersee proposed that a cabinet order should place the attachés directly under the Emperor, but this went too far; William could not yet face Bismarck with a ruling that the Chancellor was bound to oppose strongly.

[44] Witzleben, pp. 174f.; *Grosse Politik*, VI, 1183; Bülow, II, 178.

He was willing to make a start toward this "immediacy position" for attachés, and early in 1889 ordered the Paris attaché to report to him directly. He was convinced that the service attachés, these *Elitemenschen* many of whom came from his own *Flügel* aides, would render him more valuable service than did ambassadors, and that "when things become serious, they must do the main work."[45]

With Bismarck's fall (of which Waldersee had been the main engineer) the "flowering age of attachédom," as one of the Chief of Staff's admirers called it,[46] seemed to have arrived. Innumerable attaché reports were especially designed to catch the young Kaiser's eye. The "vivid fantasy and literary talents" of the ambitious and chauvinistic military attaché in Paris, Major von Huene, contributed greatly to make them interesting to the august reader, though Chancellor Caprivi thought the reports "without serious and useful content," outdone in worthlessness only by those from the first military attaché at St. Petersburg, Colonel Villaume.[47] However, the diplomats of the "New Course" were on their guard against encroachments, even if abetted by the Kaiser. At St. Petersburg, Ambassador Schweinitz kept a tight rein on his two military attachés, and Count Monts, first secretary at Vienna, also proved a sharp watchdog for civilian supremacy. Instead of allowing the attachés to move into the "immediacy position" Waldersee wanted for them, the Wilhelmstrasse, after Bismarck had gone, obtained stringent rules against military interference from the Emperor and the new chancellor. When Deines once more relapsed into political reporting, Monts persuaded the ambassador to take a firm stand and to attack a report, which Waldersee had ordered "for some dark purpose," concerning the Austrian military budget for 1891. With strong military solidarity Deines had blamed the finance ministers of Austria and Hungary for the

---

[45] Waldersee, *Denkwürdigkeiten*, II, 30f., 42; Rudolf Schmidt-Bückeburg, *Das Militärkabinett der preussischen Könige und deutschen Kaiser* (Berlin 1933), pp. 184f.; Gordon A. Craig in *Political Science Quarterly*, LXIV (1949), 78ff.

[46] H. Mohs, *Generalfeldmarschall Alfred Graf von Waldersee in seinem militärischen Wirken* (Berlin 1929), p. 240.

[47] Wedel, p. 171.

budget's shortcomings, instead of the war minister who was actually responsible. A covering report, written by Monts and signed by the ambassador, disavowed the attaché, and a battle royal ensued between the General Staff and the Wilhelm-strasse.[48] In this conflict Chancellor Caprivi, though himself a general, decided in favor of the diplomats, decreeing that "since no mission can pursue two policies in the relations with a foreign State, every report of a military attaché must be submitted to the ambassador. If the latter approved tendency and contents, his 'Read' on it means that he identifies himself with it. If, however, the military report does not conform to the policy followed by the embassy and the Chancellor, the chief of mission has the duty to turn it down." This and subsequent orders gave the German chief of mission full supervisory rights over the service attachés, and allowed him even to read their technical reports, should he care to do so. Monts, the original instigator of these measures, had to pay for them: it was Waldersee's revenge that Monts did not at once obtain one of the major embassies for which he had reason to hope, but was put on the dull round of small legations inside the Reich, such as Oldenburg and Munich.[49] Waldersee and his attachés subsequently bypassed some diplomatic control by using private letters, while reporting "little or nothing officially."[50]

Interbureaucratic feuds can be long ones: both parties may receive outside help, from the sovereign or through publicity, and the fights may be carried on like other battles after all the original protagonists have fallen. Some of the victories of the Wilhelmstrasse civilians over Waldersee and his myrmidons had been because of the Kaiser's prolonged absence from Berlin. But the military were in positions so close to him that they could nearly always obtain his support. "The

[48] Waldersee wanted to become the third rather than the second Chancellor, hoping that Caprivi would soon be used up and that his hour would then strike. Deines had implored him (February 27, 1890) not to exchange the post of Chief of Staff for that of Chancellor, which "many another man can take over as well," whereas he was indispensable in his old post. Waldersee, *Briefwechsel*, I, 350.

[49] Monts, pp. 179ff., 511.

[50] Waldersee, *Briefwechsel*, I, 388.

Emperor, who felt that he was above all a soldier, was in any case inclined to give his *Flügeladjutanten*, aides-de-camp, more credit than the diplomats of whom he did not think too highly," as a Wilhelmstrasse man put it.[51] Many of the attachés had been aides, entitled to apply to the War Lord directly if they felt that conditions warranted it. In conflicts between an attaché and his ambassador the monarch was usually ready to side with the service man, forcing the Wilhelmstrasse to strategy on the highest level in personal and interservice squabbles.

The blackest of *bêtes noires* among military attachés at this time was Lieutenant Colonel von Engelbrecht, in Rome from 1882 to 1895. The diplomats disliked him for a variety of reasons: on personal grounds, because they suspected him of aspiring to the ambassadorship, for his restless activity, which seemed undiplomatic, for his "political reports" to Waldersee, the Chief of Staff, and even for his manners. Philipp Eulenburg could never "understand how the Emperor allowed himself to be blinded by this man with the *suada* of a Jewish floorwalker who had eaten the want of tact with a big spoon."[52] The military, on the other hand, were pleased to tell one another that the diplomats resented Engelbrecht's superior knowledge of things Italian—the language and the military conditions—and also the great confidence that both monarchs reposed in him. A question on which there was violent disagreement was Italy's value as an ally, and one of the ambassadors advised Engelbrecht that "it would be well not to bare the weaknesses of this country too unsparingly, in order that gradually a higher appreciation of the value of Italy might spread amongst us." Engelbrecht would not hear of such diplomatic consideration: "For my own reporting such considerations of high policy cannot be guiding principles."[53] He would not enhance the dubious military value of Italy in the Triple Alliance.

Engelbrecht survived the fall of Waldersee by several years, but when Bülow became ambassador to Rome, on his way to

[51] Monts, p. 179.   [52] Haller, pp. 245ff.
[53] Waldersee, *Briefwechsel*, I, 59, 197; Rich and Fisher, III, 362, 473, 599, 601; IV, 44.

the Chancellorship, his friend Eulenburg finally obtained the Kaiser's approval for Engelbrecht's recall. The monarch was not won over at once: "He has my own and King Humbert's fullest confidence, and is my comrade and *Flügeladjutant!* Should he be maltreated and persecuted once more, I shall interfere with the big stick in the Foreign Office."[54] And even later Engelbrecht was never out of the Imperial favor. After the humiliating Italian defeat in Abyssinia in 1896, the Kaiser intended to send him to Humbert with a letter of consolation and an oral commission: he was to tell the King that Italy would still be considered a worthy alliance partner and might, in spite of seeming obligations under the treaty, reduce and thus reorganize and solidify its army which, considering its resources, was really too big. The Wilhelmstrasse went into action at once to stop the mission: the Chancellor, old Prince Hohenlohe, must veto it; should it go through, it would mean that the Emperor's military entourage could influence him at will; Bülow's position in Rome would be endangered—Engelbrecht wanted to go to Rome to intrigue against him, and he must be protected; Germany could not take a stand for or against the reduction of the Italian Army, for that was a completely internal question for Italy. The monarch gave in, somewhat plaintively, when confronted with some of these arguments: he had acted with the best of intentions, had hoped to give his ally some solace and quiet which he urgently needed; a military man like Engelbrecht knew the military problems involved so well, "whereas the Ambassador despite all experience is after all only a civilian and unable therefore to judge or understand military things as well as a professional soldier who in addition has conducted the whole previous negotiations regarding these things." Above all, Hohenlohe must understand that a Royal Prussian colonel and aide-de-camp would never take part in an intrigue, least of all against one of his ambassadors as the Chancellor seemed to suspect.[55] This closing word deceived no one and solved no permanent problem.

Ample documentation furnishes an exposé of the conflict

[54] Haller, pp. 87, 259.
[55] Hohenlohe, *Denkwürdigkeiten*, pp. 193ff.

between civilian and military power, specifically between civilian diplomats and service attachés in the Second Reich,
more detailed than could be painted of any other great power.
Nowhere except in Russia and the military putschist states
was the relative power position of the military as strong as
in Germany. A charitable explanation of this portentous fact
is the "unfortunate military position" of the Reich in the
center of Europe, surrounded by enemies, but historical
criticism can never overlook the fact that it was made worse
by the politics of the defense departments, and particularly
by the addition of the new navy. This procured for Germany
two additional enemies, Great Britain and the United States.
The unfortunate internal structure of class and authority
only increased the problem: every group in German society,
even peaceful Social Democracy, had its specific foreign
enemy. Nothing was more incorrect than the line of the famous war poem of 1915: "We all have only one enemy—
England." Moreover, the incompletely resolved problem of
constitutional responsibility made it impossible to apply a
general, not merely a military, doctrine of German security.
This ambiguous situation invited conflicts of which those
between civilian authorities and military officials in the diplomatic sphere were merely a part. Bismarck had not obliter-
ated or solved them, but he had at least been able to suppress
them when they disturbed his conduct of foreign affairs; his
successors lacked this power.

The monolithic governmental structure with the Kaiser
at the top invited intrigue for the ultimate royal decision
along the far too numerous channels of "immediacy." Some
forty offices, the majority military and managed by head-
strong and politically-minded men, were privileged to appeal
to the monarch,[56] not counting the equally privileged aides-
de-camp who were so often attachés abroad. "And still the
unity of leadership is wanting since His Majesty is no unity
within Himself," as the Emperor's most intimate friend of the

---

[56] Gerhard Ritter, *Lebendige Vergangenheit* (Leipzig 1944), pp. 107ff.,
in a lecture on *Kriegsführung und Politik im Reiche Bismarcks*; Vagts,
in *Military Affairs*, III (1939), 219f.; Jean M. Bourget, *Gouvernement et
Commandement* (Paris 1930), pp. 62, 165, 263.

1890's, Philipp Eulenburg, concluded. "Door and gate are opened to the *maison militaire* on which His Majesty has conferred the title Headquarters even in peacetime, with Plessen at its head who talks of nothing but 'shooting.' My God, how old Bismarck kept his big thumb on this company! . . . and now the Engelbrechts and such riff-raff, that like the little spirits of the Arabs sit on every muck-heap, spook around in all politics."[57] In spite of the impressive façade put up in Germany, impressive particularly to foreign military attachés, the constitutional-parliamentary governments of the time were actually better-run organizations, and the constitutional authorities had better control over the military. Foreign offices and ambassadors held the service attachés within intended bounds. We may not know how often there were conflicts between civilian diplomats and service attachés, but there is no doubt that, where they occurred, the civilians' superiority and unity of direction was maintained and strengthened. The attachés of the constitutional-parliamentary governments were more obedient, and therefore better tools in the hands of the directors of diplomacy than those of the Germany of the Second Reich, or for that matter in Hitler's Reich.[58]

Unavoidably, there were occasional differences of political opinion, or quarrels over procedure, between the foreign offices and the military attachés in countries like Britain. The military attaché in Berlin (1896-1900), Colonel Grierson, came to a conclusion at the end of 1897, when Germany was occupying Kioutchou, which was contrary to, or ahead of, the general direction of British foreign policy: "We must go for the Germans and that right soon or they will go for us later."[59] The earlier cooperation of the armies of Britain and Germany was changing into competition between their

[57] Haller, pp. 108f.

[58] We were told of an order by Hitler which Ribbentrop obtained in the summer or autumn of 1940, that henceforth all reports by the attachés—military, naval, air, propaganda, etc.—would have to be submitted to an embassy head, for direct reporting to the ministries in question had reached a disconcerting degree of divergence.

[59] Duncan S. Macdiarmid, *Life of Lieut.-General Sir James Moncrieff Grierson* (London 1923), p. 133.

navies, tolerated by the senior service in Germany with far too much equanimity. In March 1897 the first big German naval bill was passed, and in May Captain von Lüttwitz, of the British section in the Great General Staff and author of some anti-British articles in the *Militär-Wochenblatt*, a service journal, was appointed military attaché for London, a post that had been vacant for a number of years. Grierson and his superiors called this "an offensive proceeding." Von Lüttwitz's articles, as Grierson read them, were designed to show "that an invasion of England is not impossible, that the main obstacle to it is the British fleet, and that it is only by the possession of a powerful fleet that Germany can attain to that supremacy which it is the desire of many, especially of the Colonial party, that she should reach." British naval intelligence was even more fearful: "The appointment of this particular officer cannot be a mere coincidence—his attention having been so recently directed to showing how the invasion of England can be made possible, he will now have full opportunity of studying the practical application of his theories. There is, in my opinion, more fear of an attempt at invasion of England by Germany than from any other nation."[60]

Such opinions had to remain "private" or "secret" as far as the opinions of a director of military operations, Grierson's later position, can ever remain private—and apparently the officer who held this opinion did not try to force it upon his civilian superiors. This resulted in a comparatively greater unity in the diplomatic bodies, including the service attachés, of the powers other than Germany, or at least in obedience on the part of the attachés for the duration of their tours of duty. At the same time, Germany had some of the most disobedient and even disloyal servitors among her service attachés.

The more or less contemporaneous rise of the American and the German navies, and their rivalry, resulted in the stationing of naval attachés in the two capitals from 1898 on. The U.S. naval attaché accredited to the three com-

[60] Arthur J. Marder, *The Anatomy of British Sea Power* (New York 1940), pp. 298f.

ponents of the Triple Alliance had been making his headquarters in Rome until the first half of April 1898, when he
was ordered to move to Berlin; very soon he was accredited
exclusively to the German Government. Throughout the
1890's the reports of the officers filling this post had been almost exclusively technical, with a bare mention of the first
large German naval bill of 1896.[61] So harmonious had relations been before the war of 1898 that the attaché at the time
of its outbreak introduced the first German naval attaché
sent to Washington (the sixth to be assigned, after naval
attachés had been sent to London, Paris, St. Petersburg,
Rome and Scandinavia) very cordially, with the request to
the Navy Department that "he be accorded by the Department every facility, consistent with the situation, to see and
observe carefully what may be of interest. I ask this in view
of the uniform, unvarying politeness and cordiality shown
me as naval attaché here. I feel so profoundly that we shall
have nothing to question in Germany's attitude towards us
politically in the war that what they have done in the past
deserves the consideration of the Department."[62]

Then came the clash in Manila Bay in the summer of 1898
between Admiral von Diederichs and Admiral Dewey, who
had for some time wanted a "better enemy" than Spain; he
would have preferred France or, better still, Germany.[63] The
resulting hostility remained more deeply rooted in the navies
than in any other group in the two countries. Naval attachés
were stationed thenceforth in Berlin and Washington, while
the armies, on the other hand, gave up their attachés in
1898 and 1900. The last German soldier to be stationed in
Washington for some time to come told the U.S. naval attaché in Berlin, who was to take over the military duties

[61] U.S. Naval Attaché, Lieut. Vreeland, to Navy Department, April 13,
1896: "It is believed that the cruisers will all go through, as the 'Colonial'
party favors that kind of construction, but the battle ships are not so
sure." *National Archives.*

[62] U.S. Naval Attaché, Lieut. Niblack, to Navy Department, April 25,
1898. Niblack was called home for active duty on April 26 and replaced
by Cmdr. Francis H. Barber, ret., as attaché. *Ibid.*

[63] Vagts, *Deutschland und die Vereinigten Staaten,* pp. 1353, 1385.

as well, that "the General Staff was of the opinion that they had nothing to learn in the United States."[64]

The German naval attaché in Washington studied likely landing beaches for the plans of the *Reichsmarine,* and the United States Navy, which now had an Office of Naval Intelligence to direct and coordinate the naval attachés and their work,[65] followed all activities of the German Navy with the utmost attention. This came to a climax in 1902-1903, during the preparation and execution of the British-German-Italian action against Venezuela, which had been explained to the State Department and the President as a measure to protect the financial interests of the three powers. The American Navy, however, saw it as the final emerging into the open of German imperialist designs, and against a country within the hallowed sphere of the Monroe Doctrine. As a countermove, which was hardly called for by the definitely limited intentions of the Germans on this particular occasion, the U.S. Navy concentrated its squadrons for winter maneuvers in the Caribbean. Theodore Roosevelt himself, no matter what he had been told about the *ad hoc* allies' intentions against Venezuela, was "deeply interested in the success of this concentration and intrusted the command to the Admiral of the Navy," Dewey. The Secretary of the Navy felt "that this movement is a test of our ability to meet war demands and he will sanction all reasonable expense . . . in the preparation for this important evolution."[66]

Early in 1902 the Bureau of Naval Intelligence begged to have the tour of duty of Commander Beehler in Berlin prolonged, because "he had obtained an influence so marked as to be quite exceptional." "This post is of exceptional value to the U.S. Government. In the opinion of this office, the

[64] Barber to Assistant Secretary of the Navy, November 3, 1898. *National Archives.*

[65] Memorandum of Chief Intelligence Officer, Captain Sigsbee, for the Chief of the Bureau of Navigation, March 7, 1902, about "the fact that this office and the U.S. naval attaché system were established by the Navy Department in order to overcome embarrassments caused by the various Bureaus sending naval agents abroad independently. . . ." *Ibid.*

[66] Memorandum of the Secretary of the Navy, July 24, 1902. *Ibid.*

present is a critical time, in view of the evident policy of Germany to keep in advance of this country in the rapid building of war vessels. . . . The prospective trouble in Venezuela may also make his conversancy with German affairs of value to the Department in the near future."[67] The recently appointed naval attaché in Caracas, who remained there only from January to August 1903, was provided by the Office of Naval Intelligence with "a set of war plans for Venezuela," which gave no hints as to the likely enemy. They did, however, include topographical and economic data,[68] recently compiled from reports of consuls in Venezuela. The Navy Department had asked the State Department for them in February 1902.[69]

Service attachés turning into politicians are perhaps too few in number to warrant broad sociological or other generalizations. But apparently when they take this turn, they are disinclined to accept the usual rules of civilian politics in the nineteenth and part of the twentieth centuries: in common with most soldiers they continue to think of force and violence as *prima ratio* rather than as *ultima ratio* in politics, and of war as more probable than peace. Consequently, they tend to have but little respect for international law as an agent to circumscribe behavior in both peace and war. Germany's service attachés in Washington in 1914-1915 did not hesitate to organize criminal measures against an America that in their opinion had violated neutrality by supplying Germany's enemies with war material, while the later Admiral Canaris, when he was naval attaché in Madrid, used Spain's neutrality to incite North African tribes against their French masters. And comparable Entente personnel paid no more respect to international law or the sovereignty of the small nations. In the autumn of 1915, when Serbia's defeat and the evacuation of the Dardanelles forced the Entente powers to look for a new base in the Near East, the

[67] Memorandum of Sigsbee for the Chief of the Bureau of Navigation, January 7, 1902. *Ibid.*
[68] Memorandum of Sigsbee for the Chief of the Bureau of Navigation, January 22, 1903. *Ibid.*
[69] Vagts, *Deutschland und die Vereinigten Staaten*, p. 1555.

Russian military attaché in Athens proposed that "the only reasonable way out was to throw aside the paragraphs of all codices of law" and occupy Salonika. "The taking over of the heart of the defense of all New Greece is by itself a clenched fist and a threat neutralizing all disagreeable eventualities."[70]

Readiness to use violence in politics made the politico-attaché one of the forerunners of Fascism, insofar as Fascism took over the persistent Balkan habit of political assassination. In the Balkans this had remained a tradition; officers were constantly involved in moderating absolutism by assassination or the coup d'état, in Montenegro (1860), Serbia, Bulgaria and Turkey. In the Serbian coup of April 1893, when King Alexander had declared his majority at the age of seventeen with the help of army officers, had jailed the regents and dissolved the Skuptchina, the most decisive role was played by the commandant of Belgrade. He had been military attaché in Vienna, where he was still so favorably remembered that the Austrians hoped Serbia would remain dependent on them, rather than on Russia.[71]

The independence in politics of Russian service attachés was evident in various foreign capitals including Berlin, where the naval attaché around 1900 was considered a dangerous "diplomatic franc-tireur."[72] And a Russian diplomat in Montenegro confided to an Austrian colleague late in 1913: The Russian military agent in the country ought to be recalled, "since military attachés everywhere carry on politics," and be replaced by military instructors who were to exhibit purely technical activity, "free from all politics."[73] Russian attachés have indeed played politics most often in the Balkan countries, a habit which goes back to General Baron Kaulbars. Tsar Alexander sent him to Sofia in 1886

[70] Report of Russian military attaché, Gudin, October 9, 1915. (Gudin was involved at the same time in a scandal concerning stolen cipher telegrams.) *Die internationalen Beziehungen im Zeitalter des Imperialismus* (USSR), II. Reihe, VIII, 783, 797f. For additional cases of violation of neutrality by service attachés see above pp. 43f.
[71] *Documents diplomatiques français*, Ist ser., X, 295f.
[72] *Grosse Politik*, XVIII, 5402ff.; XIX, 5921.
[73] *Oesterreich-Ungarns Aussenpolitik*, VII, 8952.

to be the guardian of Prince Alexander of Battenberg, the first ruler over modern Bulgaria. Kaulbars had been military attaché in Vienna, but this experience had taught him nothing politically—within a few months he proved too clumsy and brutal to run a government.[74]

The Russian military attaché in Belgrade, Colonel Artamonov, was implicated in the murder at Sarajevo. He was known to his colleagues of the Central Powers as "that wild warrior who is usually the mouthpiece of the Russian Minister, Mr. von Hartwig." Hartwig had expected a European war within a few weeks early in 1913, and thought there was a good chance for Pan-Slavism, given the poor state of Austrian armaments at the time.[75] Artamonov was on intimate terms with that arch-conspirator Colonel Dragutin Dimitrijevic ("Apis"), head of the "Black Hand," who was preparing the plot against the Archduke. Whether or not he asked Artamonov what the St. Petersburg government would do if Austria should attack Serbia after the assassination, remains uncertain. In any case, "Apis" was not deterred, and after the murder the Russian paid tribute to the "heroic" plotters of the "Black Hand."[76]

Turkey also enjoyed the Balkan habit of mixing politics with military service. The French president of the Turkish *Dette publique* at the turn of the century, Commandant Berger, was the former French military attaché at Constantinople. He was known then and later to the German ambassador, patron of the Bagdad Railway, as "an intriguing gentleman," an ardent enemy of the railway, and the possessor of great influence over the Sultan. To the German's satisfac-

[74] Hugh Seton-Watson, *The Decline of Imperial Russia* (New York 1961), p. 174.

[75] *Grosse Politik*, XXXIV, 12806.

[76] Hans Uebersberger was forced to reduce the involvement of Artamonov in successive treatments of the question, from his articles in *Auswärtige Politik*, X (July 1943), and *Historische Zeitschrift*, CLXIX (1961), 296, to his book *Oesterreich zwischen Russland und Serbien* (Cologne-Graz 1958); for the doubts about Artamonov's involvement see *American Historical Review*, LXVII (1962), 693f. The activities of Artamonov were referred to by the defense in the *Trial of the Major War Criminals*, XII, 296.

tion, however, he was unsuccessful in his endeavors "to obtain for the French Army and the French armament industry the position which Germany now holds."[77]

Captain Enver Bey, who took an active part in the Young Turk Revolution of 1908 and entered Constantinople with the victorious troops, obtained as reward the appointment as military attaché in Berlin, the traditional source of higher military education for Turkish officers. He interrupted this tour of duty in April 1909, to help suppress a counterrevolutionary attempt in favor of the old autocracy, to take the capital once more and depose Sultan Abdul Hamid; later, in 1911, he went to Tripoli and organized the Senussi and other tribes against the Italians, stirring up something approaching a "holy war" on the part of Pan-Islamism.[78] He was well known in diplomatic and military circles in Berlin "as an elegant officer, of quiet exterior, reserved manners and agreeable intercourse"; his colleagues considered him "as a man of energy but also as a hothead (exalté) who would lead his country into the worst possible adventures." His relations with German officers even in his Berlin years were never quite harmonious: in a country "where discipline is honored above all" they found it hard to forgive his role in the revolution against Abdul Hamid,[79] and the revolver shot by which he personally removed the War Minister Niazim Pasha in 1913, in order to take over his office a little later. William II, in one of his marginal notes, expressed the wish that Enver "ought to be strung up pretty soon,"[80] but German diplomats and officers were able to find a modus vivendi with him, in spite of the fantastic character of some of his reforms and the unsoundness of his strategic concepts as Turkish generalissimo during the First World War.[81] Even before war broke out he had been convinced that "the Triple Alliance

[77] Marschall to Auswärtiges Amt, August 6, 1898. Grosse Politik, XII, 3341; see also ibid., XIV, 3961.

[78] Grosse Politik, XXX, 11014, 11058.

[79] Beyens, I, 97, 109, 153.

[80] Grosse Politik, XXXVIII, 15439.

[81] For details see Gen. Friedrich von Rabenau, ed., Hans von Seeckt, Aus meinem Leben, 1886-1917 (Leipzig 1938).

was militarily stronger than the Entente and would win in the case of a world war."[82] A close associate of Enver, and the second most influential leader of the Unionist officers, was Lieutenant Colonel Zekki Bey, formerly military attaché in Athens.[83] And the next Turkish generalissimo, Mustafa Kemal Pasha, who took over and salvaged part of Enver's unfortunate heritage, did a tour of duty under him as military attaché in Sofia (1913-1914), as a step in his military-political apprenticeship.[84]

After 1918

A number of former service attachés took up politics after the war, not only on the defensive right where one might expect them,[85] but on the temporarily offensive ultra-left as well. None moved farther to the left than Jacques Sadoul, attaché and member of the French military mission in Petrograd in 1917, at the outbreak of the Russian Revolution, who was intimate with the French labor leader Albert Thomas on the one hand and with Bolsheviki on the other.[86] Sadoul later became a Communist and engaged in France's party battles.

In British politics shifts in allegiance are apt to be less radical, leading no further than into His Majesty's loyal opposition. At least two former military attachés, both professionals of the professionals and hence practically born to conservatism, Arthur Ponsonby and C. B. Thompson, later Lord Thompson of Cardington, ended up as leading members of the Labor Party. Ponsonby was military attaché in Constantinople at the turn of the century, with the German

[82] July 23, 1914. *Grosse Politik*, XXXVI, 14648.

[83] *Ibid.*, XXXIV, 12670.

[84] The stationing of the politically minded officer abroad might be due to his own wish for a much coveted position or to that of his superiors, who were anxious to get him out of the country and into a splendid exile. In May 1956, Gen. Aramburu, provisional President of post-Peron Argentina, sent a number of competitors abroad to serve as attachés or ambassadors; not all wanted to go. *The New York Times*, May 20, 1956, under headline "Argentina Wary of her Generals."

[85] Gen. L. G. Kornilov, who attempted the march against Kerenski and Petrograd in September 1917, had been military attaché to Peking, 1907-1909.

[86] David Shub, *Lenin. A Biography* (New York 1948), p. 213.

Morgen; the two were again on friendly terms after 1918, when they fought propaganda lies and the exclusive war guilt ascribed to Germany by civilian peacemakers. Ponsonby was co-founder of the Union of Democratic Control, an organization intended to control the secret diplomacy of which service attachés formed so essential a part, and was made Undersecretary for Foreign Affairs in the first Macdonald Government. But when the pacifism of this "partisan de la douceur" (Sorel) went so far as to include advocacy of conscientious objectors, British ideas of *Realpolitik* put an end to his political career.

Thompson brought to a party devoid of military experts the experiences gathered during a distinguished military career. "This finished product of an English public school and Woolwich ('The Shop')" had served as military attaché in the Balkan capitals during the Balkan Wars, and was one of the few engineers to fill such a post; an attaché almost always had to be either a cavalry or an infantry man. He was already a Radical in politics, an eager follower of Lloyd George, and his ambitions were rather more political than military. He confided to a war correspondent of the time that he had a financial backer, eager to defray the expense of a parliamentary election, but the First World War intervened before this plan got under way. After the war he was a friend of Ramsay Macdonald, and ultimately became Labor's air minister; he was killed while on duty, in the wreck of an airship.[87]

The party of Stresemann, the moderately nationalistic and revisionist Deutsche Volkspartei, included two former service attachés. Corvette Captain, Ret., Werner Freiherr von Rheinbaben, once naval attaché in Rome, was Secretary of State of the Reich Chancellory under Stresemann in 1923, also a

[87] Valentine Williams, *World of Action* (Boston 1938), pp. 22ff.; Princess Marthe Bibesco, *Lord Thompson of Cardington. A Memoir and Some Letters* (London 1932). Thompson tried to recruit another military attaché, A. C. Temperley, for the Labor Party, and offered him a safe parliamentary seat, but Temperley, though he "had considerable leaning toward Labor," could not swallow the far-reaching nationalization proposals included in Labor's program. Major Arthur Cecil Temperley, *The Whispering Gallery of Europe* (London 1938), p. 11.

member of the Reichstag and generally ready with his pen; Lieutenant Colonel, Ret., and Geheimer Oberregierungsrat Arnold Kalle, under Stresemann chief press officer of the Reich, was a former cavalryman who had served as military attaché in Madrid during the First World War. Another man who was fairly close to these two in the non-conspiratorial kind of Weimar Republic politics was von Müller, naval attaché in London before 1914, who worked in the Telegraphen-Union, a major news service.[88]

The commander of the American occupation forces in the Rhineland from 1918 to 1923, General Henry T. Allen (1859-1930), had served on German soil before, as military attaché on excellent terms with his ambassador, Andrew D. White, on the eve of the Spanish-American War. He was the head of American military government and American member of the Rhineland Commission, which was, according to his understanding of its functions, "preeminently created to moderate the actions of military chiefs in the Rhineland." His sharp disagreement with the French style of pacification and postwar conquest along the Rhine was expressed in his reports to Washington, by the prompt publication of his "Rhineland Journal" (1923), and a little later by his chairmanship of an American committee to feed German children. He happened to die while visiting a member of the German embassy in Washington.[89]

None of these men could bring himself to endorse the Paris peace settlements: each had hoped for new understanding among the ex-combatants after 1918. When the so-called war guilt question was undermining postwar relations, Ponsonby and, even more incisively, General Count Max Montgelas, another former military attaché, fought this poison for the rest of their lives.[90]

---

[88] Paul Fechter, *An der Wende der Zeit* (Gütersloh 1949), pp. 108f.

[89] See necrology in *Europäische Gespräche*, VIII (1930), 572ff. See also the remarks by his former St. Petersburg colleague, Waters, *"Secret and Confidential,"* p. 240.

[90] Montgelas served from 1900 to 1904 in the Far East, first with the German expeditionary force, then as military attaché in Peking. When he returned to Berlin in March 1904, Holstein asked his views about the probable outcome of the Russo-Japanese War. Montgelas thought a

While Ponsonby and Montgelas had become dubious about the salutary effect of the sword in politics, there was no prejudice against violence and little doubt about the efficacy of force on the part of a number of former or active attachés who became leaders of Fascism. General Walter von Lüttwitz, once military attaché in London, took over the military leadership of the Kapp putsch of 1920, the first open counter-revolutionary attempt against the Weimar Republic; after its failure he fled abroad, fearing even the lenient justice of that government. Franz von Papen was less impatient. He waited until 1932 for his own application of force against the lawful Prussian Government, the "drastic methods" he boasted of later, when as Chancellor he came to tackle the involved questions of reparations and German rearmament.[91]

A younger generation of attachés were also Fascist politicos. Major Vidkun Quisling (born 1887) had entered the Norwegian Army in 1911 and served as military attaché in Leningrad (1918-1919) and Helsingfors (1919-1921) and also as Norway's war minister (1931-1933) before he founded the Nasjonal Samling, the Norwegian Nazi party, in May 1933, four months after Hitler's coming to power. He maintained intimate relations with a number of army officers, whose indiscreet letters he showed in Berlin as proof of the "untenable conditions" of Norway's politics and of military sympathies for a "national uprising." Quisling stepped up earlier contacts with Nazi organizations, some of which had been established through the German naval attaché in Oslo, and undertook to cooperate with German aggression against his country. He has thereby become the very prototype of Fascist traitor.[92]

The countries between the Baltic and the Black Sea produced many a soldier-politico between 1918 and 1945, Colo-

---

final Russian victory unlikely, judging by their initial mistakes, and agreed with Holstein that it was better for German diplomacy not to bet on Russia to win, even though the German observers in the Russian camp were inclined to back her. *Berliner Monatshefte*, X (1932), 345ff.

[91] Karl Heinrich Bracher, *Die Auflösung der Weimarer Republik* (Stuttgart and Düsseldorf 1955), pp. 555f.

[92] For details see *Trial of the Major War Criminals*, XXXIV, 273ff.; *Documents on German Foreign Policy*, Ser. D, VIII, 546f.

nel Josef Beck, a semi-Fascist like most of the colonels governing Poland under Pilsudski and later, had shown his political hand to the outside world first on an attaché assignment. The Latvian minister in Moscow in 1938 was a former military attaché.[93] The Hungarian military attaché in Berlin, Stoja, became his country's minister there at the end of 1934,[94] when the Führer's contempt for regular channels promised a better *agrément* for soldier-diplomats. Little Lithuania, which in the 1920's had employed the military attaché in Berlin to establish a common front against Poland,[95] sent Skirpa, formerly in the Berlin post and later minister in Warsaw, back to Berlin early in 1939 in order to make the inevitable surrender of the Memel Territory to the Reich as painless as possible.[96] General Antonescu, Rumanian war minister from 1937 on and virtual dictator during Rumania's participation in the war against Russia, had served for years as military attaché in London. The German minister in Bucharest early in 1938 considered him "a man of broad vision, a man of determination who has his task of building up the striking power of the Rumanian Army seriously at heart." He had as yet "no ties to Germany," and the Nazi minister repeatedly suggested the assignment of a German military attaché to Bucharest alone, and not as heretofore covering Prague as well.[97] This was eventually done, and in spite of quarreling between minister and attaché Antonescu was brought deeply and irretrievably into the Axis camp, an achievement which Hitler himself praised.

Postwar Berlin, more than Rome, became the Fascist focus of infection. Peron served as Argentine military attaché in Rome on the eve of the Second World War and acquired there many of the features which marked his own particular brand of totalitarianism,[98] but in Berlin a number of foreign

[93] *Documents on British Foreign Policy, 1919-1939*, IIIrd ser., I, 161.
[94] Friedrich Hossbach, *Zwischen Wehrmacht und Hitler, 1934-1938* (Wolfenbüttel 1949), pp. 40f.
[95] *Documents on German Foreign Policy*, Ser. C, II, 219.
[96] *Ibid.*, Ser. D, V, 485.   [97] *Ibid.*, V, 236.
[98] For a detailed analysis see *The New York Times*, March 22, 1951; the Hungarian military attaché in Rome had the entrée to Mussolini. *Documents on German Foreign Policy*, Ser. D, IV, 156.

attachés were affected. General Tojo, head of the government which ordered the attack on Pearl Harbor, had served as military attaché in Berlin shortly after the First World War; he seems to have paid less attention to the effect on Germany of an overwhelming military defeat than to the speedy machinations of the military toward a return to power. He was convinced that Japan had fought on the wrong side in the First World War, and was an early proponent of *Anschluss* to the Axis. "Overwhelmed with a feeling of austerity and joy" when his country joined Berlin and Rome in 1940, he trusted that she would now advance "with renewed strength towards Japan's fixed goal in world affairs."[99] Colonel Beigbeder, for many years Spanish military attaché in Berlin, served as go-between for Franco with the Wehrmacht, and with other organizations in the Third Reich which were to help the *caudillo* to power. Colonel M. L. Christie, former British military attaché in Berlin and Washington, became "an ardent advocate of Nazism" in England during the "Appeasement" period and managed the London visit of Henlein, Führer of the Sudeten Germans, in May 1938.[100] And foremost among the Austrians who not only welcomed but actively prepared for their *Anschluss* was Lothar Rendulic: he had been dismissed from the Austrian Army because of activities in favor of National Socialism when serving as Austrian military attaché in Paris. Hitler rewarded him well, in the end promoting him to colonel-general, the highest rank reached by any of the Wehrmacht leaders of Austrian origin.[101]

The short-lived dictatorship of Lieutenant Colonel German Busch in Bolivia (April-August 1939) may have acquired its Fascist infection through channels other than military attachés. But the putsch attempt in July 1941 was prepared

[99] *The New York Times*, July 20, 1944.

[100] *Ibid.*, May 14, 1938; *Documents on German Foreign Policy*, Ser. D, II, 404.

[101] Görlitz, p. 628. For Schuschnigg's vain attempt to keep Mussolini to his original opposition to the *Anschluss* by having the Austrian military attaché recite all the contemptuous remarks on Italy made by Hitler during the stormy Berchtesgaden interview of February 1938, see Elizabeth Wiskemann, *The Rome-Berlin Axis* (New York 1949), pp. 97f.

among young army officers, partly over long-distance wires and partly via the German legation at La Paz, by the Bolivian military attaché in Berlin, Major Elias Belmonte Pabon; he collaborated, it was said, with Himmler's *Sicherheitsdienst*. In this case they were thwarted by a combination of FBI and British secret service agents, but another putsch, later in the year, with support from the general-politicos in Argentina, was more successful.[102]

Attaché service was part of the formative years of many a Latin American politico in uniform, particularly in Argentina. The war minister (to 1936), General M. A. Rodriguez, had served in the German Army (1907-1909) and had been military attaché in Berlin in the 1920's; his successor Basilio Pertiné was stationed there in the early years of the First World War and, in common with many Latin American observers, believed that Germany would win the war. The organizer of Argentina's Military Academy (1932), Colonel Abraham Schweitzer, had also served in the German Army (in 1914) and as military attaché in Berlin (1928). Argentine belief in German military efficiency after 1919 led to arrangements for another German military mission, such as Argentina had received at various times since 1899-1900. When the mission's contract expired, two of its members became Reich military attachés in Rio de Janeiro (for Brazil and Argentina) and in Santiago de Chile, appointments which aroused some resentment in Argentina. It was thought that both men had too much inside information on Argentine military conditions to serve impartially in the capitals of two of her potential enemies.[103]

Juan Peron served his apprenticeship in at least two positions as military attaché, in Rome (1939-1941) and in Santiago de Chile,[104]—he left the latter post in some haste in the late 1930's, fearing exposure of his attempts to spy on Chile's defenses. Among Peron's competitors and enemies from 1943

[102] Associated Press dispatch from La Paz, July 20, 1941; *The Memoirs of Cordell Hull* (New York 1948), pp. 1388ff.; for Pabon's denial see *The New York Times*, July 29, 1941.

[103] Fritz T. Epstein, "Argentinien und das deutsche Heer," *Festschrift für Otto Becker* (Wiesbaden 1954), pp. 286ff.

[104] For details see *Le Figaro*, October 4 and 5, 1952.

on were several ex-attachés, men such as General (ret.) Batista Molina, who were not satisfied with Peron's brand of semi-Fascism. Molina proceeded to organize Nazi-like *Bünde*, including the Argentine Nationalist Youth Alliance, a close imitation of the Hitler Youth, and the Supreme Council of Argentine Nationalism, too military a body to be tolerated under the Argentine constitution as interpreted by Peron's government, and therefore dissolved in August 1944. Molina had made his acquaintance with Fascist methods during two years as military attaché in Berlin, and later as chief of the Military Purchase Committee, which bought most of the Argentine army equipment in Germany before 1939.[105]

There were ex-attachés among the anti-Peronists as well: Generals Dalmiro Felix Videla and Eduardo Lonardi were among the leaders of the successful rising in September 1955. Both had served in two Latin American capitals, and the latter had also been in Washington in 1947, where he was Argentina's representative on the Inter-American Defense Board. His hatred of Peron is said to have originated in 1938 when the latter left to Lonardi an unfinished bit of espionage, without telling him that Chile was on the verge of uncovering it. Lonardi was greatly embarrassed, and was dismissed from Santiago.[106]

It is not always easy to determine whether the office and the training of a service attaché or the country in which he is stationed is the more apt to nourish the germ of Fascism. Infection seems uncertain in a case such as that of the Czechoslovak military attaché in Yugoslavia in the early 1930's,

[105] *The New York Times*, August 3, 1944.

[106] *Ibid.*, September 17 and 19, 1955; *Time*, October 3, 1955. Among the more recent attachés in Latin American politics are Col. Ramon Burquin Lopez, Cuban military attaché in Washington, arrested early in April 1956 on a charge of conspiring against the Battista Government (*The New York Times*, April 15, 1956), and Admiral Larrazabal, head of the caretaker government in Venezuela after the downfall of dictator Perez Jimenez. Larrazabal had served three years as naval attaché in Washington. *Ibid.*, January 24, 1958. Others are Gen. Lott, Brazil's strong man after the removal of President Vargas by the armed forces in 1954, and Gen. Aramburu, who headed the provisional government in Argentina after the fall of Peron. *Ibid.*, November 12, 1954, and November 14, 1955. For still another case of an ex-attaché turning *caudillo* and heading an uprising see *ibid.*, November 8, 1961.

Colonel Hajek, who was subsequently associated with the Stribny League, a Czech organization of at least semi-Fascist character, and was consequently dismissed from the Prague General Staff in 1937.[107] In the case of the Syrian Colonel Mohammed Safa, endogenous causes such as the instability of his home government, which was largely military, could easily have incited his political conspiring.[108] When Safa was military attaché in Washington, he was recalled by the Government of General Shishkely, but he soon fled to Iraq where he plotted against Shishkely under the name of the "Free Government of Syria." After the latter's fall in 1953 Safa returned home, but was arrested before long for stirring up "trouble in the Army for his personal aggrandisement," and attempting an anti-government coup in September 1933. He was sentenced to a jail term of six years by a military court in May 1955.[109]

A more successful Eastern military politico was Lieutenant Colonel Ali Abu Nuwar of Jordan, the man to whom the 1956 ouster of Glubb Pasha, the British commander of the British-paid Arab Legion, has been ascribed. Nuwar, an ambitious intriguer and a favorite of the young King, was exiled to Paris as military attaché—the typical treatment meted out to soldier-politicians by unstable regimes; he was brought back at the King's insistence and over Glubb's protests. He made himself leader of the "free officers," a group to whom nationalism was more important than military efficiency, but both were cloaks for ambition. After achieving the abrupt dismissal of Glubb and other British officers he eventually won for himself the command of the "new Army."[110]

The anti-Fascist service attaché is a much rarer figure.[111]

[107] *Documents on German Foreign Policy*, Ser. D, III, 1049.

[108] For the problem of the officer-politico in the Middle East see Majid Khadduri in Sydney Middleton Fisher, ed., *Social Forces in the Middle East* (New York 1955).

[109] Associated Press dispatch from Damascus, May 18, 1955.

[110] For some details see *Time*, June 4, 1956; J. D. L., "The Jordan Coup d'état," *History Today*, January 1957.

[111] One of the few declared opponents of Salazar was Humberto Delgado, Director of Civil Aeronautics, one-time military attaché in Washington and his country's representative with NATO. In the so-called presidential elections of 1958 he openly opposed the dictator's wishes. *Der Spiegel* (Hamburg), May 21, 1958.

In Japan, for example, there was one military attaché, Ando, who became Minister of Interior in the later 1930's,[112] and Admiral Nomura might also be mentioned. When he was appointed ambassador to the United States in November 1940, it was recalled in his favor that he had served in Washington as naval attaché twenty-five years before, and had been "exceedingly popular."[113] As for his subordinates in the Washington Embassy, they assured members of the American General Staff that the Embassy personnel, including the naval attaché, were as one "in an earnest desire to better United States-Japanese relations." The military attaché, General Saburo Isoda, felt that Japan had "made a great mistake in joining the Axis"; the Army was frequently getting "out from under control of the civilian government" and had to be restrained by Imperial command.[114] It was obvious to the Americans, however, that the General "did not feel empowered to speak for the Japanese Army." The Serbian General Mikhailovitch was an enemy of both Fascism and Bolshevism, and fought them with all the weapons at his disposal, only to fall victim in the end to a temporary coalition of Communism and Western Democracy. Mikhailovitch, long a political soldier in the time-honored Serb tradition, had served as military attaché in Sofia and later in Prague, where the Nazis found him in such close league with elements hostile to them that they forced his recall.[115]

The position of service attaché may earn its incumbent a certain amount of credit which can be politically useful when he resigns from his post or from the service;[116] he may also bring to civilian life, however, the point of view frequently developed on such a post. Some of the worst alarmists of pre-1914 Europe had been attachés, and had acquired scare habits

---

[112] Geyr, *Erinnerungen*, p. 18.

[113] *The New York Times*, November 26, 1940.

[114] Memorandum of Gen. Sherman Miles, September 2, 1941. *Pearl Harbor Hearings*, Exh. 33.

[115] *The New York Times*, September 27, 1942.

[116] Robert Louis Coffey, one-time miner, fighter pilot in the Second World War, resigned the office of American air attaché in Santiago in 1948 in order to enter politics. He was elected a Congressman from Pennsylvania, but was killed in an air accident the next year. *Time*, May 2, 1949.

rather than discretion. Colonel Arthur Lee, later Viscount Lee of Fareham, Civil Lord of the Admiralty, had been military attaché in Washington at the time of the Spanish-American War, and had known Theodore Roosevelt (who admiringly called him "a trump").[117] In July 1905, when Roosevelt was President, Lee assured him "in the most certain manner that Germany was planning an attack on England."[118] This was shortly after Lee had committed an international *faux pas* of the first magnitude: in a speech of February 1905 he explained the new concentration of British forces in the North Sea by the fact that England "had now to look with more anxiety, though not fear," toward that sea. "If war should unhappily be declared, the British Navy would get its blow in first, before the other side had even time to read in the papers that war had been declared."[119] This announcement, made in an out-of-the-way place, was unauthorized by the Cabinet and afterward denied by its author and by the Foreign Office. When Lee went out of office with his party later in the year, he remained one of England's extreme anti-German alarmists, like the yellow press and Leo Maxse of the *National Review*.[120] After the war, however, back at the Admiralty, he had apparently reached years of discretion, and it was possible for him to indicate, diplomatically, Britain's willingness to agree to naval equality with the United States. "Ties of marriage and friendship, travel and years of official service in the Western Hemisphere which pre-eminently fitted this skillful exponent of Anglo-American brotherhood for his responsibility,"[121] led ultimately to the Washington Conference of 1921.

The "Military Correspondent" of *The Times* since 1914, Colonel Charles à Court Repington, had acquired some of his military knowledge and ready penmanship as British mili-

[117] Stephen Gwynn, ed., *The Letters and Friendships of Sir Cecil Spring Rice*, 2 vols. (Boston and New York 1929), I, 294.

[118] *Grosse Politik*, XIX, 6287.

[119] About this controversial statement see the conclusive article by A. Mendelssohn Bartholdy in *Europäische Gespräche*, X (1932), 185ff.

[120] Robert W. Seton-Watson, *Britain in Europe, 1789-1914* (Cambridge 1937), p. 618.

[121] George T. Davis, *A Navy Second to None* (New York 1940), pp. 274ff.

tary attaché in Brussels (1900-1902), and as head, together with Henry Wilson, of the French section in the British Intelligence Department; after he left the service, he remained the recipient of confidences from Sir John Fisher, General Grierson and other officers in high positions. He published an alarm article about Germany's threatening intentions in *The Times* of December 27, 1905, which was unjustified by any recent German actions. This earned him a visit from the French military attaché, Major Huguet, and led eventually to the Anglo-French military "conversations" of 1906 and later.[122] So high was his standing with a man like Edward Grey, an ignoramus in military questions, that his panic could sweep straight into the inner sanctum of the Foreign Office and induce a fear and a secretiveness which Grey in later years came to regret.[123] Repington became one of the leaders of the National Service League, an organization agitating for the introduction of conscription in England on account of the "German danger," and he never let up in his attacks on Germany.[124] He had originally been pro-German, like most British army officers in the 1890's, but his later opinion of the German Army sank lower and lower. In numerous articles for *The Times* he called it a mere parade mechanism, unable to endure a campaign beyond six months, and his judgment of the French army went up proportionately—a change which coincided with the views of Grierson and Sir John French.[125] According to another British ex-attaché, an enemy of both Repington and Grierson, his writing "carried immense weight" with British statesmen, who were apt to get their information from newspapers and from their military correspondents, thus allowing themselves the comfortable hope that a war with Germany, if it should come, could not

---

[122] Lieut. Col. Charles À Court Repington, *The First World War, 1914-1918* (Boston and New York 1920), ch. I; for the whole situation see Fay, I, 202ff.

[123] Viscount Grey of Fallodon, *Twenty-five Years, 1892-1916* (New York 1925).

[124] *Grosse Politik*, XXVIII, 10233; XXXI, 11314, 11567.

[125] In his agitation for strengthening British land forces against a much feared German landing attempt in 1907-1908, Roberts was "assisted mainly by à Court." Gwynn, *Spring Rice*, II, 113.

last long.[126] To Count Metternich, the German ambassador, who tried harder than anyone else in his time to keep the peace, Repington had become "one of the most dangerous and skillful German-baiters" when he published in *The Times*, at the instigation of Admiralty officers, the fact that William II had written a fatuous letter on February 6, 1908, to Lord Tweedmouth, First Lord of the Admiralty, defending Germany's naval armaments.[127] During the First World War Repington possessed "the special confidence of the Army leaders at home and was chosen by them as their special champion and spokesman in the Press against meddlesome politicians"; as Lloyd George put it, he was "the favored confidant of the General Staff whenever there were any criticisms that they wished to see directed against the War Cabinet and its policy." He and his informants did not shrink from trying to bring down a Cabinet which they considered undesirable because it had taken the liberty of "teaching soldiers how and where to make war," or from publishing Allied plans in order to make it impossible to adhere to them.[128]

After Versailles, Repington still had the confidence of many statesmen (but more often abroad than at home), and of even more military men. British and French generals agreed with him as early as 1921 that "naturally the Germans were planning a revenge and we should do the same in their place," while British and French military attachés supplied him with information for his diaries and articles, which now appeared in the *Daily Telegraph*.[129]

Service attachés, like most officers, have usually regarded war as unavoidable; and they have not always refrained from helping it on. Few of them would have an opportunity to work for the new peace. Under the treaties of the *ancien*

---

[126] Waters, *"Secret and Confidential,"* pp. 61f., 300, 310f.; Widenmann, pp. 106, 204.

[127] *Grosse Politik*, XXIV, 8181, 8186, 8190; *Documents diplomatiques français*, IInd ser., XI, 521ff.

[128] *War Memoirs of David Lloyd George*, 6 vols. (London 1933-1936), V, 267, 289, 293ff.; Lord Beaverbrook, *Men and Power 1917-1918* (London 1956), pp. 192f., 256, 376f.

[129] Lieut. Col. Charles À Court Repington, *After the War, A Diary* (Boston and New York 1922), pp. 852, 31, 364 and passim.

régime the soldiers who had fought the battles included for-give-and-forget clauses in regard to all combatants—a meas-ure humane and chivalrous, albeit in the interest of the gov-erning group in society. After the making of peace had come into the hands of civilian burghers, the concept of war guilt crept in: guilt imputed to the loser who was also declared to have been the aggressor, in order to justify the making of war by the victor, and territorial conquests and reparations payments. When the Versailles Treaty made its stipulations about war criminals, who were to be found exclusively on the losing side, practically no officer on the winning side pro-tested. An old Internationale was dead. Foch stared, hypno-tized, at the chalk line of the Rhine when General von Win-terfeldt, scion of an old Prussian family, a prewar German military attaché in Paris and member of the German Armi-stice Commission, invited him to save Europe east of the Rhine from Bolshevism and Socialism. Almost equally un-heeded went Major General Max Hoffmann's later call for an anti-Bolshevist crusade by all the Western powers, General Waters' memoirs[130] which were in effect a plea for a con-servative reunderstanding, or General Ian Hamilton's pro-posals for a "decent soldier's peace," such as earlier, pre-Wilsonian treaties had established. They had been made by soldiers "who had worked off their hate and bitterness in the field; they had been bled into a calm frame of mind; they had become very much human beings; the moment the last shot was fired they did their best they could for the fellows they had fought."[131]

Proposals for a reconciliation among soldiers, made by Hamilton, General Le Rond[132] and others, were taken up by more sinister figures such as Franz von Papen, ex-attachés all;

[130] See bibliography.

[131] Sir Ian Hamilton, *The Friends of England*. Lectures to Members of the British Legion (London 1923), pp. 111f. For Hamilton's labors on Anglo-German understanding see Geyr, *The Critical Years*, pp. 12, 99, etc.

[132] For Le Rond's visit to Hitler at Berchtesgaden in June 1938 see *Documents on German Foreign Policy*, Ser. D, II, 484f. German diplomats who knew him as military attaché in Tokyo before 1914 and as com-mander of French troops in Upper Silesia after 1918 did not consider him particularly qualified as a messenger of peace.

the more humane proposals came too late to provide a better foundation for peace. The Nazis were already in power by the time meetings of British, French and German war veterans had been arranged,[133] and they used this show of understanding among ex-enemies as a screen for the rearming of Germany and the preparation of a war.

The Russians after 1945 were far more unprejudiced and flexible than were the Western powers, especially France. Not only had they made use of German prisoners of war, from Field Marshal Paulus down, in their wartime propaganda against Hitler, something the Western makers of "political warfare" could not bring themselves to do, but they also largely disregarded the checkered past of officers useful under new conditions. General Simon Dragac had been Czech military attaché in Paris (1929-1931), later section chief in the Prague General Staff and, after the German occupation in 1939, prominent in a German-sponsored semi-Fascist organization. But all was forgiven when in 1945 he joined the Communist Party; he became commander of the Military Academy and, after the Communist coup in 1948, Chief of the General Staff (until 1950). It was said that the Russians had supported him because as head of military intelligence in 1937 he had, with the cognizance of the Beneš Government, passed on to Moscow the Gestapo-manufactured documents that were to implicate Tukhashevski and other marshals and generals.[134]

The record of the armed forces attaché in politics, whether in the service or after retirement, proves a mixture in which the bad outweighs the good. On the debit side: all too often they have not abstained (contrary to orders) from political judgment and activity, largely directed against civilian authorities, including chancellors and ambassadors. They have exhibited political sympathies and antipathies, influencing and misguiding expert military judgment, notoriously in

[133] For Sir Frederick Maurice's offer to have 10,000 members of the British Legion occupy and police the Czech territories to be ceded to Germany as an interim measure between evacuation and occupation see *ibid.*, p. 957.

[134] Ithiel de Sola Pool, *Satellite Generals* (Stanford, California 1955), pp. 43f.

regard to Fascism and Communism. More generally speaking, they have shown a preference for applying force in political strife, an idea held not only by the extreme Right, where his precedents would place the officer-politico, but also by the extreme Left.

On the credit side are the visible few who have worked for understanding between ex-enemies or between classes and groups in their own countries.[135] But this can never balance the record of a Papen, a Peron, or a Quisling.

[135] The former French military attaché in Vienna, Major de la Tour du Pin, in the late 1870's became one of the founders and animators of the *Cercles ouvriers*, organized by a group of Catholic Officers who, "penetrated by idealized memories of a Christian and corporative middle ages, were dreaming of a new alliance of the nobility and the people," thus holding up the laicizing tendencies of the Third Republic. They constituted a circle from which derived the social thought of Lyautey and other French officers. Raoul Girardet, *La société militaire dans la France contemporaine* (Paris 1953), pp. 282f.

CHAPTER 9

ATTACHÉ INTO AMBASSADOR

The usefulness of service attachés to their countries' diplomacy has been on the whole occasional and incidental; in the final balance their performance would figure on the debit rather than the credit side. They have been used by the directors of diplomacy when a powerful individual or institution proved inaccessible to or unassuageable by regular diplomatic officials—something the British met, to their dismay, after the termination of the old Anglo-Japanese alliance. To calm resentment in the Japanese services, they sent Major General Piggott, son of the foremost British expert on Japanese culture of his time, as military attaché to Tokyo in 1920 and again in 1936. They hoped to repair the "broken thread"—broken under American pressure—but it proved in vain.[1]

Such occasional employment or else the general neglect of the real or fancied talents of the politically-minded officer have excited in more than one attaché the soaring ambition to become ambassador himself—an ambition based not only on the conviction that he was as well qualified for the post as his temporary superior, but also on the theory that such a post ought to be filled by a military man in an age in which arms competition seemed the notable characteristic of great power diplomacy. Understandably, the civilians, "the frocks," did not encourage such ambitions. They avoided as much as possible having such attachés, whatever their rank, serve as chargés in the absence of the ambassador and counsellor; in fact it was considered quite extraordinary when Bismarck in the 1880's made the military attaché in Vienna, Count von Wedel, whom he considered "wood from which ambassadors

---

[1] Maj. Gen. F. S. Piggott, *Broken Thread* (London 1960) and commentary by J. F. C. Fuller in *Nineteenth Century*, 148 (1950), 52ff.

are to be carved," chargé in the ambassador's absence.[2] The few other known cases of such caretaker duties seem to have been unfortunate, and it has never become routine.[3]

Nowhere did ambitions of this sort arise more readily than in the Second German Reich, where the military was sufficiently in the ascendant to qualify an officer for almost any desirable civilian post, from postmaster to director of a Royal opera house. Civilian primacy in diplomacy was maintained only precariously, particularly under William II. About 1893 the military attaché in Rome, von Engelbrecht, was aspiring to the ambassadorship, and so hopeful did his chances appear that Chancellor Caprivi hesitated to relieve the ambassador, who was not in the Emperor's good graces, for fear that Engelbrecht might succeed him. The Chancellor was ready to submit an ultimatum if William had tried this; the old general would have resigned rather than see Engelbrecht in the ambassadorship and an unbearable military predominance established.[4]

Under the two Williams, a number of military attachés and plenipotentiaries were transferred into the diplomatic service, but it must be conceded that they were men more or less convinced of the necessity for civilian primacy in diplomacy. Von Schweinitz, ambassador in Vienna (1871-1876) and St. Petersburg (1876-1893), emphasized this so much that he was soon at odds and out of contact with his military attachés, especially when they sent reports of a warlike character to Berlin that seemed intended to captivate the young Emperor.[5]

The Kaiser wanted to have the commander of his peacetime Imperial headquarters, Count Carl von Wedel, whom he had sent to Vienna in 1890 to explain the dismissal of

[2] Wedel, p. 11.

[3] During one of the "outbreaks of political swine fever" in Austro-Serb relations—an Austrian embargo on the import of Serbian pork—the Austrian military attaché in Belgrade presented a near-ultimatum which would have made a commercial treaty dependent on Serbian orders for Austrian guns and other products. He expressed himself in such insulting terms that the Serbian minister who received the threat could hardly refrain from showing him the door. *British Documents on the Origin of the War*, V, 151.

[4] Wedel, p. 191.

[5] *Ibid.*, p. 171; Rich and Fisher, III, 473, 599; IV, 44.

Bismarck, removed from Berlin because he seemed, with the passage of time, an oppressive hangover from the Bismarck era, a veritable "conscience on legs." An embassy or legation seemed to offer the most "decent way" to get rid of him, and Wedel accepted with some misgivings. He studied for a year in the German Foreign Office and then became in turn minister to Sweden (1892-1897), ambassador to Rome (1900-1902), and to Vienna (1902-1907), where for five years he held a commanding position as representative of the strongest partner in the Triple Alliance. His presence eventually proved too oppressive for Aehrenthal; he was opposed to the adventurous policy that culminated in the Bosnian crisis of 1908 and the 1914 ultimatum to Serbia.[6]

Ambassadors such as Schweinitz, Werder and Wedel, were in a way *milites missi* with orders to cultivate what might still be common ground in the militarisms centered on the courts of St. Petersburg, Vienna and Berlin. Speck von Sternburg, however, "at the court of Theodore Roosevelt" from 1903 to 1908, was sent to the Rough Rider and his more civilian, more democratic, but still vigorous militarism to make friends for German policy, so much misunderstood in America. Sternburg had served as military attaché in Washington (1885-1890) and as First Secretary later, and he had then befriended the rising young Republican politician. When Roosevelt became president, he did not hesitate to tell Berlin that he considered Sternburg well qualified for the Washington post; the latter, in fact, owed his advancement more to this friendly aid than to any high opinion of him entertained in Berlin.[7]

The German Navy's main contribution to the category of attaché turned diplomat was Paul von Hintze (ennobled only

---

[6] For the above see Wedel, pp. 174ff., and for his position in Vienna M. Martchenko, *La catastrophe austro-hongroise* (Paris 1920), pp. 59f. Wedel returned once more to Vienna in 1914-1915, on a special mission to persuade Francis Joseph to keep Italy neutral by the cession of Austrian territory, but the Emperor would not listen. Corti-Sokol, *Der alte Kaiser* (Graz 1955), p. 457.

[7] Nelson Manfred Blake, "Ambassadors at the Court of Theodore Roosevelt," *Mississippi Valley Historical Review* (Autumn 1955); Vagts, *Deutschland und die Vereinigten Staaten*, p. 1928 and passim.

in 1908), one-time naval attaché, then military plenipotentiary in St. Petersburg (1908-1911), Minister to Mexico (1911-1915), to Peking (1915-1917) and to Christiania (1917-1918). The Tirpitz faction had wanted to make him foreign minister during the war, expecting him to seal "the victory peace," and when he finally became the penultimate foreign minister of the Second Reich for some depressing months in 1918 he was not very welcome to the civilian diplomats of the Wilhelmstrasse. They were once more realizing the fatal role that service attachés had played in foreign policy, and they took care that for the next fifteen years or so there were no ambassadors with a service attaché background.[8]

Hitler changed this to a certain extent. He agreed to continue service attachés who had been appointed before his coming to power, though in the end he came to think but poorly of them. Their reports contained too many warnings against Germany's undertaking a war, with one exception, the military attaché in Washington, General von Boetticher. Because he had refrained from warning against American war potential and preparedness, about which his naval colleague was writing worried reports, Hitler decided that von Boetticher "could not be bluffed" by the Yankees and was to be reserved for future high employment.[9]

A number of service attachés were employed by Hitler, who had little use or respect for regular diplomats; they were also utilized by the OKW, in lieu of ambassadors and in order to maintain contacts with the satellites such as Hungary, Rumania and Slovakia. In Finland the German military attaché had arranged the first visit of Mannerheim's emissary to the Führer's HQ, in order to discuss Finland's participation in the war against Russia. Through such direct channels, rather than through the Berlin Foreign Office, these military allies were informed (about June 15, 1941) on what day the attack against Russia would take place. And Mus-

[8] Hintze's last known service was a mission to Russia in May 1922. He and Col. Bauer, wartime department chief in the General Staff of the Field Army and participant in the Kapp putsch, were to study the Red Fleet and Red Army respectively. Castellan, p. 178.

[9] *Hitler's Secret Conversations, 1941-1944* (New York 1953), pp. 396f.; May 18, 1942.

solini, as early as 1942, employed the German military attaché to warn Hitler that Africa was lost, that it would be better to make peace with Stalin than bow to the Western allies, with their rigid demands for unconditional surrender.[10]

In due time, ex-service attachés were again made ambassadors, a development deplored by the Wilhelmstrasse even when it was headed (from 1938 on) by Secretary of State Weizsäcker, himself a former naval attaché. (His first post had been The Hague, in the summer of 1919, where he was greeted by his station chief with the words: "I had hoped that I would not get another Naval Attaché.") [11] The first attaché to head a legation in the Third Reich was Franz von Papen, remembered for his activities in the United States and for his tendency to lose his documents. Hitler sent him to Vienna to prepare the *Anschluss*, "without being formally subordinated to the Foreign Office," and indeed any such expert hand was absent from the written agreements Papen himself made with Austria.[12] After the Austrian *Anschluss* had been achieved (1934-1938), Papen was to bring about the *Anschluss* of Turkey; he went to Ankara as Ambassador in April 1939, but none of his attempts succeeded.[13]

From a historical point of view, Japanese adherence to the Axis was based on the wide conviction in the services—in the Army even more than the Navy—that Japan had chosen the wrong side in 1914, and that this must not occur again. In January 1919 Admiral Kato, former Japanese naval attaché in London, appeared in Berlin. He approached the German colleague who had also been stationed in London before 1914, and with whom he had had pleasant relations and had exchanged "information." Kato had two purposes: to study German substitute industries which poor Japan might also be needing in case of war and, by order of his Government, to see Tirpitz, "the only statesman Germany had had since Bismarck," to discuss a military alliance with

---

[10] Ernst Heinrich, Freiherr von Weizsäcker, *Memoirs*, transl. John Andrews (London 1951), pp. 255, 272.

[11] *Ibid.*, p. 46. [12] *Ibid.*, pp. 108ff.

[13] For Papen see his *Memoirs*, including an apologia for his Washington activities in 1914-1915.

Japan. Tirpitz could only point out the obvious: that for the time being, and in the absence of the elements of power, Germany was not *bündnisfähig*.[14]

By the mid-1930's she had acquired that quality once more, and the Japanese military, held up in their China adventure, looked for her help again. Dealing through their attachés in Europe and the German attachés in Tokyo, they sought to bring about a firmer German-Polish front against Russia and to make the Germans withdraw all help from Chiang Kai-shek. The latter attempt was the more successful. The Japanese Navy offered to return to the Germans their former South Sea colonies, now bases fortified against the United States, and then buy them back at once. Hitler and Ribbentrop, the new foreign minister, were so favorably impressed with the diplomatic talents shown by Ott, the military attaché in Tokyo, that despite his anti-Nazi past they made him ambassador. "That we are now making ambassadors out of military attachés is probably in accordance with the spirit of the times," State Secretary Weizsäcker, the former naval attaché, wrote, not too happily, to the ambassador in China who had to inform Chiang about the abrupt withdrawal of all German support. This was part of the price the Nazis were willing to pay for greater intimacy with the Japanese military.[15]

The Japanese spokesman in Berlin was General Hiroshi Oshima, who had had close relations with Berlin offices and officials, including Canaris, head of the *Abwehr*, for a long time: he had been assistant military attaché in Berlin from 1921 to 1923, was appointed military attaché in March 1934, and ambassador in October 1938. He, rather than the Japanese civilian diplomats in Berlin, pushed the Anti-Comintern Pact of November 1936,[16] thus carrying on a family tradition of close ties with Germany; his father, War Minister at

[14] Widenmann, pp. 44f.

[15] *Documents on German Foreign Policy*, Ser. D, I, 750f., 754f., 811, 818, 823, 851, 864.

[16] Joseph C. Grew, *Turbulent Era. A Diplomatic Record of Forty Years, 1904-1945* (Boston 1952), p. 1034; William L. Langer and S. Everett Gleason, *The Challenge to Isolation 1937-1940* (New York 1952), pp. 63ff., 102f.

the time, had been a pupil of General Meckel, chief German military instructor in nineteenth-century Tokyo. Oshima explained to an international military tribunal after 1945 that the service attaché was not responsible to the mission chief but reported directly to GHQ in Tokyo, and it was rather coincidental if civilian and military diplomacy agreed. They did so in the first weeks of the Nazi regime. During the Geneva discussion of the Lytton Report on the Army-provoked Manchurian incident, the military attaché, Lieutenant Colonel Banzai, told a Wilhelmstrasse official that he and the chargé d'affaires believed that Germany would be well advised to abstain from voting against Japan. The Army was trying to clear the way for cooperation with Germany, and in return the Germans could expect Japanese support, particularly in the fight against the Versailles Treaty.[17] Later, however, schizophrenia developed in Japanese foreign policy, because of dissensions between Foreign Office, Army and Navy.[18]

Oshima had negotiated much with Ribbentrop even before his appointment as ambassador, which merely formalized his position. Ribbentrop preferred him to the previous ambassador because the latter had been reluctant to grant Germany a preferential role in conquered China—Oshima, on the other hand, promised "to contact the General Staff" and thus obtain for Germany what the civilians might deny her.[19] He was, in fact, ambassador of the soldiers. His appointment, which Ribbentrop had urged, had taken place at the behest of the Army Chief of Staff and the War Minister, and probably against the opposition of the Navy. With the approval of his military superiors, he negotiated Japan's *Anschluss* to the Axis and then called upon the Tokyo Cabinet either to approve it, or to make way for another, more compliant cabinet.[20]

Japanese military diplomacy also sued Italy for a pact of

[17] *Documents on German Foreign Policy*, Ser. C, I, 6of.
[18] See Ernst L. Presseisen, *Germany and Japan. A Study in Totalitarian Diplomacy, 1933-1941* (The Hague 1958), for details.
[19] *Documents on German Foreign Policy*, Ser. D, I, 887.
[20] Herbert Feis, *The Road to Pearl Harbor* (Princeton 1950), pp. 27f.

steel, of which commodity there was more in Italian meta-
phors than in Italian war economics. Mussolini and Ciano
liked to do foreign business with service attachés, especially
those of the "succession states," Austria and Hungary.[21] The
two Japanese military attachés in Rome in 1937 were, as
Ciano was pleased to note, "both good Fascists, fanatically
pro-Italian"; they favored a military pact between the two
countries, talked hopefully "about a war with England,"
and were delighted when Ciano told them in the Duce's
presence that they ought to take Vladivostok, that pistol
pointed at Japan. Favors small and great helped to build up
intimacy: Italian arms deliveries to China, contracted and
paid for, were sabotaged; plans of Singapore, which had
come into Italian possession, were handed to the Japanese
military attaché in order to impress the Tokyo General Staff
and obtain from them "the military agreement which alone
can decide the issue with England." In October 1938 the
attachés of both Japanese services brought Ciano "a pact of
triple alliance," identical with the one that Ribbentrop had
given him at Munich in September. It was put into cold
storage for a time in order to blackmail England, even after
Oshima himself, strongly recommended by Ribbentrop, had
come from Berlin to urge the transformation of the Anti-
Comintern Pact into a Pact of Triple Alliance, and in spite
of the fact that Ciano was much impressed by him.

A perfect specimen of the Samurai as they appear in old
Japanese paintings and porcelain. Small and thickset. An
extremely proud carriage. A hard and interesting face.
When he began to speak, I realized why Ribbentrop is so
fond of him. They are the same type: enthusiasts who see
things in simple terms—I am tempted to say wishful think-
ers. He attacked Russia and said that Japan intends to
dismember her into so many small states that all thought
of revenge will be vain and ridiculous. He also said that
Japan wants to eliminate British interests entirely from
China and from the Pacific in general.[22]

21 Conte Galeazzo Ciano, *Hidden Diary, 1937-1938*, transl. Andreas
Mayor (New York 1953), pp. 85, 176f., 196.
22 *Ibid.*, pp. 29, 39, 59, 123, 185, 205.

The Hitler-Stalin Pact of August 1939 dealt a severe and un-expected blow to Oshima and his masters. They begged that Ribbentrop, on his second trip to Moscow, after the Polish defeat—and if possible the Russians too—should make at least "an appropriate gesture in favor of Japan," in order to make a future Russo-Japanese settlement somewhat easier. But Ribbentrop turned a cold shoulder, and the loss of face involved in the Nazi-Soviet deals was too much for Oshima and his superiors on the General Staff. He was recalled before the end of 1939, and replaced by Admiral (ret.) Kurusu. Oshima returned to Berlin in February 1941, however, after the military had regained the upper hand in Tokyo, and stuck it out with the Germans to the bitter end.[23]

Hitler was duly appreciative of Oshima's services on behalf of the diplomacy of militarism: he considered the Japanese one of the two ablest foreign diplomats in Berlin in 1942, and the one most assured in his position "because he has in the Japanese Armed Forces an organization at his back which has both the knowledge and the power to control the po-litical situation to the country's best advantage."[24] After the great defeat, Oshima was condemned to die, though hardly for the right reason: actually he had sinned outrageously against civilian supremacy in government, including diplo-macy, a supremacy which the elder statesmen of Japan, like Prince Saionji, had struggled in vain to preserve.[25]

The fields of activity assigned to service attachés are mani-fold, enough to occupy most of them fully. But some, in fact a relatively large number, have not found it so. They have been led astray from true office duties by other interests, notably a passion for "high" politics, for foreign affairs and their conduct, thereby irritating their civilian colleagues and superiors, and sometimes even dissatisfying their military

[23] *Documents on German Foreign Policy*, Ser. D, VIII, 146, 524f.; Langer and Gleason, *Challenge to Isolation*, pp. 193f.; Weizsäcker, *Memoirs*, p. 201.

[24] *Hitler's Secret Conversations*, p. 443.

[25] Langer and Gleason, *Challenge to Isolation*, p. 292.

chiefs. Some have become involved in "low" domestic politics, including conspiracies and revolts. The incidence of such politically-minded service attachés on record is high, compared with the total number of their kind, higher than in any other special group of officers.

II. FIELDS OF ACTIVITY FOR ATTACHÉS

CHAPTER 10

THE ATTACHÉ AS OBSERVER

... lawful espials. ...
Shakespeare, *Hamlet*
Intelligence about the enemy is the
basis of all ideas and actions in war.
Clausewitz, *On War*

All modern armed forces want to know "all about all other foreign forces." Considerations of practicality and relevancy will necessarily limit these altogether too comprehensive desires; so must "discretion," which must necessarily restrict the desire for "penetration"—the two imperatives of all diplomacy.[1] There can be too much[2] as well as too little in the supply of military information. Only through restriction to the essential can the flood of incoming "facts" be mastered by an intelligence service, the failures of which may sometimes derive from lack of clear directives.[3]

Most observers of foreign forces would be inclined to seek information in what seem at first to be direct ways, through the close and open observation of such forces or, where that would not suffice, through the employment of clandestine observers and spies. But a great deal of information about the armies, navies, air forces and war potentials of foreign countries can readily be obtained, or could before 1933, from service manuals, parliamentary reports and other papers.

---

[1] According to Henry James. Leon Edel, *Henry James*, vol. III, *The Middle Years* (Philadelphia 1962), p. 29.

[2] When Count Waldersee (*Denkwürdigkeiten*, I, 50) was appointed military attaché to Paris in February 1870, one high official in the Prussian War Ministry begged him not to report too favorably on the French chassepot rifle. "After such reports the King always makes trouble for us, but we can't change anything, for there are no funds for introducing a new model."

[3] Some good indications of a central intelligence office's directives for a spy, in this case given to Col. Wennerström, the Swedish attaché in Russian service, may be found in *The Wennerström Spy Case. How It Touched the U.S. and NATO*, U.S. Congress, Senate Committee on the Judiciary, 80th Congress, 2nd session (Washington 1964).

"The greatest part of our orientation [which is not the same as information] in England we derived from perfectly legal sources: the two British Parliaments," wrote a pre-1939 German military attaché. "The speeches delivered there were on sale. If through frequent visits to Parliament one had acquired a detailed knowledge of the individual members, their political connections, their mental and political standing, if besides one picked mosaic piece after piece out of their speeches, one acquired thanks to the detailed discussion a clear picture of many things. Public and free discussion is at the same time the advantage of democratic institutions. Of the whole diplomatic corps, I was the most assiduous visitor to the House of Commons."[4]

While the service attaché became and remained the most advanced, most open, most permanent observer for his home service abroad, every officer traveling in a foreign land was, potentially at least, an observer of its armed forces. The Regulations for the Army of the United States of 1913 and 1917, for example, laid down that "An officer of the Army visiting foreign countries, whether on duty or leave, will avail himself of all proper opportunities to obtain military information, especially such as pertains to his branch of service. He will report the results of his observations to the Adjutant-General of the Army on his return to duty, or sooner if practicable."[5] Although the observations of occasional military travelers are apt to be superficial or fragmentary at best,[6]

---

[4] Geyr, *Erinnerungen*, p. 13.

[5] *Regulations for the Army of the United States, 1913*, corrected to April 15, 1917. War Department, Document no. 454, 21 (Washington 1917).

[6] After spending a three months' leave in England in the summer of 1907, a German General Staff captain wrote an alarming report about England's warlike intentions—the Reichsmarineamt, for whom England was more *the* enemy than she was for the Army. The diplomats, seemed to agree with this and other similar reports, which could be used to give naval demands still greater urgency. However, both the ambassador and the military—though not the naval—attaché in London agreed that "the deductions of the officer in question are without value; in particular, the gentleman in question has mistaken fear of war for desire for war. The sensational write-up is a mixture of little truth and much falsehood." *Grosse Politik*, XXVIII, 282.

they may fit into the mosaic picture which the evaluating divisions of the general staffs try to form or to verify.

With such standing orders in existence, it is not surprising that even during the period of the freest international intercourse, before 1914, officers traveling in various foreign countries were restricted in their movements. In Tsarist Russia passports were required of them, as of any other foreign traveler, and certain regions, such as Russian Turkestan, could be entered only after special permission had been procured.[7] The Turks were at times anxious to keep even friendly observers out of such zones of tensions as the Caucasus frontier, partly to prevent the intrusion of others who might be less friendly. The Austrian military attaché wanted to go there on one occasion, in 1900, and the Turks protested. "I, of course, remained firm and emphasized my right of unrestricted movement," he wrote, and set off without official Turkish sanction.[8]

Franco-German tension during the 1880's led to sharp restrictions on the movements of French officers in the Reich generally and in the borderland of Alsace-Lorraine in particular. It also led to police surveillance of German officers visiting France, although, according to more peacefully inclined diplomats on both sides, these were measures "which ought not to prevail for prolonged periods between two countries which want to live on peaceful terms." The German ambassador Count Münster repeatedly urged their removal since the danger of espionage by French officers seemed negligible, but other authorities in the Reich would not extend the freedom of travel without a passport to French officers. Previous experience with them, as spies and agitators, seemed to demand continuance of the *Passzwang*; the regulation was also a measure of reprisal, to be continued as long as the French law on espionage made it almost impossible for German officers to stay in France even when they went there merely for language studies.[9] It must be admitted that it was

---

[7] See p. 133 and note 14.   [8] Giesl, p. 121.
[9] *Grosse Politik*, XIII, 3468, 3556, 3559, 5562; *Documents diplomatiques français*, Ist ser., VII, 253f., 260f.

almost a specialty of French generals before 1870-1871, and again at times after that war, to travel incognito through adjoining German territory, but they did not always escape undetected. General de Miribel, later Chief of Staff, was discovered about 1880 inspecting the German defense lines along the Rhine. The harm to Franco-German relations can easily be imagined when shortly afterward Miribel became commanding general of the 6th Army Corps at Nancy, considered to be the foremost of all military formations entrusted with *revanche*, and he took up his post with the publicly expressed hope of regaining the lost provinces.[10]

Military intelligence departments sometimes sent officers "on the spy" into "interesting" regions which had not been sufficiently covered, or where information had not been kept up to date. The time chosen for such reconnoitering might easily coincide with a period of international tension. This was admittedly the case with a trip which the later Major General Lord Edward Gleichen, then a member of the British Intelligence Service, undertook along the coast of French North Africa in 1894.[11] Happily, he remained undetected.

Actually, police surveillance of traveling foreign officers, of the service attachés, their offices, residences, movements and personal connections can be assumed far more often than any record shows.[12] The postal authorities gave similar attention to the correspondence of such officers, especially in France, with its "black cabinets," intercepting and deciphering bureaus, as well as wartime censorship set-ups.[13] All supervision naturally becomes more stringent in times of international crises and the approach of war, the very moments when an attaché would most like to make his observations. On and about July 31, 1914, the French military attaché in

[10] *Ibid.*, Ist ser., VII, 273ff.

[11] Gleichen, ch. XII, "On the Spy."

[12] For the attention given the military attachés in Paris by the Sûreté Générale early in the century see Mott, pp. 86f.; for the shadowing of foreigners, including attachés in Moscow after 1945, see Hilton, pp. 14ff. and passim.

[13] For the activities of the French postal authorities and their supervision of attachés' ciphered telegrams during the Dreyfus affair see Fletcher Pratt, *The Story of the Codes and Cyphers* (New York 1939), pp. 195ff.

Berlin realized that he had to be utterly circumspect: "It is impossible for me to prowl around the military sections and the embarkations: my comings and goings would not escape the police."[14] And with the growth of the police state in Russia, Hitler's Germany and elsewhere, supervision of all embassy personnel and actual restriction of their movements became common. By 1941 the suggestion of the War Plans Division of the United States Army "to send observer officers to potential theaters of war,"[15] if at all feasible, could hardly have been executed without such unwelcome surveillance. In fact, freedom of movement and travel was never fully restored after the First World War. Leninist-Stalinist Russia proved stricter than Tsarist Russia had been, and the former German South Sea Islands figured prominently in the restricted areas. They had been given to Japan under the mandate system, fortified by her, and tightly shut to all travelers.

The reports of regularly stationed service attachés, with a tour of duty normally not less than three years, obviously should be fuller, more consecutive, and better checked than those of occasional military travelers. Since the 1870's in most countries, attaché reports have provided the larger part of the information needed by the departments of foreign armies (*Fremde Heere*) in the General Staffs. "It is mostly procured by the military attachés at foreign courts," as an American traveling observer was told in Berlin in 1877.[16]

The service attachés "are specifically charged with the collection of information on the military situation in the countries to which they are accredited," according to a somewhat official American definition of their duties.[17] Writers on international law, in defining the attachés, have usually insisted that these officers have the task of "studying military institutions of foreign countries by observing them personally and judging the military-political situation *without seeking*

---

[14] *Documents diplomatiques français*, IIIrd ser., XI, 244.
[15] Watson, p. 358.
[16] Emory Upton, Brevet-Major General, U.S. Army, *The Armies of Asia and Europe* (New York 1878), p. 220.
[17] Major H.W.T. Eglin, in *Congressional Digest*, January 1924.

out secrets."[18] It should be noted that the (unofficial) German definition of attaché duties goes far beyond the (more or less official) American one in allowing, in fact ordering this officer to extend his reporting to the field of military politics and policy. Whether this makes him abstain from political judgment is doubtful, considering the record. But the juxtaposition of politics and policy points to the constant problem of how far the attaché may go in drawing conclusions from his own studies, particularly from sudden changes in the forces under his observation, how far this must be reserved for the home authorities and how far the attaché's propensities for political judgments must be checked by his superiors abroad and at home.

All these considerations come to a climax when a nation's intention to undertake a war or to prepare for it must be ascertained—no more momentous information or misinformation can be submitted by a service attaché. For example, on July 9, 1870, the Prussian military attaché in Paris, Count Waldersee, telegraphed: "In War and Navy Ministries large-scale preparations for undertaking a big war are under way. Reserves have not yet been called up, but it appears that troop movements would begin as early as tomorrow. Railroads have been cautioned. There seems to be inclination to start the offensive with immobile troops." Waldersee had pondered over every word of his dispatch. "It was of very great importance not to give needlessly alarming information, but above all also not to take this thing too lightly." He carefully reviewed his facts and his sources. "The most important thing was to recognize the moment of mobilization and to learn besides whether the French wanted to open the offensive at any early date." French mobilization was started on the 14th at 3 P.M.; the attaché had word of it three hours later and could report to Berlin, by way of Belgium since direct messages no longer went through unmutilated. Once this all-important piece of information was dispatched, nothing remained to be done except to make certain that a Prus-

[18] Brockhaus, *Konversations-Lexikon*, ed. 1902, art. "Militärattaché." The latest editions are without the underlined restrictive clause. For further definitions by international lawyers see Beauvais, pp. 65f.

sian intelligence service would function inside France after the declaration of war. This was Waldersee's last activity before relations were broken off.[19] He owed not a little of his subsequent brilliant career to this fortunate discovery.

The work of service attachés resembles on the one hand that of agents of industrial or commercial competitors, on the other hand that of research, but not synthesis, for a book of a historical nature never to be finished but always kept up to date. The resemblance to the former field of activity includes a certain ready accessibility of information as printed in handbooks, military literature, service regulations,[20] and a strict withholding of trade secrets. Friendly powers, as non-competitors,[21] will naturally be more ready than will hostile ones to open up sources of military information, usually on the basis of reciprocity and barter, but even forces already arrayed against one another in time of peace, in accordance with alliances, will continue to the last to exchange certain knowledge. When the British Army in 1907 had worked out new Field Service Regulations and Training Manuals, including still experimental machine gun fire tactics, the German General Staff was so anxious to obtain the most recent information "that while the Regulations were yet in draft form they were communicated to the German Military Attaché in London, in exchange for other information."[22]

For thorough coverage, the assigned field of observation

---

[19] Waldersee, *Denkwürdigkeiten*, I, 76f., 82.

[20] French applications before 1914 for certain printed Austrian regulations, which were obtainable only through the Vienna General Staff or War Ministry, were denied the naval attaché with the explanation that they were out of print and that new editions were in preparation. Faramond, p. 27.

[21] U.S. Naval Attaché Lieut. Sargent to Commodore John G. Walker, Rome, June 17, 1899. Private: "In beginning my duties here and at Vienna, I spoke plainly to the naval authorities, told them that, of course, they had no jealousy of America such as they felt for adjoining continental countries and assured them that they need feel no hesitation in giving me information as it would be regarded as inviolable by my Government and myself; that I did not intend to exchange bits of information with other attachés, or even let them know what I had been fortunate enough to receive." The promise of neutrality soon netted the lieutenant some information about gun mounts from the Italian Chief of Ordnance. *National Archives.*

[22] Lieut. Col. G. S. Hutchinson, *Machine Guns* (London 1938), p. 97.

195

must not be made too large and varied. In the interest of economy and because certain nations seemed of secondary importance, nearly all powers have frequently (though less often since 1945) accredited some of their attachés to more than one country at the same time. In the mid-1920's the United States Department of War had 22 military attachés abroad plus nine assistant military attachés, five assistant attachés from the Air Service and one from the Ordnance Department, stationed in 22 foreign countries but "grouped so as to cover 47 in all."[23] Such a distribution has distinct disadvantages, making observation accidental and disconnected and contacts with the foreign authorities no more intimate than those between traveling salesmen and their customers. Under non-competitive conditions and in relations with nations that were not immediate opponents, the makeshift institution of the itinerant attaché seemed acceptable. As late as the end of the nineteenth century, Britain thought two naval attachés "to Europe," who undertook periodic trips through the naval offices and yards, quite sufficient; in addition one such attaché was sent to Washington and one to Tokyo. This was a clear expression of British naval supremacy, since a considerable number of foreign naval attachés were stationed in London, including a German from 1886 on. The newly rising naval powers, on the other hand, thought they needed full-time attaché service in each of the great power capitals. This need had arisen for the United States, or so her naval attaché for the Triple Alliance capitals thought, during and after the Spanish War when the United States had fully entered the arena of naval competition.

England is the only European nation that has itinerant Naval attachés: but they are full captains because England wants them treated with consideration—and they are. English naval officers, however, have a fine large contempt for the navies of other nations (which they will some day regret) and their captains go around with their noses in the air principally when inspecting ships instead of look-

[23] Tracy Hollingsworth Lay, *The Foreign Service of the United States* (New York 1925), p. 154.

ing after the details. [During Barber's Berlin stay the newly appointed British naval attaché had come to him for information which his predecessor had omitted to collect.] I mention these matters because I think we are too prone to follow the example of the English Navy in preference to others especially in these days of "tommyrot" about an Anglo-Saxon alliance. Some day when we ask England to give us Bermuda as proof of this new found affection, we will see the cloven foot.

Our changed position in world politics makes it all the more necessary to accredit our naval attachés to only one great nation. . . . By our changed position, I mean that we are no longer the harmless peaceful commercial nation on the other side of the Atlantic that we once were: but have become a veritable danger to governments on this side. When Cato wished to rouse Rome to the destruction of Carthage before she became too strong, the listening senators insisted that she was too far off to do Rome any harm, beyond the sea in fact. Cato (who had a card up his sleeve so to speak) produced from the folds of his toga a basket of fresh figs gathered 40 hours before under the walls of Carthage and forwarded by a Roman Government dispatch galley. See! he said, how far they are!!

Europe has not yet arrived at the point to which the Roman Senate was roused by Cato's speech but they are thinking that way and I doubt if U.S. Naval Attachés will be allowed the free run of all the Navy yards of Europe as they have heretofore. Moreover, the possibility of national alliances has deprived our attachés of the independence they once had and made them objects of suspicion and espionage like the attachés of other nations and I am sure that in the eyes of European nations it will not do to have a man about who is one day moving into an Italian Navy Department, next day into a German, etc., and possibly exchanging points with other naval attachés. When I was in Germany I thought it was good policy never to have anything to do with my colleagues except at official functions and to exchange calls. The Frenchman made a dead set at me for some reason or other on my arrival and one day at a reception said that "he had something interesting for me": but I never asked for it. I did not want any Dreyfus, Esterhazy, Schwartzkoppen, Pannizardi business in mine. . . .

Germany is coming to the front rapidly as a Naval Power and one attaché's time would be entirely occupied with what she is doing. In the opinion of good authorities her builders will lead the world in ships, both large and small, designed for speed. Moreover she is more likely than any other nation to come into naval collision with us, for according to the present policy she is determined to have colonies in Asia, in the West Indies, and in South America and apparently our mission seems to be to thwart her. . . .

I have the impression that Japan has more naval attachés than any other nation and we should follow her example. We have no more friends than she has.[24]

Reciprocity is the first condition of free and equal diplomatic intercourse,[25] but the temptation will always be great to avoid this duty in relations with the most likely enemy of the most probable war, if not with all foreign observers. Thus, when France introduced smokeless powder in 1890, the War Minister considered the exclusion of all foreign attachés from the maneuvers of that year, when the powder would be tried for the first time in the open. Count Münster, for many years German ambassador in Paris, was much concerned with preserving good Franco-German diplomatic relations, and pointed out to Herbette, French ambassador in Berlin, the retaliation that such a measure would probably invoke from the Kaiser: he would exclude all French officers from German maneuvers, which had hitherto been freely accessible, and more tension in the relations of the two countries would result. The War Minister remained undecided for some time,

24 Cmdr. Barber to Navy Department, Rome, January 23, 1899. *National Archives.*
25 One of Tirpitz' attachés in London describes reciprocity as follows: "After the Reichsmarineamt had informed me the kind of inspection of German shipbuilding firms that the English attaché had made, I on my part applied to the Admiralty for permission to visit as many equally important English firms." Widenmann, pp. 73ff.

fearing public wrath if the press pointed out that foreigners had been watching this new and still secret instrument of war, and the diplomats had to remind him that the maneuvers were to be on so large a scale that they could not possibly be kept from all foreign observation. It would merely be done by less official observers and, everything considered, allowing the attachés to be the eyewitnesses seemed the least objectionable solution.[26]

Let them learn something about us (which they may learn in any case eventually) so that we can learn even more about them—this is the reasoning that underlies the exchange of military information. When it was being arranged that General Boisdeffre, chief of the French General Staff, come to St. Petersburg, ostensibly for the Russian summer maneuvers of 1892, actually for the far more important business of concluding the military convention which was to seal the previous political accord, it was not considered advisable to make the occasion an exclusively Franco-Russian love feast. One or two German officers were invited to the exhibition as well, "in order to have the right to send officers charged with the study of certain interesting questions to the German maneuvers." The French ambassador reassured his chief in Paris: "The presence of these Germans will not inconvenience in the least the well prepared action of our general."[27]

To what fields must the attaché as student of foreign armed forces extend his observations and studies? And on what sources, gathered in what ways, are they to be founded? The studies of the service attaché must extend to the following subjects and thereby produce a "permanent inventory of the material and moral resources of the foreign countries" under observation:[28]

The general organization of armies, navies, air forces, the ministries of defense, of commands and staffs. The organization of the various services, arms and branches of the forces, number of units, their stationings and movements,

[26] *Documents diplomatiques français*, Ist ser., VIII, no. 78.
[27] *Ibid.*, Ist ser., IX, nos. 318, 333.
[28] Lieut. Col. Rollin, *Le service des renseignements en temps de paix et en temps de guerre* (Paris 1908), pp. 16f., brought up to date.

the forming of new units, changes within the old ones. Recruitment of rank and file, non-commissioned and commissioned officers, military schools including civilian institutions in which instruction for military personnel or purposes is being given. Training of the cadres, of the reserves, forming of reserve units. Training installations such as camps, rifle and other firing ranges, testing grounds. Military missions sent to foreign countries. Combat equipment, including fire and side arms, ships, tanks, and other engines, motorization, equipment for chemical warfare, armament industries. Troop quarters, including barracks, hospitals, feeding, clothing, interior administration. Annual and extraordinary defense budgets. Morale of the troops, abilities of general officers and staffs. Mobilization (preparations, lengths and stadia of mobilization period) military and industrial, transport including loading and unloading of troops and equipment, ramps and harbors, initial assembly. Defense installations, forts, ports, arsenals, flying fields, anti-aircraft arrangements. Discoveries and inventions of military value and significance. The military geography of the host land, including the procurement of maps. Military literature.[29] Paramilitary organizations including civil defense. A power's readiness or unreadiness, willingness or unwillingness to go to war at a given time.[30]

The service attachés' studies and reports must above all possess relevance to and significance for the home country's defenses. This determines their value, their acceptability. A good deal of military progress transmitted from power to power is based on such reporting, and possibly on recommendations which may or may not be acceptable in the home offices. While some clearly superior arrangements such as

[29] Among the military writings submitted by service attachés we might note such influential works as Mahan's on sea power, which was promptly translated upon its arrival in Berlin, and Bernhardi's *Germany and the Next War* (Toronto 1914). As to the latter see Col. Samuel G. Shartle, *Spa, Versailles, Munich* (Philadelphia 1941), p. 123.

[30] In 1887, the German military attaché obtained the text of the reports of the French generals commanding army corps on whether it was opportune or not for France to go to war. *Berliner Monatshefte*, XV (1937), 965.

those of the Berlin Great General Staff were eventually embraced by most other countries—by Britain after 1906 when War Secretary Haldane had come to study its organization on the spot—there were doubts about imitating other German organizations, also highly recommended in various quarters. The U.S. naval attaché in Berlin during the Theodore Roosevelt administration, Captain Templin M. Potts, had been so impressed by the "Admiral Staff" as set up in the Kaiser's Navy (it actually proved not very successful in the First World War) that he strongly urged its introduction into the U.S. Navy. This would have eliminated any intermediary, such as the Secretary of the Navy, between the constitutional commander-in-chief, the President, and the commanding admiral, and Josephus Daniels, Secretary of the Navy during the Wilson administration, vigorously opposed all such plans for an "immediacy" position in the German style. Admiral Fiske, prompted by Potts, had recommended the plan, but Potts was transferred in order to deprive the Admiral of support, and the proposed change was omitted.[31]

The sources of information on the various points of defense interest are of varying accessibility, with secrecy most closely imposed on the preparations and plans for mobilization and initial concentration, on weapons newly invented and introduced, and on fortifications. Much can be learned and deduced from military and geographic literature[32] and from the daily press, which is usually much less discreet than the military authorities would wish it to be, in war or peace time. Opposition papers, on the whole, prove more informative

[31] Jonathan Daniels, *The End of Innocence* (Philadelphia and New York 1954), pp. 95f.

[32] An illustration of two navies being simultaneously interested in the same object of imperialism and searching for the same information: On August 31, 1898, the U.S. Navy Department cabled the Berlin attaché to compile a bibliography on the Philippines, to remedy its own ignorance about the archipelago. At the Berlin Royal Library, the attaché found that some of the literature and maps concerning the islands had already been borrowed by the Reichsmarineamt. Barber to Navy Department, September 3, 1898. *National Archives.* This little episode throws as much light on modern imperialism as would a tome of Marxist-Leninist-Stalinist literature: the imperialist urge, regardless of the object, is active before the object of its desires and its value, if any, to the acquirer are even known in detail.

than the government press. French and presumably other foreign service attachés gleaned numerous details about German rearmament between 1919 and 1933, though not about the ties between Reichswehr and Red Army, from the German Communist press; after 1933, censorship and anti-espionage legislation sealed off practically all such sources.[33] Studying governmental and parliamentary documents in print, including arms budgets, provides still further data. And so do parliamentary and other speeches: the foreign attachés gained their first detailed information about the Reichswehr-Red Army relations through the Reichstag speeches of the Social Democrats.

Many of these sources have dried up under the restrictions of the totalitarian governments, some of which, like Russia in the period of the cold war, have gone so far as to embargo, at least temporarily, the export of newspapers. But other opportunities for observation arise with the inspection of troops, or of installations such as navy yards and armament factories, State and private. In the days when there was "free trade" in arms, Krupp used to invite several hundred representatives of foreign governments, among them the attachés, to see the experimental firing with new guns on the firm's testing grounds near Meppen; on such occasions the guests were exceedingly well housed, dined and wined, and they would, as in 1878, toast the "civilization which was represented [in the Villa Hügel, Krupp's Essen residence] by the officers of nearly all European armies." Only France held aloof: after 1871 she had to buy her guns at home.[34]

On the basis of strict reciprocity, with the unit of exchange not always easily established, war ministries and general staffs handed out certain information to the foreign attachés when they applied for it. Before he left for Berlin, the British military attaché Count Gleichen (1903-1906) was advised by his opposite number, the German attaché in London: "Whatever military information you want, ask for it from the General Staff. If they can give it to you they will; and if they can't,

[33] Castellan, pp. 295, 299, etc.
[34] Bernhardt Menne, *Krupp. Deutschlands Kanonenkönige* (Zurich 1937), pp. 139f.

they will tell you they can't. But in the latter case don't try to get the information by spying, or bribery, or anything of that sort; for the General Staff will be sure to hear of it, and, even if they don't ask for your removal, they will see that you get no further information of any sort."[35] In the military capitals relations of the foreign attachés with the various military offices were increasingly restricted; certain offices received them at stated hours only. In pre-1914 Berlin personal interviews with members of the General Staff "were discouraged and if one insisted, one had to make an appointment by letter; and even then it was not very satisfactory."[36] Tirpitz had given strict orders that German naval officers must refrain from direct relationships with the foreign naval attachés, and "only the higher chiefs on whose part no indiscretion was to be feared, received, and often saw at their table, foreign officers." On such occasions they naturally met other German naval officers, but they had presumably been chosen for their discretion and lack of loquacity.[37]

Trips through a foreign country, particularly when unhampered by restrictions such as limited the movements of diplomats in the Communist-controlled countries of the 1940's and '50's, offer opportunities for the alert observer, even outside those "interesting" fortress and frontier zones which are forbidden for reasons of security. A trip in May-June 1914, which the Russian military attaché in Constantinople described, may be considered typical both as to object and results. He steamed through the Aegean islands, confirming from observation his earlier conviction that these islands, particularly those close to the Dardanelles, must be preserved for Turkey and thus for her "eventual heir," Russia, and must be kept from falling into the hands of the Greeks, who were just then threatening Turkey with war. "The English are fully conscious of the fact that whosoever owns Lemnos, controls the Dardanelles. . . . It is not in our interest that the islands in question go to Greece unless we finally give up all hope of acquiring a footing, sooner or later, in the vicinity of the Straits." He visited the coastal

[35] Gleichen, pp. 252f.   [36] *Ibid.*, p. 260.
[37] Faramond, pp. 13f.

203

regions around Smyrna which offered some military interest and, pretending a tourist's interest in the antiquities of Ephesus, he went ashore north of Scalanova where a Greek landing in a future war seemed most feasible and likely. In Rodosto he instructed the Russian vice-consul, a Greek, in the methods of collecting military information.[38] Apparently this particular attaché felt that he had kept well within the limits of professional ethics on this trip—in any case, he was not observed or discovered by the local authorities in the act of gathering information while presumably on vacation. Other officers were not so fortunate. In July 1947, with the cold war well under way, the Russian assistant military attaché in Stockholm was discovered, together with another Red Army officer, mapping, photographing and sketching in the Finnish-Swedish border region along the Torne River, which was closed to foreigners as a zone fortified against attack on Sweden from the East (the "farther East," since Finland was not an imaginable enemy); both Russians were traveling by bicycle and declared they were on vacation.[39]

Reconnoitering probable future battlefields, and camouflaging it by historical-topographical studies of battles of the past, has long been a concern of service attachés, or of their superiors at home.[40] In spite of all progress in geography and mapping, and the generally increased accessibility of militarily useful maps, which were in many countries produced by the cartographic sections of the general staff, a personal inspection of likely spots for battles, landings, or other operations seemed still more enlightening. At the turn of the century the Reichsmarineamt in Berlin had discussed the problem of "which points on the Atlantic and Gulf coasts of the United States, in the case of a warlike enterprise against the latter, would be the best points of support," and the

[38] *Die internationalen Beziehungen im Zeitalter des Imperialismus* (USSR), Ist ser., III, 184f.

[39] *The New York Times*, July 27, 1947.

[40] In December 1890, the French embassy in Rome informed Paris that the chief of staff of the Rome army corps, whose *signalement* was submitted, had just been sent on a secret mission to Tunis to report on the state of the fortifications of Bizerta, which France was then turning into a war port. *Documents diplomatiques français*, IInd ser., VIII, no. 22.

naval attaché in Washington proceeded personally to reconnoiter the New England coast during the summer furloughs of 1900 and 1901. He found Cape Cod the most suitable spot for such an enterprise.[41]

The service attachés are not their countries' only purveyors of military information from abroad. There are other official ones, such as diplomatic and consular officials, or military officers sent abroad on *ad hoc* missions,[42] and unofficial ones as well. Persons unfamiliar with governmental organization will be inclined to consider all of them as part of a country's intelligence service, directed by a central home authority. This view is illustrated by a passage in the Pearl Harbor hearings:

> Mr. Murphy: I also note, General, throughout the record, that you first state that so far as the consular officials, the Intelligence, they were directly responsible to you; that would be our military attaché at Tokyo, he would be directly responsible to you, would he not?
>
> General Miles: In the military hierarchy, yes. Of course, he was also a member of the ambassador's staff.[43]

Persons better acquainted with such a system than this particular questioner, who may not have been much enlightened by the answer he received, will query whether the service attaché is the best purveyor of information for either the armed forces or the diplomatic service. Espionage of the unofficial kind might be a superior source. Bismarck, at least, once pronounced this view, in one of his fits of irritation. When the ambassador to St. Petersburg, General von

41 *Political Science Quarterly,* LV (1940), 58.
42 In 1893, during a British-Russian crisis, the War Office dispatched a number of officers to various parts of Russia to see whether mobilization measures were under way; the ambassador at St. Petersburg knew nothing about this beforehand, nor about the orders which these officers were giving to the British consuls in Russian cities. Waters, *"Secret and Confidential,"* p. 83. The same method was followed in 1899, when the war with the Boers seemed unavoidable; but these officers in deep mufti were recognized on board the mail steamer to South Africa before the Isle of Wight was passed. *Ibid.,* p. 169.
43 *Pearl Harbor Hearings,* p. 907.

Schweinitz, was visiting him in 1879, he told his guest that diplomacy among the great powers "resembles a walk in the woods with strangers; does one of these delve into his pocket, I reach at once for my revolver; if I hear a pistol cocked, I am already shooting." He went on to say that he was thoroughly familiar with the location of the Russian troops along the frontier. But, said the Ambassador, his military attaché had reported all that quite some time ago. "Ah bah, attaché, we learn this very exactly through the Jews."[44]

Nor did Bismarck rely too much on attaché reports, though other home authorities might have done so. Such reports require constant checking against diplomatic reports, as far as the foreign office is concerned, and against other relevant information obtained by the intelligence section of the general staffs. The latter may well prove superior to attaché reports. During the autumn of 1912, in connection with events in the Balkans, the hurricane center of European politics, the German military attaché in Paris drew the conclusion from his own observations that France had provided for certain measures regarding the possibility of war. The Great General Staff examined every item, on the basis of the ample intelligence from other sources, and came to the conclusion that "it could be positively stated that no actual war preparations had been undertaken in France. Altogether there are up to now no indications from which it could be concluded that France has warlike intentions. The emergence of alarming news can rather be explained by the uneasiness caused by the general political situation. . . . There are numerous voices [from France] which, on the contrary, allow one to conclude that there is more of a fear of a German aggression and hence demands for strengthening of the frontier

[44] Schweinitz, II, 80. Bismarck explained to the French ambassador in Berlin his chief or immediate reasons for the alliance with Austria of 1879—the threatening character of the Russian concentration in the western provinces—and insisted that in spite of all Russian attempts to shroud these troop movements in secrecy, Berlin knew them in great detail. "Why should God have created the Polish Jew if not to serve as spies, and Russian officials if not to sell information to the neighbors of the Muscovite Empire?" *Documents diplomatiques français*, Ist ser., II, 585.

protection."[45] And Prime Minister Barthou did not admit such a state of alarm as at least the interior cause for more armaments, when he proposed the return to three years of military service in France in 1913. He pointed to the outside reasons for such a measure, "believing it to be his duty to take upon himself this responsibility after having read the reports of our ambassadors and of our military attachés."[46]

Published data on troop, naval, and air strength of the probable enemy, his equipment, his defense budgets, the movements of his ships, have seemed to many a service attaché (and to his superiors at home, more often than to his superiors abroad) insufficient to draw final conclusions regarding his intentions. They believe it necessary to penetrate further into the secrets of the likely enemy, and sometimes the unlikely one. Hence, if need or opportunity arises, the attaché must either spy or employ spies. Is the secret, however, always worth knowing? Is something worth knowing just because, as a defense measure, it is kept secret? Is the labor spent on exploring it and the price paid, including the worsening of international relations in case of discovery, commensurate with the actual knowledge? The vast literature on espionage seldom raises or answers these pertinent questions. Spies have often enough sold their employers worthless goods, the true quality of which could not have stood the test of an open market. Much has been pursued and bought simply because it was secret, and the buyers were "imbued with the idea that something secret must necessarily be of great value to their respective countries." The clever spy, after some study of the buyer's mentality, will often be able to invent and sell him what he happens to desire, if possible raising his price by becoming secretive about himself. The most fantastic case in this shadowy field remains that of the "avenger" who, bandaged to the eyes and pretending to be a German officer eager to revenge a slight by

[45] Moltke to William II, November 26, 1912. *Grosse Politik*, XXXIII, 12446.
[46] J. Montheilet, *Les Institutions militaires de France* (Paris 1926), p. 294.

his superiors, sold the French for 60,000 francs the open secret of the march through Belgium.[47]

The usual beliefs about espionage are based on the conviction that much that is valuable to a country's armed forces can be learned, and has in the past been learned, through spying. They are contradicted by certain judgments which, while rare, are nevertheless based upon actual experience gained in attaché service or with intelligence divisions. British Brigadier General Waters drew from his own long experience in both posts his conviction—"and experience has only tended to confirm it—that the results of secret service are usually negligible. Taking it all in all, information acquired in this manner may indeed act as a kind of boomerang, and harm the recipients by making them lose their sense of proportion, or false news may be handed out." This opinion was confirmed by General Janin, for several years French military attaché in Berlin, who told Waters in 1916 that in retrospect "no illicit military information of any real value was obtainable in Germany: the management was too efficient."[48]

Is the information furnished by the attachés as high-grade, instructive and reliable as it is supposed to be? General evaluation by the historian is difficult, even if his skepticism is challenged by the claims of attachés in their letters or memoirs. Some military men in a position to know have indicated doubts about attaché-furnished information, both as to quality and quantity. According to an American expert of the 1940's, only 4 per cent of the peacetime intelligence of the United States Navy came from attachés, as against 95 per cent from open sources and 1 per cent or less from secret

[47] Maurice Paléologue, in *Revue des deux mondes*, October 1, 1932.

[48] Waters, *"Secret and Confidential,"* p. 36. The U.S. naval attaché in Berlin (to Navy Department, June 16, 1898, telegram) applied to Washington for 1500 marks "to obtain information about intention of Germany in Sooloo Archipelago," a request the Department granted (*National Archives*). Unfortunately, the results of the inquiry are not to be found in the Archives. Since they were concerned with a policy, rather than with a technical matter, one wonders how they could have penetrated the secret of German intentions which, in addition, were vague and ever-changing.

agents' reports.[49] Such conclusions, however, represent hindsight, and will not stop the occasional or continual malpractices of service attachés. Nor are they likely to affect the widely held view that they are spies, paid and instructed by their governments, protected by diplomatic immunity, and operating under the head spy, the ambassador, in military, naval and aeronautical affairs and, more recently, in economic and technological fields.[50]

The distrust which attaché services encountered in many home commands was fairly unanimous. Exceptions are few: Captain Widenmann, until 1914 'Tirpitz' naval attaché in London, naturally the most important foreign post, was employed in the Imperial Navy's intelligence service during the First World War. Brigadier General Raymond E. Lee, U.S. military attaché in London early in the Second World War, became Director of Army Intelligence after America's entry into the war, putting to use the many contacts he had earlier established in British circles.[51] Captain Ellis M. Zacharias, USN, served more prominently. After two tours as naval attaché in Tokyo in the 1920's, he was for years (1928-1931, 1934-1936) head of the Far Eastern division of the Office of Naval Intelligence for the San Diego region, where he came to suspect a Japanese attack on Pearl Harbor or California. He returned to the Office of Naval Intelligence as its deputy

[49] Capt. Ellis M. Zacharias, USN, *Secret Missions, The Story of an Intelligence Officer* (New York 1946), pp. 117f.

[50] For an *apologia pro vita sua* by a military attaché see Giesl (p. 20), who served for 15 years in Constantinople: "The uninitiated public believes that a military attaché must, above all, undertake espionage. Aside from the fact that such an activity, maintained from ideal motives without material reward and under heavy risk, throws no shadow on one's personal honor, the profession of the military attaché has little to do with professional spying. The cases are rare when one has to use such means as disguise and false passports in the search for important matters kept strictly secret. I myself have never been asked to do that. In case members of foreign powers approached me with espionage offers, something that did happen, I either referred them to the proper place in Vienna, or I myself took over the merely businesslike agency between offer and reward."

[51] *The Memoirs of General Lord Ismay* (New York 1960), p. 213; Watson, p. 371.

209

director in 1942-1943, after service at sea, and was subsequently assigned to the Office of War Information whence he directed the endeavors to induce the Japanese, whom he knew so well, to surrender unconditionally. Admiral Alan G. Kirk, U.S. naval attaché in London 1939-1941, for a short time thereafter served as Director of Naval Intelligence (March-October 1941). He was saved from blame for the debacle at Pearl Harbor by his former superior in London, Ambassador Joseph P. Kennedy, who stated in an affidavit that Kirk had much earlier called attention to American unpreparedness at sea. After wartime commands, including much that involved close cooperation with the British in European waters, Kirk turned to diplomacy, and served as ambassador to Belgium and to Russia.[52]

[52] *The New York Times*, October 15, 1963, obituary.

CHAPTER 11

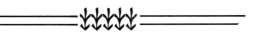

SPYING ATTACHÉS AND DIPLOMACY

In every land and language, the term
military attaché is only a synonym for
spy. Monat, *Spy in the U.S.*

The diplomats of the nineteenth and twentieth centuries received some of their rudest shocks when an espionage affair
broke involving their service attachés, and it turned out that
these officers who were "to study the military institutions of
foreign countries by observing them personally, without seeking out secrets,"[1] had disregarded not only this standing
admonition but also many an ambassador's "strictest recommendations never to indulge in that indiscreet and reprehensible curiosity which has been, at all times, more or less,
the besetting sin of the attachés wearing the epaulettes."[2] The
secrets might be small or great, might concern the technical
equipment of foreign forces, their preparations for mobilization and its execution, or—secret of secrets—their war
plans.[3] Exposure practically always and immediately brought
deterioration in relations between the two countries involved, but even such consequences have left many an
attaché himself highly unconcerned. When von Papen, declared *persona non grata* by the American Government in
1915, left the United States, he was undismayed about what
he had done. For had he not endeavored to serve his country

[1] Brockhaus, *Konversations-Lexikon*, ed. 1902, art. "Militärattaché."
[2] Ambassador Marquis de Noailles to Delcassé, St. Petersburg, March
1, 1901. *Documents diplomatiques français*, IInd ser., I, 147.
[3] The Dreyfus affair, which caused not only vast repercussions in
French home affairs, but also a serious deterioration in Franco-German
relations, occasioned rather more excitement by the fact that there had
been betrayal of secrets than curiosity about their content. William II
believed, or wanted to make others believe, that what actually had been
betrayed was the plan of the French General Staff to march through
Belgium in case of a war with Germany, "hence the great anger on the
part of the French against the traitor." *Europäische Gespräche*, X (1932),
80.

to the best of his abilities? (It never occurred to him that his ability might be slight.) If something had gone wrong, he argued, "I was a soldier, not a diplomat, and had therefore paid little attention to what the personal consequences of any of my activities might be."[4] Papen believed that a soldier could always make up for any mistakes by fighting.

Another source of friction, resulting in disregard for diplomacy on the part of service attachés, was the frequent conflict of generations between the attaché and his temporary civilian superior. While the soldier may respect the rank that goes with age in the armed forces, it is not as easily imposed across service lines. This conflict, however, seems to have abated recently, with the rise in rank and age of officers serving as attachés; by 1939 many of the French attachés, even in capitals such as Bucharest, were generals, and the difference in years between them and the embassy chiefs has considerably diminished.

Still another source of disagreement is bound to arise from the difference in value given to the technical findings of a service attaché by the officer himself and by the civilian diplomats. The third Chancellor of the Reich, Prince Hohenlohe, who had had experience with military attachés during his ambassadorship in Paris (1874-1885), stated this basic difference between the civil and the military in an exchange of confidences with the French ambassador in Berlin ten years later: "I have never been a partisan of the institution of military attachés, which is difficult to keep under control on account of their information and consequently of the more or less tempting offers made to them. When I was in Paris, I had only 12,000 francs of secret funds and at any moment I received offers which were sometimes ridiculous, sometimes rather tempting." Old Hohenlohe indicated that he turned them down, and the Frenchman promptly indicated that he would do the same, though tempting offers came to him in Berlin too.[5] Civilian diplomats might scorn such pickings by the armed forces attachés, and their importance, but the

---

[4] Papen, p. 52.

[5] *Documents diplomatiques français*, Ist ser., XI, 165, report of January 13, 1895.

latter would insist that they might even have diplomatic value. After the German naval attaché in London, Widenmann, had "accepted," as he puts it, the stolen blueprints of a Japanese cruiser which Vickers was building in 1911, he handed them to his Japanese colleague as an indication that there need not be spying between Germany and Japan. This noble gesture, Widenmann afterwards thought, laid the first small foundation of later German-Japanese intimacies[6]— and indeed, in a world run by soldiers and sailors such favors may come to mean much, or too much.

As Count Waldersee, the elder Moltke's successor, once defined diplomatic business generally, for the benefit of the military attaché in St. Petersburg, Count Yorck von Wartenburg, who in due time became involved in an espionage affair himself: "According to my own experience, the main task of the diplomats is finding out what one wants to keep from us."[7] While many diplomats might still agree with this definition from the military angle, incomplete as it is, disagreement will arise as to how far such an attempt should go, which means should be employed, and which shunned. Does the national interest, perhaps too readily invoked, justify any and all means however despicable? Do the professional ethics of the diplomat, those apparent hangovers from a more feudalistic age, limit how far the corrupting of members of the opponents' services may go? Or is the competition among states of such a cutthroat character that no hold is barred? Is there or is there not an agreed diplomatic code about unfair competition which should be respected by service attachés when they enter the diplomatic corps for a tour of duty? Are there elements in society so low that an attaché should shun them, even for the sake of national defense and security?[8]

[6] Widenmann, pp. 43ff.

[7] Adolf Hasenclever, "Militärattaché und Auswärtiges Amt um die Wende vom alten zum neuen Kurs," *Vergangenheit und Gegenwart*, XXII (1932) 589f.

[8] The British military attaché in The Hague in 1920's "had a constant stream of visitors to his office who would have formed an excellent background to a 'thriller.' It included some of the most undesirable members of the international underworld, . . . spies of all kinds, most of them

The more honorable-minded among the attachés (who were coincidentally the more feudal-minded and the sons of old families) have occasionally shrunk from the odium of dealing with espionage and spies, and have thereby sometimes involved themselves in a conflict between their own and their superiors' point of honor and the interest of the state they served. This seems to have become rarer as arms competition has sharpened, but history offers an occasional insight into such conflicts. General von Loë, a Prussian, a Catholic noble and a cavalryman, was a court general during a large part of his career, with relatives and friends among the French aristocracy before and after 1870-1871. Von Loë stated this problem and his personal solution of it to Quartermaster General Waldersee as follows:

> During my four years tour of duty as military attaché [in Paris] I have always professed and maintained the principle that the Prussian officer would have to remain loyal to the duties of his estate even in international intercourse, that is to say, that in the pursuit of his tasks he must not use any means incompatible with his character as an officer. Among these impermissible means I would have to include from my own point of view bribery as a way of acquiring state secrets. Whether or not the attempt at bribing is directed against a Frenchman or a German would be irrelevant from my standpoint, it would always be an indecent act, unworthy of any officer. . . . It would be far more important to preserve the prestige of a Prussian, abroad as well as at home, from any taint than to find out a few secrets.[9]

In order to spare his own and his peers' delicate, though perhaps obsolescent, point of honor, von Loë proposed that the Government, if it demanded such dishonorable services from any of its agents, should "entrust them to secret police agents; the uniform is not suited for such commissions." He

---

out of work, . . . inventors, mad and sane, . . . two or three offered to carry out assassinations on most moderate terms, . . . agents of German armament firms." Arthur Cecil Temperley, *The Whispering Gallery of Europe* (London 1938) pp. 16f.

[9] April 3, 1887. Waldersee, *Briefwechsel*, I, 70.

was not alone in his scruples, the German military attaché in Vienna (1885-1893), von Deines, had earlier declined the Paris appointment because *louche* dealings with espionage agents were connected with that post more often than with any other.[10]

Bismarck's main concern in regard to the military attachés was to establish and maintain control, by the Wilhelmstrasse and the mission chiefs, in all political questions. These officers were repeatedly warned to use caution and avoid all connections which might compromise their position. In practice a number of attachés disregarded this rule; if they broke it, they did so at the risk of complete disavowal by the Berlin Foreign Office. On the other hand, the Wilhelmstrasse did not interfere as long as all went well, as in the case reported by the military attaché in St. Petersburg, Count Yorck, in February 1888. One day, "a Russian officer appeared with the question whether I could not use information about the Russian Army. Naturally, I said yes, and he submitted the enclosure for which I paid him twenty Roubles, even though the information had no particular value, just in order to make a start with him. He asked whether I could use still more; I gave him some hints which he noted down, and he promised to come back with important things (fortress garrisons) in which case I gave him hopes for more money." He did come back for some price dickering and Yorck gave him 500 Roubles, instead of the 1,000 which he demanded, for data on Russian fortress garrisons in case of war.[11]

Another espionage case, which carried over from the end of Bismarck's administration, gave his successor, General Count von Caprivi, reason to promulgate stricter orders against such activities on the part of the attachés and also to act in accordance with his own principles. The German consul general in Genoa had come into the possession of blueprints of the Italian forts along the Ligurian coast, through a minor employee of the consulate who had been employed by an Italian engineering officer to make duplicates of the original drawings. The draftsman handed an extra set to

[10] Witzleben, p. 162.   [11] Hasenclever, *op.cit.*, p. 593.

the consul general on his own initiative. When this was reported in Berlin, the Wilhelmstrasse ordered that the clerk be paid 1,000 marks and removed at once to Switzerland. This was the state of affairs when Caprivi took over. His honesty, in this case at least, was quite compatible with Germany's true military interests (for what foreseeable use could she have for such plans?) and he at once resolved to return the plans to Italy, which was Germany's ally. The Italian Government did not seem much impressed by this gesture of decency; neither were many of Caprivi's subordinates, nor for that matter the German chronicler of the episode, who referred to Caprivi's "fanaticism for honesty." Actually the Chancellor's code was merely that of old-fashioned officers like Loë and Deines. This incident helped to tip the scales in favor of the civilians of the Auswärtiges Amt in the struggle for control over the military attachés, and the Chancellor composed and signed a circular, regulating their activities in general, and spying in particular.

> The military and naval attachés serving with the Imperial missions abroad, have been given the general instruction that they inform their chiefs of mission about all orders which they receive from military authorities and that in the performance of such orders they must carefully avoid steps and connections which might compromise their position. . . . Disregard of those rules and of the caution imposed upon these gentlemen tends not only to endanger the personal standing and position of our officers serving abroad but also to make more difficult the situation of the mission to which they happen to belong and to even influence unfavorably our political relations with the foreign nation in question. These consequences will appear in particularly sharp relief if the information to be obtained can only be got hold of by a severe breach of confidence and by punishable actions.

> It is therefore necessary to make it the foremost duty of the officers who are joined to our missions in a political position and with diplomatic character to avoid everything that could endanger in an unwelcome manner their own

position and the relations of their own country with the foreign one in which they serve on a tour of duty. The desire, justifiable in itself, of informing the home authorities as much as possible about all military and maritime events in the country of their activity, can only too easily lead the gentlemen to lose sight of the regard for the aforementioned points of view and the caution demanded by these.

These were the general instructions for all military attachés of the Reich, and those stationed in Vienna and Rome were also to be mindful at all times that they were residing in friendly and allied countries.[12]

Caprivi issued a still more stringent instruction against espionage on December 11, 1890: "Military and naval attachés are neither allowed to seek information about foreign armies which derive from any ignoble source nor to accept it if offered to them. In the latter case, if that which is being offered to them should seem sufficiently valuable to them, they have to report it to the proper military or naval authorities at home."[13] This ruling struck some of the attachés as too restricting: Yorck, for example, found it "so definitely prohibitive that henceforth nothing remains to do except break off all connections as soon as possible." It gave rise to part of the fight of the 1890's within the German foreign service for the supremacy of the diplomatic consideration over the military one. Several attachés, abetted by Waldersee, the Chief of Staff, simply disregarded the prohibition as contrary to what they had come to consider their most important activity, regardless of their sworn obedience to the ambassador, their temporary superior, and regardless of a concept of honor which had prevailed, at least in part, in the days of Loë and Deines.

---

12 June 23, 1890. Meisner, *Militärattachés*, pp. 55ff.; Hasenclever, *op.cit.*, pp. 608f.

13 Meisner, *Militärattachés*, pp. 73ff. In a further instruction of December 11, 1891, the attachés were told "not to be misled, in their zeal for performing their duties, into steps which, should they become known, could endanger the reputation of the German officer." *Berliner Monatshefte*, XV (1937), 963.

Espionage and Franco-German Relations

Lieutenant Colonel von Schwartzkoppen, the military attaché in Paris from 1891 to 1897, during the first phase of the Dreyfus affair, disobeyed these explicit instructions. "He had always promised me that he would indulge in no spying," Münster, the *grand seigneur* whom old King William I had once called a better nobleman than Bismarck,[14] wrote to Caprivi's successor, Prince Hohenlohe. "The whole diplomatic body is badly hurt by the wicked institution of military attachés. It will be so difficult to make this understood by the Emperor who still clings to it. All this left Schwartzkoppen quite cold, [a man] whom I had always warned against spying and whom I had told that I would not tolerate it."[15] The attaché had found it much easier to disobey his temporary civilian superior than the military hierarchy when, in 1893, he started his relations with Walsin-Esterhazy, one of the truly guilty figures in the affair. Schwartzkoppen had first warned the traitor to abstain from his criminal purpose and then had reported his offer to the Berlin intelligence service. The *Nachrichtenbureau* gave him orders to buy—the agent had threatened to sell what he knew to Russia or Italy, if Germany would not buy, since he was in need of money. The attaché never informed the ambassador of his dealings; for years he paid cash for secret information, unimportant and important—among the latter were new mobilization plans for the French artillery.

When suspicion was first aroused about members of the German embassy, the ambassador asked everyone "officially and on his oath and conscience," whether he had entertained relations with Dreyfus. This Schwartzkoppen could deny, but he remained silent about his connections with Esterhazy. And when Dreyfus was falsely accused of treason, the attaché, on orders from Berlin, could go no further than declaring that he had never had any relations with him and did not know him. Beyond that he was not allowed to testify; the traitor

---

[14] *Documents diplomatiques français*, Ist ser., VIII, no. 12.

[15] April 5 and 13, 1898. *Denkwürdigkeiten des Fürsten Chlodwig zu Hohenlohe-Schillingsfürst*, Vol. III, *Denkwürdigkeiten der Reichskanzlerzeit*, Karl Alexander von Müller, ed. (Stuttgart 1931), 439f.

must not be betrayed whatever the innocent party suffered.[16] Relations with Esterhazy must not be disclosed, Bülow decreed, "for the very reason that such an indiscretion would make it very difficult in the future to obtain information again from agents." Schwartzkoppen was recalled in 1897 to take command of one of the Guards regiments. Belatedly he gave the ambassador an account of his dealings with Esterhazy, and had to swallow Münster's reproaches that he had deliberately lied to him and thus committed a dishonorable action. The ambassador made use of Schwartzkoppen's report in order to help Dreyfus and other victims of the affair as much as he could, but the whole story went down in history as the most vicious by-product of the honorable institution of the military attaché.[17]

Most of the 1880's were years of economic recession and depression. Economic panics were followed by war scares, and armament competition among the powers increased.[18] Nerves were badly frayed, not only among the masses but also in high places, among the political directors ("we are also irritable," Bismarck cried during the Samoan crisis of 1889, on paper, wisely enough)[19] and among the supposedly iron-nerved military men. They all felt "dark forces" on the move and spying was stepped up considerably on both sides of the Vosges; some cases were uncovered and even more suspected. The tensions in French society and politics carried General Boulanger into the ministry of war and might have lifted him still higher had he possessed some "civilian courage" in addition to the military kind, but he was a man who

[16] "All the military attachés (who have the best means of knowing) hold the view of Dreyfus' innocence." Blanche E. C. Dugdale, *Arthur James Balfour*, 2 vols. (New York 1937), I, 201.

[17] The above is based on Bernhard Schwertfeger, *Militärattaché von Schwartzkoppen: Die Wahrheit über Dreyfus* (Berlin 1930); Friedrich Thimme, "Botschafter und Militärattaché," *Europäische Gespräche*, VIII (1930), 147ff.; *Grosse Politik*, XIII, 3586ff.

[18] The Germany military attaché in Paris reported (April 29, 1886) that there was expectation of an early war with Germany even beyond French army circles. Only from such a war did they "expect an improvement of commercial and industrial conditions, a way out of Socialistic disturbances and the political situation untenable in the long run." *Grosse Politik*, VI, 1224.

[19] Vagts, *Deutschland und die Vereinigten Staaten*, p. 655.

shrank more from political power than from war. In April 1886 he rammed through Parliament a more stringent law against espionage which provoked German retaliation, particularly against French visitors to Alsace-Lorraine,[20] and this and other measures made officers in subordinate positions, including Germany's military attachés in Paris, believe that France would seek an early war by provoking Germany into aggression.[21] Not only were there various actual military measures to note, but the idea of *revanche* was revived by orators, both civilian and military, who called upon the French people, "abreuvés d'humiliations imméritées," to keep alive their "fureurs vengereuses" for the favorable moment—which seemed to be approaching.

At first the Berlin General Staff was little inclined to believe in such intentions since France was, materially speaking, not really ready for war, and Bismarck agreed. But then he also succumbed to the generally prevailing armament neurosis, if only to carry a large army bill through Bundesrat and Reichstag with more conviction; however, he could still diagnose Boulanger, relatively objectively, as "a 'primer' for setting off the explosion, perhaps without wanting it, but he makes it more easy."[22] More such "primers" were prepared when, in addition to at least four espionage cases pending or recently judged in German courts, two more became known, partially, as is always the case. Early in April 1887 an employee of the French War Ministry was arrested and charged, probably with some reason, with having sold secrets to one of the German military attachés, Baron von Hoiningen-Huene. The Boulangist press, which the foreign minister protested he could not restrain under French laws guaranteeing freedom of the press, viciously attacked the attaché until the latter warned Clemenceau, the leader of the Left who had not then broken with Boulanger, that a continued press campaign might bring on war. Clemenceau's own paper then warned the general (whom he had originally "invented" and hitherto supported) against continuing such attacks on the German

20 *Documents diplomatiques français*, Ist ser., VIII, nos. 9, 12.
21 *Grosse Politik*, VI, 1223, 1228, 1232.
22 *Ibid.*, VI, 1223, 1234, 1237.

attaché, and Boulanger in his wrath proposed to the council of ministers that military attachés be abolished.[23]

Hardly had the dust settled when another espionage incident, the Schnaebele affair, brought war even closer. A German court established that Schnaebele, a born Alsatian who had opted for France after the loss of Alsace-Lorraine in 1871 and became a French police and frontier commissar, had organized an espionage system working largely in the frontier zone. It was also revealed incidentally that the French preferred to use frontier organizations and humble agents such as charwomen working in the German embassy, on such dirty business, rather than to expose any military attachés.[24] The Germans could not lay hands on Schnaebele, since he had not committed an extraditable crime, but he was finally tricked into crossing the frontier by minor German officials acting on their own initiative. He was caught and jailed, and French indignation rose to fever heat. In the council of ministers on April 23 Boulanger demanded an ultimatum to the Reich Government and the movement of troops in the direction of the frontier. The majority overruled him, however, and on April 29 Bismarck relieved the tension by ordering Schnaebele's release. Boulanger admitted later that France had never been nearer war.

The fight for and against Boulanger continued, with a prolonged ministerial crisis during which Bismarck offered to shelve, at least temporarily, a bill against espionage. This had been occasioned by Boulanger's own earlier law, and would be an indispensable tool against him, but in order not to disturb France during her prolonged ministerial crisis

---

[23] Walter Frank, *Nationalismus und Demokratie im Frankreich der dritten Republik* (*1871 bis 1918*) (Hamburg 1933), pp. 170f.

[24] During a discussion of the Schnaebele case with the French ambassador Herbert Bismarck said that it was bad enough "that an official of the French Government was organizing spying and treason for the latter." When Herbette insisted that his Government did not indulge in such things, Bismarck asked whether he seriously believed that Schnaebele had undertaken this expensive espionage work for his own pleasure, and reminded him that a press communiqué of December 1886, emanating from the War Ministry, had openly declared that the brouillon of a report of one of the German military attachés had come into its possession which proved that organs of the French Government were publicly endorsing the results of espionage. *Grosse Politik*, VI, 1262.

Bismarck was shelving it: a discussion of the bill just at that time might set off much unpleasantness.[25] In the end Boulanger did not continue in the Rue Dominique and was not a member of the new ministry headed by Rouvier.

Paris continued as a market for dealings in military secrets, until the Dreyfus affair spoiled it for a long time. Germany, whose military attaché was in it,[26] and Italy were the most eager buyers of French secrets. Russia, whose "military agent" had earlier suborned one of Napoleon III's ordnance officers, was no longer in the market since she had become France's military ally. Between Fashoda and the conclusion of the British-French entente British attachés had also been occasionally detected as receivers of stolen secrets: for example about 1902 the naval attaché received the letters of a warrant officer, giving exact information about a method of long-distance signaling then being tested, from a secret (counter-espionage?) agent of the Ministry of Marine. Rather than run the risk of endangering the tender growth of the entente, the French Government refrained from demanding the attaché's recall, which would have been the usual result of such discoveries.[27]

An American in Paris

A new buyer appeared in the Paris "thieves' market" in the summer of 1892, when a German military attaché rejected the guilty offers of an employee of the French Ministry of Marine, and the latter traded his secrets to the American military attaché, Captain Borup. The traitor was caught with plans of the Toulon fortifications at Borup's door. Borup had already bought some secrets and was ready to acquire more, perhaps even with his own funds, for he was a wealthy man. When the United States minister, Jefferson Coolidge, queried his attaché about the transaction, the officer admitted everything not only readily but with some pride, "as if it were an advantage to his Department in Washington to have these plans." The minister, more reasonably, thought it "perfectly useless for us to possess plans of seaboard fortresses in France; for even if

[25] *Ibid.*, VI, 1266, 1268. [26] See pp. 218ff.
[27] Beauvais, pp. 103f.

222

war were possible, we have not a fleet to cross 3,000 miles of ocean and attack a French city." French officials, including the foreign minister, and the French press were not only of the same opinion but concluded that the American must have bought the plans for, or sold them to, the German or the Italian attachés, with whom he was known to have been on friendly terms. This Borup and Coolidge denied vigorously (and correctly, for some of Borup's acquisitions arrived in Washington), but the press took the opportunity, as Count Münster complained at the Quai d'Orsay, to attack in the most hateful way all other attachés and in particular the German ones, who were entitled to protection by the French Government against such insults.

Coolidge obtained Borup's recall and made him leave France at once, in order to avoid personal incidents and possibly duels with French officers. The French Government, and probably Minister Coolidge, expected that Borup would be punished for his flagrant breach of international hospitality, but he never was. Actually, we know of only one case of an attaché having been punished for involvement in espionage by his superiors, except indirectly for the maladroitness that had led to his exposure.[28] The French were told by Washington that if they wanted him tried—and it would be in public—they would have to submit the evidence, and for this they were not ready even though they continued to press the case for a time. Coolidge, a "proper Bostonian," wrote privately to Secretary of State Foster that it was a mistake to send abroad military attachés who "are young and zealous but who cannot find out what they want without adopting improper means." Foster had practically no influence over the selection of officers for such posts, and it can only be surmised that he forwarded the letter to the War Department and that the latter, judging by the subsequent history of American service attachés, proceeded to dampen their zeal for espionage for a long time. It still saw no reason to disgrace Borup who was appointed in the next year, presumably on account of his linguistic abilities, to a committee

[28] The Grow case of 1951-1953; see above p. 98.

to receive distinguished foreigners at the Chicago Fair. This caused another flare-up in Paris, where resentment about the espionage episode had already made the Government veto Paris as the seat of the Bimetallic Conference, a pet project of the Americans. The French press declared the appointment another insult, doubtless a result of mischief-making at the German and English embassies, and the Government threatened to withdraw its exhibit unless Borup was removed. This was done, in order not to endanger the success of the World's Fair.[29]

For and Against Russia

The alliances for the 1914 war lessened espionage activities as far as the service attachés were concerned. It seemed useless, and a danger to the harmony of the alliance to spy on the ally. While a few gentlemen-spies, a new species of young officers on leave, scouting in the land of the future enemy with or without the knowledge and consent of their superiors,[30] were caught in the act of photographing and sketching fortifications and condemned to mild terms of honorable imprisonment, the service attachés were withdrawn from the shady side of intelligence activities by most powers. When the French military attaché in Copenhagen in 1893 overtaxed the friendly services of Princess Waldemar (née Marie d'Orleans) in order to obtain secret information on Anglo-Russian relations, the French Government recalled the zealous attaché, and indeed nearly the whole legation staff.[31]

Only in Russia did the service attachés continue to do business directly with betrayers of military secrets. Judging by the number of discoveries and revelations, Russian attachés were the most unscrupulous buyers of secrets on the eve of 1914. The German attachés had at last taken to heart Caprivi's instructions against spying, as patently more honest and

[29] T. Jefferson Coolidge, *An Autobiography* (Boston 1923); Beckles Willson, *America's Ambassadors to France, 1777-1927* (New York 1928), pp. 350-352, 358; Münster to Auswärtiges Amt, July 3, 1892; Ketteler, chargé at Washington, to same, June 30, 1892. *Archives of Auswärtiges Amt.*

[30] For such cases see *Grosse Politik*, VII, 1605ff.; IX, 2351; XXVIII, 10454.

[31] Wladimir d'Ormesson, *Enfances diplomatiques* (Paris 1932), p. 29.

certainly more practical. These rules were still in force in 1914 and apparently still respected—the last case of a recall of a German attaché for espionage seems to have been that of a naval attaché in St. Petersburg in 1893. In 1914 the military attaché in that capital had "no so-called illegal sources of information" at his disposal. "On the contrary, I had been told at the beginning of my tour of duty by the Chief of Staff of the Army that the use of such means was formally prohibited. Besides, no funds of any kind would have been at my disposal for such purposes."[32]

In Austro-Russian diplomatic relations since the early 1890's there is only one case of the recall of an Austrian service attaché, because of connections with Russian officers convicted of treason in 1902, compared with several cases of Russians recalled from Vienna for comparable reasons. Impunity, and even promotion in spite of discovery, seem to have been incentives for such activities in the Russian services, and respect for diplomatic considerations proved no check on them. Not only was the Russian attaché in Vienna in 1892, Colonel Zouiev, an ardent Pan-Slavist, according to his French colleague, but the office of "this representative of the Russian Army in Austria was not properly speaking that of a military attaché but rather approaches that of the chief of an intelligence service. Zouiev made no bones about this concept of his office duties even to the Austrians: he told them he knew all that he wanted to know, including the office secrets of their Chief of Staff, General Beck. The general allowed him the greatest liberties in his tall talk, and quietly made his *dossier* larger and larger. In the meanwhile Beck himself was directing a vast net of espionage and insurrectionary preparations in Russian Poland.[33]

Immediately after Nicholas II's first visit to Vienna in 1896, which the Austrians had tried hard to turn into a splendid affair of state, their police discovered that the Russian mili-

[32] Lieut. Col. von Eggeling, *Die russische Mobilmachung und der Kriegsausbruch* (Oldenburg and Berlin 1919), p. 8. The German military attaché in London about 1905 was under orders to refrain from spying; he even handed the offer by an Englishman to sell him information to the War Office, which had the informant prosecuted. Gleichen, p. 253.
[33] *Documents diplomatiques français*, Ist ser., X, 71ff.

tary attaché Voronin was involved in an espionage case. Goluchowski wanted to air it in public, but Beck, who had his reasons for a temporary halt in Austro-Russian arms competition, managed to keep the case from public knowledge, a discretion for which the recent visitor—the Tsar—expressed his gratitude.[34]

In 1914 occurred the infamous case of Colonel Redl, chief of staff of the Prague army corps, who remained the highest ranking traitor for quite some time. The Russian attaché had bought secrets of superior importance from him, including apparently the names of Austria's intelligence agents inside Russia.[35] And in 1910 there had been the case of Colonel Martchenko, the Russian military attaché who bought the services of a non-commissioned officer in the Vienna Arsenal. The Austrian made a full confession, but the Russians, although confronted with the evidence, declined for months to recall the colonel. By way of retaliation they trumped up a case, which they maintained was similar, against a Russian journalist who was accused of having given the Austrian military attaché in St. Petersburg secret information (it was information that could be called secret only because the Russians habitually declared very many things secret which were not so considered in other countries). But the Russians insisted that the cases were comparable and that the Austrian must be recalled simultaneously with their man.[36] When the Russian ambassador defended Martchenko, Aehrenthal demonstrated his guilt and remarked, "how desirable it would be that the Russian military attachés should receive the same instructions which ours [the Austrian] had been given some ten years ago and which forbade them any and all spying activity and relations with spies." Prince Urusov, as a diplomat of the old school, seemed to share this view and so reported to St. Petersburg,[37] but the military there were far less ready to admit any culpability.

[34] von Glaise Horstenau, p. 383.
[35] Conrad, III, 329f., 340, 345, 368; Grosse Politik, XXXV, 13370.
[36] Grosse Politik, XXVII, 9941f.
[37] Oesterreich-Ungarns Aussenpolitik, II, 2186. This directive was not always followed by the Austrian attachés. In the summer of 1909 Serbian courts condemned an Austrian commercial traveler, who had worked

When the two attachés had been removed and the question of a successor was discussed in Vienna, for a long time Aehrenthal and the Emperor could not bring themselves to agree to the candidate of Conrad, the Chief of Staff, though he seemed well qualified for the post. Less plagued by scruples, the Russians, without seeking an *agrément* first, sent as the new attaché a lieutenant-colonel whom Austrians knew to be specially charged with collecting information and with writing a handbook on the Austrian Army. In order not to appear obstinate, the Austrians gave their *agrément* after, rather than before, his arrival in Vienna.[38]

Naturally, after these incidents, the Russian encountered great circumspection, something which surprised no one but his war minister, Suchomlimov, who told the Austrian attaché in St. Petersburg that his most recently appointed attaché "did not find the kind of reception in Vienna which he had expected, and that he learned practically nothing there"; should Austria wish it, Russia would be willing to replace him. Conrad thanked Suchomlimov for his frankness. There was nothing to criticize in the new attaché, he said, but it should not cause surprise that after the unfortunate experiences with both his predecessors he was meeting with a certain reserve. In telling his story to the German attaché, Conrad ended with a sigh: "I fear we are facing difficult times."[39] A little later, the Russian Ambassador Shebeko appeared at the Ballplatz to give assurances that the new attaché had strict orders not to follow in the footsteps of Martchenko and that he himself, as a matter of principle, had never suffered in any embassy under his direction any attempt at espionage and that he would continue to adhere to this principle. He was even willing to admit that Austria had been sinned against, but hoped that a new era in the exchange of attachés might open and that bygones would be bygones.

Russia's espionage system before 1914, more under the

---

for the attaché at Belgrade, to the very severe jail term of 16 years. *Ibid.*, II, 1769.

[38] Conrad, II, 52f.

[39] *Grosse Politik*, XXXIX, 15853 (March 17, 1914).

immediate direction of her service attachés than that of any other great power, was particularly anxious to penetrate the secrets of the minor powers in her neighborhood. Both Rumania and Sweden, for example, might join with the Central Powers in case of war. The Rumanians, who were actually drifting away from the Triple Alliance, were convinced, or at any rate so assured the Austrians, that on the eve of the Balkan Wars "the whole Russian espionage service as far as directed against Rumania" had for years been concentrated in the hands of the Russian military attaché in Sofia, Colonel Romanovsky, a man who did not hesitate to accuse his Rumanian colleague of espionage in order to cover his own tracks. The Austrians knew Romanovsky as "a very capable, highly educated officer," and followed his extramilitary activities in the forming of the Balkan War alliances closely—they far surpassed those of the Russian minister in Sofia.[40]

It was widely believed in the Russian Army before 1914 that Sweden would join the Central Powers in case of a war with Russia—"Germany and Sweden are at war against Russia" was the assumption on which maneuvers of the St. Petersburg army corps in August 1910 were based[41]—so it was not surprising that she was the object of much attention on the part of the two Russian attachés stationed in Stockholm. Since Sweden was only a minor power, she found it even more difficult than did Austria to get them recalled, although she tried repeatedly, and for ample reasons, from 1912 on. It was at last admitted at the Saengerbrücke in November 1913 that the removal of at least the military attaché was justified, and he was transferred, but the diplomatic tension was not at once lessened by this act of condescension on Russia's part and still seemed to require Poincaré's mediatory service when he touched Stockholm on his St. Petersburg trip in July 1914.[42] "Never before had Russian diplomacy in Stockholm

[40] For Romanovsky see below, pp. 228 and 333f.
[41] Grosse Politik, XXVII, 9950.
[42] Die internationalen Beziehungen im Zeitalter des Imperialismus (USSR), Ist ser., IV, 278; Documents diplomatiques français, IIIrd ser., XI, 194. In July 1950 Swedish police patrols ordered the Soviet naval attaché in Stockholm to keep his motor boat away from the coastal defense

been in such a painful position," according to the last Tsarist minister in that capital.[43]

The last prewar scandal provoked by a military attaché's spying, the last also to be sufficiently clear from accessible diplomatic documents, was the involvement of the Russian military attaché in Berlin, Colonel Basarov, in the treason case of Pohl and Associates. Pohl was a quartermaster-sergeant in the Great General Staff who had sold plans of German fortresses in the East to the Russians and was subsequently condemned to 15 years of forced labor, the maximum penalty. Russian diplomacy again would not at once believe that the attaché might be guilty. When Sasonov and his Berlin ambassador were first informed, in confidence, by the Berlin authorities who were anxious to avoid scandal, they were both reluctant to admit that the removal of the colonel was advisable. Considering the admittedly bad state of German-Russian relations at the time and the fact that a similar request had been made only two years before, they expressed fear that there might be dangerous repercussions unless the Reich Government submitted irrefutable proof of the attaché's responsibility. Actually, the minister and ambassador badly needed that proof in order to face their own military men, and they would not listen to the German proposal for a discreet removal of Basarov—he might depart, ostensibly on leave, and stay away. But when Sasonov screwed up his courage to inquire in the Russian War Ministry whether the accused was guilty, he learned that Basarov "was actually culpable of a certain imprudence and that his prolonged stay in Germany seemed therefore undesirable"; for this reason he had already been told to come home on leave at once. (He departed from Berlin, but soon afterward applied for permission to return. This proved too much for even the usually deferential Russian embassy and permission was denied.)

---

installations near which he had been found cruising. *The New York Times*, August 2, 1950.

[43] Anatolii V. Nekludoff, *Diplomatic Reminiscences before and during the World War, 1911-1917* (New York 1920), pp. 265, 275f., 293.

Diplomatic hopes of keeping the incident quiet were shattered by the avidity of the press for espionage cases. On July 10 the *Berliner Tageblatt* printed details about the impending trial of Pohl and about his corrupter Basarov, protesting that official personages such as military attachés and others protected by international law were misusing their prerogatives. This set off one of several German-Russian press exchanges preceding the First World War. The *Novoie Vremia* declared that the Pohl Case showed how far morals were corrupted in Germany, where military men were ready to sell their own country, whereupon Schiemann (in the *Kreuzzeitung*) obliged with a few cases of Russian traitors.[44] For the Russians the removal of their attaché at this time had a special disadvantage: they had no one in the Embassy able to report expertly on German military measures during July 1914. The Austrian ambassador, whose home authorities were no less plagued with cases of Russian espionage, was told in the Wilhelmstrasse that it was "Unbelievable in what a widespread and at the same time shameless manner Russia was carrying on espionage inside Germany; without exaggeration, on the average one case per diem of Russian espionage inside Germany was being uncovered.[45]

Every military and naval power in Europe and Asia was spying and spied upon before August 1914, even though most of them had retired the attachés from this kind of duty. Britain was spying on German naval constructions and fortifications,[46] and was being spied on by Germany (as she had been spied on by her later allies before the formation of the *Entente Cordiale*). A set of drawings of the Dover and Channel fortifications was stolen from Campbell-Bannerman's desk when he was Secretary of State for War in Gladstone's last cabinet; they ended up in French hands. It was also a matter of record that the Russian military attaché in London at the end of the nineteenth century was in the market for secrets, and some "quite good fabricated news about guns and

[44] *Die internationalen Beziehungen*, Ist ser., IV, 31, 85f., 95, 115, 122, 181f.

[45] *Oesterreich-Ungarns Aussenpolitik*, VIII, 10278.

[46] *Grosse Politik*, XXVIII, 10454, for such a case.

other military matters" had been planted upon him.[47] According to a member of the intelligence division of the British War Office at the time, "this sort of thing was not much in our line; it was not really worth the trouble, the best plan being to assume that the potential enemy kept everything up to date, and to adopt measures accordingly if this were possible. But foreigners are often imbued with the idea that something secret must necessarily be of great value to their respective countries. In fact, my view always was—and experience has only tended to confirm it—that the results of secret service are usually negligible."[48] This could hardly, however, have been the view of the majority of officers in intelligence departments.

Espionage in the Totalitarian Age

Spying and the fear of spies were parts of political consciousness and subconsciousness in Europe and, probably a little later, in the western hemisphere.[49] Encirclement was a haunting anxiety. Fear was bound to reach its acme when the outside enemy was suspected of being in league with a domestic enemy, the traitor—or, even worse, with organized mass traitors. An American accusation of Nazi Germany, in an espionage case that was breaking in 1938, at a time of mounting American sentiment against Germany, was never fully developed; it lacked the hoped-for link with the German-American *Bund*, as the supposed agent organization directed from Berlin. The case was discussed among the diplomats, and the Germans complained that the Americans had brought "the names of high German intelligence and air service officers into the case," such as that of Admiral Canaris, head of the German *Abwehr*—something not usually done in counterespionage, for "government officials of a so-called friendly nation should not be named in espionage resistance by another nation."[50]

[47] Waters, *"Secret and Confidential,"* pp. 35f., 248.   [48] *Ibid.,* p. 36.
[49] Two Japanese assistant naval attachés in Washington, protected by diplomatic immunity, were mentioned as co-conspirators in the trial of Lieut. Cmdr. Farnsworth in August 1936. He had sold them secret naval documents. *The New York Times*, August 12, 1936, and later.
[50] Associated Press dispatch from Washington, June 25, 1938.

By this time, the sources and the channels of intelligence were firmly integrated in the Foreign, Intelligence and Security Service attached to the OKW, and its secrets were presided over by Admiral Canaris. The Central section, the *Abwehr*, took care of secret intelligence, sabotage and special duties, security, counterespionage and countersabotage; the Foreign Section (*Abteilung Ausland*) received and processed attaché reports, was responsible for liaison between OKW and Wilhelmstrasse, and between OKW and the attachés, both the German officers abroad, who were kept informed about developments at home by "a regular précis of information received," and the foreign attachés stationed in Berlin.[51]

When the Germans had started appointing service attachés again in 1933, the Reichswehr minister and the chief of staff, at the demand of the Wilhelmstrasse, had positively forbidden them to indulge in "illegal activity" of any kind, much against the wishes of Canaris, who cited one of Hitler's own orders demanding such activities. The military attaché for London, Colonel Geyr von Schweppenburg, protested strongly: nothing could be more foolish than for the first set of postwar service attachés to indulge in espionage under the watchful eyes of the British Secret Service. "I would either go to London as a gentleman or not at all and begged to suggest to the chief of staff another use for me if my unshakable standpoint in this matter should not be recognized." This honorable attitude was accepted, and helped Geyr to establish good relations with the British military, who allowed him to see what they considered safe.[52] It is doubtful, however, whether this discretion was maintained after Geyr left London in 1937—by that time Nazism had begun to

[51] Paul Leverkühn, *German Intelligence Service* (New York 1954), pp. 28, 63, etc.

[52] Geyr, *Erinnerungen*, pp. 9ff. While the British freely admitted foreign observers to their general field maneuvers, "mere eyewash" as Geyr termed them, they kept them strictly away from such special exercises as landing operations. It was known that one influential school inside the British Army laid great stress on such operations in the war to come and the German military attaché advised the home authorities to treat a large-scale British landing attempt in a *Kriegsspiel*. The warning went unheeded. *Ibid.*, p. 64.

permeate all Reich institutions, including the foreign posts.[53] At the very time that the Nazis complained in America about the decay of international manners (and perhaps with some justice, though the complaint did not come well from them) they gave orders to German missions abroad that "in view of recent developments" Reich consulates would henceforth, in peace or war, be considered part of the system for obtaining military intelligence. They were to cooperate with the service attachés, whose "judgment on military requirements is decisive." However, since "the requirements of the Foreign Service do not permit of the Service Attachés' entering into direct contact with the Consulates and giving them instructions," it seemed unsuitable that the consuls should report directly to the attachés, less direct channels of correspondence were arranged.[54]

Even fewer restraints were observed once the Second World War had erupted. "The old intelligence methods are no longer useful," the German Minister in Oslo agreed with his naval attaché in February 1940, when on orders, and with funds, from Berlin they not only financed the Quisling party, but enabled that traitor to organize an intelligence network along the Norwegian coast and on Norwegian ships, headed by Quisling himself and manned by his followers. Quisling was to transmit the reports to the German Legation, where

[53] For the order of the Luftwaffe General Staff, Intelligence Division, to the air attaché in Prague of August 1938 to reconnoiter certain Czech regions for landing possibilities personally, see *Trial of the Major War Criminals*, III, 45.

[54] Circular dispatch of June 28, 1938. Top secret. *Documents on German Foreign Policy*, Ser. D, II, 444ff. For the activities of the attachés in Washington from 1939 on see *Trial of the Major War Criminals*, XXXIV, 115f. Using consuls for purposes of intelligence was by no means a new international practice, the Nazis merely systematized it. For an older case: during the American-German tension of summer 1898, the U.S. Navy Department regularly received newspaper clippings from Kiel and Wilhelmshaven about the movements of German navy vessels. When the Department censured the attaché in Berlin for not having reported the departure of the transport SS. "Darmstadt" to Manila on May 4, he explained the oversight: he had arrived at his post only on the 3rd, "which hardly gave me time to 'catch on'; however, the U.S. consul at Singapore where the 'Darmstadt' passed through, ought to have reported." Cmdr. Barber to Navy Department, August 9, 1898. *National Archives.*

the naval attaché "promised himself a great deal from these facilities. In Norway we have an opportunity to operate through a political movement, the followers of which act by conviction"—hence they are more reliable and also cheaper than the old system of paid agents.[55] The Nazis could hardly have been unaware that the Communists had preceded them in using agents who spied from political or religious conviction,[56] and who indulged in activities from which the Soviet service attachés were excluded, at least on the surface.[57]

The Western powers began, a little late, to imitate the totalitarians, though their contacts with and use of the German Resistance, which might have been the counterpart of the totalitarians' organization behind the enemy lines, were half-hearted and remained so to the end. These contacts were probably fewer than the Nazis expected; from the beginning the regime was convinced that "secret information [about German rearmament] is being daily received in great quantity by the foreign military attachés here" in Berlin.[58] Not until 1940-1941 did the United States Chief of Staff, General Marshall, give orders "to initiate legislation to improve U.S. espionage and counterespionage."[59] The United States Embassy at Vichy, with an admiral at its head, became the center of intelligence in Europe, and agents in the disguise of naval and other attachés were stationed there for spying purposes. According to Ambassador-Admiral Leahy, "our attachés had excellent contacts and kept me completely informed of what they were doing. An Ambassador may choose to 'forget' some of the things he is told. Intelligence is not a subject to be discussed freely at any time. No mention of this

[55] *Documents on German Foreign Policy*, Ser. D, VIII, 797f. About the actual value of the intelligence furnished by the Quislingists see T. Kingston Derry, *The Campaign in Norway* (London 1952), pp. 17f.

[56] For the activities of such "modern, Puritan types of spy, motivated entirely by idealism and devotion," see Arthur Koestler, *The Invisible Writing* (Boston 1955), pp. 301ff.

[57] Voroshilov assured the German ambassador that in spite of the deterioration of German-Russian relations after Hitler's coming to power, "he had ordered his military attachés on pain of severe punishment not to carry on any espionage activity of any sort whatsoever." *Documents on German Foreign Policy*, Ser. C, I, 422.

[58] *Ibid.*, Ser. C, II, 72.   [59] Watson, p. 54.

important activity was made in my conversations with the President when we discussed the Vichy appointment."[60]

The declared moratorium on class warfare among the so-called democratic powers during the war against the Axis was never an altogether honest one, except on the popular level where complicated diplomatic considerations and procedures were simplified into a sort of "Mission to Moscow" film. To such a mentality the thought of spying on a coalition partner would have seemed unjustified indeed. This condition of mind, outlasting the war, was rudely shaken when on February 15, 1946, the Canadian Government publicly stated that personnel of the Russian Embassy in Ottawa under the direction of Colonel Nicolai Zabotin, principal military attaché, and in cooperation with Canadian and British nationals, had engaged in espionage activities against Canada and to a lesser extent against the United States, at least since March 1945. They had tried to obtain minutely specified information, including data on the atomic bomb. The discovery, made with the help of a Russian on the embassy staff, was so shocking to the Canadian official mind that the statement was given out before an official complaint had been made to the Russians. For once following the usual diplomatic practice, Russia complained that this statement about a fairly common incident had been made without "previously asking an explanation from the Soviet Government, as is expected between countries maintaining normal relations." The military attaché was recalled at once by Moscow "in view of the inadmissibility" of his activities, and it was maintained that "the Soviet ambassador and other members of the Soviet embassy in Canada had no connection whatsoever with the matter." The Russians also tried to emphasize "the insignificance of the circumstances," since they already possessed the information brought to them by eager Canadian traitors without the incitement of pay (a disquieting innovation in espionage?), but insignificance is certainly not the *mot juste*, from any mass-psychological viewpoint.[61]

[60] William D. Leahy, *I Was There* (New York 1950), pp. 22, 57, 69ff.
[61] *The New York Times*, February 16, 21 and 22; March 5, 1946. As an eager defender of the Soviet case, former ambassador Joseph E. Davies

Traffic with spies is most often a sign of official national hostility, more rarely the outcome of zeal—of a defense department or, more rarely still, of a service attaché. The rationale of spying lies in the presumption that war between the countries involved is not beyond the bounds of possibility; it is an adjunct of secret diplomacy. Though it may often lie outside the knowledge of the diplomats themselves, the latter will know better than the general public where the line is drawn. When the public learns that an espionage case has "broken," it is inclined to presume that relations between the two countries must be bad indeed, if spying is required. It is an additional shock when one's compatriots or neighbors are suspected or convicted of giving aid and comfort to the potential enemy. Hence the terrific impact of the Canadian spy case and of the Coplon, Hiss and Rosenberg cases of 1946 to 1952.

Another espionage case received, in comparison, little attention. The American military attaché at Buenos Aires in 1946 was buying military information from a clerk in the Argentine ministry of war; this was discovered and the attaché recalled, while the clerk was sentenced to a prison term. While diplomatic relations between Peron and the State Department were obviously bad, were they so bad at the time that war, and the procuring of information necessary only in the case of war, had to be undertaken? Or did the information wanted refer to warlike intentions on Peron's part against one or more of the South American Governments? Or was it another Borup case?

The theory that service attachés or other members of embassies, legations, or trade commissions do not spy, a theory

---

maintained publicly that "Russia in self-defense has every moral right to seek atomic bomb secrets through military espionage if excluded from such information by her former fighting allies." Such a statement, considering the Russians' own declaration about "inadmissibility," was more than a student of diplomacy would have expected, least of all from an experienced lawyer after his client had made this admission in court. For Russian intelligence activity directed against atomic research in the United States in 1944-1945, a question never raised with the State Department by Russian diplomacy, see Edward R. Stettinius, *Roosevelt and the Russians* (New York 1949), p. 34.

strengthened by actual practice at certain periods, for example immediately before 1914, was one of those polite fictions by which diplomacy has been carried on in the past. It was finally torn to shreds by the spy trials which various satellite governments instituted, and which were in most cases intended to compromise foreign service attachés. The testimony elicited in the Vogeler case, for instance, was used by the Budapest Communist Government to demand the recall of two British and three American service attachés as no longer *persona grata*. The two Western governments complied, in accordance with diplomatic practice, while "wholly rejecting" Hungary's stated reasons for the recall, which included reduction of the "overswollen number of the staff" of the American Legation (seven officers and no less than 103 Hungarian employees).[62] Such treatment was paralleled in Poland,[63] and was one of the features of the cold war. Indeed, within the Russian orbit all foreign service attachés came to be considered most untrustworthy, as spies above all other spies. The Soviet general who conducted all Moscow business with the attachés told one of them: "Every foreign service attaché, no matter how he conducted his life in Moscow, was regarded as a spy by the Soviet authorities."[64]

The opposition camp, and the remaining neutrals, felt much the same way. Sweden, in her exposed position on Russia's flank and in spite of her reaffirmed neutrality, was the object of much Russian spying: from 1948 to 1952 she asked nine Russian embassy members to leave Stockholm because of espionage, which had been supplemented by the work of service attachés from such satellite states as Poland[65]

[62] *The New York Times*, February 19, March 11 and 12, 1950.
[63] For the "vivid" concepts entertained by the Polish Reds about the spying activities of American, Canadian and British service attachés in their country since 1947 see *ibid.*, December 12, 1950. Tito, *per contra*, early in 1951, for the first time since the close of the war, invited the military attachés of the United States, Britain, France and Italy to witness exercises based on the idea of "carrying on guerrilla warfare after the inevitable retreat from the plains," that is to say, the likeness of the second stage of a war with Russia and the satellites. *Frankfurter Allgemeine Zeitung*, January 17, 1951.
[64] Hilton, p. 8.
[65] *The New York Times*, July 17 and 18, 1952.

or Czechoslovakia. A British engineer was sentenced in July 1938 to fourteen years imprisonment—a stiff sentence—for having "sold secrets of vital importance for the safety of the country," thereby jeopardizing "the lives of thousands of citizens," to the Czech military attaché. By the time the case came to court the Czech had left London.[66] The satellites, in fact, were helpful both as assistant spies and as assistant bouncers—after the upheaval of 1956 Hungary expelled first a British and then an American military attaché, accusing both of having taken an active part in the revolt.[67] NATO members such as Denmark, Belgium and France attracted similar Russian attention, and found it necessary to ask Russian and Czech attachés to leave; Czechoslovakia retaliated by demanding the recall of Belgian and French military and other attachés.[68] When the supply of military attachés was exhausted—or their assistants who were sometimes considered more expendable[69]—commercial or other attachés were accused of military espionage and expelled. In one case, at least, the United States retaliated in kind.[70] Never, of course, was any impropriety admitted by either side. When the cold war abated, after the Geneva summit meeting, restrictions on the service attachés could be eased: in December 1955, the United States Army, without insisting on reciprocity, took the Russian and four satellite attachés to Louisiana, together with attachés of 30 other nations, and let them watch at least the first half of the country's biggest postwar maneuvers.[71]

Whenever the cold war became hotter, it was usually marked by the discovery of a spy case and the request for the recall of some diplomatic personnel, not always service attachés.[72] They were usually accused of having been caught in

[66] *Ibid.*, July 19, 1958.

[67] *Ibid.*, January 19, April 14, May 3, 1957.

[68] *Ibid.*, February 2, 1952, January 24, 1953, January 29, February 28 and October 14, 1957.

[69] For the break-up of a Soviet spy ring in Italy, headed by the secretary to the military attaché of the Soviet embassy, see *The New York Times*, April 24 and May 20, 1958.

[70] *Ibid.*, April 19, 1958, and later.   [71] *Ibid.*, December 12, 1955.

[72] For the case of a Russian military attaché in Ottawa caught while handing money to a Canadian citizen for supposed secrets see *ibid.*, December 12, 1961.

the act of spying on defense installations or of suborning some minor personnel of the armed services—sometimes, more ominously, the higher-ups. It has been said, somewhat smugly, that "secret service is such a dirty business that only a gentleman can safely deal with it." Service attachés, as gentlemen-spies, have withstood the corruptive milieu of espionage and counterespionage, as far as the record is known, at least to the extent of not selling themselves to the enemy, until the cold war. Then, in 1962-1963, two cases (or was it one?) were revealed: former service attachés, one on each side, who had sold themselves to the enemy. Oleg P. Penkovsky, deputy head of the Foreign Department of the State Committee for the Coordination of Scientific Research in Russia, was arrested in the autumn of 1962 for spying in the interest of Great Britain and the United States, and sentenced to death by a military tribunal in May 1963. He confessed the betrayal of technological secrets to a British agent, who was also caught and sentenced, and to members of the two Anglo-Saxon embassies in Moscow, who were asked to leave or not return to their posts. Penkovsky's earlier services included a tour of duty as military attaché in Turkey in 1956.[73] His body had hardly begun to molder in an unmarked grave when Swedish authorities divulged the case of Colonel Sig Wennerström, ret., a former air attaché. Wennerström had served in Moscow in the 1940's, doing some spying for the Germans; after his return to Stockholm he offered his services to the Russians for 5,000 Kroner as a starter, and continued to work for them during his second assignment to Moscow, from 1948 on, and still later in Washington (1952-1957). In the American capital he became the senior service attaché and was decorated by the Americans, who fondly supposed that as the emissary of a neutral power he was working in their interest. For a time he felt like "a double agent," when "in fact he was selling 'a lot of information' about American defense to the Soviet Union." Much of this was confided readily by various Americans, some of whom, after the close of the Korean War, were eager to sell Sweden air weap-

73 *Ibid.*, December 14, 1962, May 12 and 14, 1963.

ons through this friendly member of a purchasing commission.

Sweden employed Wennerström after 1961 as a disarmament expert in their Foreign Office, which thus also became a source of information for the Russians. Only slowly and reluctantly did the Swedish officials become aware of his treasonable activities, but at last they prosecuted him for "gross espionage," for having sold the secrets of Sweden and of friendly powers to Russia for some fifteen years—and "for financial gains," as the prosecution stressed, much as if ideological motivation would have been less despicable. The Colonel readily admitted much of this story, perhaps even embroidering on it. He claimed the character of an idealist seeking "to preserve the peace and the power balance of the world," threatened as it seemed to him by American preponderance and such "offensively oriented" American intelligence work as that undertaken by men like General Grow, whose notebook on targets inside the Soviet Union had been denounced by the Russians. The Russians, so Wennerström declared, were acting "purely defensively," the same argument used by Klaus Fuchs and another Western spy for Russia. The rewards for Wennerström included the strange, because in the nature of things secret, honor of the rank of major general in the Russian Intelligence Service, and a number of medals which he could never display.

The scandal, without precedence in the institution of service attachés, rocked the Swedish Social Democratic Government, which was accused with a good deal of justification of negligence in its supervision of the Colonel. The damage done to the Swedish defense system, which had to be rearranged at vast cost, staggered the military imagination. After a trial, most of it in secret session, the traitor was condemned to hard labor for life, which under the humane Swedish regulations makes him eligible for parole in ten years. While waiting for release he is said to ask for ever more spy stories for his reading.

Enough about the man's motivation and psyche has become known through the published portion of the Swedish investigations to describe Wennerström and his milieu—though not all his assertions have been acknowledged by his presumed American partners. The image emerges of an aviator not very good at flying and hence passed over for promotion—in such a situation "one soon feels distinctly that one has been slighted," as he himself expressed it. Resentment against his superiors and against his homeland in general developed weaknesses apparent to the Russians, who offered him, besides material rewards, honors that fed his ego such as the code name "the Eagle," supposedly conferred by a Military Intelligence Service general assigned as his "handler." This "handler," a term probably taken over from the sporting world of dog shows into this twilight world of "intelligence work," knew very well how to manipulate Wennerström; he was able to instill a kind of enthusiasm in the traitor through an "almost hypnotic ability to carry people along," and to induce "a significant feeling of loyalty, towards himself and the Russian intelligence system." Wennerström became such an "eager beaver" that, as he told his interrogator, at times his "ability to deliver was much greater than the receiver's capacity to work upon the material," and he was often left "with a very strong sense of having accomplished something and of having reached a high level of prestige."

That such a spy could continue his work so long was largely because of his position, his "insider" connections as the son of a military family, and because he was a man of impeccable manners and an artist in protective coloration who could remain inconspicuous in the most exposed situations. He also had on his side that solidarity, prevailing nationally and supranationally among men in uniform, that leads to confidence and confidences; this esprit de corps left him generally above suspicion to his comrades—but not to his Swedish charwoman.[74]

[74] *The New York Times,* June 26, 1963 and after; July 29, 1963 (Hanson Baldwin); May 27 and 30, 1964; *Time,* May 8 and June 13, 1964; 88th Congress, 2d. Sess., Senate Committee on the Judiciary, *The Wennerström Spy Case. How it Touched the U.S. and NATO.* Washington, December 1964. A first "history" of the Wennerström case is H. K. Rosenbloem, *W. Spionen,* Stockholm 1965. In English there is Thomas Whiteside, *An Agent in Place: The Wennerström Affair,* New York 1966.

CHAPTER 12

ATTACHÉS AND WAR ECONOMY

Wars were part of that force that served as midwife to the progress of capitalist production—capitalism as consequence of war, not as its cause.[1] To a certain extent they still are. And yet, warmakers of the last 150 years, including their most advanced agents, the service attachés, as a rule realized but little of the war function or potentiality of a nation's economy until after war had started—or until after it was over, its history being written and its lessons contemplated.[2] War economy, economy as part of purposeful preparation by the war specialists, is a late concept, after 1914, unless it be considered a recrudescence of older concepts such as formed part of Mercantilism.

The diplomacies should be prepared to envisage a country's economic potential in a war. It is startling to realize, however, that nineteenth-century diplomats paid less attention than did the Venetians of the Renaissance to the various factors which comprise a nation's war potential, or to movements of capital from one country to another and their influence on the warmaking ability of the powers concerned. Such international movements were, in fact, considered by nineteenth-century diplomacy as a kind of golden lubricating system which helped to keep the peace. As long as there were peaceful relations between Germany and Russia, for example, including rather intimate relations between the two armies, Berlin gave little thought to the consequences of another Russian

[1] For this problem see Werner Sombart, *Krieg und Kapitalismus* (Leipzig and Munich 1913).

[2] For the economic preparation of the First World War in Berlin see Reichsarchiv, *Der Weltkrieg 1914-1918. Kriegsrüstung und Kriegswirtschaft*, 2 vols. (Berlin 1930). For the remarks of a German banker on "financial readiness for war" and his surprise at the neglect of the problem, see Max Warburg, *Aus meinem Aufzeichnungen* (n.p. 1952), p. 23.

loan of 60 million marks which accompanied the renewal of the Three Emperors' Alliance in 1884.

Estrangement between Russia and Germany began with the soldiers—the Russians first—rather than the diplomats; it never extended to the bankers. German attachés and the Great General Staff began, from 1882 on, to question whether German capital export to Russia ought to continue, since the recipient, if not already an enemy, seemed on the verge of becoming one. Soldiers, and above all the military attaché in St. Petersburg, rather than the Wilhelmstrasse and its representatives, drew attention to the military dangers inherent in this continued German capital export to Russia. Finally, in the late 1880's, governmental measures were devised to at least slow up the outflow of capital to Russia, although Bismarck believed as late as 1889 that "the strengthening of Russia for war was far less dangerous than Social Democracy" (that common enemy which would in the end induce reconciliation with Russia).[3] Instead, militarism gained the upper hand in Berlin and St. Petersburg, and proceeded to manipulate the Chancellor's dismissal, which had had its beginning in the clash of civilian and military opinion over German capital export to Russia. The young Emperor read military attaché reports about how dangerous this flow of capital might be to Germany's military security, and would not listen to the Chancellor's explanations.[4]

German investments in Russia never stopped completely, but most of the necessary foreign capital, particularly in the form of government loans, was henceforth supplied by the Paris market, which was more strictly under government

[3] *Historische Vierteljahrsschrift*, XXXI (1936-1937), 760f. Occasionally a service attaché would touch on Socialism and "class war," which were usually considered to be factors tending to weaken a great power's potential or perhaps to incline it toward war as the way out of internal troubles. After the Zabern affair of 1913-1914, the French naval attaché in Berlin wrote that "it reveals to us suddenly a silent understanding between the bourgeoisie and military Pan-Germanism. Frightened by the progress of Socialism, the propertied classes draw closer to the Army." Faramond, p. 132. This view could be found in Socialist publications at the time.

[4] Waldersee, *Denkwürdigkeiten*, I, 223; II, 54ff. and passim; Georg Johannes Friedrich Freiherr von Eppstein, *Fürst Bismarcks Entlassung* (Berlin 1920), pp. 31, 100ff.

control than was the German one. French savings opened the way for the Franco-Russian alliance, and the military rather than the diplomats to a large extent arranged the channels into which the French savings would run—the construction of strategic, though "highly uneconomic" railways from the interior of Russia in the direction of the Central Powers, and the manufacture of millions of Russian rifles in French factories. This order was engineered by the Russian military attaché and the French Ministry of War, and was part of the understanding between the soldiers which preceded that between the diplomats. It was the soldiers, including the Assistant Chief of Staff, General Boisdeffre, with his connections as former military attaché in St. Petersburg, who obtained the necessary control over the Tsar, and his final signature.[5]

Greatly to the satisfaction of the Great General Staff, though hardly under its direction, some of the German capital export in the early 1890's found its way into Italy, to support the shaky economy of the third partner of the Triple Alliance;[6] though the French ambassador in Berlin assumed, in 1891, that this would not long suffice. He was convinced that by 1897 Italy would be bankrupt, would drop out of the Alliance, and thus "disrupt the coalition which hems us in."[7] Before 1914 the alliance system was increasingly paralleled by control over the outflow of capital, so that only friends and allies, actual and potential, could be recipients. This government-controlled capital movement was part of the financing of the alliances; in the end it was even more onerous to some national economies, especially that of France, than outright taxation for military purposes.

Although older statesmen, and a few later ones like Caillaux, may have thought the export of capital to have a peace-

---

[5] *Documents diplomatiques français*, Ist ser., VIII, 226, 439ff. and passim. For Russian strategic railway construction see Wilhelm Treue, "Die russische Verschuldung an Frankreich zum Zwecke des strategischen Eisenbahnbaus," *Preussische Jahrbücher* (May 1935); for the role of French loans in the forming of the military agreements see William L. Langer, *The Franco-Russian Alliance, 1890-1894* (Cambridge 1929), pp. 34f., 40f., 121, 210f., 221f., 238, 397, 404.

[6] Waldersee, *Denkwürdigkeiten*, II, 125, 315.

[7] *Documents diplomatiques français*, Ist ser., VIII, 475.

preserving function, twentieth-century nationalism and militarism would not allow any such tendencies inherent in at least certain sectors of capitalism to take effect.[8] In 1910 French financial interests were inclined to grant Austria-Hungary a loan, but the French naval attaché in the capitals of the Central Powers protested vigorously and successfully: "It would be generous folly on our part to help out with our money in the development of the Austro-Hungarian Navy," the purpose to which the loan was to be applied. It would merely add to the strength of the Central Powers as a whole.[9]

Part of the customary tie-in of capital export was the sale of armaments to the debtor by the creditor. Aristocratic nineteenth-century diplomacy traditionally remained aloof from a large part of the dirty business of economics, but sometimes it would be rudely disturbed by orders from home to take an active interest in such supranational industries as armaments.[10] Often this meant that the diplomats had to back up the service attachés, who acted as advance salesmen for the producers of explosives, warships, guns or rifles. In spite of indignant outcry about "merchants of death," the diplomats had become very much aware that foreign orders for such home industries strengthened their own country's war potential, that foreign sales in fact helped to keep these war industries on a stand-by basis, and sometimes at the expense of the international capitalist from whom the foreign buyer was obtaining the loans necessary to pay for his orders.

Competition in the sale of arms intensified as 1914 approached. Since it was the sector of a national economy with

[8] In 1863 an Austrian diplomat wrote: "I remember very well the time [the 1830's] when it was said there can be no war, Rothschild does not allow it. And Rothschild was only the first presentiment of capital, before it showed itself as a great power, and still it needed only a Prussian *Landrat* [Bismarck] to override its veto." Alexander von Villers, *Briefe eines Unbekannten*, 2nd ed. (Vienna 1917), X, 27.

[9] Faramond, p. 30.

[10] A French ambassador reported from Berlin in 1886 that the Krupp Works were considered there "a great establishment in the national interest," hence the use of artifice on the part of the Reich Government in all parts of the world to obtain orders for it, particularly at this time of overproduction and a worldwide crisis of the metallurgical industries. *Documents diplomatiques français*, Ist ser., VI, 282.

which officers, and service attachés in particular, were most familiar, the cutthroat competition only served to confirm the ancient military view of *Händler und Helden*, heroes and hucksters. Conveniently oblivious of their own role in sharpening international competition, the officers often claimed that traders eager for profits "caused" the wars that soldiers had to fight. Colonel Pellé, military attaché in Berlin from 1909 to 1912, later chief of staff and ambassador, and one of the most incisive French military minds, concluded from his observations of Germany's industrial structure that, considering the increasing closing of markets against her, "German industry's need for expansion, combined with the conviction of their military superiority, will lead the Germans to war in the more or less immediate future."[11] Lenin came to approximately the same conclusion at about the same time.

The salesman role of the attaché was perhaps better understood or appreciated by the home authorities, and even by the frequently ignorant political parties,[12] than by the diplomats, some of whom had to be forced into the business or else removed from their posts as unhelpful to the homeland's armament interests.[13] But the majority proved pliable in this service. The teamwork of diplomacies, armed services, armament industries, bankers and the press in international com-

[11] *Ibid.*, IInd ser., XIII, 328, 387.

[12] After the Reichsmarineamt in February 1914 had promised the Catholic Center Party in the Reichstag a Catholic chapel for Navy personnel on Helgoland, the Party in return voted a naval attaché for Buenos Aires. The naval correspondent of the *Berliner Tageblatt* wrote at the time: "They were told the post was necessary in the interest of our industry, particularly the torpedo-boat building shipyards. For Argentina was buying her boats from Schichau and the Germania Shipyards. That is to say, she bought them already *before* an attaché was active there. Wouldn't it have been more just that the two interested firms paid the extra costs for an attaché out of their own pockets? For Krupp's paying 14% dividends, 15,000 mark means very little." Capt. Lothar Persius, *Menschen und Schiffe in der kaiserlichen Flotte* (Berlin 1925), p. 99.

[13] For the case of the German minister in Peking during the 1890's, Schenck zu Schweinsberg, who was replaced by a more energetic man after his support of the interests of German armament makers and traders had been found insufficient, see George W. F. Hallgarten, *Imperialismus vor 1914*, 2 vols., 1st and 2nd eds. (Munich 1951 and 1963), I, 352f.

petition before 1914 is so well known[14] that it will suffice to mention only a few cases here.

When the ever-needy Balkan nations sought loans, the governments and banks of the capital-exporting countries were usually inclined to consider expenditure on armaments (if the money was spent in their own countries) as "productive," and would therefore grant the necessary permission and facilities. In such cases the military attachés served as salesmen, in addition to other, less official agents for the home industries; sometimes they even exerted pressure on the home banks, which tended to bicker lengthily over loan terms. With this purpose in mind Ferdinand of Bulgaria told the French military attaché at Sofia in October 1904 that he wished that "the deal about guns should be concluded as soon as possible with French industry." He was anxious to provide his well-trained artillery personnel with up-to-date materiel, "did not want to give in to the pressing solicitations in favor of Krupp who was almost out of his mind at the idea of losing the Bulgarian market, and deplored the attitude and excessive appetite of international finance, which was so contrary to the interests of French industry, and the loss of time connected with it. The Prince knew about and appreciated Delcassé's and Rouvier's active intervention in order to move the Banque de Paris et des Pays-Bas to grant him acceptable conditions, but he was now near the end of his patience."[15]

The same kind of thing happened in the opposite camp. Germany's military attaché and her ambassador to the Porte were arranging for the Liman von Sanders military mission that was to reorganize the Turkish Army; at the same time they supported Krupp's offers of new field artillery materiel for that Army, to be paid for by a loan from the Deutsche Bank. They ran up against the corresponding French team of ambassador-attaché and bankers, and the attaché, in a moment of relative good will, actually declared that "in case France is

[14] The most profound piece in this category is Hallgarten's *Imperialismus vor 1914.*

[15] *Documents diplomatiques français,* IInd ser., V, 446.

not excluded from the sale, the German mission [of Liman von Sanders] is endurable."[16]

Much the larger part of the competition between armament firms paralleled the pre-1914 alliances—German shipbuilders versus British, Krupp versus Schneider-Creusot or Vickers-Armstrong. But some embarrassment within the camp of the Central Powers arose from competition between Krupp and the Austrian Skoda Works, occasionally between Krupp, Skoda and Schneider, as happened in Serbia in 1906, or between Mauser and Mannlicher, in countries such as Serbia, Bulgaria or Turkey. And in Greece in 1905 the Austrian riflemakers won out, after William II himself had strongly recommended the Mauser product to his brother-in-law, the Greek Crown Prince. In order to explain the product better to the buyers, Baron Giesl, the Austrian attaché serving in the Balkan capitals, used his leave in 1902 to study the Skoda Works; later he investigated the Krupp Works as well. This enabled him the better to cry down the Krupp product.[17]

But concern with war potentials, one's own and that of enemies and neutrals, and with war economies in general, remained sporadic rather than systematic before 1914. And if it was neglected at the centers of war preparation, not too much blame can be pinned on neglectful attachés—though occasionally a superior such as Kitchener did blame them, and wanted to have them reformed when the war was over.[18] The attachés had simply not received directives for the necessary observation and reporting. The age of "economic espionage" had not yet arrived; it was, in fact, proclaimed by the Bolshevists in the 1920's.

After 1918 the movement of international capital served the defense interests of the exporter in a different way, by strengthening the armed forces and war potential of allied or friendly powers—after his disastrous experience with Tsarist bonds the French private investor could no longer be expected

[16] *Grosse Politik*, XXXVIII, 231.

[17] Giesl, pp. 21, 75, 170; Constantine Dumba, *Dreibund- und Entente-Politik in der alten und neuen Welt* (Zurich-Vienna-Leipzig 1931), pp. 218f.

[18] Knox, p. 364; see above, pp. 42f.

to underwrite such alliances. While French bankers made considerable investments in Polish and Czech armament industries[19] (selling out their Skoda interest after Munich), other financing, designed to help the allies closer to war-industrial autarchy, had to take the shape of "loans" from government to government—a loan such as France was willing to grant Belgium during the 1930's if the latter were to construct a system of fortifications beyond the left wing of the Maginot Line.[20] This was a form of support approximating the ancient system of subsidies. It was essentially what the United States did, perhaps not consciously, in aiding friendly nations (even if not called allies) during the cold war. Orthodox capitalist arrangements could no longer suffice for the production and procurement of armaments now that "wars were to be decided inside factories"—or at least more so than ever before in the history of war.

Between the two World Wars, as before 1914, those military powers in which capitalism and capitalist ideas and practices best survived, relied on foreign arms sales in order to keep their national arms industries going; this seemed to involve the least amount of *faux frais* for war preparations. As an Air Board appointed by President Coolidge and headed by Dwight Morrow, of J. P. Morgan and Company, put it in a report of December 2, 1925: "The Board urges the encouragement of civilian aircraft and the sale of planes to foreign countries so as to lessen the number of planes which the Government must order to keep the industry in a strong position."[21] In 1934 the Swedish Chief of Staff rejoiced that the Bofors Works, for years controlled by Krupp, was once again Swedish-owned; it was "a lucky thing for Sweden, freeing her of the need to maintain ruinously large stocks."[22] It is this modern concept of the "national interest" which the accusatory "merchant of death" literature usually ignores, overlooking the fact that keeping national war industries on a stand-by basis in peace

[19] Data on this in *Neues Tagebuch*, October 8, 1938.
[20] Maurice Gustave Gamelin, *Servir*, 3 vols. (Paris 1946-1947), II, 69.
[21] Emile Gavreau and Lester Cohen, *Billy Mitchell* (New York 1942), p. 166.
[22] Castellan, p. 283.

time is one of the aims of the service attachés and the military and naval missions to underdeveloped countries, who act as salesmen for the international armaments industries.

But capitalistic considerations of the conventional, pre-1914 kind never functioned freely or fully in a number of countries after 1919. Some of those in need of arms supplies from abroad were too poor to pay for the increasingly costly weapons of modern wars; poverty and industrial backwardness strengthened dependence on some great power, often France, the diplomatic-capitalistic patron of the countries of the Little Entente. The two chief "have-not" powers after the First World War, Russia and Germany, undertook rearmament on the basis of barter, with Germany providing the industrial know-how and Russia the locale for that arms production and testing which was forbidden in Germany. Later Russia provided raw materials as well.

Incongruity of the two socio-economic systems did not hinder the Reichswehr in its dealings with Russia, and anti-capitalism in Russia had its distinct advantages in German officers' eyes. As Seeckt, the original founder of this military cooperation, reminded them early in 1933, when it was feared that the Nazis might institute a change: There was no longer the danger of the end of the last century, when "France had succeeded in drawing Russia into her golden nets," thus placing Germany between two fronts.[23]

German-Russian relations, military and industrial, presented military intelligence of the victorious powers with their no. 1 puzzle. It proved relatively easier to uncover the secrets of German rearmament within the Weimar Republic: the puzzle pieces were more numerous and characteristic; there were more voluntary and involuntary helpers contributing to the jigsaw, including parliamentarians, pacifists, Communists and the anti-Reichswehr Left—until 1933 when very strict anti-espionage laws cut off these sources. The information they furnished the attachés in Berlin, together with the findings of the French intelligence service, allowed the latter to compose a fairly complete and accurate picture of German

[23] *Deutschland zwischen West und Ost* (Berlin 1933).

rearmament. Its full implementation, including plans for total mobilization, did not get under way until the Four Year Plan of 1935, when the war industrial potential (by French estimate already greater than ever before in 1929) was pushed into more kinetic shape.[24] German military attachés, whether called by that name or not, took care of the knotty problems that such rearmament on foreign soil produced—and more problems than actual equipment were produced during the times of General von Seeckt.[25]

When German rearmament came to be undertaken on a really large scale, new problems arose, such as the financing of buying the necessary foreign raw materials, which were often at the disposal of impecunious states, in need of arms themselves. Elaborate barter arrangements were made with under-industrialized countries such as Russia and China, by which the Nazis paid for raw materials, at least in part, with arms of German manufacture. Later, from 1938 on, they also paid with Czech-made materiel. Similar barter arrangements were made with the Balkan states, where the Nazis replaced France as supplier of arms and capital. To illustrate the function of service attachés in such deals, and incidentally the clashes which could arise between diplomats and the military: in February 1939, Yugoslavia, which was estranged from France, expressed to the German air attaché in Belgrade through the Prince Regent and the Chief of Staff a desire for rather large arms deliveries, including 300 planes plus ground equipment, to be bought on credits that the Reich was to guarantee. The Luftwaffe, and Goering himself, took the deal under consideration at once without informing the Wilhelmstrasse people; they learned about it eventually, however, and complained that this secrecy was keeping them from the "political exploitation of the armaments transactions." Ribbentrop got hold

[24] For numerous details, reported by French attachés, and general conclusions by the French General Staff, see Castellan, passim.

[25] For details see Gustav Hilger and Alfred G. Meyer, *The Incompatible Allies: German-Soviet Relations, 1918-1941* (New York 1953); George W. F. Hallgarten, "Seeckt and Russia, 1920-1922," *Journal of Modern History*, XXI (1949), 28ff.; Edward Hallett Carr, *German-Soviet Relations between the Two World Wars, 1919-1939* (Baltimore 1951); Helm Speidel, "Reichswehr und Rote Armee," *Vierteljahrshefte für Zeitgeschichte*, I (1953), 9ff.

of the case; he was then "engaged in a lively struggle over his jurisdiction on all sides," and wanted to reassert "a tight, unified conduct of foreign policy," but he had only indifferent success. Goering and the Luftwaffe continued their efforts to bring Yugoslavia over to the Axis—the prospect seemed promising as the Yugoslav air force "was completely oriented toward Germany," but the army was not yet fully emancipated from its old pro-French attitude.[26] Similar motivations, procedures and intra-German conflicts occurred in the extension of control over Rumania, its oil fields and its armed services.[27]

In spite of the endeavors of the powers great and small to create war industries of their own, hardly one of them has ever become self-sufficient, especially for a long period. Certain orders for materiel important in war or for raw materials had to be placed in foreign markets, which were often highly competitive. This market situation made many a service attaché the purchasing agent for his home department,[28] a precarious position and not always conducive to the highest morality; the big arms makers offered largesse to those who visited their factories and proving grounds, and to those who inspected their goods.[29]

After observing foreign materiel, the attaché must draw his own conclusions as to its value for the home force or the need for a weapon equalling or surpassing it. Should an article used by a foreign army or navy or a specific feature be imitated, im-

[26] *Documents on German Foreign Policy*, Ser. D, V, 396ff., 400ff., 409f.
[27] *Ibid.*, VIII, 602.
[28] U.S. naval attachés "also act as representatives of the Navy Department in purchasing materiel abroad and conduct the required inspection of such materiel; the volume of this work in certain countries is such as to require the assignment of officers as assistant naval attachés." Cmdr. W. W. Galbraith in *Congressional Digest*, January 1924.
[29] See George W. F. Hallgarten, *Vorkriegsimperialismus* (Paris 1935), II, 273 and passim. The most recent scandal of this sort concerns the Swiss military attaché in Washington, Col. Hans Rieser, who learned that his country intended to buy 100 Vickers-Armstrong tanks, and informed his brother of the impending deal. The brother promptly became the Vickers-Armstrong agent for Switzerland and saw the deal through, netting a $100,000 commission, of which $12,500 went to the attaché. When the whole thing became known, Rieser was dismissed from the service, but no criminal charges were brought against him. *Der Spiegel* (Hamburg), January 27, 1957; *The New York Times*, June 18, 1957.

proved upon, or acquired by outright sale from the foreign manufacturer (provided it is for sale)? Or should its use be shunned?

The armament buyer's side has been underpublicized. The reports of the U.S. naval attaché in Berlin during the Spanish-American War concerning a deal with the German firm of Schwarzkopf, manufacturers of torpedoes, in the production and use of which the United States had been rather backward, should therefore be of interest. In May 1898 the firm suggested that the American Government place an order for 200 torpedoes, to be delivered within the next two to four years at a price of £500 each, or a royalty of £50 per torpedo if manufactured in the United States on the basis of the firm's plans, experience and information, which would be freely given. The firm's manager declared that "his directors were nearly all bankers who would prefer a large money indemnity as the United States is so rich." The naval attaché told him that "the richer the man the more he would fight over small matters," but submitted the proposal to Washington with the remark,

> that it will be better to order torpedoes—say 150—than to pay cash for we are going to want a great number in the future but I would have them made as quickly as possible in view of possible complications with Germany, and I would cut the royalty down to £30. I would also be inclined to increase the period for royalty to 15 years rather than to cut it down below ten, as the improvements over here will always be valuable and the unpaid royalty will secure us the free run of the place and give us a continuous sight hole, so to speak, into the torpedo system of Germany itself. The manager says that they will make no arrangement with any private firm in the United States as that will only insure a possible rival in the future, and I infer from the Department's letter that it is the intention to establish a Government factory. I hope this is so as it will prove more economical.[30]

During and between wars the service attachés act as buyers only temporarily, as when for example the Czech air attaché

[30] Cmdr. Barber to Navy Department, May 14, 1898. *National Archives.*

in Rome on the eve of the Munich crisis of 1938 asked the Italian Air Ministry whether the Government would allow the sale and export of some 150 planes. The export license was denied, though the loss of the sale was regretted, and the Italians promptly informed the Germans and expected credit for their good deed.[31] Usually, purchasing commissions from home took over after the attaché had made the initial move in exploring the arms factories, but the attaché could make what use he wished of the knowledge gained—he could trade information with other countries' attachés, enabling them to judge more accurately the war readiness and war potential of the seller nation. Both the Japanese and Spanish military attachés in Berlin could tell their French colleague in 1932 about the strength and readiness of German industry after their own countries had placed orders with it.[32]

Selling or buying, or merely serving as broker and transmitting agent for arms, munitions and raw materials gave the service attachés new and important functions in a *Wehrwirtschaft*, such as the Germans established before 1939, in part on the basis of military studies,[33] or the military sectors of either capitalist or Communist economies. Were they to prepare themselves for these activities by economic studies, in addition to languages and other fields? It would seem necessary enough. For what they meant by "economic" might turn out to be something merely militaristic or imperialistic, ancient and destructive in character.[34]

Modern war has brought the service attaché two new tasks belonging in the economic sector, tasks clearly too big to be handled by him and his office alone: the supply of arms and war materials essential from abroad, and the detection and description of the sources of such material, in enemy or neutral countries, which are among the targets for sabotage, bombing and guided missiles. Since the war of 1870-1871, or

[31] *Documents on German Foreign Policy*, Ser. D, I, 1171.

[32] For details see Castellan, pp. 77f.

[33] See for this the *Schriften zur kriegswirtschaftlichen Forschung und Schulung*, Maj. Dr. Kurt Hesse, ed. (Hamburg 1935ff.).

[34] The Japanese military attaché in Paris explained the Japanese army ventures in Manchuria in 1932 as "due to economic necessity." Gamelin, *Servir*, II, 84f.

even earlier when Bismarck thought of buying war vessels in the United States, that country has been considered by the European powers and Japan as a supplier of war goods. As the First World War approached, von Papen warned in Berlin that the United States was not only a potential arms supplier, but that its industrial capacity would enable the Americans "to expand their Army almost without limit within a very short time."[35] After the Marne battle of 1914, which indicated that the war would not be a short one, the belligerents went to this market for supplies. Germany was greatly handicapped from the outset by the tightening blockade, and hence inclined toward measures like preemptive buying, ("cornering the munition market," as Papen called it in his bolder moments), sabotage, and the fomenting of strikes. Most such attempts, often clumsy, by von Papen and by the naval attaché, came to the attention of the Western allies, including the British naval attaché in Washington, who had planted a Czech agent among the Austrian officials. Eventually even the "idiotic Yankees," as Papen called the American authorities in an intercepted private letter, learned of their activities. Without being able to pin many specific misdeeds on Papen and his naval colleague Boy-Ed, the Washington Government at the end of 1916 declared them both *persona non grata* for their "unwarranted military and naval activity," and succeeded in having them recalled.[36]

Other neutrals as suppliers of war materials were kept under strict surveillance by the belligerents, and the service attachés were among the foremost watchdogs. This part of their wartime activities is best illuminated by the observations and proposals of the British naval attaché in Stockholm, Captain Consett, who throughout considered Sweden's neutrality as favoring Germany and British blockade measures against her as too lenient. His superior, Minister Sir Esme Howard, favored a more lenient treatment in order not to provoke German sympathies, which were far from weak in that northern country and even favored entry into the war on the side of the Central Powers.[37]

[35] His *Memoirs*, p. 19.   [36] *Ibid.*, chs. 2 and 3.
[37] For details see Montagu W. W. P. Consett, *The Triumph of the*

The most important targets of economic warfare at the beginning of the war in 1939 were the Swedish ore deposits, the Rumanian and Russian oil fields and the transport routes to the Reich, the main beneficiary of these deposits. Allied plans to obtain control of either the deposits or the transport routes were made; they were bold or overbold: to help struggling Finland the Gelleväre ore fields were to be taken over; the Russian oil fields near the Caucasus were to be bombed by planes based in the Near East, and extensive sabotage was to bring Rumanian oil production to an end. The French High Command proposed "to give our military attaché in Bucharest the mission to set afoot the whole organization that will be necessary for the possible (*éventuel*) destruction of the Rumanian oil fields," through a large-scale sabotage action directed by the same engineer who had guided the destruction work in those fields in 1916, before the Germans won control.[38] The Nazi victories of 1940 put to an end all such plans for the continuance of the *Sitzkrieg* by economic strangulation of the Reich, and Germany promptly strengthened her hold on Rumanian oil production, defying not only the Allies but also Soviet Russia.

The choice of targets for bombing in Axis territory appears to have been made by the engineers and economists among the makers of economic warfare, rather than from data supplied by service attachés who had served in Axis capitals. This, at least, is the impression gained by one member of the Washington Board of Economic Warfare. Experience gained during the Second World War put great stress on the reconnoitering and selection of targets in case of another war, and service attachés seem to have tried to make good their earlier deficiencies. The intercepted diaries of the U.S. military attaché in Moscow in 1951 are replete with "good targets" in Moscow and elsewhere,

---

Unarmed Forces (1914-1918). An Account of the Transactions by which Germany during the Great War was Able to Obtain Supplies Prior to Her Collapse under the Pressure of Economic Forces (London 1923).

[38] *Les documents secrets de l'État-Major Général Français* (Berlin 1941), p. 35. This is a German White Book published by the Auswärtiges Amt, of captured French military documents which outline most of these plans.

such as railroad and other bridges, anti-aircraft positions, industrial and other plants.[39] Subsequently, in spite of the U-2 reconnaissance flights over Soviet territory and other detection methods, the Pentagon had to admit, publicly, to inadequate knowledge of Soviet missile sites as preferred targets for the retaliatory use of long-range nuclear-armed bombers and missiles. The Russians had succeeded in keeping their bases secret.[40]

[39] Richard Squires, *Auf dem Kriegspfad. Aufzeichnungen eines englischen Offiziers* (East Berlin 1951), pp. 214ff.
[40] *The New York Times*, December 1, 1960.

CHAPTER 13

OBSERVERS OF BATTLE

Reporting, and usually commenting, on military matters came more and more exclusively into the hands of the military themselves, whether they reported peacetime technological progress or backwardness, or whether they described war in its latest shape. During the nineteenth century military observers, either the attachés in the capitals of the belligerents or special observers sent out by the neutral war ministries and general staffs, tried to survey the latest war at the closest possible range—on the battle line, along the supply lines, and occasionally even on the barricades of civil war.[1]

Prussia had her military attaché accompany the French army to Mexico, and France sent her Berlin attaché, the Comte de Clermont-Tonnerre, to follow the Prussian and Austrian armies to the Duchies in 1864.[2] Most of the military powers of Europe kept observers on both sides of the American Civil War, which had at first been dismissed as of no interest or significance to European armies or to the science of warfare. As a power interested in colonial warfare, France had two observers on the staff of Sir Robert Napier during the Abyssinian campaign of 1868. There was a full score of neutral observers in the German GHQ in 1870-1871—fewer on the French side, as if there were more to learn from the winner. Of the great powers only Austria was unrepresented, because either she herself or the Prussians distrusted her neutrality.

[1] For the reports of the Russian military plenipotentiary in Berlin, Count Constantin Benckendorff, on the street fighting during the March revolution see Veit Valentin, *Die deutsche Revolution von 1848-1849* (Berlin 1930), I, 431.

[2] At the storming of the Düppel lines by the Prussians one of them remarked about the observers: "It was interesting, indeed, to watch our guests, Gablenz [the Austrian], von der Tann [the Bavarian], and the French military attaché Clermont-Tonnerre. The latter was unable to restrain his tears, so touched was he by the childlike obedience and yet heroic behavior of our young men." Schweinitz, I, 167.

For the neutrals without direct and recent war experiences of their own such observing was the most immediate way of learning about the newest methods and weapons, and most belligerents were willing to learn and let others learn from their own experience. Such observers became, in one way or another, the instructors of their home forces—exemplified probably most literally in the case of General Dragomirov (1830-1905), Russia's greatest tactician under the last Tsars and in Russian military history the link between Suvorov and the Red Army. Not a little of his teaching, in military schools and in his writing, was based on observations in the Italian GHQ during the War of 1859—after which he became a professor of tactics, and later the director, at the Nicholas Academy for officers—and on his experiences with the IInd Prussian Army during the battles of 1866 in Bohemia.

Requests to admit such observers and allow them to follow the field armies were usually granted during the nineteenth century as a matter of courtesy and on the basis of reciprocity, with some exceptions—no one was allowed, for example, near the Russian Army during Sevastopol. There were also occasions when the observers were more hampered than helped by the authorities of the belligerents. The Italians in the War of 1866 decided to let the observers on their side shift for themselves, and obtain their own transport, food and quarters; it seemed one way of keeping them away from the inglorious battle of Custozza. During the night after the defeat, when it was expected that the victorious Austrians would start an energetic pursuit, the foreign military attachés acting as observers were awakened and hurriedly conducted to Cremona, well in the rear. An aide of Victor Emmanuel told them: "I have seen the King at three o'clock this morning; he is much dejected, but we are still more so, for we fear he might be forced to abdicate."[3] This information, for foreign observers, seemed even less suitable than eyewitness reports of the military defeat.

As a rule such observers shared the privations and dis-

[3] Germain Bapst, *Le Maréchal Canrobert: Souvenirs d'un siècle*, 6 vols. (Paris 1898-1919), IV, 40f.

comforts of the staff officers of the belligerents. General Grant warned the French who were to come to his headquarters that "the campaign was conducted with the greatest neglect of personal comfort,"[4] and indeed some belligerents have found it advisable to make the restrictions imposed upon foreign observers as irksome as possible. When the British military attaché at Paris went to the French army in Italy in 1859, he was kept waiting for eight days in Genoa before being admitted to the Imperial HQ; by that time things had been straightened out sufficiently, after an original *décousu* of improvisation and disorder, to be safe for foreign eyes. As the Comte de Fleury, one of the court generals in the camp, remarked about the Britisher, "It is a *drôle de mission* to look on in the name of a government which has its observers on both sides; also, he seems a bit annoyed at what he has to do. I shall cultivate him the best I can in order not to sour him and to maintain good influences on that side." (Fleury himself was rather an Anglophile, and entertained hopes for the French embassy in London.) [5]

Sharing the discomfort of a belligerent might even go so far for the neutral observers as to share, if only for a moment, his captivity.[6] As a rule, they were freed promptly by the captor according to the customs of war, usually in the expectation that they would not return to observation duties with the enemy. To cite an exception: when General Gurko, a son of the Gurko of 1877-1879 fame, was captured by the British while serving as military observer with the Boers in 1899-1900,

[4] Beauvais, p. 28.

[5] *Souvenirs du Général Comte Fleury*, 2 vols. (Paris 1897-1898), II, 20f. The Russian observer in Napoleon's camp in 1859, Count Paul Shuvalov, later ambassador to Berlin (1885-1894), received such handsome treatment that he remained a decided Bonapartist and hostile to the Third Republic. *Documents diplomatiques français*, Ist ser., IX, 152.

[6] Two German and one French attaché-observers stayed voluntarily with the defenders of Port Arthur in 1904, anxious to learn about the recent developments of siege techniques. The Japanese, early in the siege, offered them free exit, and William II gave orders to the Germans to leave. One of the latter crossed the lines safely, the other and his French colleague departed on board a Chinese ship and disappeared without a trace, apparently murdered by the crew. Maurice Bompard, *Ma mission en Russie* (Paris 1937), pp. 57f.

Lord Roberts passed him back to the Boers by way of neutral Lorenco Marques.[7]

It was considered good manners for such observers never to change sides and thus avoid even the semblance of carrying information about one camp into the other. When a Prussian observer, General von Willisen, appeared in Radetzky's headquarters after having first followed the campaign of 1849 on the Italian side, the Piedmontese became quite resentful, and this breach of military good manners was still a source of annoyance when Austrians and Piedmontese met again under Prussian observation in 1859.[8] Two American observers, however, General Burnside and Colonel Forbes, braved this prejudice. After having spent some time in the German HQ early in October 1870 they appeared at a Paris defense outpost and asked for admission to the beleaguered city as carriers of information from their government to United States Minister Washburne. Many Frenchmen, including Gambetta, considered that diplomat as hostile to the effort of the *Défence nationale*, but Trochu, the commandant of Paris, and others, succeeded in having the Americans admitted. They told Trochu and others among the besieged that Bismarck was counting heavily on the effects of sedition among the people, but Trochu assured them, and through them the Germans, that more was needed, hunger for example, to bring about surrender. Jules Favre's attempt to establish a new line of negotiations with Bismarck through the Americans, after their return to the German side, came to nothing.[9]

Hardly a war between 1815 and 1914, in Europe or beyond the seas, escaped this neutral observation.[10] The last large-scale conflict before 1914 to be so observed was the Russo-Japanese War, during which all great powers and some minor ones had observers on both sides. In the Russian camp there

[7] Knox, pp. 400f. See Beauvais, pp. 166ff., for a discussion of the captive neutral attaché from the point of view of international law.

[8] *Die auswärtige Politik Preussens*, I, 250.

[9] Louis Jules Trochu, *Oeuvres posthumes*, 2 vols. (Tours 1896), I, 308ff.; for the German side Moritz Busch, *Bismarck. Some Secret Pages of his History*, 2 vols. (London 1898), I passim.

[10] Prussia's military attachés in Paris observed the fighting of French troops in Mexico in 1863 and in Algeria in 1864. Gordon A. Craig in *Political Science Quarterly*, LXIV (1949), 68.

was a group of 27 officers, with a British lieutenant general as doyen whose "position with our army was rendered especially delicate by the fact that Great Britain was then a military ally of Japan," according to the Russian general staff officer who was bear leader and liaison officer between this group and GHQ. The French representative, General Sylvestre, was deeply disappointed, if not offended, that Kuropatkin was far from anxious to receive his advice, advice from an ally which considered itself further advanced in military science. The German and Austrian observers, including the former German military attaché at St. Petersburg, Major von Lauenstein, an old partisan of the Three Emperors' Alliance, "knew more about our army than any of the others," according to the liaison officer, who might well have drawn this conclusion from his control over outgoing mail. The truly tactless observers were the two sent by Switzerland, one of whom calmly remarked in the presence of the Russian liaison officer, one day when Russian railway guns appeared on the scene and stirred the curiosity of the observers: "What are you so excited about? Anyway, the Russians are only getting these guns ready so as to be able to hand them over quicker to the Japanese!" The senior representatives of the neutrals promptly obtained the recall of the two Swiss.[11]

Some other observers with the Russians left for home in the early autumn of 1904—there seemed not enough to learn professionally about the war to make the discomforts of a prolonged stay worthwhile—much to the chagrin of the Russian war minister who thought they regarded the outlook for his army as hopeless. He particularly resented the fact that the representative of allied France also intended to leave. This officer, in the opinion of the French military attaché in St. Petersburg who favored the war à outrance, wanted to tell the authorities at home, French and perhaps also Russian, the "interesting" things which he could not well put in writing because of censorship, including his firm conviction that an immediate peace at almost any price was imperative for

[11] Ignatiev, pp. 171ff.; Waters, *"Secret and Confidential,"* p. 262, confirms this story.

Russia if the army, which had had some valuable tactical experience, and "the authority of the Tsar" were to be saved.[12]

The results of such neutral observation can be read in military literature,[13] some of it official in nature, such as the work of the historical sections of the general staffs—the most famous piece in this category is the Prussian General Staff's work *Der italienische Feldzug 1859* (1862), practically dictated by Moltke himself on the basis of incoming reports—and some of a more private character, though that can never be quite conceded to the writings of officers still on active duty. Some times this private literature, particularly when unflattering in its treatment of one or both of the belligerents, has aroused resentment. When one of the two Austrian observers with the Russian Army in Manchuria gave a public lecture on his experiences to his colleagues at the *Militärkasino*, the officers' club, immediately after his return to Vienna, he included some sharp criticism of the Russian Army and command, and the longstanding ill will between the Austro-Hungarian and Russian armies received new fuel.[14]

The result of such experiences with foreign observers was that the belligerents restricted their movements on the theater of war, and especially their opportunities to see the less creditable events and conditions. Journeys to the battle zones took on more and more the nature of planned tours. In Libya in 1911, Italy, always touchy about military criticism which might puncture the make-believe of her great power status, resolved to keep foreign observers of her aggression against Turkey under the control of military *ciceroni*. She turned down the request of her ally, Austria, to have some officers take part in the campaign. Instead, she invited the attachés of the powers to come to Tripoli aboard an Italian man-of-war; there she kept them shut up, permitting only an oc-

---

[12] *Documents diplomatiques français*, IInd ser., V, 543f.

[13] The reports of the British attachés on the war of 1904-1905 are in *The Russo-Japanese War: British Officers' Reports*, War Office 1908, the American reports in *Reports of Military Observers*, General Staff USA, 1906. The British General Staff wrote and published the official *History of the Russo-Japanese War* (London 1906ff.), and the German the *Russisch-Japanischer Krieg* (Berlin 1907ff.); an English translation of the latter was made by K. von Donat.

[14] Glaise-Horstenau, p. 387.

casional peep at whatever seemed most innocuous in that far from glorious enterprise. Conrad, the Austrian chief of staff, thought it was a famous joke to get rid of neutral snoopers in this manner but he was determined not to fall for it; instead he ordered his military attaché in Rome to go to Tripoli for a short stay and then to find a suitable pretext to return to the capital, where there was far more to learn about the war.[15]

The Balkan Wars, which had not been correctly foreseen and diagnosed[16] by the military attachés, also proved of limited accessibility to neutral observers, attachés and other officers, as well as newspaper correspondents. Reliable news about the siege of Adrianople during the winter of 1912-1913 was hard to obtain, "since military attachés and correspondents up to now have received no permission to follow the war operations and the Bulgarian General Staff on its part naturally would give out only news favorable to itself."[17] The defeat of the Turks was so shameful that they would have no observers at the front. The Greeks allowed such observers to see a little more, at least temporarily, when peeping seemed safe, as in their campaign in Macedonia in November-December 1912; they took all the military attachés in Athens to the front, including a special German observer since the Reich maintained no attaché there. Two of them had left the Turkish side earlier, because they had not been admitted to the theater of war. "Among all of us there reigned constantly good fellowship in the best sense of the word, even though we made no secret about the separate character of the interests of Triple Alliance and Triple Entente. In spite of that our living together remained always harmonious, and curiously enough groupings resulted which were by no means identical with the political groups," as the German observer wrote. But they soon ran into difficulties with a Greek commander who was an ardent Venizelist and suspected the attachés of leanings toward Greek royalty or toward the Turks; he censored and destroyed their mail and favored instead the newspaper correspondents, who would spread the fame of a good Venizelist.

[15] Conrad, II, 176ff.

[16] *Oesterreich-Ungarns Aussenpolitik*, IV, 4064.

[17] Report of German Minister in Sofia, February 4, 1913. *Grosse Politik*, XXXIV, 12795.

Most of the attachés returned to Athens after a few weeks near the front, and there learned more about the events in Epirus than they had on the spot.[18]

The belligerent under observation resented, either openly or covertly, the presence of representatives of powers which, for good or bad reasons, were not considered quite neutral. The British military attaché in St. Petersburg, Colonel F.-A. Wellesley, who was in the Russian camp in 1878, suffered much for the favors which his Government and the British press showed the Turk; insults were offered him by some of the grand dukes and others, and the Russian foreign office and the Tsar had to apologize. The indiscretion of a cabinet minister did not mend matters. He spoke of Wellesley's reports about the many shortcomings of the Russian mobilization to the French ambassador in London, who reported to Paris, and when it became known that he had expressed such unfavorable opinions Russian feelings were further inflamed. The various incidents were so handsomely smoothed over, however, that Wellesley was sent on a mission to London by the Tsar, to find out whether the Disraeli Government was ready to mediate peace under conditions formulated by the Russians. But the latter suffered a setback while Wellesley was en route to London, the Russian forces were held up for months at Plevna, and Disraeli was not ready to act on these conditions—which were actually much more favorable than those of the peace of San Stefano.[19] Part of the Russian fury was due to the activities of the British military attaché in the Turkish camp on the Caucasus front, General Sir Arnold Kemball. According to contemporary newspaper reports he gave the Turkish commander, Moukhtar Pasha, much sound advice which the latter neglected, to his own detriment. In discussing this case of un-neutrality, the foremost Russian international lawyer at the turn of the century, F. de Martens, commented: "If the commander-in-chief of the Russian army in Transcaucasia had possessed irrefutable proof as regards the participation of Sir Arnold in the operation of

18 Maj. Gen. Gerold von Gleich, *Vom Balkan nach Bagdad* (Berlin 1921), pp. 27ff., 51, 54, 56 and passim.

19 Col. F.-A. Wellesley, *With the Russians in Peace and War* (London 1905), chs. XVIIIff.

the Turkish armies, the latter, in case he should have been captured, would necessarily have been treated as a Turkish prisoner of war, and not as a British general or as the military attaché of the British Government. Sir Arnold Kemball seems to have realized this himself for in consequence of setbacks suffered by the Turkish army and when it turned tail *en masse*, he took care not to be with the rear-guard."[20]

During the Russo-Japanese War American friendliness toward the Japanese, the "monkey men," particularly as demonstrated by the press, was greatly resented by the Russians; they told the American military attaché, T. Bentley Mott, that it was a sign of ingratitude toward "an old friend."[21] Benevolent neutrality, on the other hand, was well rewarded during that same war when British naval observers were permitted, as no others were, to embark on Japanese warships and even go to battle with them, a quite unique opportunity. In order to gain or preserve American friendship during the opening phases of the First World War, Kitchener on his own initiative gave orders that none but the American military attaché in London, Colonel Squiers, was to be admitted to the zone of the BEF from the outset. He hoped that this would help to win benevolent neutrality, and eventually more, from the United States.[22] At the same time, American neutrality was considered so insincere by the Central Powers that they extended a scanty welcome to American observers anxious to watch the war along their fronts. After the first shells of American manufacture had fallen on his troops in Poland in 1915, Mackensen excluded five American observers, who had come to study trench warfare, from the list of the guests taken care of by his HQ at Lodz. The officers most immediately

[20] F. de Martens, *La paix et la guerre* (Paris 1901), pp. 505f.; Valentine Baker Pasha, *War in Bulgaria* (London 1879), I, 7 and passim, for British and French attachés in the Turkish camp.

[21] Mott, p. 125. According to Theodore Roosevelt, *The Letters of Theodore Roosevelt*, selected and edited by Elting E. Morison, 8 vols. (Cambridge, Mass. 1951-1954), IV, 1086f.; 1115, the officers serving with the Japanese Army "grew to dislike the Japanese, although they greatly admired them as soldiers." The U.S. military attachés with the Russians thought that the latter were "colossal in their mendacity and trickery, and do not fight as well as the Japanese."

[22] Callwell, I, 195f.

concerned seem to have understood his sentiments better than did the American ambassador to Berlin.[23]

Showing favors to the service attachés of an ally or a friendly neutral had become part and parcel of the European system of alliances well before 1914. During the 1890's, when Great Britain was a non-signing member of the Triple Alliance, a great deal of military information about Russia, the common potential enemy, was exchanged through the British military attaché in Berlin, Colonel Grierson. While the ultimate secrets of the French army might never have been revealed to the Russian ally, innumerable favors were shown to her attachés which the Russians returned, such as exclusive admission to special maneuvers. And when in preparation for the power grouping at the Algeciras Conference French and German diplomacy competed for the favor of the United States, France decided that American Army officers, including the Chief of Staff, General Chaffee, who was traveling in Europe at the time, would be the only foreign officers permitted "to witness the cavalry engagement which opened the maneuvers and the only foreign officers who were allowed to be present at the critique following each day's maneuvers."[24]

Such neutral observation became a true *pépinière* for future warmakers, almost the realization of the international academy of warfare of which an eighteenth-century military *grand seigneur*, the Prince de Ligne, had dreamed.[25] The intellectually most impressive group of such observers ever assembled was on the Japanese side in the war of 1904-1905. It included several great military figures of the First World War: Sir Ian Hamilton, the unfortunate commander of the badly prepared Dardanelles expedition; Colonel Enoch Crowder, director of the American draft in the First World War; Captain Peyton March, later Chief of Staff, and Captain Pershing, both of them American military attachés in Tokyo (1904-1905

---

[23] August von Mackensen, *Briefe und Aufzeichnungen des Generalfeldmarschalls aus Krieg und Frieden*, Wolfgang Foerster, ed. (Leipzig 1938), p. 192; James W. Gerard, *My Four Years in Germany* (New York 1917).

[24] William Harding Carter, *The Life of General Chaffee* (Chicago 1917), p. 272.

[25] Max Jähns, *Geschichte der Kriegswissenschaften vornehmlich in Deutschland*, 3 vols. (Munich and Leipzig 1889-1891), p. 2094.

and 1905-1906) ; Major Caviglia, later Italian minister of war, and Max Hoffmann, later Chief of Staff of Germany's eastern front command. They were all sent out to study war in its latest manifestations, war that had not occurred on such a large scale in over thirty years. That they personally gained useful experience in Manchuria is far more certain than whether they succeeded in making their home governments accept their conclusions about the fundamental changes in warfare (use of machine guns, field fortifications, extended fronts, "invisible" uniforms, etc.) .[26]

These men were predestined to leadership in the First World War, because of age and other qualifications, except where gerontocratic conditions stood in the way, as in Hoffmann's case. They were sent out by the home authorities, most often not as military attachés—Pershing's and March's attachéships were merely formal and of short duration. Study of them and of many military attachés emphasizes the fact that service as observer is far more conducive to military leadership than prolonged service as military attaché. None of the German and French army leaders of the First World War had ever served as attaché; such service would seem as deleterious in its effect on commandership as overly-prolonged staff duty.[27]

For one thing the military attaché lived abroad for long

[26] For Hamilton's experiences in the Far East see his book, *A Staff Officer's Scrap Book*, 2 vols. (London 1906-1907); Hoffmann's notes on Manchuria are in his *Aufzeichnungen*, Nowak, ed. (Berlin 1929).

[27] "My own view is that staff work is definitely bad training for a commander. This does not mean to suggest that a commander should never have been a junior staff officer. Some training in that direction is definitely desirable; but an officer who has served nearly all his life on the staff hardly ever makes an outstanding commander. His years of training as a staff officer have made him see so many difficulties and point them out; it is the duty of the commander not to allow himself to be unduly influenced by them. This is definitely difficult for a staff officer who has spent most of his life doing so." Sir Giffard Martel, *The Problem of Security* (London 1945), p. 82. The author is an engineer and tank specialist. Another likely result of such duty may lie in the former attaché's inclination not to obey too strictly. The Russian military plenipotentiary in Berlin, Prince Dolgoruki, proved a failure in the field. Driven by the desire to take a Turkoman position before the other assault columns could arrive, he set out an hour before the general attack was to take place, with the result that his column was defeated and nearly wiped out. Rich and Fisher, II, 91f.

periods. Several services tried to limit the term to three or only two years, but many an attaché managed to stay longer —and came to learn, or believe that he had learned, the foreign army in question better than his own, a knowledge quite inadmissible in the commander. For another thing, the attaché, originally a technician chosen for his language knowledge, his good manners, his ferreting abilities, too often became obsessed with politics, particularly foreign politics. While a certain amount of political judgment and talent proves helpful to the officer placed in positions such as war minister and chief of staff, particularly in his unavoidable dealings with civilian politicians, it has seldom improved commandership—except where a gift for politics and diplomacy could be helpful in circumstances such as those of coalition warfare.[28]

Among the military attachés who subsequently became chief of staff the following might be mentioned: Alfred Count Waldersee, military attaché at Paris before the war of 1870-1871, Moltke's quartermaster-general (1882-1888) and successor (1888-1891), field marshal and commander of the army contingents assembled against the Boxer rebels (1900-1901); or General Boisdeffre, 1882 military attaché in St. Petersburg, later chief of the General Staff, reorganizer of the army together with Freycinet, and negotiator of the Franco-Russian military convention; or General Pellé, Joffre's chief of staff from April 1915 on, former military attaché in Berlin and high in the graces of the Quai d'Orsay, which made him ambassador to Kemalist Turkey after the war. According to an admirer Pellé was "the prototype of the general staff officer, of remarkable intelligence and rare erudition, a man of charming courtesy. He possessed an extraordinary faculty of assimilation and treated with equal competence questions of organization, military or diplomatic problems and foreign affairs," and

---

28 Part of the conflict between Navy Secretary Josephus Daniels and Adm. Sims derived from the Admiral's inclination toward "placing shore duty above sea duty in the danger zones" of the First World War, a propensity influenced by his own past as naval attaché. In his 25 years of service, he spent only nine at sea. Jonathan Daniels, *The End of Innocence* (Philadelphia 1954), pp. 303f.

still with all these talents was "a victim of political hatred."[29] The Italian Chief of Staff, General Pollio, who died suddenly in July 1914, had been military attaché in Vienna for many years, where he had married a lady *née* Gormadz, alias Goldman. He was considered "thoroughly loyal" as regarded Italy's military obligations arising from the Triple Alliance, even by such skeptical judges as Ambassador Count Monts.[30] General Maxwell D. Taylor was for a short time assistant military attaché in Peiping (1939), after having studied the Japanese language—and presumably the Japanese Army as well—in Tokyo since 1935. After commanding an airborne division in the Second World War, he held a variety of posts that indicated the great trust his superiors put in him; he was Superintendent of the United States Military Academy, until he became Assistant Army Chief of Staff, and then (until 1959) Army Chief of Staff. He retired from that post in order to express publicly his great concern about the shortcomings of American defenses in *The Uncertain Trumpet* (New York 1960). His contemporary and opposite number as Air Force Chief of Staff, General Thomas Dresser White, had served in earlier years as attaché in China, Russia, Italy, Greece and Brazil.[31] All in all, judging by the record, attaché training seems not to be conducive to generalship, but rather to intelligence, instruction[32] and staff duties at best, and, at the other end of the spectrum, to politics. Colleagues often considered the returning attaché as lost and spoiled for further front line duties.[33]

Both world wars with their tremendous changes from earlier conditions of warfare and preconceived ideas about

[29] Lieut. Col. Jean Fabry, *Joffre et son destin* (Paris 1931), pp. 78f.

[30] Monts, p. 253.

[31] *Forbes' Magazine*, June 1, 1960.

[32] Brig. Gen. Joseph E. Kuhn, President of the U.S. War College, the Army Staff College, since 1916, had gained some of the war experience which he was to teach prior to America's entry into the war as military attaché and observer both in the Russo-Japanese War, and the first two years of the World War in and around Berlin. Frederick Palmer, *Newton D. Baker: America at War*, 2 vols. (New York 1931), I, 38f., 82.

[33] Lothar Persius, *Menschen und Schiffe in der Kaiserlichen Flotte* (Berlin 1925), pp. 101, 152, gives several examples of former German naval attachés becoming "estranged from their proper profession."

war, would have offered much to the eyes of observers from allied, associated, or neutral powers. The belligerents of 1914 to 1918, however, severely curtailed the opportunities for neutrals, or for most of them, and in the Second World War they strictly limited the occasions for even allied and associated observers to see the war. They feared the revelation of the *parties honteuses* of their warfare, or they were afraid of an unneutral passing of information to the enemy. In the First World War allied observers stayed in the headquarters of the belligerents, but neutral ones—in Paris placed under the guardianship of the War Ministry—were only on rare occasions admitted there, and were taken to inspect the front lines under more or less peaceful conditions and after battles were well over. The Paris attachés of the neutrals were taken over the Marne battlefields of 1914 afterward, and received on-the-spot lectures about the *peripetia* of that battle by members of the French general staff.[34] This might have resulted not in better military history, but in better propaganda, which had become the main aim of the belligerents in taking the neutrals on guided tours to the front lines.[35] An inspection tour by neutrals along the whole length of the Italian front, from the Isonzo to the Swiss frontier, was described in great detail by the Swiss participant; his report was designed for the eyes of Swiss officers only, but it was communicated to the Austrian and German attachés at Berne who found precious data in it.[36]

Between the two great wars, the small wars which took place in Ethiopia[37] and in Spain were perhaps a little more accessible; in the former, American, Austrian, Hungarian, Japanese and Albanian military attachés were reported to have inspected certain front positions and the arrangements in the debarkation port of Massaoua. In Spain, the British

[34] Beauvais, pp. 161f.

[35] Max Schwarte, ed., *Der grosse Krieg 1914-1918* (Berlin 1921), VIII[1], 503.

[36] Beauvais, pp. 85f. This author, p. 159, observes, quite correctly, that the literary record of the neutral observers during the 1914-1918 period is exceedingly meager; this strikes one particularly when compared with the rich military literature on the Russo-Japanese War.

[37] Beauvais, p. 162.

military attaché with the Republican Government fell into the hands of the Franco forces while observing the fighting around Aranjuez in November 1936. They allowed him to return to Madrid by way of Burgos and France, but he could not compare notes with a British attaché in Franco's camp because none had yet been appointed there.[38] The last time neutral attachés functioned as observers on the eve of the Second World War was when the British and Italian military attachés accompanied the Germans who took over the Czech "Maginot Line" (it was much stronger than anyone expected); the French attaché was not taken along, to spare the feelings of the Czech ex-allies—besides, his Government ought to have known the works well enough, as the French themselves had inspired the construction.[39]

Per se, the presence of neutral attachés in opposing camps might have been made to serve the cause of peace, at least in the first steps of leading to suspension of hostilities and an armistice. Actually, the history of war and diplomacy seems to furnish very few examples of their activities in this respect,[40] but some of these will be discussed in the next chapter.

[38] *Ibid.*, pp. 180ff.

[39] John W. Wheeler-Bennett, *Munich: Prologue to Tragedy* (New York 1948), p. 333.

[40] *Documents diplomatiques français*, Ist ser., VI, 151ff.

CHAPTER 14

ATTACHÉS AND THE
LIMITATION OF ARMAMENTS

The most hateful labor, in all probability, for service attachés
to perform has been in connection with the several attempts
at international armament reduction. While the diplomats
concerned have usually been skeptical about the outcome of
such proposals, the typical soldier and sailor officer—the aviator has hardly yet been put in this quandary—has resisted or
sabotaged such attempts, except in occasional situations
where the interest of one power lay in a temporary halt
or slow-up of arms competition. What professional military
man would wish to commit professional or national suicide?

For obvious technical reasons, international disarmament
conferences included a goodly number of actual or former
service attachés as members of the national delegations,
officers with international experience and linguistic ability.
The delegations were often headed by an ambassador who
might happen to be the attaché's permanent chief. The French
and Prussian military attachés in St. Petersburg assisted their
chiefs as "military commissaries," in the highly technical conferences on the use of explosive bullets held in that capital in
1868, one of the first conferences to deal with the restriction
of armaments and also one of the first to employ these experts,
who were in the future to play an increasing, complicated—
and also complicating—role.

The arrangements for technical assistance to be rendered
the chief delegates were much the same in subsequent conferences dealing with the laws and customs of war and the
limitation of armaments. Sometimes the nucleus of a delegation was an ambassador-attaché team which had worked
together satisfactorily in the city where the conference was
held, or in some other capital. The British delegation to
the First Hague Conference included the minister at The

Hague as Second Delegate, and the military attaché in The Hague and Brussels, Lieutenant Colonel Repington, later military correspondent of *The Times*, as military member, in addition to the Director of Military Intelligence in the War Office.[1] The Reich delegation was headed by the Paris Ambassador, Count Münster, whose military-technical assistants were Captain Siegel, his naval attaché, and Colonel Gross von Schwarzhoff, former military attaché in Paris. All the military men were chosen, as Emperor Francis Joseph explained at the time, as "men who were in a position to give information in technical questions"; actually, the positions given them allowed far more independence. There were six service attachés as members of the First Hague Conference, ten at the Second, and four at the London Naval Conference of 1907, and on the whole they employed their international know-how toward an international understanding against disarmament. The German military delegate at The Hague in 1899 used his talents in a different direction: in excellent French, the Conference language, while the other military delegates sat tongue-tied, he blurted out his own and his profession's aversion to the idea of disarmament in almost the first session of the Commission which was to deal with the limitation of armaments, and was composed exclusively of military members. ("That nonsense," as Admiral Lord John Fisher put it in talks with the Germans, but he begged them not to quote him to his country's first delegate, a civilian.)[2] The wish of the Wilhelmstrasse to avoid at least the appearance of opposing the disarmament proposals, highly popular then and later, and the almost equally widespread public indignation at obstructionists of disarmament could be turned against Germany. After the damage had been done the German military delegates excused themselves: they had been forced to play the leading role in the military and naval commissions, much against their original intention. They had at first tried to leave that to others; "but partly because the British and Americans knew no French, while others remained

[1] For one of Repington's reports on the results of the discussions on the limitations of armaments see *British Documents on the Origin of the War*, I, no. 82.

[2] *Grosse Politik*, XV, 4274.

silent, we were therefore forced to lead the debates."[3] The usual military taciturnity was thus turned into a diplomatic-political asset and the unusual military eloquence into a liability. Other attempts to have attachés serve the cause of arms restriction and control, such as the British proposal of 1911 that the naval attachés of the embassies in Berlin and London visit the governmental and private shipyards periodically, observe the progress of ships under construction and thereby remove at least some mutual suspicions,[4] proved no more acceptable than The Hague proposals for the limitation of armaments.

Other attaché services in the interest of peace were somewhat more successful. On at least one occasion neutral attachés became the mediators of a peace, or at least of an armistice as the first step in that direction: the armistice between the Serbs and Bulgarians in December 1885. The initiative was taken by the Great Powers. The Austrian Foreign Minister Count Kalnoky thought it "impossible to allow the belligerents to debate any longer the conditions of an armistice if one ever wants to come to the conclusion of peace." Together with Italy he therefore proposed to the Great Powers that they charge a commission of their military attachés stationed in Vienna with the settling of the purely military questions, the conclusion of an armistice and the drawing of demarcation lines. Serbia and Bulgaria were made to promise beforehand that they would accept the decisions of this international military commission. The powers agreed, with varying amounts of skepticism about such an unprecedented body, but it proved quite successful. Within a week after the start of its work an armistice was obtained, evacuation measures agreed upon, to be begun by Serbia as the losing side in the war, and the immediate appointment of peace negotiators was promised by the belligerents.[5]

[3] *Ibid.*, XV, 4256, 4259, 4351. For more details on the employment of service attachés at international conferences see Beauvais, pp. 63f.

[4] *Grosse Politik*, XXVII, 10429 and passim.

[5] *Ibid.*, XVIII, 5524ff., 5579. For another, perhaps dubious, claim of an attaché, see Papen, *Memoirs*, p. 18. In 1913-1914 he was German military attaché for both Washington and Mexico City. He happened to be in the latter during the Vera Cruz episode, supporting "the moves by the

Operating at a distance from the embassies but still under their authority, groups of military attachés have been employed on such peace problems as the neutral delimitation of new boundaries provided for in peace treaties. Attachés of the neutral Great Powers established the new lines laid down in the Greek-Turkish peace of December 4, 1897, and the settlement was then rammed down the throat of the recalcitrant, because victorious, Turks.[6] The majority of the diverse commissions established to draw the boundaries of the new principality of Albania in 1913-1914 was likewise composed of military attachés of the Great Powers. Their attachés at the Porte were given, from 1903 on, the task of organizing and supervising the international *gendarmerie* in Macedonia, where their presence, it was fondly hoped by British diplomacy, would end the continued bloodshed in that troubled region.[7] On these and a few similar occasions such attaché groups became the organs of a temporarily functioning "concert" of powers, but they have not been too favorably remembered. The Paris Peace Conference, an international body with a somewhat more earnest intention of reducing armaments, at least one-sidedly, showed little respect or use for attachés in the service of disarmament or boundary-drawing; their services in disarming the conquered were dispensed with and the necessary supervision was put in the hands of special interallied missions of control.[8] At certain moments, at least, moments of actual or

different diplomatic representatives to get Huerta to resign, as a means of preventing the conflict with the United States from spreading."

[6] *Documents diplomatiques français*, Ist ser., VI, 151ff.

[7] *Grosse Politik*, XII, 3240.

[8] Francis Leveson Bertie, 1st viscount, *The Diary of Lord Bertie of Thame, 1914-1918*, 2 vols. (New York 1924), II, 320. In October 1919, the Germans proposed to the Peace Conference that the Allied officers serving on control missions when on duty in Germany should wear civilian clothes, "which is customary for officers exercising their functions in foreign countries, for example for military attachés." This seemed to them the best way of avoiding incidents. The Peace Conference, or rather its successor, turned down this sensible proposal, Pichon declaring that "there was no possible analogy between the position of members of the Commissions of control and military attachés. Moreover, military attachés wear the uniform when on duty." (It would be more correct to say: when on certain duties.) Crowe agreed: the Germans merely wanted to diminish the prestige of Allied officers and rob them of the respect that always went with a uniform in Germany. *Documents on British Foreign Policy*, Ist ser., I, 964, 968.

apparent civilian supremacy, diplomats would be willing to agree with pacifists that entrusting military men with disarmament is like choosing cobblers "to deliberate on how men could give up wearing footgear."[9]

Problems that were occasionally, as at The Hague before 1914, coupled with the limitation of armaments, such as the codification of rules of warfare, fared somewhat better, especially when they concerned a supranational problem in future wars, for example, the treatment of prisoners of war, including officers. Other questions, if inconveniently raised during international conferences where soldiers participated, would be passed over as indiscretions: when the Austrian military delegate at the Second Hague Conference, Baron Giesl, a military attaché, touched on the knotty problem of the rights and duties of a military commander in neutral territory and wanted it discussed, he received no support from either the German or the French delegate. Both had neutral Belgium and possibly Switzerland on their minds. "As could be well understood, Germany did not want anyone to look into her cards," and the Frenchman was silent when Giesl asked him "whether in a future war France would definitely renounce all offensive movements beyond her frontiers that might have to cross neutral territory."[10] Such a query, involving a fairly open secret and coming from a military attaché, must have struck Giesl's colleagues as highly undiplomatic and more properly that of an *enfant terrible.*

The discussions and negotiations of disarmament proposals between 1919 and 1939 were more resolutely than before taken in hand by civilians, particularly in Washington in 1921-1922 and in Geneva, where there were "experts" at their elbows. Active or former service attachés, though qualified in various ways, were sedulously kept out of disarmament meetings, as if that would aid in maintaining the often false optimism about these discussions. There was only an occasional ex-attaché among the experts at Geneva, such as Major General A. C. Temperley—"qualified presumably by my previous experi-

9 Bertha von Suttner's comment after the naming of Col. Schwarzhoff to the chairmanship of the Military Committee of the First Hague Conference. Merz Tate, *The Disarmament Illusion* (New York 1942), p. 283.
10 Giesl, p. 181.

ence as a military attaché" (at The Hague, 1920-1925). Temperley served as military adviser to the British Foreign Secretaries, as an observer of disarmament problems for the British General Staff and as member of the Permanent Advisory Commission in Geneva. This had been set up under French pressure as a sort of International General Staff for the International Force which never materialized, but which the French governments tried to foist on the League of Nations as a sop to those idealists who believed that if arms could not be turned into ploughshares, they might at least be internationalized, thus ending arms competition.[11]

[11] For details see Arthur Cecil Temperley, *The Whispering Gallery of Europe* (London 1938), passim.

CHAPTER 15

ATTACHÉS IN THE SERVICE
OF AUTOCRACY

The authoritarian structure of armies and at least some navies has given rise, even in modern times and in unsuspected
places, to a strong tendency on the part of officer bodies to
countenance absolutism. As the German political jingle has
it: "Und der König absolut, wenn er *unsern* Willen tut"
("Let the King be absolute, as long as he does *our* bidding").
Vast powers were left to the not always merely nominal sovereigns in the exercise of their function as commander-in-
chief or Supreme War Lord. Even England's constitutional
ministers allowed Queen Victoria a certain residuum of
absolutism, particularly in her relationship with the British
Army, including the military attachés.[1]

As the number and influence of the attachés increased,
they, rather than the diplomats proper, were sometimes
chosen to approach some of the absolutist holders of thrones,
or to serve as intermediaries between them.[2] These rulers
were only too often inclined to honor the attachés, rather
than civilian diplomats, with their confidences,[3] and in the
process usually strengthened them in their autocratic lean-

[1] According to a report of the Prussian military plenipotentiary from
St. Petersburg, Victoria had telegraphed "her" military attaché there *en
clair* that the fall of Plevna had had "a very painful and depressing
effect in England." *Berliner Monatshefte* (September 1939), p. 767.

[2] For the readiness of the governors of democratic France to exploit
the absolutist leanings of constitutional monarchs, and the latters' strivings for independence from their ministers through the medium of
service attachés, as for example in dealings with Alfonso XIII, see *Documents diplomatiques français*, IInd ser., XII, nos. 205, 315; XIII, nos. 159,
321.

[3] Both Tsar and Tsarina, who had not wanted the peace concluded
at Portsmouth, N.H., in 1905, confided to the British military attaché
in October that Russia had been tricked into the bad peace. Thomas
W. L. Newton, 2nd Baron, *Lord Lansdowne, A Biography* (New York
1929), p. 326.

279

ings. It was through the French military attaché in St. Petersburg that War Minister General Boulanger in February 1887, at a very dangerous moment in Franco-German relations, endeavored to get a letter of an alarming nature to the Tsar —greatly to the horror of his ministerial colleagues.[4] Even the heads of democratic states were sometimes thought to be open to this sort of approach, including the President of the United States. After his skirmish with the powers of the Second Reich, Count Gleichen was transferred to Washington in 1906, and Roosevelt's friend Spring Rice thought him, and not the ambassador, "the best person to keep in touch with the President. . . . A military attaché is the very man to get at him." Spring Rice added this rather morbid recommendation: "As Gleichen has been shot in the stomach and the neck, he is quite certain to meet with a favorable reception, . . . would certainly get on there, although he is rather apt to be scandalized by the unexpected."[5] In spite of such an advantage it does not appear that Gleichen got on overly well in Washington or with Theodore Roosevelt.

Naval attachés, in spite of the slightly more liberal traditions of the junior service, proved equally ready to serve modern absolutism. According to one version of the court history of the Russian Revolution of 1905, the German naval attaché in St. Petersburg, Hintze, who was high in the graces of Nicholas II, not only ordered German torpedo boats to Kronstadt and put them at the disposal of the Tsar should he be forced to leave the country, but also persuaded that autocrat to end all further concessions "to the street" and instead to try force. This advice proved successful for Tsardom and to a certain extent for Hintze as well, although he acquired numerous enemies among the envious members of the German embassy, and among chauvinistic Russians who resented their own failure of nerve against a "nervy" foreigner.[6]

[4] Adrien Dansette, *Le Boulangisme, 1886-1890* (Paris 1938), pp. 63ff.
[5] Stephen Gwynn, ed., *The Letters and Friendships of Sir Cecil Spring Rice* (Boston and New York 1929), I, 23ff.
[6] Johannes Fischart, *Das alte und das neue System* (Berlin 1919), pp. 324ff., where this episode is included in an account of Hintze.

Prussian and Russian Military Plenipotentiaries

The two European armies which, for sixty years after 1815 and in spite of all "geopolitical" circumstances, thought least in terms of competition and hostility were the Prussian and Russian. Although what military institutions they borrowed or exchanged were more the trappings of autocracy than features of true military progress—Prussia took over "taps" and other arrangements about military music, and the Russians introduced the spiked Prussian helmet which was not discarded until the reign of Alexander III—but there was also a constant exchange of officer personnel. The supreme war lords of both armies had for some ten years before 1815 lived on terms of great, if not always sincere, intimacy, and their armies had cherished a similar companionship in arms —sometimes imbued with tutelary condescension on the part of Russia, still the stronger force, a spirit of "c'est la Russie qui a fait la Prusse puissance européenne."[7]

To preserve and cultivate these ties the two monarchs from 1819 on, and more continually from 1834 or 1838, maintained so-called military plenipotentiaries (*Militärbevollmächtigte*) in the brother sovereign's entourage. The officers were usually from the guards regiments, they were always noblemen and of elevated rank, in most cases generals who had been aides-de-camp of their own monarch; they were court generals rather than front officers, and the aide-de-camp position conferred on each of them the privilege of "immediacy," of writing directly to his sovereign whenever he felt moved to do so. The title of the Prussian officers was "aide-de-camp or aide-de-camp general of His Majesty the German Emperor assigned to personal duty with the Emperor of Russia."[8] During most of the nineteenth century these men were the most uncontrolled and irresponsible agents in diplomacy, serving autocracy[9] as long as autocracy understood its own interest.

[7] Otto Hoetzsch, *Peter von Meyendorff* (Berlin and Leipzig 1923), I, 286.
[8] For this institution in general see Meisner, *Militärattachés*, pp. 67ff.
[9] In 1880 the Tsar told the Prussian plenipotentiary that he had a letter from his uncle William I expressing concern with the Tsar's reported intention to grant a constitution; William advised his nephew,

In the fulfillment of their duties they remained independent of their country's embassy, using their own ciphers and addressing their reports directly to the monarch at home. The foreign and war ministers might receive them later—sometimes too late for usefulness, as Bismarck thought—or might never receive them from the sovereign's hand. When the Prussian minister at St. Petersburg was on leave, it was usually the military plenipotentiary, and not the first secretary of legation, who took over as chargé d'affaires. At various times they carried the most important messages and the most intimate exchanges of ideas between the two autocrats (the one in Berlin was relatively more under ministerial control). The success of this inter-sovereign communication, this "aide-de-camp diplomacy," as one of the military plenipotentiaries called it, depended altogether on the maintenance of the monarchs' mutual trust and of the trust they put in their agents, who "had nothing to do with any authority, any superior, only with the two sovereigns." In the words of General von Schweinitz, a sturdy conservative who held this office from 1865 to 1869: "I reported to nobody except the King, and was under no necessity of accepting orders from the Ministry of War or the Foreign Office which I thought were not in keeping with the considerations which my altogether exceptional position imposed upon me."[10]

As high-ranking members of the monarchs' military entourage the plenipotentiaries often met the earlier Tsars, at all court and military events and at the tea table of the Tsarina. "The Prusski Fligeladjutant, as he was called at the court, saw the emperor almost daily, at any rate oftener than Gortchakov did;[11] the emperor discoursed with him not only about

---

on the strength of his own experience with constitutionalism and considering the backward state of the Russian people, not to do this. The Tsar was very much gratified by this friendly avuncular advice and assured the Prussian general that he had no constitutional intentions. Schweinitz, II, 8.

[10] *Ibid.* I, 181.

[11] Gortchakov dreaded the Tsar's dealings through the plenipotentiaries. As he told Bismarck when the latter was Prussian minister to St. Petersburg (1859-1862), in thanking him for not having used all the byways that might have been available to him in that capital: Münster, one of these officers, had under Nicholas I "a position which for a foreigner to

militaria and the greetings from him to be transmitted to our master were not restricted to family affairs" (Bismarck). This position enabled the plenipotentiaries to defend Prussian policy to Nicholas I, the protector of the counterrevolution, whenever Prussia was in disgrace; Nicholas told one of them, Count Münster (1850-1856), "every day how miserable authority was in Berlin as long as that whole constitutional rubbish 'of the 1848 Revolution' was not removed" (1852). He held that as weakness in his brother-in-law, Frederick William IV, who, the plenipotentiary advised in Berlin, was so much in disgrace that he should refrain from writing letters to the Tsar for the time being. "Believe me, it is better if they do not write to one another," an *avis au lecteur* that William II would not have understood though it was published during his reign. The Prussian had to defend and justify Prussia's policies, for example during the crisis in December 1850 that led to Olmütz, which the Tsar found insufferable and contrary to the spirit and best interest of the Holy Alliance as far as it still survived. Prussia's position during the Crimean War again made "for difficult hours with the Tsar," who had become such a sick man that "one now often catches glimpses of Papa Paul," that is to say, of that earlier Tsar's madness.

The plenipotentiary was often called "a representative of the Prussian Army with the Russian," and he could at times feel more reliance on the Army than on the Tsar. For the Army had chosen Austria as *the* enemy, largely on the basis of experiences in Hungary in 1849, where the conditions of coalition warfare against the Revolution had estranged the participating armies and had also given the Russian generals a low opinion of Austrian bravery; Austria's unfriendly, "ungrateful" attitude during the Crimean War strengthened not only this hostility, but also the friendliness of the military toward a better-behaved and much more neutral Prussia. Even during the Olmütz crisis when the Tsar had sided with Austria and had partly mobilized against Prussia, the pleni-

---

hold, even if he belongs to a related court, is quite unbearable in the eyes of every Russian." Maximilian Harden, *Von Versailles nach Versailles* (Dresden 1927), p. 488.

potentiary found that "no reasonable man inside the Army would like to oppose us in favor of Austria, since the sympathies for the Prussian Army are still almost as powerful as the hatred everywhere expressed against Austria. This the Emperor also knows full well and will have to consider."[12] Even the highest respect for autocracy did not blind the Prussian officer to the fact that it was the Russian Army which could still make or unmake a tsar; his successors were to see still more of that power.

Bismarck, having been Prussian minister to St. Petersburg himself, knew only too well how the system worked on either end of this extradiplomatic wire. While it offered advantages, it also had inconveniences: "The activity of two independent political agents at the same court has undoubted disadvantages for the Royal Service, particularly if the one does not know what language the other uses when talking to the people on the spot," he wrote from the Neva to the man he would succeed in the Berlin foreign ministry.[13] In spite of the dangers of dual agents in St. Petersburg, he boldly proceeded to make the best use of the system, remembering only too well that occasionally in the past Prussia's plenipotentiaries were more important negotiators than the "rather helpless" Prussian ministers accredited there at the same time.[14] Several times when he wanted to get some information or a request to the Tsar directly, either because time was pressing or to by-pass Gortchakov, he made use of the Prussian plenipotentiary, and he found the autocrat of all the Russias by no means averse to this procedure. The Tsar told Bismarck on one occasion, in his own Chancellor's presence, that "when military men negotiate with one another, everything always goes well; as soon, however, as diplomats mix in, nothing but imbecilities happen."[15]

When the war of 1866 approached and the Tsar remained

[12] The above is based on "Politische Briefe des Grafen Hugo zu Münster an Edwin von Manteuffel," *Deutsche Revue* (January-June 1913).

[13] *Bismarck's Briefwechsel mit Schleinitz* (Stuttgart 1905), p. 164.

[14] Otto, Fürst von Bismarck, *Gedanken und Erinnerungen*, 3 vols. (Stuttgart and Berlin 1919-1922), II, 253.

[15] Report to William I by Col. von Loë, March 1, 1863. *Die auswärtige Politik Preussens, 1858-1871*, III, 330f., 337.

uninformed or misinformed about Prussia's policy—the Prussian minister practically never saw Alexander II and besides was an opponent of Bismarck's policy, and the Tsar would be enlightened only by the ill-willed Gortchakov—Schweinitz, the Plenipotentiary, took it upon himself to explain to Alexander the "forceful motives" of Prussian policy. He had disagreed with many of Bismarck's opening moves, "as an officer and man of honor"; but in his opinion the military intermediary of the two sovereigns still had "the task of representing the immutable laws of honor and nearly sacred friendship even when state reason was in conflict with them."

"My conservative views, my abomination of the Revolution were known to Emperor Alexander, and it could therefore not remain without some impression upon him if even I pointed out to him certain national desires of Germany as justified and imperative." The Tsar called such a war, which could actually only hurt dynastic interests, "a general misfortune; the common enemy of all, the Revolution, against whom all governments ought to maintain a common front, would be the only winner. . . . My task was limited to convincing the Emperor that we represented the true, actually realizable conservative interest with which went certain concessions to the national party." Schweinitz depicted to the Tsar the dangers with which the Revolution was threatening everything high, everything in the existing order, not forgetting the status of Prussia's and Russia's common enemy, Poland, and finally won him over to the view "that the Prussian army was truly the only firmly closed phalanx which could restore orderly conditions." In doing so, Schweinitz felt fully conscious of "the great responsibility which was weighing on me, although not before the law, public opinion or the Ministry, because for these I was non-existent, officially I had only to do with the two sovereigns."[16]

Bismarck was much impressed by Schweinitz' initiative and diplomatic talents, and made him ambassador to Vienna after the war of 1866, although he was aware that aristocratic Viennese society would feel slighted by the appointment of a

16 Schweinitz, I, 193f., 200f., 220f.

mere colonel from the lower nobility,[17] who in addition married the daughter of an American clergyman. His successor on the Neva, first as plenipotentiary and later as ambassador, was General von Werder (1869-1886), from the First Guards, like Schweinitz. The King himself had wanted to send a Colonel von Rauch, son of a former plenipotentiary and minister, as tradition in the relationships between the two courts and two armies had become a weighty factor.[18]

In Russian accounts of this system it was always Prussia that came begging to the Tsar on her way to great power status, invoking his approval and assistance in the wars she undertook. Immediately upon the outbreak of the war of 1870-1871, William I sent the Russian plenipotentiary to the Tsar with a confidential letter appealing to their ancient friendship and expressing the hope that he would intervene, should Austria show signs of entering the war on Napoleon's side.[19] Even before the letter could have arrived, Alexander had informed his uncle through Werder that he would place an army of 300,000 along the Austrian frontier, and that he would possibly even occupy Galicia if Austria abandoned her neutrality. Russian sentiments early in the war were generally very favorable to Prussia. "Most people hope that victory will follow the banners of Your Majesty. The public takes it quite for granted that Russia will not permit Austria's participation in the war," Werder reported. And the Russian plenipotentiary, Prince Kutusov, in the Prussian GHQ at Sedan, wept tears of joy over the downfall of Napoleon III. This feeling changed somewhat later in the war, when French propaganda aroused the fear that the now much stronger neighbor might some day take away Russia's Baltic provinces.

The Russians, overlooking Prussia's friendly neutrality during the Crimean War, inclined to think that she was repaying such "services" with rank ingratitude by her attitude toward the Russo-Turkish War of 1878-1879. On the eve of the

[17] Emile Ollivier, *L'Empire libéral*, 18 vols. (Paris 1895-1918), XII, 299f.
[18] Excerpts from Werder's reports to William I were published in the *Berliner Monatshefte* (September 1939), under the title, after the recent Nazi-Soviet Pact, "Aus Jahrzehnten deutsch-russischer Freundschaft."
[19] Ollivier, XV, 419f.

war, Bismarck evaded as long as possible answering the Tsar's question of October 1, 1876, whether Germany would remain neutral if Russia should get into a war with Austria. The channel of communication was Plenipotentiary von Werder. Together with Gortchakov he had followed the Tsar to his *villegiatura* in the Crimea and without protest had accepted the fearful query and transmitted it to Berlin. Bismarck was enraged:

> Von Werder is rather worse than awkward when he allows himself to be used as a Russian tool in order to extort from us an inconvenient and untimely answer. . . . To present us now with the insidious question about Austria, demanding a yes or no, is one of Gortchakov's traps. If we answer "No," he spoils things for us with the Tsar; if we answer "Yes," he makes use of that in Vienna. Does Werder consciously or unconsciously help to set the trap? He must be prohibited from lending himself to the posing of questions at the address of his own Government. If and when the question: whether or not we promise to remain neutral in a war against Austria, should be submitted to us by Russian organs contrary to our expectations, we must in any case evade the answer. We ourselves have not asked for or received such guarantees from Russia in '66 or '70.[20]

As Bismarck saw it, Werder was in Livadia "so to speak under the power of Gortchakov who, through the channel of Werder, under the mask of *bonhommie,* can ask us for more than is fair, for something so imprudent that it cannot even be submitted in the official diplomatic way. . . . What Werder was moved to transmit was so irresponsible and evasive in its nature that it would be an easy thing to afterwards disavow it as mere confidential conversation with just the Tsar's own 'aide.' " While the Chancellor saw no immediate usefulness in the removal of Werder from Livadia, he told him to refrain from all political business, about which he seemed to know less than was desirable in his position, and to remind all Russian interlocutors of the existing regular diplomatic channels.

[20] *Grosse Politik*, II, 240.

For if things should go on in this manner, we either get into concessions fraught with the heaviest consequences, or in *mésententes* with Emperor Alexander, just the thing Gortchakov expects, but which we can escape much more easily or almost certainly through the regular course of business. A political military plenipotentiary at St. Petersburg who is sympathetic to Emperor Alexander can form a very useful complement to the diplomatic relations of the two courts; if, however, a totally unpolitical officer who by and by has come to be closer to Russian than to home conditions, should become the exclusive representative of German policy in Russia, with such a clever and for us so unreliable a diplomat as Gortchakov to face, that would amount to a diplomatic calamity, and no representation at all would be preferable.[21]

Bismarck gave orders that henceforth all Russian queries, demands and claims, when reported through Werder, would be treated by the Auswärtiges Amt as non-official and would be dealt with by the King's Military Cabinet or the Ministry of War. Werder himself was to refrain in future from transmitting such highly political communications and to point to the non-political character of his mission. The ambassador in St. Petersburg, von Schweinitz, who had been on leave, returned to his post to take over the task of answering or evading such embarrassing Russian questions. Bismarck trusted that at least Gortchakov would no longer be able to present them "under the guise of amicable informality" and through agents who were not fully responsible.[22] In 1880 Werder expressed through Schweinitz his desire to be transferred from the Neva, and Bismarck thought it a good thing to see him go, telling Schweinitz that Werder had "behaved like a Russian general, whereas in fact he was an official of the Foreign Office." Schweinitz was fully aware that both statements were wrong, "but the Prince had worked himself gradually into such a state of excitement and gesticulated in such a manner with his long pencil that I no longer interrupted him."[23] Werder had sinned unforgivably against one of the maxims of Bis-

---

[21] *Ibid.*, II, 242.   [22] *Ibid.*, II, 239-251.   [23] Schweinitz, II, 136.

marckian—if not of all—diplomacy: "Do not transmit awkward wishes of foreign governments to Berlin. Leave it to the foreign government to bring forward such requests through their own representatives in Berlin where they can be more easily refused if need be."[24]

Both Schweinitz and Werder, that pair of military diplomats, came to realize the increasing limitations on the Tsar's omnipotence, imposed on him by the Army. Ostensibly to compensate for the German Army's superior and more rapid mobilization, the Army was constantly putting more troops into the Western provinces; Prussia wanted their number reduced, in the interest of friendly relations, but the Tsar could not make the Army agree. Werder convinced himself early in 1880 that, although the wish for peace might be close to the Tsar's heart, such a concession for the time being was "impossible and dangerous because the war party, principally recruited from among the officers of the General Staff, would make use of it at once for its own profit. This would rob the Emperor of the respect which he still possesses but which, unfortunately, has been deeply shaken due to the complete bankruptcy of the regime, and particularly so in the Army. A demand, however, put forth by a foreign power, especially one heretofore friendly like Germany, which might hurt patriotic feeling—and the retiring of troops from the border zone would amount to that—might lead to a war or make governing impossible for the Tsar."[25]

The latent dictatorship exercised by the Russian Army came further into the open during the agitation of Skobelev, who impressed Werder as belonging to the type of people's tribune or military dictator—"a role he seems eminently fitted for." Skobelev was bold enough to pronounce in Russian society that "the only salvation for the Emperor was to put himself at the head of his [the Pan-Slavist] party," but only after long hesitation did Alexander II make up his mind to censure him and order him to abstain from further speechmaking. Germany in the early 1880's had become a very

[24] Bülow, IV, 289.
[25] Immediate reports to William I of March 26, 1880, February 10 and March 9, 1882, November 23, 1883. *Berliner Monatshefte* (September 1939), pp. 69ff.

"possible enemy" in many circles of Russian society, but when Werder asked who really wanted such a war, he was told: "Only those who have nothing to lose or risk nothing in it, and some ambitious General Staff officers who incidentally will not expose themselves overmuch." To these Germanophobes Werder thought it necessary to add the Pan-Slavist party, which dreamed of a great Slav empire and would play a great role in the future.[26]

Berlin still tried for a time to keep the exchange of plenipotentiaries alive and to make it useful, but the institution was losing strength, especially with the death of Alexander II (1881). There was talk of ending it altogether. The German Crown Prince, who had long since found this completely irresponsible position incompatible with his own ideas of Liberalism and constitutionalism, told Schweinitz that he intended to give it up when his day came, and the Ambassador himself, by 1883, was persuaded that the institution had had its day.[27] The death of William I (1888) was the *coup de grâce* —only a pious tradition had kept it alive since Alexander's death.[28]

It had first suffered a diminution in 1880 when the two plenipotentiaries, General von Werder (in *ancienneté* ranking above the ambassador, von Schweinitz) and General Prince Dolgoruki, were simultaneously replaced by mere colonels, aides-de-camp of their respective monarchs— Colonel von Villeaume, heretofore military attaché in Paris, and Colonel Golenitschev Kutusov. The latter was made particularly welcome in Berlin because his father had served there in the same position; the fact that he had died by a stroke in the presence of Emperor William I was mentioned among the son's qualifications. French diplomacy foresaw, rightly, that with a team of such minor rank the prestige of the office would tend to decline.[29] Much to the satisfaction of the French, Alexander III terminated the institution of 75

[26] *Ibid.*, pp. 77f.
[27] Schweinitz, II, 250.
[28] *Ibid.*, II, 265; III, 431. For Bismarck's admission of 1887 that the post was no longer what it used to be see Lucius von Ballhausen, *Bismarck-Erinnerungen* (Stuttgart 1920), p. 382.
[29] *Documents diplomatiques français*, Ist ser., VI, 344, 350f.

years' standing by recalling the Russian plenipotentiary in 1892 and appointing no successor, which forced the Germans to follow suit. To the French, waiting for the Russian alliance, "this was not one of the smallest signs of the spirit of independence on Tsar Alexander's part and of the little inclination he has for everything that might tighten the links uniting the two courts."[30] To mask the inner break in German-Russian relations, however, which had come with the start of Franco-Russian negotiations, the Tsar insisted on having Werder in St. Petersburg again, this time as ambassador; he assured William II that he put "an absolute and unlimited trust" in him. The Kaiser, persuaded by his friend Eulenburg to preserve at least the appearance of harmony between the two courts, readily assented.[31]

Practically all these plenipotentiaries, Russian and Prussian, had upheld the traditional non-competitive relations between Berlin and St. Petersburg, particularly as far as the armies were concerned; both armies, in fact, deprecated competition, with its revolutionizing effects. The sentiments of the Russian partners in this relationship are less well documented, but certainly the plenipotentiary in Berlin from 1879 to 1884, Prince Nikolaus Dolgoruki (with whom Alexander II was said to share more secrets than with his foreign minister, Giers) represented such conservative views that he even defended and furthered the Three Emperors' Alliance, the whipping-boy of the Pan-Slavists in and out of the Army. Giers assured the Bismarcks that the Pan-Slavists were "your enemies as well as ours. . . . But we want to stand together against the Revolution and therefore seek to lean on the world's strongest monarchy, Germany. We can reckon only with monarchies; it would be suicide for us to get involved with a gang like Grévy, Clemenceau, Floquet *et toutes ces canailles.*" At that time the vast majority of politicizing Russian officers would have agreed to the closest possible alliance with Germany, but only *à deux*, without Austria, the oppressor of Slavs.[32] But to that Bismarck and his successors could not agree, for good reasons,

---

[30] *Ibid.*, IX, no. 281, and X, no. 18; Toutain, p. 147.

[31] *Grosse Politik*, VII, 1639-1641; Haller, p. 85; *Documents diplomatiques français*, Ist ser., X, no. 57.

[32] *Grosse Politik*, III, 617; V, 1118.

including military ones. And soon there was no holding back of the insidious work of officers agitating for a Franco-Russian alliance, wrecking the old-fashioned political structure which the military plenipotentiaries had once helped to support.

The officers of the Russian General Staff were particularly satisfied with the disappearance of this institution. They had long resented, as they confessed to their new friends, the French, the presence of the Prussian plenipotentiary at all Russian parades, reviews and maneuvers, where he had "finally become something like an indiscreet, inconvenient and dangerous supervisor." French diplomacy was equally satisfied, although for a time the institution of a similar post was considered. And the Russian ambassador in Berlin was relieved that he was no longer overshadowed by a *grand seigneur* like Dolgoruki in the office of military plenipotentiary.[33] The latter had wanted to become ambassador himself, for the great purpose of saving Russia with the help of Germany; he told her diplomats that she "had it in her power to preserve the Russian dynasty and save Russia from the otherwise inevitable Panslav or Nihilist revolution." She could do that by proposing a revision of the *status quo* in the Balkans, which would give the Russian governmental policy such prestige that it "would cripple all attempts to overthrow the dynasty for a considerable time to come."[34]

The pseudo-absolutism of William II, who could never quite forget ancient Prusso-Russian intimacy and dreamed of restoring it, was never more active along this line than in 1904 and 1905, the years of the Russo-Japanese War, the Russian Revolution and Bjoerkoe. Among the institutions to be revived were the cooperation of the two police systems against "the Revolution" (which had never quite lapsed),[35] and that of the military plenipotentiaries.[36] Several times

[33] Toutain, pp. 147, 276f. Dolgoruki tried in later years to return once more to Berlin, as ambassador, but was sent to Rome instead (1909). *Grosse Politik*, XXVII, 406.

[34] Rich and Fisher, II, 15, 92, 96.

[35] See Kurt Eisner, *Der Geheimbund des Zaren* (Berlin 1904).

[36] For the later story of the military plenipotentiary see Gustav Graf zu Lambsdorff, *Die Bevollmächtigten Kaiser Wilhelms II. am Zarenhofe, 1904-1914* (Berlin 1937).

after 1894 "Willy" had proposed to "Nicky" that they once more exchange aides-de-camp as members of their *maisons militaires,* to facilitate their exchange of thought; but the Tsar either paid no attention or answered that "it would provoke all kinds of gossip."[37] The Kaiser intended "through his personal influence on the Tsar to tie the latter closely to himself and to Germany. But the Tsar did not want to be animated, but rather to be left alone. . . . He was thoroughly conscious of the mental superiority of William II, felt it to be oppressive and avoided meetings with him as much as he could" (Lambsdorff). Only the disasters of 1904 made him somewhat more accessible to the Kaiser's importunities. In October 1904 the Kaiser appointed one of his *Flügel* aides-de-camp, Gustav Count von Lambsdorff, as military plenipotentiary—in order to revive that ancient institution of their forefathers' times, as he wrote the Tsar. Again this soldier was to be "a direct link between the two of us," was to report only to the Emperor and was to have no official connection with anyone else at home, General Staff, Ministry of War, Foreign Office, or Chancellor.[38] The Tsar agreed and followed suit.

At the outset, the renovated institution seemed a success, at least to the diplomats of the Entente who thought that "the Plenipotentiary-General-Aide-de-Camp would be a very important person, more important than the Ambassador," as had so often been the case in the past. It appeared that "the Kaiser has got the ear of the Emperor here, has his adjutant always bringing him messages and making all manner of suggestions," so that the easily alarmed Spring Rice wrote to his friend Roosevelt from the British Embassy in St. Petersburg: "The Kaiser has enormous influence here and has through the Russian and German military attachés direct access to the Emperor's ear—which he uses. . . . They say here 'Berlin is the capital of Russia.' Of course, the policy of

37 *Denkwürdigkeiten des Fürsten Chlodwig zu Hohenlohe-Schillingsfürst,* Vol. III, *Denkwürdigkeiten der Reichskanzlerzeit,* Karl Alexander von Müller, ed. (Stuttgart 1931), p. 9.
38 Walter Goetz, ed., *Briefe Wilhelms II. an den Zaren 1894-1914* (Berlin 1920), p. 129; *Grosse Politik,* XIX, 6035; *Documents diplomatiques français,* IInd ser., V, 47off.

Kaiser Wilhelm is a secret to nobody now. It is to have the hegemony of Western Europe and leave the East to Russia. At home he is to crush the Socialists and Liberals with the sympathy and support of Russia whom in turn he is to help to crush her own internal enemies." To Roosevelt the Britisher depicted the threat of an anti-Liberal world dominion, established and run by the autocrats in Berlin and St. Petersburg, whose close cooperation would be arranged through the two military plenipotentiaries.[39] These agents seemed immensely powerful to others as well: Delcassé suggested in 1912 and again in 1913 that France and Russia imitate the Prusso-Russian arrangement by an exchange of aides to the heads of State. But better advice prevailed: Paléologue pointed out that French public opinion would not tolerate it, and would accuse Poincaré of still stronger autocratic temper than he was already charged with possessing.[40]

The renewal almost immediately proved a senseless anachronism. The first incumbent, Count Lambsdorff, was chosen partly because his family had a Russian branch to which the Foreign Minister, Count Lamsdorff, belonged. Instead of reviving ancient supranational and inter-Junker connections, however, the appointment merely aroused the suspicions of modern nationalism, which forced the Russian Lamsdorff to cut the German Lambsdorff, and avoid meeting him. The lack of success of this renaissance soon became so obvious that the French could easily refrain from imitating it, as Loubet and others had been anxious to do.[41]

With the one exception of the Dogger Bank incident, the Tsar never made the confidential use of the military plenipotentiary which William had anticipated, and the various German plenipotentiaries repeatedly told him that it was a futile hope. Besides, the retired way in which the Tsar preferred to live gave them very little occasion for speaking to

[39] Gwynn, *Spring Rice*, I, 436, 439; II, 22, 156.

[40] Georges Maurice Paléologue, *Au Quai d'Orsay, à la veille de la tourmente: journal de 1913-1914* (Paris 1947), pp. 120f.

[41] Goetz, *Briefe*, pp. 220, 386ff.; Russia, Foreign Office, *Un livre noir, diplomatie d'avant-guerre d'après les documents des archives russes, novembre 1910-juillet 1914*, 5 vols. (Paris 1922-1934), I, 36; *Grosse Politik*, XIX, 528.

him directly, while the Russian counterpart at Berlin, who was far more often seen in the Emperor's military entourage, had ample occasion to witness that monarch's impetuosities and indiscretions.[42] The new exchange proved still more unfortunate when it was discovered that the Russian plenipotentiary in Berlin, Colonel Shebeko, was engaged in espionage. He had been military attaché there in 1904, and subsequently attached to the person of the Emperor. Now, feeling well protected in a more honorable position, he went on with his old activities and had to be recalled at German suggestion in November 1905. A suitable successor was not at once found, since the Russian War Ministry insisted that the candidate must have "absolute qualifications for the general staff service." "For better spying?" queried the disillusioned Emperor on the margin of the report.

The conditions under which the military plenipotentiary could be a harmonizing influence in the relationship between Russia and Germany, and particularly between their armies, never returned. Somewhat reluctantly, at least on the slightly more conservative German side, they were caught up in the unrelenting process of military competition. Early in 1908 Russia, not yet fully recovered from her Manchurian defeat, "feared" Turkish preparations for war against Persia, preparations that seemed confirmed by a trip of von der Goltz Pasha to Constantinople. General Roediger, the war minister and no Pan-Slavist, told the second in this new series of plenipotentiaries, Major General von Jacobi, that speaking quite openly as a soldier the challenging attitude of Turkey could only be explained by Germany stiffening her back. Jacobi answered, "as a soldier and officer, that he as well as the ambassador could give the assurance that the insinuation that Germany was driving Turkey into war was a grotesque

---

[42] *Grosse Politik*, XXV, 8808. Only occasionally did William II realize that the exchange favored the Russians almost exclusively. Then he would wax very indignant that Tatitchev should abuse his position of trust and bandy about imperial indiscretions, though he did expect, but rarely received, the same sort of indiscretion in reports from his own plenipotentiary near the Tsar. Robert, Graf von Zedlitz-Trützschler, *Twelve Years at the Imperial German Court* (London 1924), p. 243.

and tendentious piece of vituperation."[43] The antagonism of the once friendly armies went so far that the Russians saw the mailed fist of Germany behind any move contrary to her own policies in the Balkans, even if in fact Turkey, Austria or Bulgaria was acting far too much on her own to please Berlin. The German Army was everywhere suspected of greater imperialist drive than it actually possessed.

In 1908 General von Jacobi found all Russia united against Germany, in spite of the anti-revolutionary support she had lent the Tsarist regime in 1904-1905. Grand dukes from Nikolai Nikolaievitch down, reactionary Muscovites, liberal Pan-Slavists, court, society and army were agreed. "Of course, there are still among them persons who have preserved their pro-German sentiment, but whereas formerly they appeared on the scene joyfully and assuredly, using every opportunity to give expression of their sentiment to me, to speak of traditional friendship, comradeship-in-arms, yes, even of the possibility of fighting shoulder to shoulder, they now almost avoid me, at least as soon as they think they are under observation, weigh their words carefully and at the most bring themselves to characterize a war against Germany as foolishness, as an impossibility."[44] For a military man, for a member of two societies that were once in many respects one, this shows an unexpected awareness of an alienation process that could only end in mutual destruction.

Such a man could not last long in this equivocal post. After less than a year he was replaced by a naval officer from the Kaiser's entourage, Captain von Hintze (1908-1911), who had been Diederichs' flag lieutenant at Manila, diplomatic negotiator with Dewey, and later (1918) for a short time foreign secretary. Finding little to do as member of the Tsar's entourage, and excluded from the business of the regular military and naval attachés, he composed long reports on foreign affairs, and found it very hard to avoid so-called diplomatic questions. His activity was more or less integrated with the regular diplomatic service of the Reich, however: he used the embassy cipher for his telegrams, which went through the

[43] *Grosse Politik*, XXV, 8597, 8723, 8732, 8826, 8850.
[44] *Ibid.*, XXV, 8740.

Wilhelmstrasse; he let the ambassador read his reports (at least some of them), and the latter on occasion gave the plenipotentiary directions which the Wilhelmstrasse thought necesary.[45] The Wilhelmstrasse employed him where one "who knew the peculiar qualities of the Tsar so well" could be of service, reminding him, when necessary, that the autocratic power of Nicholas must be considered as much diminished, that he "was after all only a more or less irresolute tool in the hands of his responsible counsellors and that the personal sympathies for the person of his Majesty the Emperor which he undoubtedly possessed, are without influence on our relations with official Russia."[46]

The complete estrangement of the armies, which a naval man had been sent to mend, culminated in the Russian summer maneuvers of 1910, when Germany, already considered "the supposed enemy in all maneuver exercises of army and navy since Alexander III," was openly, in printed orders, called *the* enemy. This was a "quite extraordinary manner of expression" for which the Grand Duke Nicholas or his staff were responsible, and which was intended to make the maneuvers "more lively and more understandable for officers and men."[47] It marked the end of a tradition which sentimentalists date from the oath of eternal friendship sworn by Alexander I and Frederick William III at the tomb of Frederick the Great on November 3, 1805, and it also signalized a deterioration of international courtesy which was not again apparent until after the two World Wars.[48]

Increasingly, Hintze found that in spite of the absence of a true conflict of interests between Germany and Russia—when the actual conflict was between Germany and the Western powers, and between Russia and Austria—the "old tradition-

---

[45] *Ibid.*, XXVI, 9573.   [46] *Ibid.*, XXVI, 786, 866.

[47] Report of German military attaché, August 12, 1910. *Ibid.*, XXVII, 9950ff.

[48] The first German military attaché to Brussels after 1929 found to his surprise that in the Belgian maneuvers of 1938 the supposed enemy of the Belgian forces were two divisions with which he himself had recently served. "That was no accident. Beyond the limits of the Third Reich there were also people with sometimes doubtful taste." Geyr, *Erinnerungen*, p. 134, also p. 160 for a Dutch exercise based on a theoretical Japanese invasion of the East Indies.

ally friendly relations" between St. Petersburg and Berlin were at the Russian end "consciously used to put Germany to sleep when she might become suspicious or resentful." Even the memory of them vanished with the older generation, which was accused by the younger *outre tombe* that it had suffered the unification of Germany and Italy to the detriment of Russian interests.[49] The Tsar could not have helped this, even if he had wanted to. After the Bosnian crisis the Kaiser and Chancellor Bethmann Hollweg agreed that the former's endeavors to exert an influence over the Tsar, personally or through military plenipotentiaries, had had no tangible effect as far as Russian policy toward Germany was concerned.[50]

Hintze came to be considered an ultra-pessimist, in regard to German-Russian relations, both by the Wilhelmstrasse and by the Kaiser's entourage. The Tsar and the German embassy had also tired of him, and he was recalled early in 1911, taking leave of St. Petersburg with the conviction that the institution of the military plenipotentiary, begun under totally different conditions, had outlived its usefulness.[51] The embassy was glad to see this doubter of its own peace-preserving efforts go, and the Countess Pourtalès, the ambassadress, expressed the general relief in the words: "Enfin nous avons réussi à nous débarrasser de Hintze."[52]

The last incumbents of the office of military plenipotentiary on each side, Lieutenant General von Chelius (1911-1914) and Major-General Tatichev (1905-1914), were faithful adherents of the ancient, outdated tradition. The Russian was characterized by the French as "a guard officer accustomed to the high life of St. Petersburg,"[53] and later by the Belgian minister to Berlin as follows: "a court and *salon* soldier, living in the entourage of William II, overloaded with attentions by him, was won over by German propaganda into admiring Germany, to favoring the renewal of an alliance between Russia and her powerful neighbor. He reflected, as in an unconscious mirror, the inmost sentiment prevailing in part of the Tsar's

[49] *Grosse Politik*, XXVI, 864. [50] *Ibid.*, XXVI, 9571.
[51] *Ibid.*, XXVII, 9956f. [52] Lambsdorff, *op.cit.*, pp. 190f.
[53] *Documents diplomatiques français*, IInd ser., VIII, no. 271.

entourage and of Petersburg high society who were much more attracted towards monarchical Germany and her autocratic Emperor than towards Republican France."[54]

Such anti-Republican inclinations, however, were not sufficient to restore Prusso-Russian understanding. The two armies no longer wanted it and made that clear to men like Tatichev.[55] During the July 1914 crisis he happened to be on leave in St. Petersburg and was to carry one of the last-minute messages in favor of peace which the Tsar and Kaiser exchanged, whether sincerely or not. This one was to be dispatched after the Tsar had ordered mobilization against Austria, and after the Kaiser had come to think it "childish" to go on with his role of mediator in the face of Russian mobilization.[56] But Tatichev's departure was held up at the St. Petersburg railway station, for reasons not well known, by Sasonov, with whom he witnessed, on July 30, the Tsar's last struggle against the final step into war and his decision to order immediate mobilization of all Russian forces.[57]

It is in the light of the last flicker of tradition that one must consider these two plenipotentiaries, now quite without power, in July 1914. They made gestures to maintain a peace which meant, as they and some "effeminate" courtiers realized, the preservation of at least two dynasties, and of their own institution and way of life. Officers in the Tsar's entourage, good monarchists, suggested to Chelius on July 26 that he urge the Emperor to telegraph the Tsar "as the best way of preserving peace among the great Powers . . . appealing to the Tsar's own monarchical feelings and pointing to the severe shock which the monarchical idea had suffered through the Sarajevo murder and the dangers which threaten the monarchies in the case of a general European conflagration." Chelius, who transmitted this appeal to Berlin, found St. Petersburg full of "the fear of being forced to make war

[54] Beyens, II, 55.

[55] *Grosse Politik*, XXXIV, 12605-12606, 12609; *Oesterreich-Ungarns Aussenpolitik*, V, 5150, 5168.

[56] Auswärtiges Amt, *Die deutsche Dokumente zum Kriegsausbruch . . . 1914*, Max Montgelas and Walter Schücking, eds., 4 vols. (Berlin 1919), nos. 390, 399.

[57] Fay, II, 301, 472.

while in all Russia the revolt of the laboring masses is burning," a fear "still ranking higher with many than the interest
in Serbia"; among "the old gentlemen at headquarters" there
was still little love for the entente with France and "great
inclination towards monarchical alliance with Germany."[58]
As late as July 30, with almost the coolness of the historian,
Chelius was able to see that "they have mobilized here out
of fear of coming events, without aggressive intentions, and
are now frightened by what they have started."[59] But by that
time more reckless forces had taken over, leaving behind
military men who still thought war between Germany and
Russia was untraditional.[60]

William II and the Foreign Attachés: The Irresponsibles

> The foreign military attaché seemed to Him a par-
> ticularly congenial public, in front of whom He
> need not feel any constraint. Erich Eyck, *Das per-
> sönliche Regiment Wilhelms II.*

At many European courts before 1914 the service attachés
ranked above most diplomats, as far as accessibility to the
sovereign was concerned. The two "old emperors," William I
and Francis Joseph, had been disposed to keep these attachés at
arm's length; the latter only gave them a chance to address
him on such public occasions as parades and military inspec-
tions,[61] and William I reduced such contacts to a well-regulated
minimum. He told the French attaché, the Duc de Polignac,
during the "War in Sight" episode of 1875, that "they [who-
ever that might have been] wanted to embroil us; that has
been due to the nonsense of newspapers. But it is now all over,
completely over."[62] But the younger monarchs were far more
inclined to admit attachés to their intimacy.

The Tsars, down to the last somewhat timid one, almost
always had closer relations with the service attachés than

[58] *Deutsche Dokumente,* nos. 229, 291.

[59] *Ibid.,* no. 445.

[60] Tatichev was with the Tsar's family at Ekaterinburg and was shot a
few days after they were killed. Post Wheeler and Hallie Erminie Rives,
Dome of Many-Coloured Glass (Garden City 1955), pp. 566f.

[61] *Grosse Politik,* VI, 1226.

[62] Erich Eyck, *Bismarck,* 3 vols. (Erlenbach-Zurich 1941-1944), III, 162.

with the ambassadors. Nicholas II sometimes preferred to discuss even serious diplomatic conflicts, and possibly settle them, with an attaché rather than with his chief. In 1898, when war with Britain seemed to threaten over the seizure and fortification of Port Arthur by Russia and a deadlock had been reached, the Tsar called in the British military attaché, whom he knew rather well, rather than the ambassador whom he knew but slightly. The attaché wrote later: "Diplomatists were not, as a body, viewed favorably at the great military courts, St. Petersburg or Berlin, while some military attachés had fairly frequent opportunities of seeing both rulers and of bringing up any subjects which it was desired to discuss."[63]

Even after 1905, when the Tsar had become still more of a figurehead, he was allowed to entertain certain "immediate" relationships with foreign attachés. Nicholas had shown Prince Gottfried Hohenlohe "repeated signs of personal sympathy," when he served as military attaché at the Russian court in the earlier 1900's, and the Austrian Government, nominally Francis Joseph himself, banked on this when they sent him to St. Petersburg again, during the Austro-Russian crisis over the Balkan settlement early in 1913. There had been certain measures of preparedness, if not mobilization, on both sides, and Hohenlohe (later ambassador to Berlin, 1914-1921) was to explain Austrian motives, much misunderstood on the Neva and elsewhere, and was if possible to bring about mutual demobilization. It was announced that peace, and the agreement to demobilize along the Austro-Russian frontier, had been achieved through an understanding between the two emperors, with Hohenlohe as intermediary.[64]

The last German Emperor made the foreign attachés virtually a part of his military entourage, which he liked to call GHQ even in peacetime. Most of them took his camp ceremonial—or unceremoniousness—as part of their duties and in their best diplomatic manner. The Army, through Waldersee and Schlieffen, had made it painfully clear to William II that, for personal rather than constitutional reasons, he could not lead the German troops in a war in the style of Frederick

[63] Waters, *"Secret and Confidential,"* pp. 238f.
[64] *Oesterreich-Ungarns Aussenpolitik,* V, 5584, 5599, 5675ff., 5751.

the Great. But the diplomats had been unable to exclude him to a similar extent from the direction and handling of foreign affairs, though they had good reason to regret his trespasses, which culminated in the *Daily Telegraph* affair of 1908-1909. They had felt constrained to allow William certain "immediate" relations with the foreign service attachés in Berlin, although they regretted it. Even before his accession, William II had toyed with the evil dream of a British-Russian war, in which Germany would prove the *arbiter mundi* and the savior of Britain. To help bring it on he had sought out the Russian military plenipotentiary, Prince Dolgoruki, when there was danger of war over Herat in 1885, and had expressed the view (if not the hope) that this was the time and the opportunity for Russia to settle accounts with Britain. When the Tsar learned this, and detected the German desire for such a war and the hope to profit by it, he became much more conciliatory.[65]

Thus this Hohenzollern began early to play with the high tensions between East and West, and each side watched him closely. The English military attaché in Berlin, Colonel Swaine (1882-1889 and 1891-1896), who tried to maintain good relations not only between the two armies but also between the two related royal families, reported to the Queen on the development of her grandson, his narrow-mindedness, his anti-English upbringing, the limitation of his interests to the military, but also his hard-working nature. On the whole Swaine found him "a right good young fellow, deserving the great future he has before him. . . . He requires very careful leading" (1885). He reported the Prince's denial of his rumored Anglophobia: William said he was misunderstood by his English relations and insisted that he was just as little pro-Russian as he was anti-English. He remembered far too well that Germany and England "should go hand in hand in all political questions and we two being strong and powerful should uphold the peace of Europe. You with a good fleet and we with our great army can do this and if my English

[65] According to the story told Count Carl von Wedel by Herbert Bismarck during the Chancellor crisis of 1890. Wedel, p. 42.

relatives will only give me the opportunity I would tell them this myself" (1889).[66]

During the first half of his reign William contrived, with self-satisfaction, to make his previous *agrément* necessary for the appointment of a new foreign attaché to Berlin, or at least for permission to recall him, a routine which had earlier been observed only between the three empires. Even the most democratic powers played up to this imperial whim. On one occasion he expressed "with considerable feeling" to the always obsequious American ambassador, Charlemagne Tower (1902-1906), "his personal disappointment at the suddenness of the recall" of an American naval attaché. He reminded Tower that "military and naval attachés do not occupy the same position in the embassy as that of a secretary for instance, but that as these gentlemen are officers of the U.S. Army and Navy they are received here upon the footing of personal guests of the Emperor himself and are so considered. 'I feel that I am entitled under the circumstances to be informed of the intention upon the part of a government to remove its attaché who has been accredited here, just as I feel that I ought to be consulted in regard to the appointment of any particular officer intended to be sent here to occupy that place.' " In the recent and sudden removal of an American naval attaché "he was inclined to feel that a personal discourtesy had been shown to him." The ambassador assured him that his Government had no such intentions, that the removal was due to service considerations, and the Department of State gave a similar assurance to the Auswärtiges Amt, where the recipient of this information remarked "that it was a marked characteristic of the Emperor that he disliked changes amongst the persons about him."[67]

The French Government, at least occasionally, went as far as the American in complying with the Emperor's whims. When

[66] Arthur Ponsonby, *Henry Ponsonby. Queen Victoria's Private Secretary* (New York 1943), pp. 290f., 360f.

[67] Tower to Hay, confidential, June 21, 1904; Hay to Tower, July 21, 1904; chargé Dodge to Hay, August 10, 1904. *Archives of Department of State.* For a conflict between William II and the French ambassador Herbette over the recall, which Herbette had caused, of the French military attaché whom the monarch wanted to retain, see *Grosse Politik,* XI, 349; also *Documents diplomatiques français,* IInd ser., VIII, 24.

their naval attaché at Berlin, a Lieutenant Buchard, left his post early in 1897 without leave, in order to fight a much discussed duel with another officer, the French President, without the knowledge of the ministers, went out of his way to ascertain whether the attaché was still *persona grata* with the Emperor and could return to his post. Welcome back, said William II; he would judge Buchard simply as an officer and a comrade, in accordance with the rules of his own Army which thought as little of an officer who had touched the honor of a comrade as of one who did not know how to preserve his own honor. Buchard was doubly welcome, as a duelist and as the proponent of a French-German understanding which, he told the Emperor, was favored by the French Navy rather than the Army with its diehard sentiments.[68]

As soon as Delcassé had been dismissed from the foreign office (by Berlin and by his own cabinet colleagues) the Emperor, once more triumphantly chasing the rainbow of a continental alliance, congratulated the French naval and military attachés in Berlin: Delcassé's dreadful policy had been leading France toward a catastrophe and too close to England. When he paused in his fulminations the military attaché could only say that he was not *au courant* with general politics, a field much too high for him; the Kaiser, patronizingly, told him: "Yes, but I, I know and I tell you that you were running into the worst possible adventures."[69]

In conversations with French naval attachés, or rather monologues directed at them, William proposed a common front against the parliamentarians who must furnish the necessary money for navies—"They will give it to me because they are afraid; and if they won't, I shall send them home"— as well as against pacifists and against the British. He had resurrected the hoary idea of a naval alliance of the continentals against the unbearable preponderance of British sea power,[70] even after the conclusion of the Anglo-French en-

[68] *Grosse Politik*, XIII, 3453-3455, 3552, 3576.
[69] *Documents diplomatiques français*, IInd ser., II, 52, 56f., 66.
[70] In May 1897, the Kaiser took the French military attaché apart at a luncheon for the attachés and told him: "You in France can't make up your minds to shorten the bridle on the British. Perhaps it is your newspapers that stand in the way. I have to make up my mind, however,

tente of 1904 had made this notion utterly unrealistic. Impelled by what French diplomats called "the urge to speak, a constitutional intemperance," and also to unburden himself of some nasty remarks about France's new friends, the British, the Emperor talked to the attachés, who listened politely and reported faithfully, rather than to the ambassador. He put the case on a soldierly level of reasoning, decency, honor, pointing out the errors of the French government in neglecting the Navy or in not entering the war on Russia's side and thereby protecting their Indo-China possessions against the "Yellow Peril"; he assured them that the British would not interfere because they had not yet recovered from the South African War, and also (shades of Napoleon!) because they were above all just merchants.[71]

William liked the foreign military attachés to form part of his military suite, riding in their pre-1914 array behind him[72] at maneuvers, parades and entrances, or meeting him, as the naval attachés were expected to do, on various occasions offered by the annual Kiel Yachting Week.[73] They were all comrades-in-arms, members of an international society whose ideas of international understanding could deceive only

---

just the same. I can do that now since I have Russia with me." The ambassador reported the encounter as "a matter of psychology." *Documents diplomatiques français*, Ist ser., XIII, 399.

[71] *Documents diplomatiques français*, IInd ser., V, 192f., 398f., 201f., 401f.

[72] Boulanger loved the same *mise-en-scène*, with the foreign military attachés behind him on horseback as features of the parades which were making him popular. Walter Frank, *Nationalismus und Demokratie im Frankreich der dritten Republik (1871 bis 1918)* (Hamburg 1933), pp. 154f.

[73] U.S. Naval Attaché Beehler (to Navy Department, June 16, 1900, *National Archives*) found "that it is expected that Naval Attachés shall attend during that week. . . . The Emperor will be there and he regards the Naval Attachés as members of his staff. He has the greatest personal interest in this and in the Navy, and it is important for me to be there as I have been so informed, though I cannot state what will be done. French, Russian, Japanese and Turkish Naval Attachés are at present on duty there. . . . The Emperor wants to converse about naval affairs with Attachés and from this combination the U.S. Naval Attaché ought to appear to advantage, and therefore I must not fail to be present at Kiel during that week." According to his report of June 29, Beehler "had opportunities to cultivate the acquaintance and friendship of German Navy officers and was the recipient of the most cordial hospitality, . . . had three audiences with the Emperor, who is very anxious to have American Yachtsmen visit Kiel and compete for the prizes." *Ibid.*

Romantics—which many of them were, demonstrating their common world outlook in small talk and pleasantries. On one occasion William II asked the U.S. naval attaché, Lieutenant Commander Beehler: "What is this Schley and Sampson trouble?" The American replied that it was "an unfortunate way we have of washing our linen in public." Said the Emperor: "I do not do that. All your officers did well and I cannot understand this trouble."[74]

With the great number of military events in and around Berlin particularly during the summer season, an attaché had "much more often occasion to speak with the Emperor than the ambassador himself."[75] Meetings on the training grounds, in regimental messes, at military dinner parties, offered many occasions (with no diplomats present) for royal indiscretions and the attachés' more discreet answers; in fact their special task at this post was to receive and transmit these outpourings to their diplomatic and military superiors and thus serve as an additional channel of diplomacy. Sometimes the Kaiser was visibly carried away by a personal success on the training grounds which displayed his not very genuine "physical vigor and military judgment" to the attachés and other foreign visitors. It was under the impact of such a success that he approached the French military attaché with the strange request for information about a new paint the French navy used on armored cruisers.[76] He cultivated the French attachés continually—attempting Franco-German reconciliation[77] without paying the price of Alsace-Lorraine on which the French insisted. The Emperor told these French officers: "We are the only two military peoples. Together, we could do what we wanted to do in the world."[78]

He entertained the strange idea that such confidences to military men might take the edge off French *revanche* sentiments, which were nowhere stronger than among these officers. They ought to realize, he thought, that Germany had neither

---

[74] Beehler to Navy Department, November 19, 1901. *National Archives.*
[75] Stürgkh, p. 180.
[76] *Documents diplomatiques français*, Ist ser., IX, no. 348.
[77] *Ibid.*, Ist ser., X, no. 40.
[78] *Ibid.*, IIIrd ser., II, 453, November 1911, to Col. Pellé, later Joffre's Chief of Staff.

reason nor intention to make war against France—unless the French alliances necessitated it—that he wanted peace with her, a peace which might be sealed by a joint war of the continental nations against Britain,[79] and which ought not to be disturbed by espionage affairs. When the case of a French spy ring in Germany broke in 1908, he told the military attaché that the Paris General Staff ought to stop that sort of thing, "and that it was very unfortunate to have this incident occur at this very moment when Germany and France might show one another signs of good will and lend one another support in the Orient, for it was of a nature to excite public sentiment in Germany." The colonel answered, as a matter of course, that the General Staff had nothing to do with it, a reply even less convincing than many so-called diplomatic replies.[80]

Contrary to the policy of his own foreign office, William let the French see that to him Morocco was not worth a war, a possibility which the Bülow-Holstein Moroccan policy had not excluded; he told a French military attaché during the first Moroccan crisis that the danger of anarchism and socialism, just then raising its ugly head in Russia, was all the more reason for France and Germany to end the crisis. After his return from Tangier, where Bülow and Holstein had exposed him on the world stage rather against his will, he confided to the French military attaché: "I have not the least intention of going to war with France about this Moroccan business"— and this at a time when Bülow, with whom the Emperor was not on the best of terms, was still trying to intimidate France. Realizing at once the importance of the imperial statement, the attaché, a marquis who "had all the instincts of a gentleman," asked whether he was permitted to make use of it, or whether it was to be considered as confidential. The Emperor answered without hesitation that he might use it,[81] and the Frenchman actually did stress with his superiors in Paris his own conviction that William sincerely wanted peace, appearances to the contrary notwithstanding.[82] The intransigence

[79] *Ibid.*, Ist ser., XIII, 399.
[80] *Ibid.*, IInd ser., XI, 851.
[81] Zedlitz-Trützschler, *Twelve Years at the Imperial German Court*, pp. 200f.
[82] *Documents diplomatiques français*, IInd ser., VIII, 145ff., 371ff., 397f.

of French diplomacy at the Algeciras Conference could safely be based on this supposition, while the Emperor's more public and more bellicose utterances could always be invoked to justify further armaments, or to call on the British for diplomatic assistance.

Remarks of this sort by this "modern central person," as one of his contemporaries called him, were duly passed on to ambassadors and home offices, where some eyebrows were doubtless raised by the monarch's want of restraint and of tact. When Bismarck prepared to visit Vienna in 1892 for the wedding of his eldest son, the Austrian Government inquired in the Wilhelmstrasse what they should do in case the ex-Chancellor should apply, as he later did, for an audience with Emperor Francis Joseph. The first answer was that they were not interested. "All the greater was the surprise on the part of the Austrian military attaché Steiniger when Wilhelm II one day later at some cavalry exercise at Potsdam took him aside in order to tell him how incomprehensible it would be for him if his high ally should receive a rebel for whom the prison fortress of Spandau was standing ready." To please his invaluable military ally Francis Joseph was absent from Vienna when the Bismarcks arrived there, conveniently absent on a trip not previously planned.[83]

Britain's military attachés in Berlin during the 1880's and 1890's were relatively important persons in the diplomatic scheme. In addition to maintaining good relations between the two courts, the contacts they kept up between the military officers in both sides of the North Sea, including a continued exchange of information about the potential common enemy, Russia,[84] were more of an earnest of England's probable intention to join the Triple Alliance in case of war[85] than were

[83] Glaise-Horstenau, p. 346.

[84] See, for instance, the information given to the German military attaché in London about the plans of operations of the British Army command in case of war with Russia in 1885. *Grosse Politik*, IV, 778.

[85] Cf. Swaine's letter to the Queen's private secretary, November 9, 1892: "Germany is terribly handicapped by her two allies and unless our fleet extricates the Italians, a war between the Triple Alliance on one side and Russia and France on the other will in my belief end in the victory to the latter—and then God help the rest of Europe." Ponsonby, *Henry Ponsonby*, p. 362.

the vague assurances of the diplomats. Chancellor Caprivi, of whom the British thought highly, and others in Berlin understood it this way, but the Emperor could not leave well enough alone.

He would send the British strange counsel, well-meant perhaps but certainly ill-considered, preferably through the military attaché. After the death of the Khedive in 1892 the Sultan, nominally still the suzerain of Egypt, hesitated to accede to British wishes and hand down a *firman* installing the new ruler. William II advised Salisbury, through the attaché Colonel Swaine, that British men-of-war should steam through the Dardanelles at night, anchor below the Sultan's palace and train their guns at its windows; this threat and that of an immediate British annexation of Egypt would force him to sign on the dotted line. Should Russia protest this breach of treaty and such a rough-and-ready solution of the Oriental Question, he would guarantee that neither Germany nor France would fight. "This is an opportunity which may never recur for England to make herself feared at Constantinople." Salisbury did not consider that this proposal called for an answer. Instead he suggested that the Queen, who was visiting relatives in Germany, recommend to her grandson "calmness both in his policy and in the speeches which he too often makes." This invocation of grandparental authority, this elderly headshaking over a guardsmanlike solution of *Weltpolitik*, seems to have been reported to its originator, and to have contributed greatly to the complete about-face in the Emperor's feelings toward Salisbury. From almost child-like and eager confidence he switched to the hostility which he showed when the latter once more came to power in 1895.[86]

At that time the Kaiser still considered himself Britain's only true friend, and felt forced to tell her ministers that she must align herself more closely with the Triple Alliance; she must stop "insulting and fooling" Germany and the Alliance, as she had done for the seven years since he had come to the throne. Otherwise, he would simply be forced to make common cause with France and Russia, each of which had a

---

[86] Lady Gwendolen Cecil, *Life of Robert, Marquis of Salisbury*, 4 vols. (London 1921-1932), IV, 370ff.

million soldiers along his frontiers ready to break in, while England was not even friendly with him. England must abandon her policy of selfishness and bullying; she must come out on the side of the Triple Alliance with treaties signed and sealed, or else take her stand openly against it.

In his impatience and without consulting Chancellor Hohenlohe and the Wilhelmstrasse, the Kaiser made the experienced British military attaché, Colonel Swaine, the recipient of these fulminations. According to the monarch's own story the Colonel " 'winced' as they do in English novels" when the Kaiser gazed at him sharply, and was "deeply shaken and moved" at the end of their conversation. And so were the officials of the Wilhelmstrasse, probably more genuinely; they were forced to excuse and soften the imperial outburst, which was "the most important document you have ever sent us from Berlin," as one member of the Salisbury cabinet wrote to Swaine, although another minister thought the attaché was definitely not the man to discuss such questions as the settlement of the Straits problem.[87] Swaine was and remained, however, the darling of the Queen—in her more imperialistic moments and because she doted on her grandson who, through Swaine, wangled an honorary colonelcy in the British Army out of her.[88]

Three months later William, unrestrained by the Wilhelmstrasse, again berated British policy as vacillating, again through the medium of Swaine—and again the diplomats had to smooth things out. The powerful Holstein raised the question of whether this direct interference on the Emperor's part "had not brought out into the open a situation which could not continue without the most serious dangers to the Reich" which the Chancellor must point out to him. To the latter, however, this early prelude of the *Daily Telegraph* affair "seemed insufficient to bring on a row with the Emperor."[89] He and his underlings preferred a row between the

[87] *Grosse Politik*, XI, 2579 with notes; Alfred George Gardiner, *The Life of Sir William Harcourt* (London 1923), II, 324.

[88] G. E. Buckle, ed., *The Letters of Queen Victoria*, 2nd series, 3 vols. (New York 1926-1928), II, 345ff., 395.

[89] *Grosse Politik*, X, 2572ff.; Haller, pp. 182ff.; Hohenlohe, *Denkwürdigkeiten*, III, 146.

Emperor and England (the Krüger dispatch, dating only three weeks after William's last talk with Colonel Swaine) to a row between themselves and the Emperor.

To forbid or even to advise the Kaiser to moderate his talks with attachés and other little-authorized persons was beyond the courage of the Wilhelmstrasse civilians. Such talks went on until William II had broken his diplomatic wisdom teeth— late in his reign, if ever. He made Swaine's successor, Colonel Grierson, the recipient of similar confidences, much as if a firmer understanding between Germany and Great Britain could be best appreciated and brought about by the company of soldiers. He had somewhat repented of the churlishness of the Krüger despatch, and again wanted to see Britain draw closer to the Triple Alliance. Together they would face Russia, England's worst enemy and now in close league with France, which "had prostituted herself into the arms of Russia." The two great Protestant-Germanic powers must stand together against the threat of Europe swamped by the Slavs with French assistance. William convinced Grierson, a newcomer, that "in spite of appearances, his friendship for Great Britain and his desire for a British alliance had never wavered and that his great wish now was to replace matters upon the friendly footing upon which they were before the present regrettable estrangement took place."[90]

These were not the tactics to draw a Salisbury out of a policy of isolation, however un-splendid. The threat of a continental alliance need not disturb him, France would never join it. He remained unmoved when the Kaiser pleaded with him once more, through Grierson, reciting his version of the futile wooing of Britain in the past (January 15, 1898). For eight years he had tried to gain her alliance, but she had not cared for it. There was no more chance of it now, with the continental alliance in the offing. And what was British policy anyhow? Grierson thought it was aloofness from either continental group, a position safe enough since the two would never

90 Duncan S. Macdiarmid, *The Life of Lieutenant-General Sir James Moncrieff Grierson* (London 1923), pp. 117ff. For a word picture of Grierson see Gwynn, *Spring Rice*, I, 207f.

join. "You are mistaken," the Kaiser replied. "They can combine, and they *shall* combine. Socialism and other causes will force the Monarchs of the Continent to combine for mutual assistance and the yellow races of the East are our greatest danger."[91]

By this time Grierson had made up his mind that Germany was England's enemy and no longer her secret military ally, that he need no longer be impressed by the Kaiser's complaints and "frequent tirades" about the Salisbury Government, with its "two minds" on questions touching Anglo-German relations, and Salisbury's delaying tactics in such negotiations as the division of Samoa.[92] According to his colleague, in Vienna, Dawson (1890-1895), who was in lively correspondence with Grierson and equally convinced of the reality of a "German danger" for Britain in which people at home would not believe, no one distrusted the Germans "more cordially" than Grierson did by the time he left Berlin, "which is important, for he knew more about the German Army and their military policy than any British officer of his day." Dawson, who served from 1895 to 1901 as attaché in Paris, during the Fashoda episode, kept up an exchange of views with Grierson "as to the coming struggle which we were both absolutely convinced must come before long."[93]

Grierson's successor in Berlin, Major Waters, almost desperately endeavored to halt the deterioration in Anglo-German relations when the Kaiser took him into his confidence in mess hall style. Well aware that the monarch "was rather fond of saying things to a military attaché—if he had confidence in him—which, if said to an ambassador, would have been necessarily official, and might sometimes have far-reaching consequences," he listened to the Emperor's threats that Germany and the other Continental powers might intervene in the Boer War, but felt constrained to reply that "while he and his Allies might succeed in pulling us down, this would not make Eng-

[91] Macdiarmid, *Grierson*, pp. 134ff.; *British Documents on the Origins of the War*, I, no. 62.

[92] November 5, 1899. *British Documents on the Origins of the War*, I, no. 154.

[93] Dawson, pp. 161f., 219.

land stop the struggle, and that we would do our utmost to drag Germany down with us."[94]

Historical discussion of the break in Anglo-German friendship has left the relations of the two armies on either side of the North Sea in the main unconsidered. For a time they had been intimate, hence the constant appeals of William II to the attachés as useful and understanding diplomatic agents.[95] Schlieffen, the Chief of Staff, was not the man either to cultivate or to spoil such intimacies; he did not believe that the German Army could be helped by diplomacy in achieving its war aims, and the split in Anglo-German relations only occasionally received a contributory impact from the military side during the late 1890's. A Captain von Lüttwitz (twenty-five years later, as a general, the military leader of the Kapp putsch) wrote an article in favor of a stronger German navy, a stand that few army officers at the time cared to take, a navy necessary to acquire colonies and to cope with an unfriendly Britain. The article, thoroughly unimportant as regards ideas and arguments, appeared in a translation in a British service journal in 1897 as "proof" of German designs against England.[96] Soon afterwards the same Lüttwitz was appointed military attaché to London, conceivably as a "humorous" expression of the Emperor's displeasure with British policy.[97]

In the nature of things, the Wilhelmstrasse learned of only a fraction of the imperial indiscretions in talks with foreign attachés; when they did hear, it was usually by way of the repercussions they provoked.[98] What should or would they

[94] Waters, "Secret and Confidential," pp. 252f., 146; Grosse Politik, XVII, 5072.

[95] Col. Swaine was employed as late as March 1906 as the bearer of a conciliatory message from Edward VII to his nephew, "as he believed I was persona grata at Court here," as Swaine told Holstein. British Documents on the Origins of the War, III, 280f. Waters was a frequent visitor at Doorn, the Kaiser's home in exile, during the 1920's.

[96] William L. Langer, The Diplomacy of Imperialism, 1890-1902, 2 vols. (New York and London 1935), p. 426.

[97] See above, p. 110.

[98] After the Kaiser had told Col. Waters that if the Boer War should last much longer, intervention on the part of the suffering continental powers might become necessary, the British ambassador, before writing his report on the conversation, inquired in the Wilhelmstrasse whether anything was known there about such intervention plans. Without

have thought had they known of his unneutral utterances—
unneutral towards both sides—during the Spanish-American
War? Answering the Navy Department's query as to whether
he could learn anything of the whereabouts of a Spanish
squadron passing Cape Verde, the U.S. naval attaché at
Berlin cabled that the Emperor had just told his French colleague that there was no news about this squadron, but that the
German military attaché at Madrid had reported that in
Spain no arsenals were ready for war. He was also told,
probably by the same source, that the Emperor's "sympathies
are strongly with Spain but he has no patience with their
manana policy."[99] These imperial remarks were apt to be
repeated where they could do the most damage, for example
the Kaiser's contemptuous observation about Italy, still a
nominal ally, to the French military attaché, Colonel Pellé,
during the unduly dragged-out Tripoli compaign: "If one
does a bad deed, it must be done fast and it must succeed."[100]

This imperial irresponsibility and lack of caution may
have been "good for the Navy," but at times it went too far
even for the father of the German Navy, von Tirpitz. When
the British naval attaché, Captain Dumas, told him early in
1907 that the Emperor had asked him point blank, the summer before, whether Admiral Fisher was actually working for
an attack on Germany, a remark which he felt in duty bound
to report to London, Tirpitz cautiously protested "that it
was not so sure that His Majesty had put a really serious
question in that direction up to him," but the Englishman
insisted that he had.[101] Bülow, while more determined and
successful than Chancellor Hohenlohe in his attempts to restrain the Kaiser's talks with foreign attachés, still could not
fully curb this dangerous loquacity.[102] There were relapses.

disavowing the monarch, Bülow emphatically assured the ambassador
that no such step could be expected on Germany's part. *Grosse Politik*,
XVII, 5072.

[99] Barber to Navy Department, telegram, May 6, 1898. Five days later
Barber could report that the Cape Verde fleet was back in Cadiz. "This
news had been received officially at the German General Staff only two
hours before." *National Archives*.

[100] Faramond, p. 80.

[101] Tirpitz to Bülow, January 12, 1907. *Grosse Politik*, XXIII, 7779.

[102] For his endeavors see *Documents diplomatiques français*, IInd ser.,
XI, 145, 242 (1907).

Bülow had to "note new proof of the political indiscretion (*Unbesonnenheit*) of His Majesty" when, in spite of previous bad experiences with the Austrian military attaché at St. Petersburg Prince Hohenlohe, a determined Russophile, the Kaiser poured his heart out to this princeling and also used him at least once, rather than the Prussian military plenipotentiary, to carry a letter to the Tsar.[103] It might have calmed Bülow had he known that one of these foreign attachés, Grierson, could no longer "attach very much importance to statements from His Majesty's mouth."[104]

This conclusion, on the whole a sound one, was unfortunately not shared by one of the later British military attachés in Berlin, Count Edward Gleichen (1903-1906), the son of a Prince Hohenlohe who had emigrated and married into British society. Gleichen was one of several Edwardian Britishers with the wrong father or mother or fatherland, wrong because German: these men felt they had to make up for a prenatal faux pas by British ultra-nationalism (Eyre Crowe, Lord Cromer, Sir Alfred Mond, etc.)—an earlier generation under similar circumstances had thought it their duty to promote good Anglo-German relations. Gleichen was also a direct cousin of the German Empress who, according to Bülow, gave him the opportunity to hear "more than was good" in Berlin, and a favorite of Edward VII, his godfather, to whose attention he sedulously brought German expressions of hostility to England, including those of the Emperor himself.

The Emperor did not like him, Gleichen thought, because he had twice ventured to disagree with His Majesty, once over the unmilitary British habit of putting civilians in the office of Secretary of War, and the second time over a book by a German subaltern (*The Military Interpreter*, by Jecklin). The author (subsequently punished by a transfer to a poor frontier garrison) had included a translation exercise dealing with the brutal treatment meted out by the British to the Boers and their women during the South African War; a similar piece was a "proclamation of the Kaiser when he had entered London at the head of a victorious army—also most offensive."

---

[103] 1906. Bülow, II, 26of.
[104] *British Documents on the Origins of the War*, I, 130.

As a matter of routine and for their information Gleichen had submitted a copy of this work to the Intelligence Division at home, where Grierson got hold of it. He showed it to the War Secretary Arnold-Foster, who took the thing very seriously and discussed it with Edward VII; the King brought the book along on a trip to Germany and jokingly showed it to his nephew: "Nice things you say about us." The Emperor was furious with Gleichen who, he declared, "had done a most outrageous and unfriendly thing in sending the book home to the King"; if the attaché had come to him about it at once, he would have suppressed the obnoxious work. "And here he was, having just made friends with England, and I [Gleichen] had spoilt it all again." Since the Kaiser did not want to hear his explanations, the attaché went to Chancellor Bülow and explained everything, but the Kaiser insisted that Gleichen had shown the work to his Uncle Edward with evil intent (Bülow also gives this version in his *Memoirs*), and Gleichen was grieved that his word of honor was not believed in Berlin.

By 1904 the rift between the governing classes in Britain and Germany had proceeded so far that Bülow thought it "doubly necessary, since we meet with so much trouble in England at the court, in society and in the press and when again and again disturbing incidents occur [Gleichen], to convince the broad masses of the English people that we harbor no hostile or aggressive intentions against England"[105]—an appeal from the higher classes to the lower. After several clashes over Gleichen and with him, the Wilhelmstrasse in the summer of 1905 demanded his recall, but this did not take place until January 1906 when he was transferred to Washington with a promotion in rank. His removal had become absolutely necessary after he had touched a hypersensitive nerve in the German federal constitution. On orders from London and without any previous notice to the Reich government (according to Gleichen's own version, on his own initiative and with the permission of the ambassador, who "considered that it would be rather a good thing") he had presented himself as British military attaché to the courts of Southern

---

[105] Bülow to William II, July 15, 1904. *Grosse Politik*, XIX, 6043.

Germany and Saxony. Such a British official had not been seen there in a long time, and in Dresden he was not even admitted. Gleichen never consulted "the Prussian authorities as he imagined they had no say in the matter," and assumed blandly that "both Saxons and Bavarians were pleased at the idea of having a real foreign military attaché accredited to them, for it emphasized their military separation from Prussia—whom, of course, they loathed." After visiting two capitals Gleichen planned a third trip of homage to German federalism, but the Wilhelmstrasse complained to Lascelles about this strange encouragement given to "States' rights" sentiments, and there were no more visits. Neither Gleichen nor his superiors realized the dangerousness of the ground on which they allowed him to tread, and the episode was one of those diplomatic gaffs which are usually imputed only to German diplomacy before 1914.[106]

One of Gleichen's successors, Lieutenant Colonel A. V. F. V. Russell, in Berlin from 1910 on, had at least "one rather serious row" with William II, "and we both more or less called each other liars! I regret to say that I lost my temper completely and so did he." It was over an article by Repington, sharply criticizing recent German military maneuvers. According to Russell, the Kaiser, "of whom it may most justly be said *L'État c'est moi*, invariably paid special attention to the military representatives of foreign Powers. The number of parades, military functions, gala operas, etc., to which we were invited, was larger than at any other court and on nearly all these occasions the foreign military attachés were . . . 'made a fuss of' by the Emperor." In spite of all his martial gesticulations Russell found the monarch "constitutionally averse from war"; he even heard German officers "exclaim with exasperation: 'We shall never have a war under this Emperor

---

[106] *Ibid.*, XIX, 6220; XX, 6866f., 6870; Bülow, II, 253; Gleichen, pp. 262ff. Gleichen did not allow resentment over his treatment in Germany to interfere with his military judgment. Contrary to the feeling of panic that swept across England in 1907-1908, he did not believe that concentration for a German attack on England could take place "without our knowing it, or that the Government or the Kaiser desire to bring on war, or that the Navy is being formed for our destruction." Gwynn, *Spring Rice*, II, 113. A rich documentation of the Gleichen case from the Bavarian (the Federal) angle is in the Munich *Geheimes Staatsarchiv*, MA 50238.

he is entirely for peace. He is too much a coward to go to war!' "

The Crown Prince, attempting to gain the popularity with the army which his father no longer possessed, began to play up to war sentiments in the Prussian officer corps. He thought he was growing up politically when he demonstrated in uniform in favor of the Pan-Germans. During the Imperial maneuvers of 1912 he passed Russell and the other foreign military attachés, and shouted in English: "Hello, Russell, is there going to be a war? I do not want to fight against my dear 11th Hussars, but I should love to have a go at those dirty Frenchmen." Luckily, according to Russell, his colleagues, and the Frenchman in particular, did not understand English.[107] But there were other ways of learning that the young man had begun much as had his father, when the latter was Crown Prince.

Later absolutist governors, the various totalitarians, had relatively little use for the go-between services of attachés in uniform, in spite of their vaunted militarism. As a category, service attachés had nothing to do with the rise of Duces and Führers, into whose entourages they would not fit, except in the case of King Alexander of Jugoslavia who, during the last, absolutist phase of his rule, chose for his court marshal and confidant General Alexander Dimitriye which (sic), recalled from his post as military attaché in Paris to be used on numerous political and military errands.[108] Mussolini, as early as 1923, did use the Italian naval attaché in Berlin to establish contact with the German militaristic rightist elements; at first he found no welcome from Stresemann, but instead from Reichswehr generals such as von Seeckt. The latter urged German support for the Italian case in the Fiume imbroglio and eventually brought Stresemann to consider German-Italian cooperation, which included the dispatch of Italian arms to weapons-starved Germany in December 1923.[109] It was part of later "Revisionism" when the Duce gave free entry

[107] Lieut. Col. Hon. A.V.F.V. Russell, "Reminiscences of the German Court," *The Fighting Forces*, I (1924), 58ff.

[108] Obituary in *The New York Times*, September 5, 1963.

[109] Alan Cassels, "Mussolini and German Nationalism, 1922-1925," *Journal of Modern History*, XXXV (1963), 141.

to the service attachés of such countries as Hungary,[110] or when shortly after the Nazi purge of 1934 he expressed to the German military attaché, and through him to the Reichswehr chiefs, his hope that the army would maintain its strong position in the Third Reich and "would exercise a decisive influence with the Führer in major questions not only of a military but also of a political character." The attaché "naturally encouraged him" in this view, which would help to keep down the Party theorists "who were out of touch with the realities of politics."[111] These were the hopes of comparative conservatism, in military or party uniform.[112] In events leading up to the Second World War the service attachés of the European totalitarians, as distinct from their Japanese peers, played far less of a war-accelerating role than did the civilian diplomats, who were more often employed as go-betweens by the Duces and Führers.

[110] *Documents on German Foreign Policy*, Ser. D, IV, 156.
[111] *Ibid.*, Ser. C, IV, 669ff.
[112] For German attaché warnings as to British suspicions of German rearmament, especially in the air, which might "jeopardize German land armaments," from the summer of 1934 on, see *ibid.*, Ser. C, III, 174ff., 189ff., etc.

CHAPTER 16

MISSION CHIEFS AND
SERVICE ATTACHÉS:

THE CIVILIAN-MILITARY STRUGGLE FOR SUPREMACY

A military attaché's post is essentially
a subordinate one, involving strict reticence. Dawson, *A Soldier-Diplomat*

Service attachés are members—temporary, even if sometimes
for as long as twenty years—of the diplomatic corps in a
capital,[1] but they are not as a rule members of their country's
foreign service. They are attached to a mission, originally to
the suite of an ambassador, and detached for the requisite
time from the services of which they are usually life members.
No embassy and few legations seem complete without at least
one of them, even when their usefulness has sometimes seemed
dubious.[2]

They are expected to behave diplomatically, in keeping with
established diplomatic usage, whether they have been selected
primarily for diplomatic and "social" talents or for more
definitely known professional abilities. In the latter case, the
service attaché will often feel out of his element among diplomats, and more at home in his relations with the defense
offices in the country to which he is assigned.[3] He will main-

---

[1] Occasionally a service attaché or an assistant service attaché may be
stationed outside the capital, or a naval attaché may be detached from
the embassy in a landlocked capital. The Germans had an assistant military attaché stationed in Istanbul during the Second World War, to cultivate old and new contacts with the Arab world. Paul Leverkühn, *German
Intelligence Service* (New York 1954), pp. 12f.

[2] According to Mott, p. 141, the United States kept service attachés
in some South American capitals "largely as a matter of prestige. We
have nothing to learn and nothing to fear from these countries. But
we like to have our own estimate of their military resources, and they
like the implied recognition."

[3] Early in 1907 the British naval attaché Commander Dumas paid
Tirpitz a visit, prefacing the very frank message he was to bring from
Admiral Fisher by stating that "he was no diplomat and had never
learnt to express himself diplomatically, but he begged to speak a few

tain direct relations with these offices, channeled in various ways, as do other men on special duty, such as the labor and commercial attachés.[4] In order to assure their acceptability, several countries, including the United States, do not send service attachés abroad until after the *agrément* of the home foreign ministry, the mission chief and the foreign government in question have been obtained.[5]

The attaché is a subordinate of the head of the embassy or legation in which he serves, under the arrangements made by most powers, and nowadays he usually ranks after the first counsellor or first secretary of embassy or legation, the presumptive chargé d'affaires.[6] Countries such as France, Great Britain,[7] Prussia-Germany from 1867 on, Italy, Tsarist Russia (where actual compliance was apt to be weak)[8] and the United States make his subordination complete and definite. Some other countries, such as old Austria-Hungary, Japan,[9] Finland, Greece and Uruguay extend this subordination only

---

words in honest language about the relations between England and Germany." When Tirpitz informed Bülow about their conversation, he added that Dumas, before coming to Berlin, had served at sea for ten years without interruption. *Grosse Politik*, XXIII, 7799.

[4] Potiemkine, III, 802.

[5] The Brookings Institution, *The Administration of Foreign Affairs and Overseas Operation* (Washington 1951), p. 252.

[6] For the most recent American directives for intra-embassy precedence see *The Army Almanac* (Washington 1950), p. 14.

[7] Service attachés abroad correspond with the naval and military authorities at home only by way of the Foreign Office; they have to follow the instructions given by the latter. *Parliamentary Debates* (Hansard), House of Commons, Official Report, Vol. 102, 844, 988; Vol. 103, 353. Julius Hatschek, *Englisches Staatsrecht* (Tübingen 1905), II, 218.

[8] The Russian military attaché in Paris in 1914 corresponded directly and in special cipher with the War Minister in St. Petersburg. Gen. Adolphe Messimy, *Mes Souvenirs* (Paris 1937), p. 191.

[9] In Japan the reports of the service attachés went "directly to the War and Navy Departments, and not to the Foreign Office. Thus it is possible that a military or naval attaché may make a report to Tokyo contradicting that of the ambassador stationed in the same country. This practice of direct report of the service attachés to their respective superiors in Tokyo without the knowledge of ambassadors and ministers has occasioned several parliamentary interpellations concerning the unity and harmony between the representatives of the Foreign Office and those of the military and naval authorities." Of course the heads of government never admitted to the Diet that a lack of harmony between the various departments existed. Tatsuji Takeuchi, *War and Diplomacy in the Japanese Empire* (Chicago 1935), p. 79.

to the attaché's personal conduct and questions of etiquette, though the chief may call on him for advice in military and naval problems.[10] Under the first arrangement, the attaché keeps the head of the mission informed about his activities and intentions and submits for his inspection all information, written or oral. The head of mission can even veto or suppress his reports, although they are addressed as a rule either to the general staff or the minister of war of the homeland[11] (but an English attaché addresses his reports to the head of the embassy or legation). They are then sent in the diplomatic pouch to the foreign office at home, which will read and may retain, in the original or in copies, those which seem altogether political in nature (a French habit), at the same time informing the original addressee about them. The general staff or the war ministry thus receives the attaché reports indirectly except in certain countries like the United States, where the reports, after being passed by the ambassador, are sent on without further participation by the Department of State.

Not much can be said in favor of the independent service attaché, except that the problem of conflicting loyalties is avoided to a certain extent. This arrangement gave a relatively young officer, who had always been under strict orders and had led a highly circumscribed life, an independence which was potentially dangerous and irresponsible; it was so complete, as one Austrian attaché put it in retrospect, that "it was somewhat unearthly . . . with no one in sight who had the right to give me an order. As regards the performance of my duties and the obligations of my post, there were only very general directives. No superior, no order, no body of rules defined and fixed for me the time, the nature, the direction of my work. I was, as the one specimen of my kind in the whole foreign country, in all these respects to rely completely on myself."[12]

[10] Beauvais, pp. 118ff.
[11] Waldersee (*Denkwürdigkeiten*, I, 67), as military attaché in Paris in 1870, wrote on the average one report every fortnight. "I have to hand them in to the ambassador who made his remarks, but cannot change anything in them."
[12] Stürgkh, p. 102.

The ambassador cannot use—or at least cannot order—the independent service attaché to examine certain information of a military nature the value of which a layman might find hard to judge[13]—the regular procedure within a completely hierarchical embassy.[14] The same problem arises when military measures are undertaken in the country of residence, and a professional opinion is needed.[15] A strong desire for independence from ambassadorial authority has been expressed from time to time by service attachés and their superiors, but it has been granted only in Russia and the Austria-Hungary of Francis Joseph[16]—an index of the ascendancy of the military which Metternich had been able to avert. As far as Britain is concerned, the Foreign Office "always refused firmly to change our plan," as one former military attaché remembered, adding:

> And in my opinion it was quite right. . . . The other system has great drawbacks, and offered no counterbalancing benefit. It happened at times that the Ministry for Foreign Affairs, or the Ministry of War of some particular country kept each other in the dark as regards the line of policy which one of them was pursuing. Austria and Russia are

[13] When the ambassador happened to be a former military man, as in the case of Schweinitz in St. Petersburg, relations between him and the attachés were decidedly cool; the ambassador disbelieved their reports or trusted his own judgment more. Wedel, p. 171. The diplomats of the Central Powers in St. Petersburg early in 1909 explained the recently diminished bellicosity of the British ambassador, Sir Arthur Nicolson, by the fact that he had made his own inquiries about Russia's war readiness, independent of those of his military attaché; the results were presumed to have been negative, discouraging the ambassador in his earlier tendency to drive Russia toward war. *Grosse Politik*, XXVI, 9196.

[14] For this procedure see *ibid.*, XXXIII, 12519.

[15] Learning about some measures that seemed to point in the direction of a Russian mobilization, the German ambassador in November 1912 requested that his military attaché, on leave for the past six weeks, be sent back, "since I am not in the same manner as an expert in a position to examine information of this kind as regards correctness and value." *Ibid.*, XXXIII, 12411.

[16] While the London Ambassadors' Conference was trying to work out a peace order for the Balkans, Chief of Staff Conrad (II, 413) informed the Austrian military attachés in London and St. Petersburg (December 30, 1912) "strictly confidentially," that his own "purely personal view was that a warlike settlement with Serbia was the only solution of the problem that promised success."

cases in point. Considerable trouble could, and did, sometimes result, while it happened occasionally, within my own
knowledge, that a military agent criticized directly to his
Chief of State the ambassadorial behavior. The dual plan
was also bound to prejudice harmonious politico-military
co-operation.[17]

In the French service the tendency to make the service
attaché independent of the authority and control of the
foreign office and the chiefs of mission was strong only at the
time of Boulanger. Early in February 1887 that tempestuous
general proposed to enter upon a direct correspondence with
the Tsar, and began with a letter which the French military
attaché in St. Petersburg, on leave in Paris at the time, was to
deliver secretly. In vain the attaché pointed out the incorrect-
ness of the proposal, but he added incautiously that perhaps
such a letter might be handed over in connection with a
present, such as a sword or one of the General Staff publications. The War Minister ordered at once that such a present
be bought. On second thought the attaché went to confess to
Foreign Minister Flourens, who brought the matter before
the council of ministers and complained that this sort of thing
made the conduct of foreign affairs entrusted to him and his
ministry quite impossible. Boulanger denied everything.[18] The
French ambassador in Berlin, Herbette, who called it a "ba-
roque idea" for the General to write directly to the Tsar,
proposed that something should be done "to fix more precisely the relationships of subordination on the part of military attachés vis-à-vis the chief of the diplomatic representation." Under current regulations, the attachés traveled to
Paris at the beck and call of Boulanger more often and more
publicly than seemed advisable at that very critical moment;
furthermore, they sent direct telegrams to the war minister,
the contents of which were unknown to the ambassadors, instead of corresponding through them. "This lateral diplomacy is full of inconveniences." Their correspondence ought
to be made part of the embassy archives—there was none in

[17] Waters, "Secret and Confidential," pp. 46f.
[18] Adrien Dansette, Le Boulangisme, 1886-1890 (Paris 1938), pp. 63f.

the Berlin embassy, and its absence embarrassed both the ambassador and later military attachés.[19] While no specific details about new and more stringent regulations appear in the printed French documents, a tightening of the system of ambassadorial authority seems to have taken place as part of the civilian supremacy generally reestablished in reaction to *Boulangisme.*

During his service as minister plenipotentiary at Frankfurt and St. Petersburg Bismarck had found this independence of Prussia's military plenipotentiaries and attachés not only irksome to himself but positively dangerous to a unified direction of Prussia's foreign policy.[20] By no means everywhere had Prussia's civilian ministers had such loyal attachés as von Loë, for example, in the important post in Paris. Serving as attaché from 1863 to 1866, he was twice independent of the minister, as attaché and as *Flügeladjutant,* and reported directly to the War Minister and the King. Von Loë realized that this dualism in the reports from Paris, that of the minister plenipotentiary and that of attaché and aide-de-camp, was apt not only to produce constant irritation and disharmony, but also to puzzle or misguide the directors of affairs at Berlin, so on his own initiative he submitted all "immediate" and other reports and even private letters to the Minister, Count von der Goltz, with whom he was on very good terms.[21] Bismarck's own less fortunate experiences led to the order of 1867, which placed the attachés (but not the plenipotentiaries) under the heads of mission and the Auswärtiges Amt itself. This extended even to disciplinary matters: Herbert Bismarck found it necessary on one occasion to reprimand attaché Major von Deines for overstaying his leave.[22]

But the officers considered this subordination irksome and tried to shake off the yoke imposed by civilians—and civilians who were not always even "temporary gentlemen." Loë himself, who had once been sharply reprimanded by Bismarck,[23]

---

[19] *Documents diplomatiques français,* Ist ser., VI, 451.

[20] Adolf Hasenclever, "Militärattaché und Auswärtiges Amt um die Wende vom alten zum neuen Kurs," *Vergangenheit und Gegenwart,* XXII (1932), 598f.

[21] Schlözer, p. 41.   [22] Witzleben, p. 182.

[23] Rich and Fisher, I, 31.

thought in his later years that it was derogatory to an officer's honor that a military attaché could be censured by the ambassador, even if he acted in a manner contrary to his duties; such a reprimand, he wrote Waldersee, must be called "the culmination point of nonsense."[24] The thought of officers rendering even temporary obedience to the highest ranking representatives of their country's foreign policy was unbearable, so firm was the conviction that military considerations outranked all others. For Loë, as he put it in April 1890, shortly after Bismarck's fall, "the most important factor in the embassy in France is and remains the military attaché"[25]—at the time this happened to be a Major von Huene, an officer whom Chancellor Caprivi considered "dangerous, because ambitious and chauvinistic."[26] Bad relations between station chiefs and service attachés were almost axiomatic in the German service. When Berlin naval circles considered sending an attaché to Tokyo soon after the Sino-Japanese War of 1895, the matter was postponed, "since we know from experience that Freiherr von Gutschmid [the minister in Tokyo] does not know how to get along with naval officers." And though William II noted on a report that "if the minister is unable to get along with the naval attaché, *he* must go," nothing was done, not even when Tirpitz, stationed in East Asiatic waters at the time, urged such an appointment (1896). None was made until long after Gutschmid's departure.[27]

It must have made things more irksome still for the German officers to realize that the attachés of their Austrian ally worked under no such restrictions or temporary authority. The Austrians corresponded directly with the chief of the General Staff,[28] who communicated some of their reports to the foreign ministry—which of them was left to his own choice—as "pieces for their perusal." It was an exceptional position, as the Austrian attaché at Constantinople from 1895 to 1910, Baron Giesl, admitted, but it was "always a ticklish problem; one knew perfectly well that nearly all these reports were sub-

[24] Waldersee, *Briefwechsel*, I, 364.   [25] *Ibid.*, I, 363.
[26] Wedel, p. 171.   [27] Meisner, *Militärattachés*, pp. 23f.
[28] There are numerous Austrian attaché reports in Conrad's compilation *Aus meiner Dienstzeit*, particularly in vols. II and III.

mitted to the Emperor. My ambassador made this task easier for me from the first day by permitting me to inspect the political archives." In his memoirs Giesl, though emphasizing that within the Austrian embassy there was none of the friction and jealousies which marred so many others, particularly the German embassy, does not say whether he reciprocated by letting the ambassador read his reports. It seems doubtful. Giesl created quite a position for himself at the Golden Horn, and the Austrian ambassador, who was not his chief, complained occasionally to his Russian colleague that Giesl had "completely escaped from his control."[29]

While a weak central authority might consider the separation of the incompatible civilian and military as the best way out of a continuous conflict, and hence more efficient, the lack of unity within an embassy is in the final analysis not conducive to the proper conduct of diplomatic business. Information gathered and forwarded separately by the military component might often have diplomatic significance, sometimes unsuspected, while the reverse might less often be true. Perhaps nine-tenths of attaché reports are concerned with purely technical matters, but in the remainder the ambassador might find matters to interest him, or reason to interfere with the attaché's activities; or he might draw conclusions from the reports of a broader nature than the reporter himself had inferred. The pre-1914 Belgian minister to Berlin, Baron Beyens, gives from his own experience an example of what the diplomat may find. He was glancing over a report one November day in 1913, before putting it into the diplomatic mailbag, expecting to find only technical information, when he read much to his surprise about a meeting of his own attaché and the Russian military plenipotentiary with Moltke, the German chief of staff, at a state dinner. He was not overworked, Moltke had said. "It is sufficient to keep the machine from getting rusty, to put some oil into it. However, since

[29] Giesl, pp. 19f., 146 and passim. It was on the basis of Austrian experiences that a modern handbook on diplomacy speaks of the "deplorable picture which the parallel activity of the envoy and the military attaché presents." See Baron J. de Szilassy, *Traité pratique de diplomatie moderne* (Paris 1828), pp. 201ff. For an illustration of Giesl's independent diplomacy see *Grosse Politik*, XXVII, 9780ff.

Agadir we have had relatively more work to do. We have been constantly on the alert. One cannot exactly know what will arise from the Balkan War. Even if one is ready, arch-ready, as we are, it is necessary to take precautions in order not to be surprised by the events." When the Belgian officer suggested that there seemed to be a lull in Balkan affairs and one could therefore look forward to a prolonged period of peace, Moltke protested: "Don't deceive yourself. The war with France is inevitable and much nearer than you would believe. We do not wish it. We have nothing to gain on that side. But we have had quite enough of these continued alarums which hurt our [the army's?] development. It is absolutely necessary that France put an end to hurting and provoking us; if not, we shall have an explanation with her. The earlier the better. . . . I repeat we do not wish war. We shall make it in order to have an end of this." (Does this mean seeking open war because the war of nerves had become unbearable? Moltke was somewhat of a neurotic type.) The Belgian minister thought this out-burst of the highest importance; it ought to have been re-ported to him at once, he told the attaché, who had not him-self taken it too seriously; in the future he was to remember this admonition as well as the fact that "a military attaché at Berlin sometimes has occasion to be informed on subjects which touch politics, and to help the chief of mission to make his own investigations more complete."[30]

Little remains today, as far as formal rulings go, of the old-time attaché independence. Well before 1914 most home governments had unequivocally laid down the relative stand-ing of mission chief and uniformed attaché. As Ribbentrop put it, they wanted to make every embassy and all its members "a sworn unity" (*verschworene Einheit*).[31] There were still so many conflicts, however, that they could be considered normal, and mutual understanding and harmony atypical. Even in the French diplomatic service before 1914, which had fewer conflicts of this kind on record, complete harmony be-tween diplomat and service attaché seems to have been the exception.

[30] Beyens, II, 110ff.
[31] Geyr, *Erinnerungen*, pp. 120ff.

Most of the trouble probably arose, and may still arise, from the double allegiance enforced upon the attaché by the authorities of his original service, to which he would eventually revert and in which he hoped to continue and end his career. Generally speaking, it was impossible for the ambassador to make or break one of his temporary subordinates, particularly if the attaché's ambitions were military, and not political or diplomatic.[32] Other intra-mission conflicts, such as one reported case of a fist fight between ambassador and military attaché in the Turkish embassy in Moscow in the summer of 1939,[33] might have arisen from the conflict of generations or from the attaché's political ambitions, which his temporary civilian chief might have considered dangerous or out of place.[34]

Relations between embassy chiefs and service attachés in the last hundred years or so were far more harmonious in the democracies than under the empires or Fascism. Conflicts within the former, if and when they did occur, were as a rule personal, rather than a fundamental civilian-military disagreement. In any case, it was wise to look ahead and try to avoid them, though some specific instance may have occasioned the following typical instruction. The American Secretary of State, on the eve of his country's entry into world politics which must not be impeded by interservice squabbles, reminded the officials and officers concerned that

each military attaché is, in a sense, an aide-de-camp to the ambassador or minister to whose embassy or legation he is

[32] For the case of a military attaché breaking the ambassador: Count Hülsen-Haeseler, later head of the all-powerful Military Cabinet in Berlin, had been military attaché in Vienna under the ambassadorship of Ph. Eulenberg (1894-1902). Eulenberg considered the attaché and his wife unfit for the post, and delivered his judgment in a report both witty and malicious that reposed in the files of the Military Cabinet's personnel office. There Hülsen-Haeseler read it after he had taken charge; infuriated, he swore revenge and helped in the scandalous downfall of Eulenberg in 1907. Robert, Graf von Zedlitz-Trützschler, *Twelve Years at the Imperial German Court* (London 1924), p. 287.

[33] *Nazi-Soviet Relations*, p. 43.

[34] The disciplinary power of the chief of mission over service attachés seems nowhere definitely established or claimed. The Bismarcks, father and son, the latter as Secretary of Foreign Affairs, did claim and exercise it.

appointed. The orders of the ambassador or minister will be obeyed, unless they manifestly conflict with orders or instructions given by the Secretary of War. In the latter case, the military attaché will respectfully notify the ambassador or minister of the circumstances which prevent a compliance with his orders, in which event the full particulars of the case must at once be forwarded to the Adjutant-General. It is the earnest wish of the War Department that the most harmonious relations should exist between the military attachés and their chiefs in the Diplomatic Service. Any military attaché whose relations with the chief of embassy or legation to which he is assigned are not most cordial will request a recall. A dignified appreciation of his own position and courteous respect for his diplomatic chief will be expected of each attaché.[35]

The need for such an instruction promptly became manifest. In the struggle among American politicians of all sorts over "imperialism" and the disposition of the spoils of the Spanish War, the ambassador in Berlin, Andrew D. White, and his naval attaché, Lieutenant Commander Barber, found themselves in opposite camps. Barber realized it more clearly than did White, and took the liberty of reporting at once to the Navy Department, saying that the ambassador seemed inclined to approve of Germany's wishes for "Samoa, the Carolines and naval stations in the Philippines in return for her goodwill." Without showing his cable to White, who had told him about these German desires, he wired: "I advise immediately doubling Dewey's squadron via Suez Canal as unofficial reply to avoid future complications. Strictly confidential." The next day the Navy Department, on the whole as empire-minded as its Berlin representative, gave him clearly to understand that he had "unintentionally" exceeded his attaché duties, to which he replied: "Very sorry, but as Ambassador consulted me officially I thought it my duty, but did not intend to precede him. The mistake will not occur again."

[35] Secretary Sherman to Ambassador John Hay, London, October 14, 1897. John Bassett Moore, *A Digest of International Law* (Washington 1906), IV, 437.

It did, though, almost at once. Within a few days of his cable, Barber wrote the Navy Department, defending his stand

> on the professional side of the matter, based upon considerable experience in the Orient [where he had been stationed as attaché in 1894-1895] and upon a profound conviction that whatever may be our foreign policy, only an overwhelming naval superiority and an evident willingness to use it will even command the respect of Germany whether we ever give her anything or not. The German Navy is a rising power with good officers and good men and as only *one* officer in it has been in action on board ship, they are thirsting to fight somebody and they don't care whom. This one officer is Admiral von Knorr. . . . The opinion of German Army and Navy officers expressed both in private and in print is not favorable to us in this war although they do concede that we whip the Spaniards once in a while. We are simply better than the Spaniards, that is all. . . . The press of the country teems with all sorts of malicious exaggerations. . . . The idea seems to be that mutinies, disease, riot etc. etc. have demonstrated not only that the war is unpopular but that native Americans neither know how nor want to fight—and never could meet German soldiers and sailors. The latter is seldom expressed but the inference is always obvious.
>
> Finally there seems but little doubt that the development of the Navy and Colonial expansion is the ambitious dream of the German Emperor. The Monroe Doctrine is gall and wormwood to him because he has "views" in America and the apparent lines of progress marked out by the United States and Germany are likely to intersect each other in time.[36]

The experience with Barber, who had been recalled from retirement whence he had brought his strong political opinions, accounts for the fact that his successor, Lieutenant Commander Beehler, of the recently formed Office of Naval Intelligence, was admonished by his superiors to show him-

[36] Barber to Navy Department, July 14, 1898. Confidential. *National Archives*. Admiral Knorr had fought a French man-of-war off Cuba in 1870.

self an obedient subordinate of the ambassadors with whom he had to deal: "During your service as naval attaché, you will regard our Ambassadors at Berlin and Rome and our Minister at Vienna as your superior officers and will, at all times, comply with such instructions as they may give you."[37]

In later American diplomatic history the relations between mission chiefs and service attachés seem to have been on the whole harmonious. They were so good and so intimate between Ambassador Herrick and Colonel T. Bentley Mott during their ten years of association in Paris that Mott became Herrick's authorized biographer. Another example of excellent cooperation was that between Ambassador Joseph E. Davies and Attaché Colonel Faymonville, whom Davies publicly praised as "a very careful and able man" in his *Mission to Moscow*, and apparently in still more glowing terms elsewhere. This proved almost awkward for Faymonville, who was eventually recalled for his too favorable opinions of Russia's military strength; actually his views proved truer in the end than many other judgments submitted to Washington.

But did a change in this diplomatic relationship take place after 1945 when the military security of the United States had become the foremost concern of its foreign policy? Did that change tempt service attachés to show greater independence of their (not always civilian) superiors? There are indications of such a trend, of the fact that "many of them" were looking at "the Foreign Service and the State Department with ill-disguised contempt and making themselves virtually independent of the ambassadors under whom they should work."[38] The most tangible and damaging proof of such inclinations was furnished by the Communists when they stole and published the highly indiscreet diary of the U.S. military attaché in Moscow, Major General Grow, which revealed among other things an outspoken dislike of the writer's temporary superior, the ambassador.[39]

In comparable conflicts in Tsarist Russia, civilian-diplomatic primacy was less easily secured, if at all. Russian GHQ

[37] Instruction for Beehler, signed Long, January 27, 1899. *Ibid.*
[38] Hanson W. Baldwin in *The New York Times*, April 13, 1952.
[39] See Chapter 6 above, p. 98.

in 1914-1915 was much dissatisfied with the inability of the
Minister at Bucharest, Poklevski, to bring Rumania into the
war on the Entente side; the Russians abetted by the British
Secret Service, accused Poklevski, who happened to be of
Polish descent, of being "in the hands of the Austrian Polish
party which was subservient to the interests of Germanism"—
the old Pan-Slav accusation against the Poles. Foremost among
his accusers was the military attaché in Bucharest. Sasonov's
Ministry ascertained that Poklevski was innocent, and therefore the officer must have lied. But Grand Duke Nicholas's
chief of staff told the foreign office representative at GHQ that
his ministry would never be able to get rid of the attaché. The
diplomat was properly overawed: "It is quite astonishing that
Sasonov has succeeded in defending Poklevski. To irritate
GHQ even more would mean entering upon an open fight
with it. That is undesirable from the standpoint of general
interests and might also turn out fatally for Sasonov since it
is not easy to get the Grand Duke down."[40]

In a general summing-up of diplomatic history it might be
said that many of the contests between ambassadors or ministers and service attachés, apart from the usual conflict of
generations with the attaché always the junior, arose from
the professional bellicosity of the military man and his disbelief in the power or value of conciliation and persuasion. He
inclined to see war as more immediately impending than did
the diplomats, and to propose measures in the interest of
readiness for war or to strengthen defenses, measures which in
themselves might tend to bring war nearer. During his fifteen
years in the Paris embassy Count Münster never expected war
between his country and France as often as the attachés
serving under him did. The Russian military attaché in Sofia
in 1911, at the time of the founding of the Balkan alliances,
Colonel Romanovsky, contributed far more to their bellicose
character than did his superior, Minister Nekludov, whose
inclinations were peaceful. "Russian policy wears two masks,"
wrote the Austrian minister from Sofia during the Balkan
Wars when Romanovsky continued to oppose peace and

[40] *Die internationalen Beziehungen im Zeitalter des Imperialismus*
(USSR), IInd ser., VII, 292ff.

diplomacy, completely ignoring the rather unenergetic minister and relying on his high credit in St. Petersburg. He represented the military party in Sofia and, according to the departing Turkish minister, it was he more than anyone else who had brought the Bulgarians to mobilize in 1912.[41]

In the same capital at nearly the same time the German minister and German military attaché were in violent disagreement. The latter was thoroughly convinced of the vital strength and military efficiency of the Bulgarians and reported as much, while the minister, "in his well-known fanatical Turkophilia," could for some time see no reason to support Austrian endeavors toward a Bulgarian-Turkish alliance after the end of hostilities.[42] Occasionally, however, there was an exceptionally peace-minded service attaché, such as the Russian naval attaché at the Porte in 1911-1912. He must have found himself in conflict with the majority of his diplomatic superiors and their concepts of Russia's vital interests, including control of the Straits, when he wrote: "If, in the next few years, Russia fights China, Turkey, or Germany, this will by no means signify that Russia needed that war, but will merely serve to prove the government's incapacity and frivolity. That will be cruel and unjust toward the Russian mushik."[43]

Diplomatic and military judgments must often disagree—on the significance of another power's move of a military character, on the military strength of a diplomatic opponent, on the value of another power as alliance partner. The British military attaché in St. Petersburg during the 1890's, who also reported on naval matters, was thoroughly convinced for professional reasons that the Russian naval forces in the Black Sea were insufficient for a *coup de main* against Constantinople, while the ambassador Sir Nicholas O'Conor was constantly agitated over the strengthening of this fleet and its moves. The fact that the attaché proved right about the outcome of a sortie of that fleet, which had particularly worried the ambassador, worsened rather than improved the relations between the two. Unlike others under whom the attaché had served, O'Conor

[41] *Krasny Archiv*, VIII (1927), 62ff.; *Oesterreich-Ungarns Aussenpolitik*, III, 3907, 4145.

[42] *Oesterreich-Ungarns Aussenpolitik*, VII, 8399.

[43] *Journal of Modern History*, XII (1950), 71.

kept him "in the dark regarding diplomatic affairs, although it was difficult, especially in a country like Russia, always to separate them from military matters." Consequently the attaché proposed and secured his own transfer before the idea had occurred to the ambassador.[44]

French embassies and legations before 1914 usually presented a united front to the outside world and were, in fact, more compatible bodies than many others. Since the Russian alliance, French diplomacy, the French army command, and the French public generally had put their trust and their money in the armed power and manpower of Russia. French ambassadors, military attachés, and various military missions to Russia during the period of reorganization after the Russo-Japanese War were unanimous: Russia had profited from that lesson; materiel was being restored; officers were giving up their old habits of laziness and debauchery; there was no better soldier than the Russian private, well disciplined, frugal, inured to fatigue and suffering. In this chorus of approval there was one dissenting voice: an assistant military attaché at St. Petersburg, a captain of engineers with the Alsatian name of Wehrlin and one of the few "mechanics" ever made attaché, consistently expressed doubts about the solidarity of the whole Russian structure. The ambassador repeatedly demanded that he be recalled.[45] Thus even in the well-disciplined French service frictions arose between ambassador and service attachés, conflicts between diplomatic considerations and military urgings. One ambassador invoked "the strictest recommendations which had been made [to a newly appointed military attaché] never to indulge in that indiscreet and reprehensible curiosity which has been, at all times, more or less, the besetting sin of the attachés wearing the epaulettes."[46] While these struggles seem seldom to have bordered on the scandalous or the anarchic as they did in the German foreign service under William II, they must have been fairly frequent if an exception was worth noting: the French minister at Athens at the beginning of the century, d'Ormesson, was on terms of friendship and high esteem with the military attaché of the legation. "The

[44] Waters, "Secret and Confidential," pp. 180f., 237.
[45] Messimy, Mes Souvenirs, p. 179.
[46] Ambassador Marquis de Noailles to Delcassé, March 1, 1901. Documents diplomatiques français, IInd ser., I, 147.

case is worth citing," remarks his son, "for it is, all in all, rather rare that a military attaché is on good terms with his ambassador or minister. With that superb disdain which so many military men betray for the 'civilians,' it happens, in fact too often, that the military attaché strives to take a stand opposite to the policy of his chief of mission, and to snipe at him."[47]

One of the recurrent basic conflicts between ambassador and attaché was always over the war strength and war readiness of the country to which they were assigned. The Austrian diplomats, Chancellor Beust and Metternich, the ambassador in Paris, as well as the army commander Archduke Albrecht were all eager for *revanche* after the defeat of 1866, and all in favor of the Austro-French-Italian alliance. They thought far more highly of the French readiness for war than did the military attaché in Paris and not nearly as well of the Prussian army as did the attaché in Berlin (he had served in Paris before and could compare the two armies).[48] Both attachés were opposed to the alliance; both of them, Count Uexküll and Count Welsersheimb, were members of Austria's high aristocracy and were consequently quite outspoken about it in their reports. On July 12, 1870, Uexküll wrote from Paris that within a few days it would be decided whether there was any spark left, in the French Government, of that *grandeur* "which is always sung here in all keys and *ad nauseam*. I myself have considered it my duty during the last four months to openly declare that I have no confidence either in the French Government or the conditions in this country. This much I believe I am allowed to say, that utmost caution in negotiations with this Government is an obligation for every State and the only insurance against being suddenly left in the lurch." On the 13th he was quite convinced that the "unreliable French Government" had decided on war with Prussia and was stirring up the masses with chauvinistic appeals, that it was ready to blame them for the war rather than the Emperor and his Government, "a procedure as immoral as it is dangerous," and one they would not hesitate to apply to any

---

[47] Wladimir d'Ormesson, *Enfances diplomatiques* (Paris 1932), p. 140.
[48] Schlözer, p. 67.

power which might engage itself precipitately. When Uexküll complimented his own Government for their wise decision
against entering the war, Beust may have winced, if a diplomat ever does such a thing.[49]

If the home authorities are undecided about war, differences
of opinion between ambassador and attaché are apt to make
confusion worse confounded. This happened, as a Russian
General Staff officer complained, when "the awkward confusion between the reports of our ambassador in Japan [A. P.
Isvolsky] and of our military attaché there" obscured the
pros and cons of the war with Japan. For once, it seems that
the military judgment of the civilian was the better of the
two.[50] Isvolsky was ambassador in Paris in 1911, and he still
had "too good a memory of the terrible consequences of the
lightheartedness which our military attaché at Tokyo exhibited" to refrain from complaining to Sasonov about his
attaché in Paris, and "the astounding manner in which he
understands business."[51]

The uninitiated may have believed in the effectiveness and
strictness of authority and obedience in the autocratic empires
before 1914 (witness Marcel Sembat's *Faites un roi, sinon
faites la paix* of 1913, with its thesis that the organization for
successful war demands a monarchical head of State), but
in reality there was far more disobedience, indirection and
even indiscretion than existed in the armed and diplomatic
services of the parliamentary countries. Independence, diso-

[49] Oncken, *Rheinpolitik*, III, 428, 433.
[50] Ignatiev, p. 160. Isvolsky left Tokyo in 1903.
[51] Specifically Isvolsky complained that the attaché had been absent
on leave during the Agadir crisis; after his return he had busied himself
exclusively with the visit of one of the grand dukes, who was unwelcome
in France at the time, but whose visit had been engineered by the attaché and his wife, "a bold American." "To my questions about France's
military preparations he answered that he did not know about them at
all; the French generals at present in Petersburg, without doubt, had
given all necessary information. As for that, I should like to know why
we have a military attaché here. . . . The French war minister has
given me to understand how little importance he attaches to the presence
of an officer who is so little competent as Count Nostitz is in military
affairs. All this is far from being in the interest of our prestige" (Letter
of September 14, 1911). Russia, Foreign Office, *Un livre noir, diplomatie
d'avant-guerre d'après les documents des archives russes, novembre 1910-
juillet 1914*, 5 vols. (Paris 1922-1934), I, 133f.

bedience, even disloyalty of the service attaché, in his relations with ambassadors and foreign offices, was a distinctive feature in this successfully concealed anarchy. It seems likely that this disobedience was strong in direct ratio to the degree of autocracy, and hence most prevalent in Russia, though the greater amount of documentation might give superiority to the empire of William II.

German diplomacy had known this particular Russian anarchism long and well and probably counted it a negative element in Russia's war potential, but it chagrined and scandalized the French when they realized it. The French minister at Bucharest in 1901 gave Delcassé a graphic description of the conflicts raging in the Russian legation there, particularly unfortunate in a country which must one day be detached from the Central Powers. Russian diplomacy was by no means centered in the Russian legation, which had been directed for ten years by M. de Fonton. "It is complemented or perhaps complicated by the intervention of diverse agents, independent of one another, representing distinct or rival interests which, as is apt to happen in such cases, choose means of action which are often conflicting, and spend the best part of their efforts in attacking one another and exonerating themselves." The Russian minister was discreet and zealous, and wanted to establish friendly relations with the downtrodden Rumanians, but he was not quite anti-German enough to please his French colleague. He made discreet use of the Orthodox Church, which he subventioned, and of Pan-Slavism, but he had not yet been very successful in efforts to dissociate Rumania from Austria. This, at any rate, was the contention of the Russian military attaché in Bucharest, Colonel Leontovitch, "who openly attacks the policy of the chief of legation under whose authority, by the way, his functions do not place him. He treats the Rumanians with an extreme rudeness and without any consideration. He does not hide in any way his most menacing and aggressive understandings with the Serbs and Bulgarians. He underlines his sentiments which are anti-German and very much in sympathy with France. His antagonism towards M. de Fonton has reached the breaking point, but it seems that the Russian Government had kept its

338

confidence in its military agents for it has recently charged him, together with Admiral Birileff, with a diplomatic mission to Belgrade and Sofia and it has added Bulgaria to the countries over which his military surveillance extends. A third person, more influential perhaps than the two official representatives of Russia, has been acting in the shadow at Bucharest for several years: he is Colonel Grabo, whose secret mission consists in informing the Petersburg Government about all the facts which interest Russian policy, not only in Rumania but in the whole Balkan peninsula." This Colonel had considerable funds at his disposal, and was not interfered with by the helpless Rumanian Government; he was the representative of the Russian police.[52]

Exponents of German Militarism and Navalism

Hardly less violent but not quite so complicated conflicts of opinion occurred within the German embassies throughout the reign of William II. The ambassadors in capitals like Constantinople, Rome, Paris—and later London, after Anglo-German naval competition had gotten under way—tried valiantly to keep the service attachés within the bounds of assigned duties and diplomatic restrictions as understood in the days of Bismarck, but again and again they encountered the predilections of the Emperor, and also of the General Staff,[53] in favor of the recalcitrant or outright disobedient attachés. This conflict, incidentally, was also one of generations—the Emperor and the attachés vs. the generation of Caprivi, Hohenlohe, Münster, Marschall and Metternich—as well as of good manners, of general interest vs. service interest.

Münster, when confronted by the French Government with dossiers of certain espionage cases in which the German attaché Major von Hoiningen-Huene had been involved, was forced to propose his recall in the autumn of 1890. The major did not feel that his superior had adequately defended him and his honor against the accusations; he vowed revenge and constituted himself the ambassador's main critic when a conciliatory gesture—the visit of the Emperor's mother to Paris

52 *Documents diplomatiques français*, IInd ser., I, no. 347.
53 Rich and Fisher, III, 362.

in the spring of 1891—went awry and Münster was blamed for the failure. The wrangle occurred during a particularly bad period of imperial neurosis. When the ambassador serenely reported that the political scene as viewed from Paris seemed quiet, and promised to remain so for the approaching summer (the summer of Kronstadt), the Emperor declared that this report and one by the new attaché, successor to Huene, could not be surpassed in "naïveté and childlike confidence," that both men must go and that Münster must be replaced by a general. He telegraphed the Wilhelmstrasse: "In order to be quite sure I have summoned Major von Huene and queried him about the whole situation. He proved himself as well informed as ever and knew decidedly more than the whole present embassy together. He himself had such staggering news from his own absolutely reliable Paris sources that he had been on the verge of submitting a report to me. His general impression was that it was not unlikely that the French will seize the initiative this summer" and would possibly attack Germany even before the Russian alliance was perfected. The Wilhelmstrasse had to utilize the often required but complicated *démentir* machinery, in order to disabuse the Emperor and crush the major. They forced the ex-attaché to put his observations and sources for them on paper, and then made Münster, the new attaché, and some members of the foreign office point out for the Emperor's benefit the unlikely character and highly dubious sources of Huene's information.[54]

This treatment seems to have improved the patient for quite a while to come—when the next conflict between ambassador and attaché came to his attention, he was even inclined to decide against the soldier. At Constantinople, the ambassador Baron von Marschall and the first military attaché ever sent there (in 1897), Captain Morgen, were not on the best of terms, partly because Morgen, appointed *Flügeladjutant* during the Emperor's Orient voyage in 1898, reported home about the activities among the civilians of the embassy.[55] He

[54] *Documents diplomatiques français*, Ist ser., VIII, no. 356; VII, 1563ff.
[55] Giesl, p. 63. When Morgen reported that the Sultan was no longer sending officers to Germany to receive military instruction because he

represented a new type of Prussian officer—the non-noble "Colonial" or "African," the man who had seen service in the German colonies, driven thereto by comparative poverty, abundant energy and the feeling of frustration at home— in the line of Lettow-Vorbeck, Epp and others, early trail-blazers of Hitlerism. After nearly ten years of service in the *Schutztruppe*, he had participated as observer on the Turkish side in the Greco-Turkish War, had helped the Turks after the war to a somewhat more favorable boundary line, and had then become attaché in Constantinople.

From the outset, Morgen considered Turkey a potential military ally for Germany in future wars. "The essential task of a military attaché, observing the army of a State as regards its organization, armament, training and readiness for war, did not satisfy Morgen's restless mind." He was not pleased with the work of German instructors in the Turkish army, and took every opportunity to point out, to highly-placed Turks, the faults in their military organization and above all in their fortifications along the Straits and the Russian boundary, and he pressed them to make improvements. He gave advice on the route of the later sections of the Bagdad Railway and advocated obtaining a shipping monopoly in Mesopotamia for the Railway Company. He undertook to direct cavalry exercises and *Kriegsspiele* for Turkish officers, among whom was Enver Bey, and he studied conditions along the Caucasus frontier during long horseback trips, thereby exciting Russian suspicions.

At first the Emperor, who received Morgen's reports only after the Wilhelmstrasse had intercepted them and added its own warning commentaries, was inclined to adhere to the earlier German policy of disinterest and non-interference with Russia's designs. She was "after all already reigning at Stambul. Morgen shall keep quiet and leave these questions untouched," he decreed. He agreed with the diplomats' argument that "compromising our relations with Russia and having this counterbalanced by the military advantages which could be gained in the future" by a stronger Turkey, according to

---

feared they might become infected by Social-Democratic ideas, Marschall showed how erroneous that was (summer 1898). *Grosse Politik*, XII, 3341.

Morgen, was sheer illusion, and that for general political reasons Morgen's "bustling and zealousness" must be dampened.[56]

This was before the Kaiser's voyage to the Orient in the autumn of 1898; after his return, he was far more inclined to listen to Morgen's arguments.[57] When the Russians, always eager to paralyze genuine Turkish intentions to reform, whether military or economic, complained that Morgen and other German officers had inspected Turkish troops at Erzerum and had participated in their maneuvers, thereby indicating that Germany's interests in Turkey were no longer merely commercial, but military as well, the Emperor was outraged. He wished to tell the Russians that not only had he kept German instructors from being stationed at Erzerum, where Russian suspicions might have been aroused, but that Morgen had gone there merely to study old theaters of war. (Military history seems to be about the only field of interest which that versatile officer ever neglected.) "To attribute other motives to my *Flügeladjutanten* is an impudence which I forbid and Muraviev shall be told that. . . . The Russians have nothing to seek in Turkey and my aides shall move there as I please. Regardless whether that pleases Muraviev or not. I have never forbidden any foreigners to travel over the battlefields in Lorraine or under the very walls of Metz which is something still more suspicious." The complaints were rejected, though not in the Emperor's words, but the Russians remained unconvinced: their own reports indicated that Morgen was inciting the Turks, pointing out the inevitability of war with Russia, and giving advice on how to meet a Russian attack in Asia Minor.[58]

Further trips undertaken by the restless Morgen came to grate on the nerves of the cautious German diplomats almost as much as on those of the Russians. He undertook an inspection of the Bulgarian-Turkish boundary and one of the Red Sea region, where he went with a commission from the Reichsmarineamt. As a result of this trip he proposed the Reich's acquisition of the Farsan Islands, to control shipping

---

[56] *Ibid.*, XII, 3341f. [57] *Ibid.*, XIV, 3976, 3980.
[58] *Ibid.*, XIII, 3548; XIV, 4023ff.

lanes in the Red Sea. (Tirpitz had to forego this acquisition for general diplomatic reasons in spite of his general hunger for naval stations.) Morgen's activities finally gave sufficient cause to obtain his recall in the autumn of 1901, when he was transferred to the Great General Staff, section "Foreign Armies," subsection "Balkans." From that vantage point he continued his attempts to improve Turkish army conditions, in such an indiscreet manner that the Wilhelmstrasse caused his removal from the General Staff and his transfer to front duties.[59] Here he rose to the rank of lieutenant general, and was much feared by officers and men in the First World War on account of his exacting demands.

For some years German diplomacy kept the Reich's service attachés under control, at least while it was under the direction of Bülow who remembered Bismarck's sharp reprimand of the unfortunate Deines in 1887.[60] Schlieffen seems to have recognized the limitations which diplomacy must needs impose upon the activities of service attachés far better than did the Kaiser or Tirpitz. Besides, the German Army was in a way "saturated," trusting to the timetables of its mobilization plans, but not the new German Navy. The latter needed funds and arguments to obtain such funds, arguments which its attachés were to furnish in addition to technical information, and which were to be drawn from the activities of the competing navies, the British and the American.[61] The "flowering age" of the naval attachés brought back the vices of their military colleagues under Waldersee—private letters from the attachés to Tirpitz in order to bypass foreign office control; general contempt for the diplomats and their considerations; winning of the Kaiser's ear. Without reproof from Tirpitz they wrote him that "it is an old experience that when the inky diplomats want to obtain something, concession-making

[59] *Deutsches Biographisches Jahrbuch*, 10 (1928), art. "Kurt von Morgen" (1858-1928). The title of nobility dates from 1904. Rich and Fisher, I, 178.

[60] Bülow, II, 179.

[61] In October 1897 the German military attaché in Washington received an order from the Reichsmarineamt, where propaganda was in need of new arguments, to submit American naval literature; he promptly subscribed to the services of a clipping bureau. Later in the year he submitted Mahan's latest work. Vagts, *Deutschland und die Vereinigten Staaten*, p. 1272.

begins"; Stumm, a diplomat who was anxious to maintain an understanding with Britain, was called "the type of diplomat in the bad sense, that is to say, the name which must unfortunately be applied to our corps diplomatique."[62]

They could rely on Tirpitz' approval of their disrespect and on his backing against the Reich diplomacy—though he was the son of a civil servant, he claimed that that service was composed of a "degenerate nobility or sons of big businessmen unable to continue their fathers' work."[63] Group conflicts within the governing classes are not always so clearly revealed or so crassly and materialistically explained as in this particular bureaucratic clash. Germany's naval officers were made to feel that they rode the wave of the future in a Reich whose progress was declared, by Tirpitz and by the Kaiser himself, to lie upon the waters. To the monarch the diplomats were mere "bureaucrats" and always backward, most of all in their reporting. Shortly before the outbreak of the First World War he said: "The hiatus in reporting between the civilians and the military men is historic. . . . The civilians never want to admit or to understand danger whenever the military warn against it. As soon as the relations between two countries reach a point where they must be judged from the standpoint of military possibilities as well, the military viewpoint is always underrated and ridiculed by the mortified diplomats."[64]

In this *progressio rei militaris* there was still another victory over the diplomats to be won: the recall of an ambassador because he displeased one or both of the services. This result had never been achieved before, but the cooperation of Tirpitz and the London naval attaché Widenmann, obtained the removal of Count Metternich, German ambassador at the Court of St. James since 1901. For years Metternich had warned that German naval construction would bring England into the war against Germany; he fully realized the hostility of Tirpitz for whom, as Metternich put it, "it was not

[62] Alfred von Tirpitz, *Politische Dokumente*, Vol. I, *Der Aufbau der deutschen Weltmacht* (Stuttgart and Berlin 1924), pp. 355f. and passim.
[63] Freiherr von Freytag-Loringhoven, *Menschen und Dinge wie ich sie in meinem Leben sah* (Berlin 1923), p. 146; Gordon A. Craig in *Political Science Quarterly*, LXIV (1949), 86.
[64] Tirpitz, *Aufbau*, p. 367.

pleasant to hear that our building program and our relations with England depend on one another."[65] Tirpitz himself held that industrial and commercial competition was responsible for the deterioration of Anglo-German relations (for the services it is easy to hold the merchants responsible, as in Napoleon's day). William II did not want to hear such warnings from the ambassador any longer—"I do not agree with the judgment of the ambassador! The naval attaché is right!"[66] he said, throwing to the winds the time-honored pretense that the attaché was not supposed to judge in political questions. Actually, the attaché's views were kept exactly identical with those of Tirpitz in order to impress the monarch even more by their unanimity.[67]

When Bülow retired from the Wilhelmstrasse, abandoning the interdepartmental struggle with Tirpitz, the resistance of Germany's diplomats to service egotism and navy megalomania weakened more and more. They were dimly aware of the consequences of competition with British sea power, but, obeying the Emperor's craving for big ships, they were soon past observing the rules of a supreme State reasoning. Metternich reminded them that this prevailed in England, where "navy and army are considered the most important stakes of policy, as means to a purpose, not however as the determinators of the course of policy." Metternich appealed to the new Chancellor, von Bethmann Hollweg, to follow this rule and back him up in his demand for the recall of Widenmann. "The latter's mail order propaganda campaign" could only be terminated if he were immediately returned to front duties.

The naval question is of military and political nature. Where the separation line is to be drawn, is not easy to say and a matter for interpretation. Under normal conditions a chief of mission will be able to bring the military and naval attachés to follow the orders of their superior as regards reporting. The present naval attaché, however, feels completely safe under the protection of Herr von Tirpitz and H.M. the Emperor, and he does not think of changing his reporting and restricting it to the merely technical side.

[65] *Grosse Politik*, XXVIII, 167.   [66] *Ibid.*, XXXI, 11315.
[67] *Ibid.*, XXXI, 25.

Rather does he state openly that he thinks it his duty to use the rest of his London stay to warn incessantly against the English danger in his reports.

There is only one way open for me, to demand of him to remove tendentious information from a report of his. To this he will not submit, for the above stated reasons. I then have to apply the additional means at my disposal and declare to him that I shall not hand on the report in question. He will then complain, with his naval chief, who will submit the complaint to His Majesty. His Majesty, probably, will call for the suppressed report. Even though the report is politically flavored, but will, at the same time, discuss the naval question, I am in no doubt that H.M. will declare the naval attaché in the right and myself in the wrong.

Would the Chancellor back him up against the attaché with all the authority of his office? Would he have the attaché removed?[68] The weakest of all Chancellors threw up his hands: it was quite impossible to get rid of the obnoxious attaché, and conflicts with the Emperor must be avoided. The existing regulations regarding attachés should be applied in such a way that any of Widenmann's reports, to which exception must be taken, should not be held back; instead they should be refuted in covering letters in a very positive and sharp form, possibly also in a satirical manner.[69] A little later, the Chancellor pointed out to William II that the attaché's activities, at the moment designed to sabotage Haldane's visit to Berlin, which might result in curtailing the German naval bill, were endangering the singleness of purpose of the Reich's foreign policy; he wanted permission to tell Captain Widenmann that his action was disapproved. The Emperor said: "No! He is an officer and can be reproved only by the Supreme War Lord, not by his civilian superior."[70]

These decisions by the Emperor and indecisions on the part of the Chancellor, who neither resigned nor threatened to do so over this fundamental reversal of Bismarckian principles, mark the deepest bow that diplomatic authorities ever made

[68] *Ibid.*, XXXI, 11328.   [69] *Ibid.*, XXXI, 11329.
[70] *Ibid.*, XXXI, 11337; Tirpitz, *Aufbau*, p. 294.

before service attachés and their backers. It was logically followed in the spring of 1912 by Metternich's recall, a triumph for Widenmann and Tirpitz. "If only Metternich were away from here. He is a national misfortune for us."[71] It was Widenmann who wrote and Tirpitz who received this expression of utter disrespect—not only for a superior, but also for the amenities of a bureaucracy considered well disciplined by its contemporaries, but actually torn apart by departmental jealousies and egotisms. Bismarck called this "cavalry troop patriotism," the mentality which makes the leader of the third troop indifferent to the want of forage for the second troop, as long as his own horses are well fed.[72] The German diplomats were denied even the small satisfaction of seeing Widenmann recalled before the ambassador was. The attaché remained in London until September 1912, and he doctored his reports in such a way as to omit reporting and discussing the clear declarations of British statesmen about the influence of the big German naval bill of 1912 on British estimates for that year; he continued to maintain boldly that the German bill had actually improved the outlook for peace.[73] This was the line that Tirpitz and the Tirpitz biographers were to take, putting the blame for war and its outcome on the diplomats, the merchants, the industrialists and the bankers.

Widenmann's successor, a Captain von Müller of very recent vintage in the *Almanac de Gotha*, was groomed no differently by Tirpitz. Müller promised his chief to be "on his guard" that in Anglo-German negotiations "no conditions are proposed and maintained by our diplomats that we [the Imperial Navy] cannot agree to."[74] Before he submitted his official report on a first conversation with Churchill about a naval holiday, he consulted Tirpitz on how he should report it, and whether it was wise to mention it at all in a report which would be read by the Wilhelmstrasse and the Emperor. The Admiral, evading direct responsibility, wrote him by a subordinate hand that considering the "universal desire for a permanent understanding with Britain," the Wilhelmstrasse and the Reichstag might, alas, be receptive to the holiday

71 Tirpitz, *Aufbau*, p. 322.   72 Bülow, I, 109.
73 *Grosse Politik*, XXXI, 11578.   74 Tirpitz, *Aufbau*, pp. 335f.

idea; it would be best to report the meeting very briefly and to convey the impression that Churchill was only seeking to delay or impede the expansion of Germany's navy insofar as it was likely to endanger Britain's own superiority. The result of this consultation, eighteen days after the meeting with Churchill had taken place, was another "mail order" report to Berlin, as Metternich had termed these Tirpitz-inspired documents. It was greeted by the Emperor's "Bravo! very good! We are on our guard! *Caveant Consules!*"[75]

The intramural conflict in the London embassy, with no umpire of Bismarckian caliber to intervene, sharpened into a continual "two fronts' war," as the participating service attachés called it—one against Britain and one against the German navy. All civilian staff members, from about 1905 on, were "officially anti-Navy," according to one of Tirpitz' men. So violent became this clash at one time that the military attaché, a pro-Navy man, was on the verge of challenging the Counsellor, later Secretary of State, von Kühlmann, to a duel. Kühlmann was neo-feudal and rich, and hence to be suspected by a Tirpitz man; he had stated outright that the unsatisfactory state of Anglo-German relations was altogether due to the "painful construction" of the Reich Navy, and that Tirpitz must be fought as a danger to world peace.[76] In addition to naval disputes, however, the conflict between the civilian and the military-naval outlook, which rocked the Second Reich, included subsidiary, crisscrossing fights between old, high and rich nobility, mostly serving as diplomats, and the newer and lower nobility, plus non-nobles, who officered the armed services. Of the ten naval attachés serving in London between 1888 and 1914, only three were noble, and they were of the lowest and newest creation. Tirpitz never thought highly of the governing nobility, and looked to commoners for the best heads among his men—his "wily Ulysseses," as Kühlmann terms them, with some respect for their abilities rather than for their politics and habits of conducting business[77]—to serve

[75] *Ibid.*, pp. 395ff.; *Grosse Politik*, XXXIX, 15573.
[76] Widenmann, pp. 20, 37ff.
[77] Richard von Kühlmann, *Erinnerungen* (Heidelberg 1948), p. 290.

under "the mandate of representing the interest of the German Navy in London." There was none higher.[78]

A more detailed analysis of the backgrounds, views and activities of the service attachés of the German, and to a certain extent the other pre-1914 monarchies, would show that as a rule the greater bellicosity, the less conciliatory attitudes, were exhibited by the commoners, men who aspired to higher military rank and also to an eventual patent of nobility; the possession of such a patent from birth would make the noble officer, and particularly one from an old and rich family, less ambitious for himself and for the State which he served.[79] The pushing urge for the Navy had some of its strongest roots in the non- (and neo-) nobility of its officer body,[80] who, from Tirpitz down, saw in contemporary Reich diplomacy mostly degenerate nobility or effete sons of big businessmen. If a venturesome scion of the older nobility, by a sociological mistake so to speak, entered upon a naval career, his promotional chances would still be quite excellent, but Tirpitz and his aides would keep him out of positions where his inborn tendencies toward international conciliation might harm the Navy. When Lieutenant Commander Widenmann, who came from a family in trade and administration, had to leave London several months after the recall of Ambassador Count Metternich, he obtained one great satisfaction from Tirpitz: his successor was Erich von Müller, of a most recent vintage in the *Almanac de Gotha*, who "in addition to excellent professional knowledge, possessed also the necessary strength of character which guaranteed that he would be equal to his difficult London job." Another candidate, Baron von Rheinbaben, a member of Stresemann's party in the Reichstag during the Weimar Republic, had disqualified himself, during repeated visits to London, by his tendency "toward running after Englishmen, rather than letting them come," an attitude that would never do.[81]

There could be no change or let-up in the attachés' Anglo-

---

[78] Widenmann, p. 62.

[79] Frederick the Great had no use for officers of the higher nobility, such as counts.

[80] See *Journal of the American Military Institute*, III (1939) 214ff.

[81] Widenmann, p. 83.

phobia. Tirpitz himself had made it a touchstone for the growth of the German navy,[82] and "very disagreeable" it was to German diplomats who sought to reach agreements in other than the naval field. "These eternal baitings and accusations of English policy are extraordinarily disturbing, particularly since *en haut* this is always used against me as an argument," the harassed Secretary of State von Jagow wrote to Ambassador Lichnowsky in February 1914. Couldn't he put his naval attaché "on a somewhat shorter leash"?[83] But Lichnowsky, a true scion of the "degenerate nobility," could not or would not undertake this task. Unlike his predecessor Metternich, who was a stronger character, he wanted to believe in the possibility of an Anglo-German understanding "in spite of the fleet" (*My Mission to London*), and in spite of the naval attaché whom he never mentioned in his reports or his apology.

We have already established that service attachés are more warlike or more skeptical as to the preservation of peace—the two need not logically coincide—than diplomats. The soldier or sailor (the air attaché is hardly yet in the documents) will with great readiness consider the best-motivated strivings for peace as mean and dishonoring. For example Widenmann, although he was writing after two world wars had been lost by his country, could not refrain from describing and condemning Bethmann Hollweg, "in anguish wringing his hands." The attaché had been brought from London to Berlin in support of a new and much larger naval bill in 1911, and the Chancellor told him: "You bring us the war!" The sailor "suffered this pitiful outbreak of fear for some time and with the deepest contempt," then, "filled with scorn that escaped the miserable Chancellor," he replied: " 'It is not I that brings the war, but the British will do that as soon as they have found the necessary allies on the Continent.' " To avert this, so ran the sailor's logic, nothing availed but more German ships, and the bigger the better.[84] He remained oblivious of the possibility that shipbuilding might make enemies—it was the business of the

---

[82] For the beginnings see Vagts, *Deutschland und die Vereinigten Staaten*, pp. 911ff.

[83] *Grosse Politik*, XXXVII, 14697.

[84] Widenmann, p. 187. One epithet he used for the Chancellor on this occasion remains unprintable.

civilians to avert such consequences of the German Navy as a world war.

Cases of disobedience in an hierarchical system are considered *scandalosa* by officialdom and hence are not too amply documented. They usually arise from a struggle for supremacy, which is itself the outcome of a fundamental disagreement on policy, and they are apt to shock the citizen more if a member of the armed forces, from whom he expects implicit obedience, is involved. In milder cases disobedience, such as an attaché's in relation to his ambassador, may stem merely from the difference in the style of giving orders between diplomats and soldiers. The initial disagreement between Sir Robert Morier, British ambassador at St. Petersburg (1884-1893), and one of his military attachés, Colonel Gerard, arose when Morier suggested that the colonel should not join an exclusive club which had recently blackballed a civilian member of the embassy out of sheer Anglophobia; the colonel joined nevertheless, not willing to understand that "this intimation was merely the Foreign Office method of giving an order, whereas military departments were more bluff."[85]

The fronts in these internecine conflicts are nearly always drawn in such a way that the diplomats, from foreign minister and members of the foreign office to the ambassador and his youngest civilian attaché, are opposed by army or navy personnel from the chief of staff and (less often) the war minister to the service attaché abroad. The exceptions are few and curious, for example in the alignment of French ministers and officers during the Agadir crisis of 1911. For the first six or seven weeks after the "Panther jump" the negotiations with Germany did not progress; they were exclusively in the hands of the professionals at the Quai d'Orsay, whose policy proved stubborn and bellicose. Ambassador Cambon in Berlin became concerned about this dangerous delay and, in order to bypass the bureaus of *Affaires étrangères*, he made his military attaché, Colonel Pellé, the channel of communication to the war minister and the prime minister. Pellé had warned against any provocative measures such as retaining one year's

---

[85] Waters, *"Secret and Confidential,"* p. 47.

contingent under the colors; he wanted no war at that time since Spain might go along with Germany. Caillaux then took the direction of the negotiations into his own hands, with results satisfactory to most participants including the military attaché, who told the war minister that "in order to make a a good war, one must not commence it by bad diplomacy."[86]

The German Revolution or breakdown of 1918 was long in the making. Of longer duration, perhaps, than any other contributing factor was the basic disorder in the governmental structure, culminating in the altogether un-Bismarckian military dictatorship of the OHL of Hindenburg and Ludendorff to which the weakness of Chancellor von Bethmann Hollweg opened the way. The Chancellor could not make the Austrians agree to the concessions necessary to keep Italy out of the war, concessions absolutely necessary in the opinion of Bülow, the ex-Chancellor and ambassador to Rome, and in that of his military attaché, Major von Schweinitz. The latter expressed his convictions on this vital point somewhat more bluntly than had Bülow himself, and the Chancellor, unlike his predecessor who had known how to keep attachés in their place, neither censured nor reprimanded him; he merely complained about the attaché's lack of "competency and good taste" when he used such terms as "with somewhat more energy," or *Berlin est faible*," with regard to his own government's policy. "The language of Major von Schweinitz probably finds its explanation in the little familiarity he possesses with political things and the resulting want of judgment about what is attainable through political pressure. We have gone to the limit in Vienna, as regards the language which is permissible in relations with an ally whom threats might have brought in the end to giving up the fight and leaving us alone in the battle with our adversaries." The dilemma of the stronger of the two partners was to be solved, as in the Austro-Serbian conflict of 1914, by surrendering to the greater wilfulness of the weaker one, even though both German and Austrian chiefs of staff had stated their conviction that "an intervention on Italy's and Rumania's part on the side of our enemies would be tantamount to the loss of the whole war for us."[87]

[86] Messimy, *Mes Souvenirs*, pp. 61ff.
[87] Bethmann to Bülow, March 16, 1915. Bülow, III, 231f.

The 1918 Revolution brought out into the open the numerous and violent cases of conflict between the old Reich's diplomats and service attachés. The effect of these revelations on post-1918 German politicians and officialdom, and in particular on the diplomats of the Weimar Republic, was a stubborn opposition to the restoration of the service attaché of unfortunate memory even after the Versailles powers had agreed to that particular revival. It was only under a general as Chancellor, von Schleicher (December 1932-January 1933), that it finally took place, and even then the attachés were not made welcome in all Reich embassies. The experiences, in 1933 and later, of the first post-1918 London military attaché, Colonel Geyr von Schweppenburg, were typical:

> The tension which has always existed between German diplomacy and the representation of the *Wehrmacht* I also came to feel at the outset. When my first ambassador in London, Herr von Hoesch, heard that military attachés were to be sent out once more, he muttered, rather unpleased: "What shall they do? Making politics, perhaps?" There were experiences at the bottom of this. In addition, the Chancellor at the time, von Schleicher, was a soldier and the Wilhelmstrasse seemed to fear military influences in some ways and might find them disturbing to its own circles. Reception in the London Embassy was, therefore, cool and help to the service attachés on its part at their arrival and during their accommodation scant. But Herr von Hoesch, one of the outstanding personalities of Germany's foreign service, was wise enough soon to recognize how useful for the information of the ambassador the loyal cooperation of older and experienced service attachés could be in a world where armaments were in such an unstable state.[88]

In general, the more conservative service attachés soon got on working terms with the more conservative ambassadors who survived from pre-Hitler days, but disagreed with later comers like Ribbentrop. Men like the latter wanted the officers to be or to become Party men, loyal only to the Party, and not also to their military superiors such as General Beck, Chief of Staff

[88] Geyr, *Erinnerungen*, pp. 15, 31f., 40.

and chief military opponent of Hitler's war ideas. The more upright service attachés insisted on reporting everything worth knowing to the military offices, including warnings about the consequences of Hitler's policies, and not merely what Hitler wanted to hear. The Führer in any case read but little of their reports, but his servitors wanted *Gleichschaltung* of all judgments, and thus wished to make the embassy, as Ribbentrop put it, "a sworn unity" (*verschworene Einheit*).[89]

Where ambassadors and attachés failed to agree, the old independence or disobedience appeared again—even the unsystematic documentation currently provided by the destroyers of Hitlerism allows us to say that much. But there had to be some order, and there were attempts to bring the multifarious special attachés employed by diplomacy back under the control of the chiefs of missions, attempts which resulted among other things in the co-signature of service attaché reports, when of a political nature, by the ambassador or minister—in itself a desirable innovation.[90] But these regulations were imperfectly obeyed. One illustration: by mid-November 1941, the Japanese militarists had decided that "conflict was inevitable, even if the United States should make greater concessions in the very last minute," and had informed the German naval attaché in Tokyo about this extremely important decision. The latter informed the ambassador, but to a limited extent only; he cabled more complete information to his superiors in Berlin, who were besought not to hand it on to Ribbentrop's Foreign Office. As one of the defendants at the Nuremberg trials testified, so much along the German-Japanese Axis "had been talked about and threshed out by the military and naval attachés,"[91] but *Gleichschaltung*, where it was most imperative, in a wartime embassy, had not been achieved.

[89] *Ibid.*, pp. 120ff.

[90] See the numerous attaché reports from Prague in 1938 in *Documents on German Foreign Policy*, Ser. D, II.

[91] *Trial of the Major War Criminals*, XXXV, 622, 632; see also XXXV, 323, for the participation of the Japanese service attachés and military offices in the diplomatic negotiations with Germany in November 1941.

CHAPTER 17

SERVICE ATTACHÉS AND
THE ALLIANCES

Before 1914

The military and naval attachés were essential cogs in the alliance system that prevailed after 1871, and helped to prepare and preserve it. It was part of their legitimate business to submit expert judgment on the military strength of another power and hence its potential value as a partner[1] or its strength as a potential enemy,[2] or even its inclination, as far as they could determine it, to become an ally of their own, or of another, hostile country. The attachés might go further, and counsel for or against an alliance with the power in question; for example, on the eve of the war of 1870-1871 the two Austrian military attachés in Paris and Berlin, on the strength of their acquaintance with the French and Prussian armies, both opposed the alliance with Napoleon III which the Vienna diplomats were negotiating.[3]

In 1879 the Austrian military attaché in Berlin, a Prince Liechtenstein, who had been excluded from the negotiations and from any detailed knowledge of the Austro-German alliance, confided to his British colleague that he did not think the alliance would be of much use to Austria. Berlin had

[1] In 1888, as well as several times before, the French military attaché in St. Petersburg expressed his "absolute conviction that the military strength of Russia is not what it ought to be in the interest of France, and neither is it what it could be, and quite easily," if only the financially handicapped Russian Government could dispose of 400 or 500 millions (Rubles?) more. *Documents diplomatiques français*, Ist ser., VII, 647.

[2] Whatever other judgments might have been passed by Germans about the "contemptible" BEF, the pre-1914 military attaché in London warned from 1911 on that the British field army, contrary to many continental beliefs, was a force well trained in the field which could be of considerable assistance to the French in case of war. *Grosse Politik*, XXIX, 68.

[3] Schlözer, p. 67; Oncken, *Rheinpolitik*, III, 428, 433.

never, he said, had the friendship for Austria that she had for Russia, and Austria could not forget that all her misfortunes were due to Germany.[4]

The Austrian military politics, led by Chief of Staff Conrad von Hötzendorf, continued to presume on their influence on the alliance-forming process, and brought Bulgaria closer to the Central Powers after the Balkan Wars. They had failed in this endeavor during the Bosnian crisis of 1908-1909, when they had competed with the Russian military attaché in Sofia, and with Pan-Slavism generally, for the favor of the Bulgarian military politicos.[5] The German military attaché in Vienna observed this rapprochement, and reported in April 1913 that "in the General Staff sympathy for Bulgaria is on the increase of late. The Bulgarian military attaché is visiting there oftener than before." Soon afterward, the Austrian war minister spoke favorably of a military convention with Bulgaria, a convention guaranteeing her the territories in dispute between Bulgaria and Serbia-Greece. This was so dangerous that William II wanted it "under no circumstances."[6] At the same time Rumania was beginning to veer away from her nominally still valid alliance with the Central Powers. The Rumanian military attaché in Berlin, according to the reports from his Bulgarian colleague and well ahead of any public decisions by his home government, "expressed himself in the most violent and hateful manner about Austria-Hungary and declared positively that Rumania would not go with the Double Monarchy but rather, on account of her national interests, with Russia."[7]

Bismarck never allowed the German military attachés to exert such influences in the forming of his alliance system; in fact, after he had decided to conclude the alliance with Austria he made Moltke submit a statement supporting it from a military point of view. This exclusion of the soldiers was in keeping with the original peaceful purpose of the alliance as a sort of international cartel, not for war but for

[4] Winifred Taffs, *Ambassador to Bismarck, Lord Odo Russell, first baron Ampthill* (London 1938), p. 350.
[5] *Oesterreich-Ungarns Aussenpolitik*, I, 736, 1012.
[6] *Grosse Politik*, XXXIV, 13214.
[7] *Oesterreich-Ungarns Aussenpolitik*, VII, 8432.

peace—a peace against France, as the fulcrum of the possibility of war. The service attachés' subsequent military judgment on either of the alliance partners, particularly Italy, was often unfavorable, while the diplomats, still eager to keep Italy away from France, with a few exceptions thought more highly of her value. The diplomats were thinking more in terms of war prevention, the military more in terms of war preparation.

The more autocratic a regime, the more liberty in regard to its foreign policy the military are apt to take: Russian generals such as Skobelev, Obrutchev, Dragomirov, Bogdanovitch,[8] rather than diplomats, prepared the way for the Franco-Russian alliance.[9] Early in 1880 the Grand Duke Nicholas, the Russian commander in the Balkan War, came to France for a visit and was taken in hand by the former French military attaché in St. Petersburg, General Gaillard, who in 1878 had observed the war in the Russian GHQ and had been a favorite of the Grand Duke ever since. Gaillard put the visitor in touch with the French Army "as the most vivid embodiment of the French nation"; he showed perhaps too much zeal to please the Russian military attaché in Paris, Baron Fredericks, but he was able to discuss with the Grand Duke the idea of a political alliance between their two countries. For further negotiations he was less well qualified, at least as far as French politics were concerned—he was too well remembered as the president of a court-martial which had condemned numerous *Communards,* a role, however, that could only recommend him to the Russians.[10] More useful was another ex-military attaché to St. Petersburg, Boisdeffre, later *sous-chef* of the French General Staff, who was invited to return to Russia in the summer of 1890 "for

---

[8] *Grosse Politik*, VI, 1213.

[9] This two-mindedness or anarchy left Giers, the foreign minister, "without protection on the part of the war ministry against generals who, as troop commanders or as high administrative officials, directly oppose his policy, approved of by the monarch" (*Grosse Politik*, VI, 1216). It also made Bismarck ask, when told by Austria in 1888 that "the war was being prepared by Russia": "But *who* is Russia?" *Ibid.*, VI, 1190.

[10] Kurt Koerlin, *Zur Vorgeschichte des russisch-französischen Bündnisses 1879-1890* (Hallische Forschungen zur neueren Geschichte, no. IV, Halle 1926), pp. 56f.

the maneuvers," but also for intimate conversations with the war minister and the chief of staff, thus to establish "contact between the two general staffs."[11]

Well ahead of Kronstadt, the Russian military attaché in Paris, Baron Fredericks, "fed the fires of the Russo-French alliance and friendship" by public speeches and gestures,[12] and more secretly negotiated the French manufacture of millions of rifles for the Russian Army. The French Government readily consented, persuaded that these rifles would never fire at France. Fredericks had transmitted an early French proposal, made by the Chief of the General Staff, General Haillot, in 1887, during a period of Franco-German tension and "war danger," which aimed at concerting troop dispositions and possible cooperation, "notably in the case when Germany should make war." The Russian Ministry of War provided him with a special cipher (to bypass the Foreign Ministry) for all correspondence on the matter, and indicated its own intention to proceed with it.

Nothing came of it at that time, but Fredericks remained ready, as he told an agent of the Quai d'Orsay in March 1891, "to take up this question between the two war ministries, provided, of course, that the Tsar agreed to it. But one must know in this case whether that desire still existed on France's part. . . . A *military* convention, if kept absolutely secret and laying down certain important points, could be useful even if a *formal alliance* should not exist. . . . An alliance, in fact, based on a community of interests and dangers, was easily worth a written alliance."[13] Actually, a minimum at least of political understanding had to precede the military convention. And such understanding was considered too important to be negotiated by mere military attachés, who were only allowed to arrange the journeys of the actual negotiators, the chiefs and under-chiefs of staff. The French envoys in St. Petersburg were discreet but nonetheless effective, as they listened to the expression of Russian military sympathy for France and "profound hatred for Germany" and especially

---

[11] *Documents diplomatiques français*, Ist ser., VIII, 226, 234ff.
[12] *Grosse Politik*, VII, 1510.
[13] *Documents diplomatiques français*, Ist ser., VIII, 441.

for her military attaché in St. Petersburg;[14] the Russians were more indiscreet or brutal. Russian attachés in Berlin told members of the French Embassy there, during the Boulanger crisis of 1887, that "they would prefer to hurl themselves directly against the Germans instead of making a beginning with the Austrians" (nothing could have been more welcome to French strategy)—that they might be beaten at first, but that the conflict would last eighteen months or two years, much longer than Germany would be able to sustain a war. They made no bones to the French about their resentment against Germany, their military inferiority complex. "It weighs them down to feel in some way to be under the hand of Germany"—thus the French ambassador in St. Petersburg diagnosed the malaise of the Russian Army in 1885.[15] They were hardly more diplomatic to the Germans and their allies; the Russian military attaché in Vienna told the Austrian Chief of Staff in November 1891, when additional Russian divisions were being crowded against the Western frontiers: "If Germany gets into a quarrel with France, we shall let go, and that means: with passion against the Germans, and since you are obliged to help the Germans, of course against you as well." The Austrian answered with more dignity that if that was how things stood, the preservation of the peace depended on the Paris mob, and not upon the Tsar.[16]

The service attachés were, so to speak, the maintenance personnel servicing the military machinery of the alliances and ententes. They shuttled information back and forth, queries and answers between the general staffs and war ministries about operation plans, technical developments, in the field of arms or communications (wireless connections between Russia and France in case of interruption of the traditional communication by wire), about intentions to strengthen, or, more rarely, to reduce an army or navy, observations

14 Toutain, pp. 272ff.

15 *Documents diplomatiques français*, Ist ser., VI, 504, 155.

16 *Grosse Politik*, VII, 1511. The German attaché reporting this scene called his Russian colleague "doubtless a very able brain, but occasionally blurting out his innermost thoughts with Slavic childishness. He is a protégé of Obrutchev and Dragomirov; his views would be close to those of these generals."

about the forces of their common enemies, the peacefulness or war-mindedness of an enemy or an ally. But even among the Allies there remained a certain guardedness as to the ultimate secrets, such as operation plans or the intention to go to war. The Austrians never learned the exact strength of the German forces which would remain on the Eastern front at the start of a war—Berlin feared the secret might be betrayed to the Russians by an officer of the Redl type. And when the Russians planned or intended a coup against the Dardanelles in 1895-1896, the French ally was told nothing. France considered a war at that time and for that purpose highly undesirable, and French service attachés had to travel to the Black Sea to find out how far actual embarkation and landing operations had been prepared.[17]

Only to a limited extent were the attachés made liaison men between the intelligence sections of allies and coalition partners. These offices, on the whole, preferred direct contact, including the exchange of visits by their respective heads. During the Austro-Russian tensions of 1912-1913, a reflex action of the Balkan War, the German military attaché in Vienna observed something he had not been told about, that the *Evidenzbureau* "was in a lively exchange of information with Section III B of the Great General Staff." Knowing something about the sources of the intelligence in question, he recommended that it be reexamined in Berlin, since it might have been "seen too much through the eyes of Polish agents."[18] Inside the Axis the intelligence offices (the *Abwehr*, headed by Admiral Canaris, and the *Servizio Informazioni Militari*, headed by General Roatta in 1936), were in direct connection, doing without the service attachés.[19] On the other side, some of those charged with liaison work found nothing more exasperating than the reticence or suspiciousness of Russian intelligence; it had been far more communicative during the period of Reichswehr-Red Army interchange, when data about Polish armaments and plans were

[17] *Documents diplomatiques français*, Ist ser., XIII, 41, 85, 89ff., 275ff., 315f.

[18] *Grosse Politik*, XXXII, 12393.

[19] Enno von Rintelen, *Mussolini als Bundesgenosse, Erinnerungen des deutschen Militärattachés in Rom, 1936-1943* (Tübingen 1951), p. 10.

exchanged to the end of the Weimar Republic. One of the strongest links between Warsaw and Paris, which survived even the German-Polish flirtation between 1933 and 1939, was the direct line established between the two intelligence services. Originally established on the basis of a secret protocol of March-April 1926 as a sort of reinsurance against Locarno, this nexus, which had been dropped in 1927 and resumed in 1932, provided the French with the first concrete details of German-Russian military cooperation; on the other hand, the exchange of information about German rearmament arranged between the French and Italian intelligence services as part of the Stresa front and lasting from January 1935 to April 1936 netted the French but little that they considered new or interesting.[20]

The military conventions were followed by naval conventions, and naval attachés followed the examples of their military colleagues. In 1889 the Italian naval attaché in London (where Italian hopes for the safety of their coasts against France were centered) suggested that the German and Italian naval commands should have constant relations as the two armies did, and an exchange of naval attachés was agreed on. This was soon followed by Crispi's proposal to unite the Mediterranean fleets of the three Triple Alliance partners as a precaution against France, which Rome suspected of planning a surprise attack on La Spezia,[21] a sort of early and miniature Pearl Harbor raid. Bismarck, however, told Crispi that Italy must first come to an understanding with Britain for naval assistance against France; this, Crispi indicated somewhat mysteriously, he had already done. For Bismarck, who knew how difficult it was to obtain binding promises from Britain, that was sufficient; there was and remained an exchange of naval attachés but no naval conventions between Berlin and Rome[22] until 1900, when a rather empty instrument was signed. It was replaced by a very elaborate one in 1913 which provided for the reciprocal assignment of naval officers to the three supreme headquarters in case of

[20] Castellan, pp. 467, 474f., 478; Maurice Gustave Gamelin, *Servir*, 3 vols. (Paris 1946-1947), II, 467.
[21] *Grosse Politik*, VI, 1278.   [22] *Ibid.*, VI, 1320-1327.

war, if not before. "For this service the naval attachés are indicated, as they appear to be specially suited thanks to their personal relationships with the Navies of their Allies." It was also agreed that they were to be informed of the existence of the Naval Convention and, if necessary, of the details.[23]

The Triple Alliance, as time went on, with *Italia fara da sè*,[24] became a triangle with only one solid side, the Berlin-Vienna one. The German and Austrian military attachés endeavored from the outset to strengthen at least this side. The first condition necessary to establish confidence was to give up spying on the power which was now an ally (something which the Russians could not bring themselves to do, at first, in their relations with their new ally, France).[25] When the Austrian military plenipotentiary in Berlin (1880-1895), Baron von Steininger, was offered that appointment, he declared to his superiors that he would not assume the role of a spy, should they think it necessary to have such an agent in Berlin. Even so, Steininger worked at first under the shadow of suspicion; Berlin thought that he was employing a German ex-officer suspected of spying, and the government offices gave him no more information than they allowed the French and Russian attachés. This attitude changed only after the Austrian had sought and obtained an open explanation from the War Minister, and William II himself soon showed "astounding frankness" toward his ally's military representative.[26]

[23] Alfred Francis Pribram, *The Secret Treaties of Austria-Hungary* (Cambridge 1920), I, 286ff.

[24] According to Austrian information, Italian opposition to Austrian policy in the Balkans after 1907 (the year which marks Italy's turning away from the Triplice in the military field and making military preparations in the direction of Tyrol and Istria) went so far that her military attaché in Belgrade in 1908 worked out plans for the concentration of the Serbian Army "in case some constellation or other action in the direction of Greater Serbia should become possible," as well as a plan for Italian military support to Serbia. *Grosse Politik*, XXVI, 8921, 9090. How far this was a private performance, or whether it had official sanction, is unknown.

[25] *Ibid.*, XIII, 3577.

[26] *Preussische Jahrbücher*, 201 (1925), 264ff. According to one of Steininger's successors, there prevailed by the turn of the century "for considerable time past a state of confidence and the greatest frankness, particularly as regards the most important war preparations, between the German and the Austrian army commands. There was, then, nothing

From then on there was great intimacy between the two General Staffs, including arrangements as to initial operations in case of war, constant exchange of information, even extensive division of labor—too extensive in the opinion of some critics. Germany, for example, allowed military observation in such Balkan capitals as Belgrade, Athens and Cetinje to be an Austrian preserve, and even abstained from sending an observer to the Serbian armies during the Balkan Wars. This was partly for reasons of economy, but also because Vienna had a permanent military attaché at both Belgrade and Cetinje, and "perhaps put emphasis on the fact that the military conditions of Serbia should be judged by us [the Germans] in agreement with Vienna." This might not have come about had Berlin had its own lookout-man there. The result was an unfavorable opinion of Serbia in Berlin, including the *Rotes Haus*, and the wrong guess as to the outcome of the Balkan Wars. The military judgment was to a large extent "a reflection of our diplomatic relations. The Rumanian Army was therefore considered as by far the best, the Bulgarian, probably mainly on Viennese recommendation, as satisfactory. On the Serbian, not to mention the Greek, Army official judgment had little that was favorable to say and extra-official judgment was outspokenly negative," while Turkey's strength was vastly overrated.[27]

The estrangement of Italy from the Triple Alliance led to restraint and less and less communication, to the resumption of fortress construction along the Austro-Italian frontier and to Conrad's proposals to make war on the ostensible ally. Germany, however, and the Ballplatz people from Aehrenthal down, would not allow him to do this, in 1907 or later.[28] There were numerous signs of this estrangement in the military field, including the relations between the service attachés of the Triplice. When the Italian military attaché in Constantinople, "always so apathetic," suddenly and repeatedly

to inquire about on this point, to espy or to learn in circuitous ways. All that one side or the other wished to learn from the other was asked for in the open, official manner." Stürgkh, p. 181.

[27] Maj. Gen. Gerold von Gleich, *Vom Balkan nach Bagdad* (Berlin 1921), pp. 9f.

[28] Conrad, IV, 188.

in 1902 came to his German colleague for information on Tripolis, the German thought it best to show great reserve.[29] In 1906, the Austrian attaché in Turkey wanted to undertake a journey through Tripolis, which was still under Turkish sovereignty but already permeated by Italian propaganda; the Italians protested, and succeeded in getting him stopped en route by order of his war minister.[30] While the diplomats continued the pretense of the Triple Alliance, the military and naval offices in Berlin and Vienna had largely written off Italy as an ally.[31] The Italian naval attaché in both capitals around 1910 was considered as "a suspect rather than an ally." And when the French naval attaché once mentioned to him the possible collaboration of the Austrian and Italian navies, "he shrugged his shoulders, and both of us, presuming what the future would be, agreed to help one another out."[32] Another Italian service attaché completely estranged from the Triplice well before 1914 or 1915 was the military attaché in St. Petersburg, Lieutenant Colonel Abati, who received Russian queries during the Balkan Wars as to what stand Italy would take in a war between Germany and Austria-Hungary and the Triple Entente. He answered that his country would never actively interfere on the side of her allies; the most the latter could expect from her would be neutrality. Turning his ostentatious Russophilia to good use, however, Abati was able to obtain information at the Russian war ministry which was usually given only to the French ally.[33]

In keeping with Conrad's policies, most Austrian military men, including attachés, were far more suspicious of Italy's loyalty and military usefulness long before 1914 than were the Berlin generals and admirals who tried to preserve a military purpose in the Triple Alliance. The German Admiralty proposed in 1913 that the two Mediterranean partners arrange that in case of war their fleets would together

---

[29] *Grosse Politik*, XVIII, 5856.   [30] Giesl, p. 172.

[31] The Kaiser's "joke," always to send very tall officers as attachés to Rome and thus to remind the King of his small size, could hardly prove helpful. Eugen Schiffer, *Ein Leben für den Liberalismus* (Berlin 1951), p. 117.

[32] Faramond, p. 30.

[33] *Oesterreich-Ungarns Aussenpolitik*, IV, 4346.

attack French army transports from North Africa; a successful attack, eliminating all or part of the three army corps which France was expected to bring across during the first days of mobilization, would enable Germany to assist Austria on the Eastern front with that greater strength for which the Austrians hoped so much. This idea was strongly and successfully opposed by the Austrian military attaché in Rome, who warned repeatedly against a naval agreement with the Italians beyond the existing naval convention—it "might unveil to them much that is unknown."[34]

The military part of an alliance is relatively the more mechanical, more automatic part, and this became more firmly arranged between Berlin and Vienna than were the diplomatic ties. Bismarck, for one, had wanted to keep the latter as unfettered as possible. He was well aware that once military alliances, conventions, understandings have been concluded, the tendency of the military authorities of the signatories would be directed toward "timely conversations about detailed military measures" for the *casus foederis*, the occasion against which the alliance had been prepared; in such case, the military argued, neither partner "must be surprised by events." Aside from the plans of operations to be concerted at least in a general way, numerous other things were in need of minute peacetime preparatory work, such as the use of railways, possibly an identical first day of mobilization, the simultaneous declaration of war and opening of operations, with all the necessary timetable arrangements.[35] Inherent in these prearranged minutiae is the danger that general staffs and their leaders tend to look forward to the point where the *casus foederis* has become a *casus belli*. Or they may find that the arrangements for cooperation have become so tight and automatic that one step toward war by one alliance partner can trigger only a prearranged reaction by the other partner or partners. The desire to lead the war

[34] Report to Chief of Staff, March 29, 1913. *Ibid.*, V, 6366. It was communicated to the Foreign Ministry, which did not get to see much material of this nature, at the urgent request of Archduke Franz Ferdinand, as *Einsichtsstück*, for their inspection.
[35] *Grosse Politik*, VI, 1162, 1185.

offensively does not always know how to conceal itself behind a policy of apparent non-aggression.

When these alliance problems plagued Bismarck during the "war danger" period of 1887-1888, the elder Moltke protested. He was fully aware that, regarding the *casus foederis* between Austria and Germany, it was *exclusively* within the province of the Chancellor, and not of the general staff, to decide when that point had been reached. Bismarck, however, would not allow Austria ("certain military circles of Vienna," to be more precise) to change this *casus foederis* in such a way that it would exist at all times, and not only, as specified, in case of a Russian aggression.[36] After Austrian proposals for discussing the war with Russia had been submitted by the Austrian attaché, the Chancellor admonished Kalnoky that "we two must take care on our part that our privilege of advising our two monarchs politically, does not actually slip from our hands and pass to the General Staffs." He begged the Austrian foreign minister to support his stand that "international understandings and the foundations of them are not formed by purely military parties" without his knowledge and permission and that of Kalnoky. "It is in the interest of peace to adhere strictly to this way of conducting business since both ministers will naturally be more peacefully inclined than their military compatriots."[37] The military proposal, which Kalnoky had embraced more wholeheartedly than he later cared to admit, was "to lay down precisely the conditions under which the *casus foederis* would have to arise." The Chancellor termed it "squaring of the circle, impossible of definite clarification and not capable of being solved by any treaty text as long as one does not trust the bona fides of an ally more than the text the clauses."[38]

This retention of the German Chancellor's having the final decision on the *casus foederis,* and the insistence upon political-civilian supremacy grew weaker with the years, while the military ties between Berlin and Vienna were tightened. The later chancellors allowed what they mistook for a more clear-cut division of labor to take place, between the military

[36] *Ibid.,* VI, 1183, 1184, 1186.   [37] *Ibid.,* VI, 1185-1187.
[38] *Ibid.,* VI, 1192.

and the diplomats, but it actually amounted to losing control of what the military did among themselves. The Wilhelmstrasse could have seen this developing in the reports of the German military attaché in Vienna, though more was apparent in the correspondence between General Conrad and his attachés and in Moltke-Conrad correspondence. It came to a climax on July 31, 1914, when Moltke told the Austrian attaché that

> he regards the situation as critical if the Austro-Hungarian Monarchy does not mobilize immediately against Russia. Russia's announced declaration concerning mobilization she has ordered, makes necessary counter-measures by Austria-Hungary, something that must also be quoted in the public explanation. Thereby would arise the *casus foederis* for Germany. With Italy, do come to some honorable arrangement, assuring her compensations, so that Italy will remain actively inside the Triple Alliance; by no means leave even one man on the Italian frontier. Do decline the renewed advances made by England for the maintenance of peace. The firm seeing through of a European war is the last chance of saving Austria-Hungary. Germany goes along unconditionally.[39]

With this telegram in hand, Conrad surprised Berchtold, the foreign minister, who cried out: "That is capital *(gelungen)*! Who is governing: Moltke or Bethmann?"[40] The milder judgment would prevail, but the military element, from William II down, betrayed to and through the service attachés, both German and foreign, a bellicosity that the diplomats could not stifle. As one example from many, in the later years of the Kaiser's reign: before the German military attaché at St. Petersburg returned from leave in November 1912, at a time of growing Austrian-Russian tension over the Balkans, he was received by the Emperor who, as the Austrians at St. Petersburg were told, seemed "particularly warlike and had expressed the view that if Serbia and Russia behind her should prove unreasonable *à tout prix*, the present moment might

39 Conrad, IV, 150.

40 *Ibid.*, IV, 152. For the July 1914 setting of this episode see Fay, II, 506ff.

not perhaps be an unreasonable one in which to remove by force once and for all the many antagonisms which had successively piled up on all sides and which formed a constant danger for Europe." The Austrian ambassador at St. Petersburg could not at all perceive "what advantage Austria-Hungary could derive even from a victorious war with Russia," but the Ballplatz people saw, even at that time, that "the advantage would lie in the settlement of the South Slav [Serbian] problem!"[41] They were booking such imperial statements as deposits to the common account on which they were to draw a blank check in 1914.

The intimacy and cooperation established between Russian and French military leaders, with the help of the attachés as permanent intermediaries was on the whole more lively, more detailed than the contacts between Berlin and Vienna. On one side the military backwardness of the Russians, their tendency to cheat the alliance partner by earmarking more forces against the Austrians than had been promised, and more than seemed advisable from strictly military reasoning,[42] their setbacks resulting from defeat in 1904-1905, and on the other hand the French urgency to remedy these shortcomings crowded the wires and pouches with suggestions from the French and explanations and demands from the Russians. The attachés carried desires and suggestions about the other partner's armed forces, his defense installations, his equipment and mobilization plans. After 1905 the French concentrated their proposals on the strategic railroads which Russia was to construct with French loans, and which were to bring the Russian masses faster to the German frontier and thus ease the pressure of the German masses on the French frontier. Even before the military convention had been signed the Russians had kept the French informed, through their attaché in St. Petersburg, about increasing troop concentrations against Germany.[43] Later, this officer participated in discussions of where to garrison the troops designated to fight Germany; it had been realized that far too many had been crowded

---

[41] *Oesterreich-Ungarns Aussenpolitik*, IV, 4727.
[42] *Documents diplomatiques français*, IInd ser., X, 492.
[43] *Ibid.*, Ist ser., IX, 199ff.

into garrisons west of the Vistula, which might offer the Germans another Sedan.[44] The last of the meetings of the two chiefs of staff accompanied by the two military attachés, in August 1913, confirmed the need for more mutual information. "Since the exchange of information between the two allied armies can only be advantageous, it is to continue regularly and frequently."[45]

At times it was an effort for the French ambassador and military attaché in St. Petersburg to persuade themselves that they had no reason to suspect the good will of the Russian General Staff—this was in 1910—but on the whole mutual confidence grew as 1914 approached. This trustfulness was merely part of the conviction, prevailing by 1914 in both diplomatic camps and among military men as well as diplomats, that one's own side could win the war, hence need not shrink from it. The Entente need postpone it no longer, now that Russia had regained her strength, while the Central Powers believed that they could win in spite of that.[46] The service attachés shared these convictions: the British military attaché in Vienna, a "good man," Major Sir Thomas Cunningham, told an Austrian civilian politician in November 1911 "that the German Army would be beaten by the French if it should come to war." The recipient of this confidence found it "curious how this conviction has recently spread in France and England."[47] Confidence in the Entente camp was also produced by the Franco-Russian Naval Convention of 1912, complemented by a Convention for the Exchange of Information between the Russian and French Navies. This provided that information was to be applied for through the two naval attachés, who were to call on the admiralty staffs; the attachés themselves, however, were not to be directly questioned by the authorities in the country of residence.[48]

[44] *Grosse Politik*, XXVI, 806.

[45] Auswärtiges Amt, *Der diplomatische Schriftwechsel Iswolskis, 1911-1914. Aus den Geheimakten der Russischen Staatsarchive*. Friedrich Stieve, ed., 4 vols. (Berlin 1926), III, 276.

[46] For this thesis see Vagts, *Defense and Diplomacy*, pp. 365ff.

[47] Josef Redlich, *Das politische Tagebuch* (Graz and Cologne 1954), I, 110.

[48] Ministère des affaires étrangères, *Documents diplomatiques: L'alliance franco-russe* (Livre jaune) (Paris 1918), pp. 136f.

The French tried not to be condescending, but they considered themselves, with good reason, the more advanced military nation. French achievements, if embraced by her partner, offered all that was required to turn the vast Russian manpower potential into kinetic war energies. The French were deeply chagrined when Russian officers suggested various French military reforms; they felt that while their own proposals derived from technical and organizational progress, those of the Russians stemmed from political reaction. On one occasion, when directed against a much too liberal war minister, General André, a champion of Dreyfus, the Russian ideas became so indiscreet that the military attaché in Paris had to be recalled: he was airing in the Paris press the irrepressible conflict between himself and the Rue Dominique (1901). The Russian, Colonel Mouraviev-Amourski, bore a name famous in Russian imperialism, on which he had banked, and he was a cousin of the former Russian foreign minister. He declared in a farewell press statement, a quite unusual thing for an attaché to give out:

> I have never made any secret of my opinion about certain projected reforms of the French Army. This opinion is completely my own; and since I am a soldier, and not a dipomat, I have believed that I ought not to hide it in my various conversations with your ministers and notably with M. Delcassé. I believe as ever that the united military force of our two peoples is the surest guarantee of the European peace, and if I have not approved of certain changes brought about in the French Army, it has been due alone to my solicitude for the solidity of the Alliance. . . . And what justifies me in this belief is the fact that the German newspapers have been unanimous in expressing their satisfaction about my removal which they, on their part, attribute to my hostility to French military reforms.[49]

In spite of a few such incidents the position of the Russian attaché in Paris was by 1911 so firm and so formalized that,

49 *Documents diplomatiques français*, IInd ser., I, nos. 121f., 205. For some later political activities on Mouraviev's part see *Oesterreich-Ungarns Aussenpolitik*, VII, 9261.

although the British military attaché visited the French War Ministry very frequently, he still had to go on days assigned for the reception of foreign service attachés, while the Russian had his special *entrée* at all times. The German military attaché thought this nuance "characterizes perhaps the difference between alliance and *entente cordiale* as far as military matters go."[50]

In foreign posts, particularly in Berlin and perhaps less so in Constantinople, French and Russian attachés were as a rule on friendly or intimate terms, "en rapports de vraie camaraderie," as one French military attaché in Berlin described his relations with his Russian colleague. The latter, recalled in December 1905, confided that by the end of his tour of duty he had come to the conclusion that the German Army had passed its peak and was now on the downward slope; the Frenchman agreed: "There was no longer the same spirit of devotion and discipline in the officer body; and among the rank and file, Socialist agitation had not remained without some effect."[51] This judgment, incidentally, raises a difficult question: on which signs and indications will a foreign military observer base his opinion about the morale and other imponderables of another country's armed forces?

As alliance partners the French, including their military attachés, showed infinite, admirable, and at times pathetic patience with the vagaries of their Russian ally, whose Far Eastern policy was nothing but a waste of effort and *faux frais* by any French standards. This determination to let the ally go as far as he cared to go in his reckless way, and thereby even relax temporarily the pressure on the Germans (the only thing which really counted in French military considerations) probably reached its highest point in the conclusions of the French attaché at St. Petersburg, General Moulin, in the autumn of 1904, after the first ominous Russian defeats in Manchuria. The French observer on the spot had already

[50] *Grosse Politik*, XXIX, 67.
[51] *Documents diplomatiques français*, IInd ser., VIII, no. 271. For an exchange of views between the French military attaché in Berlin and his Russian colleague, "an ally and collaborator," in 1910, particularly as regards the probable distribution of the German forces along the two fronts of a future war, see *ibid.*, IInd ser., XII, 608ff.

concluded that an immediate peace was imperative in the Russian interest and that "from the point of view of *real* power Russia could only gain by abandoning the Far East," but Moulin thought it best to have the Russians slug it out, not only to their last officer but also until a still larger amount of French francs, provided by French capitalists buying Russian bonds, had been spent. "Since the interest of France is that Russia should persevere to the end of this enterprise, it is the duty of every Frenchman, in his own sphere of action, to contribute to this perseverance by his word, his pen, his counsels, and if need be by his money." Nothing would be spent in vain if only the alliance survived the war and the Kaiser's wooing. William was willing to substitute for France as Russia's benefactor, an eventuality against which the Russian war minister and the French attaché combined and conspired as early as November 1904, long before Bjoerkoe.[52]

The service attaché has often been the most undiplomatic member of a diplomatic team.[53] He has shown the greatest readiness to express convictions, and bluntly, about a recently or presently impending war and to describe conditions "more realistically" than do the diplomats proper. He has confided his views to friends and neutrals, and sometimes to the prospective enemy, regardless of the possible aggravation of diplomatic crises. While the Algeciras Conference was sitting, the German naval attaché in Rome, who had been a member of the Kaiser's *maison navale*, a position which gave him great prestige among his colleagues, pronounced his views on the possibility of war to a small circle of friends, one of whom reported them to the French naval attaché. "I do not believe we shall have war," the German sailor had said, "but you may be sure that we have envisaged the eventuality of one without any

[52] *Ibid.*, IInd ser., V, nos. 364, 450.

[53] An anecdote on attaché—and national—diplomacy: "Seven foreign military attachés, on an inspection tour through a Canadian artillery training center, were asked a recurring question: Did they think Russia had the bomb yet? Their answers: *The American*: 'I haven't been to Russia'—*The Chinese*: 'It's hard to say'—*The Czechoslovak*: 'How should I know? I'm not stationed at Ottawa'—*The Frenchman*: 'I am not a Russian'—*The Swiss*: 'All I can say is, we have no atomic bomb'—*The Turk*: 'Myself, I'm for democracy'—*The Briton*: 'I'm an old-fashioned gentleman who prefers not to be quoted.'" *Time*, February 14, 1948.

emotion for we are certain of success, even on the sea. We don't want to declare the war but, if we see it as inevitable, we shall arrange it so that it will be declared on us at the very moment when we judge it most advantageous to us." (The arch-secret of professional diplomats before 1914, the planning ahead of war guilt, was blurted out by the temporary diplomat.)

England, the German continued, "in the disdain which she affects, looking down from the heights of her pride as the world's foremost naval power, has not bothered to form a superiority decisive in the first hour by maintaining a squadron clearly superior to ours. In spite of the new distribution of the English naval forces, directed against us, the Channel squadron is perceptibly inferior to our fleet as regards tonnage and artillery power. England needs but 48 hours to reverse this ratio, but before these 48 hours are over, we shall have destroyed the Channel squadron and burned London; after that we will retire to our bases for refitting and repairs and then victoriously face the second English squadron." The French Atlantic squadron could be left out of consideration, it was completely outmoded, and anyhow France would not march. "It is the business of our diplomacy to tie her arms by the play of our alliances and the salutary fear of our action on land." This boast met another from across the North Sea, furious sound waves caught by history as they crossed one another. For at the same time the English naval attaché in Rome, Commander Keyes, told his French colleague that he had word from the Admiralty: "We are lying in wait for the German fleet like the cat waiting for the mouse."[54]

The diplomatic tension between Austria and Russia on the eve of the First Balkan War was reflected, *inter alia*, in a strong antagonism between the Constantinople embassies of the two powers. The Russian military attaché confided to the German ambassador that, should Austria attack Serbia, "the Russian Government would at once be swamped by public opinion and forced to intervene."[55] And the Russian military attaché in Berne during the prolonged Balkan crisis of 1912-1913, Colo-

---

[54] *Documents diplomatiques français*, IInd ser., IX, no. 87.
[55] *Grosse Politik*, XXXIII, 12216.

nel Gurko, who played a considerable role in the Russian intelligence service and had been involved in various espionage cases, told a member of the Austrian delegation with a frankness "surprising even in a Russian soldier":

> From the Russian standpoint it was quite desirable for the Turks to keep Constantinople. Should they be pressed back into Asia Minor, they would have a much better chance to regain their strength and might become troublesome for Russia. A quick ending of the war would therefore be in the Russian interest. But public opinion in Russia, extraordinarily excited, did not understand such practical considerations. It wanted to assure the Balkan States of a full success, something to which only Austria was opposed. The same mood prevailed throughout the Russian Army. Since a settlement of accounts with Austria-Hungary was inevitable in any case, the present moment was most favorable for Russia to break loose. Her Army had completely recuperated from the Japanese campaign, her artillery was equal to the German and superior to the Austrian, Italy was still engaged in Tripoli, France at the height of her war-readiness, and as regards Britain, her superiority at sea could only grow less as time went on.[56]

Another "wild warrior," as German diplomats called him, was the Russian military attaché in Belgrade, Colonel Artamonov, who had his "luggage packed" for a European war as early as 1913.[57] It could only encourage the Serbs in their resistance to Austrian demands to hear him say that the Double Monarchy, with her military backwardness, was in no condition to make war in 1912.[58]

The incomplete separation of military and civilian authority and activity in the Balkans offered the foreign military attachés in the Balkan capitals, such as Artamonov, many political opportunities. None grasped them more eagerly than the Russians, whose activities in this region provide new reminders of the close ties between Russian officers and Pan-Slavism. "There's where the war instigators are to be found,"

---

[56] *Ibid.*, XXXIV, 12790.   [57] *Ibid.*, XXXIV, 12806.
[58] *Oesterreich-Ungarns Aussenpolitik*, IV, 4353.

as William II observed in one of his more lucid marginal remarks on the eve of the Balkan Wars.[59] The military attaché in Sofia, Colonel Romanovsky, was a tireless mediator in the making of the alliances preparing those wars, "driving eagerly for war, contrary to the officially peaceful endeavors" of the Russian Minister, as we saw in the last chapter.[60] Further Russian encouragement was received when the Tsar sent for the Bulgarian military attaché in St. Petersburg to give him a message for the war minister in Sofia. He, the Tsar, "would view with favor a successful termination of the Serbian-Bulgarian negotiations," concerning agreements which obviously constituted a war alliance largely fathered by military politicos. Among them moved the Italian military attaché in Sofia; he was on intimate terms with Romanovsky and with Bulgarian officers who had gone to Italian military schools, and from them he learned of the Serb-Bulgar alliance. The Turks had hitherto been stubborn, but this piece of information hastened the conclusion of the Turkish-Italian peace on terms highly favorable to Italy.[61]

Essentially, the service attaché is intended to be an observer and reporter, and not a negotiator. On specific occasions of a military nature, however, and on the basis of clearly defined instructions given him by his home offices or by his ambassador, he may undertake negotiations, which can result in military conventions or in more limited understandings. Only under primitive or reckless conditions such as prevailed among the Balkan nations did military attachés act as negotiators and signers of the most important treaties, for example those between Serbia and Bulgaria in April 1904, the prelude to the Balkan alliances.[62] The Franco-British understandings of 1905-1906 and later, about military support of France in case of war with Germany, were arranged through the French mili-

[59] *Grosse Politik*, XXXIV, 12806.
[60] *Ibid.*, XXXIII, 12219; for further activities of Romanovsky see *ibid.*, XXXV, 13564, 13566. See also above, pp. 228, 334.
[61] Ernst C. Helmreich, *The Diplomacy of the Balkan Wars* (Cambridge, Mass. and London 1938), pp. 52, 156; Anatolii V. Nekludoff, *Diplomatic Reminiscences before and during the World War, 1911-1917* (New York 1920), pp. 75, 82ff., 194.
[62] Helmreich, pp. 5, 464ff.

tary attaché in London, Colonel Huguet, who turned first to a British ex-attaché, Colonel Repington.[63] The proposed Anglo-Russian naval convention of 1914 was to be negotiated on the Russian side by the naval attaché in London on the basis of oral instructions which he had received at St. Petersburg; this was partly because "the trips of the naval attaché, even if repeated, would not strike the public as something exceptional whereas the arrival of higher officers of the Imperial Navy at London would certainly become known and would be commented upon in an undesirable manner."[64] In spite of the secrecy, which was in accordance with British desires, this "important step towards attaching Great Britain to the Franco-Russian Alliance" (Sasonov), became known in detail to the Wilhelmstrasse through M. de Siebert in the Russian embassy in London, and through the *Berliner Tageblatt* to all the world.[65]

The service attachés of friendly powers have often exchanged information gathered in the country of their residence.[66] When there were alliances or other understandings this exchange would become more intimate, more exclusive,[67] in fact practically obligatory, and attachés stationed in the capitals of other powers would cooperate no less closely than their chiefs, the ambassadors. Friends must remain friends and enemies

[63] For details see Fay, I, 203ff.

[64] *Die internationalen Beziehungen im Zeitalter des Imperialismus* (USSR), Ist ser., III, 5; for these negotiations see Vagts, *Defense and Diplomacy*, pp. 126ff.

[65] Theodor Wolff, *The Eve of 1914* (New York 1936), pp. 380ff.

[66] During the Balkan crisis (November 1912) the German military attaché in Paris was told by his Spanish colleague, "who has been here for five years and is a good observer," that the French Government, in order not to be surprised by events, had taken all precautions that were possible without provoking foreign countries or public opinion at home more than necessary. The Italian attaché told of orders to accelerate the training of recruits recently called to the colors, in order to get them ready sooner than usual for field service. *Grosse Politik*, XXXIII, 12436.

[67] When the alliances and ententes occasionally became a little looser, the exchange of information between attachés from the two camps dividing Europe was resumed. The German embassy at St. Petersburg concluded that some Anglo-Russian estrangement over Persia was taking place in 1913. "In favor of this view are the numerous visits which the always so reserved English military attaché is paying the Austrian attaché, whom he tries to pump on rumored Russian troop movements in the South." *Ibid.*, XXXIV, 12649.

enemies—that is the categorical imperative of alliance diplomacy. When at the close of the First World War the newly appointed military attaché for Tokyo came to ask Sir Henry Wilson, Chief of the Imperial General Staff, for instructions to guide him during his four years' tenure, the General told him: "You ask me to give you a general line, or policy, to pursue in Tokyo. Well, I cannot do better than recommend to you my own motto, which I have always tried to live up to. *Stick to your friends and kill your enemies.* You will know how to interpret this in Japan. I have always hoped and believed that the Japanese are our friends, and that it is of vital importance to keep this friendship. I hope that your associations with their army will result in your being able to report that they and we can still stand together, representatives of law and order."[68]

The exchange of military information can come to stand almost in lieu of an alliance. At various times since the 1880's this has been a specifically British way of secretly overcoming the publicly declared resolve to remain unallied; indeed, the imparting of information by Britain to isolationist America, during two world wars, became a way to overcome the latter's tendency to shy away from diplomatic agreements. The most tangible part of the quasi-alliance between Britain and the Triple Alliance before and after 1890 lay in the exchange of information about possible common enemies, Russia in particular.[69] Captain Grierson, head of the Russian section in the War office and military attaché to Berlin during the 1890's, "was on very friendly terms with several members of the Great General Staff at Berlin, whence we acquired much interesting military information about Russia." The British were able to return the favor and give the Germans information which they declared most valuable.[70]

Again, though the British avoided a written alliance with France and Russia, they confirmed their real entente by an exchange of information—so lively that the German military attaché in London, observing it early in 1912, was led to believe that there must be "a kind of defensive and offensive

---

[68] Callwell, II, 307f.   [69] *Grosse Politik*, IV, 778.
[70] Waters, *"Secret and Confidential,"* pp. 25, 33.

alliance between England and France," and therefore British observers of the forthcoming German maneuvers should be put under the same restrictions as the French ones.[71] The British military attaché in Berlin in February 1912, where the French and British naval attachés were "in daily communication," informed his French colleague of certain changes in the German mobilization plans which he had just learned; to the Frenchman they seemed of an alarming nature and were communicated as such to St. Petersburg and London by his home office.[72] Later in the year, during the Balkan crisis, the British military attaché in Vienna informed his Russian colleague that the British embassy had information about the energetic pressure exerted by Germany to prevent aggressive Austrian measures in the south, against Serbia.[73]

It was for information that the British War Office, in 1906 and again in 1912, approached the Belgian chiefs of staff through the military attachés in Brussels: The British could not be bound by their "conversations," which were "entirely provisional and non-committal"—but what were the Belgian preparations against a German invasion? Which would be the best locations and which the best arrangements for unloading and detraining a British force coming to Belgium's aid in case of a violation of her neutrality? Maps? Liaison? Interpreters? etc. etc. What did the Belgians know about military activities in the neighboring Rhine province of Germany? Belgian information was incomplete; the chief of staff in 1906 regretted that he was denied secret service funds and that Belgium kept no military attachés abroad. In a report to the Minister of National Defense he "thought it his duty to point out this situation which put Belgium in a state of flagrant inferiority with regard to her neighbors and potential enemies." But not until 1913 did Belgium station some military attachés abroad.[74]

The chiefs of the general staffs concerned, and the attachés whom they had come to consider their foreign representatives, were convinced that the Triple Entente was a firm al-

---

[71] *Grosse Politik*, XXXI, 11552.
[72] *Documents diplomatiques français*, IIIrd ser., II, nos. 13, 56.
[73] Stieve, ed., *Der diplomatische Schriftwechsel Iswolskis*, II, 275.
[74] *British Documents on the Origin of the War*, III, 186ff.; Beauvais, p. 77.

liance for war purposes, but such isolationist members of the British cabinet as Morley and Burns were not. By the beginning of 1912 at the latest, the elastic character of the entente, which Grey pretended to maintain, no longer existed for those military men who were privy to the arrangements made for the *casus belli*. Some Russian doubts as to English obligations which survived at first, and perhaps sporadically until the outbreak of war, had to be dispelled. When Lieutenant General Jermolov, Russian military attaché in London (1891-1895 and 1907-1917), voiced such uncertainties late in 1911, the French Chief of Staff General Dubaille gave the Russian attaché in Paris, Count Nostiz, "renewed and altogether categorical" assurances about the reliable character of the expected English help on the Continent; in case of war, everything military was arranged and, to round things out, additional agreements were under negotiation between the two naval staffs. Nostiz's English colleague confirmed the French information: in case of war the landing of British troops in France would certainly take place, in spite of the unfortunate recent opposition to this idea in some British newspapers. The Englishman had that very day received definite assurances from the War Office regarding English readiness to help France on the Continent, in the manner arranged in the autumn of 1911, "and thus it will remain in the case of new complications" with Germany. He admitted that, outside the military, there were persons unsympathetic to the idea; even in the Admiralty there had been some doubters, but they had now been removed. With these firm and apparently authoritative assurances from the British side Nostiz, and many other officers and diplomats, envisaged a safe margin of victory for the Entente. France was in the best strategic situation since 1870, and had lost the old fear of Germany's might: a high French officer had recently assured Nostiz "On n'a plus peur du Prussien en France."

To dispel Jermolov's doubts his French colleague in London, Colonel Huguet, paid him a visit at the same time that Nostiz received his assurances in Paris. England's readiness to intervene on the continent in case of war could not be doubted: the recently improved connections between General Staff and Admiralty were further proof of it. In France, and hardly less so in England, the expectation of an early war with Germany was increasing; and Germany, where the Emperor's peace-mindedness would soon lose control of the war-minded, must fight England via France.

Joffre, who succeeded Dubaille in January 1912, confirmed the latter's assurances, adding that the War Ministry was working assiduously to prepare for a German war in the spring; cooperation with the British was now so definitely agreed upon that they would be on the spot in time for the first battle. The German march through Belgium was to be expected and on the whole to be welcomed. To complete the triangular watch over Germany the Russian military attaché in Berlin, Basarov, discussed Jermolov's report and the whole situation with his French colleague Pellé. They agreed that while German press polemics were less acrid than before, "the politically mature circles of society as well as the Army were in a bad temper against France and particularly against England" owing to the failure of the German policy in Morocco; the two original Entente partners also agreed that the break would come first between England and Germany and would then involve France—a belief that must also have reassured them about England's participation in war on the continent. Germany was increasingly preparing for war in the near future. "At the same time there was no doubt that neither the Emperor nor a large part of the German people *at the present* desired war. Should they realize, however, the complete unavoidability of the war, it is more than probable that the start of military operations will be on Germany's part since only suddenness on her part can equalize to a certain degree the chances of success in the battle with the British Navy and guarantee the final preponderance in the battle against France. The organization of Germany's land and sea forces offers every chance for this."[75]

Such exchanges of confidences could not fail to strengthen French and Russian belief that the British were "in this with

[75] These Russian attaché reports of January and February 1912 were considered as highly important and were communicated by the General Staff to Sasonov, in addition to the interchange among the various attachés. German translation from the publication in *Krasny Archiv, Berliner Monatshefte*, VII (1929), 931ff.

them" and could safely be counted as military allies in spite of the reserve, greater in public than in private, of British diplomacy. They were bound to strengthen the war readiness of the military on the Entente side, which increased as 1914 approached, and communicated itself to many of the diplomats. They made what were called "understandings for certain cases" more binding than politicians such as Grey were willing to realize or, later, to admit. The sharing of secrets usually has this effect, at least among gentlemen and those who, like soldiers, consider themselves more gentlemanly than most other men.

But reservations remain among gentlemen, some secrets are usually withheld. Even among alliance partners there remained suspicion that a partner was pursuing his own specific interest, rather than the common one. Almost as soon as the negotiations for the Anglo-Russian naval convention in 1914 had started, the British naval attaché in Berlin, probably knowing about the unabashed spying done there by Russian attachés, suddenly approached his Russian colleague with a proposal to cooperate with him in securing information. The Russian was puzzled by the offer. He finally concluded that this was the Britisher's devious way of getting Russia to increase her military preparations, and thereby force Germany to arm even more strongly against her—on land, needless to say, which would mean diverting funds from sea armaments to land armaments, and would ease the burden of competition for Britain. The Russian military attaché in London was similarly concerned. He feared that the Haldane Mission to Berlin in February 1912 might lead to an Anglo-German agreement to reduce naval expenditures, which in turn would cause the Germans to spend more on their land armaments against Russia.[76] This, if nothing else, made the failure of that Mission so highly desirable in Russian eyes.

Information exchange through service attachés was only one aspect of keeping friendships and alliances in repair. When the military applied pressure politics to the hesitant diplomats, service attachés were often the conduit—between Vienna

[76] *Journal of Modern History*, XII (1950), 85.

and Berlin,[77] Paris and London,[78] and Paris and St. Petersburg—and they served as such on all three lines during the
July crisis. On July 28 General Henry Wilson and his pro-
French friends in and out of the Army "began to suspect that
the Cabinet was going to run away" and leave France in the
lurch, in spite of all understandings arrived at among the military; he advised General Vicomte de la Panouse, Huguet's successor, to get Ambassador Cambon to go to Edward Grey that
very night and threaten "that, if we did not join, he would
break off relations and go to Paris."[79] Cambon was too subtle
a diplomat to use the blunt words the soldier considered appropriate—instead he appealed to "the honorable expectations . . . that in a just quarrel England would stand by her
friends."[80] At about the same time the Russian military attaché
in Paris sent a last note: "The French War Minister has declared to me in a tone of hearty enthusiasm the firm decision
of the French Government for war, and begged me to confirm the hope of the French General Staff that all our efforts
will be directed against Germany, and that Austria will be
treated as a *quantité négligeable.*"[81]

After 1918

Only occasional glimpses are as yet permitted us of the role
of the service attaché in the forming or maintaining of alliances after 1918. The much suspected doings of an attaché-
politician such as Colonel Beck, stationed in Paris in the early
1920's, were more suited to wreck than to confirm the Franco-
Polish alliance, which was further weakened after Beck had

---

[77] Conrad, IV, 152; see above, p. 367.

[78] In March 1911, Sir Henry Wilson, Director of Military Operations,
opened up to the French military attaché during a visit to Berlin. He
said that for years he had had "no doubt that we will have war ere
long"; that Belgium's neutrality would be violated by the Germans and
that consequently her army would join the Western side; that the German
infantry need not be feared; that the individual German was neither
brave nor combative and that after the first defeat his morale would
crumple. Since he gave details on what help France could expect from
Britain, the report was treated with the greatest discretion in Paris. *Documents diplomatiques français*, IInd ser., XIII, 326ff.

[79] Callwell, I, 189.   [80] Fay, II, 536.

[81] August 1. Fay, II, 531; Gen. Youri Danilov, *La Russie dans la guerre
mondiale* (Paris 1927), p. 179.

become Pilsudski's foreign minister. The service attachés of Soviet Russia, even if originally called by other names, first reappeared in the military relations with Kemalist Turkey in 1919-1920, and with China and the Reichswehr. German business with Russia, Seeckt insisted, must "in its details be handled by officers only," without the participation of the Moscow embassy.[82] Colonel Köstring, Seeckt's emissary, acted as Germany's first postwar military attaché in Moscow long before he was given that title. Russian attachés once again served as channels to foreign general staffs, and became *verhandlungsfähig*, fit to conduct negotiations, after original Bolshevist agitators such as Krassin and Radek had died or disappeared. They may not have regained the liberties they had taken under the White Tsars, but there was an occasional glint of the tiger's eye in the political jungles. The German military attaché in Moscow (or his predecessor who did not as yet enjoy the title) were the main agents for the close Reichswehr-Red Army ties which included the testing of forbidden German arms on Russian soil. When the rise of Hitlerism terminated this intimacy, the Russian military heads at first tried hard to maintain or restore "friendliness toward Germany," and it was not the fault of the German attachés that these efforts were in vain—until 1939.[83]

Inter-staff relations carried on by attachés seemed due for a revival when the French generals, faced with a new German peril in the 1930's, put their conservatism aside and seriously contemplated another military alliance with Russia. An exchange of attachés had been arranged between Paris and Moscow very soon after Hitler's coming to power.[84] Even though the Poles would not join in, and the Quai d'Orsay aspired to nothing beyond an Eastern Locarno, the Army started De Lattre de Tassigny, then a colonel, on an interminable exchange of views with the Russian military attaché in Paris, General Wenzov.[85] The resulting Franco-Russian Treaty of May 2, 1935, never fulfilled the hopes of the military, not merely because of Laval and Bonnet but for a variety of other

---

[82] Friedrich von Rabenau, ed., *Hans von Seeckt. Aus seinem Leben, 1918-1936* (Leipzig 1940), p. 317.
[83] *Documents on German Foreign Policy*, Ser. C, II, 376ff.
[84] *Ibid.*, Ser. C, I, 71.   [85] Pertinax, II, 43.

reasons, including the fear of Red imperialism and its high price. Shortly before Munich, when Gamelin called in the Red Army attaché in order to send word to Voroshilov about France's military dispositions, and to ask whether Russia was ready to act "in accordance with the events," the Red Army man did not conceal his belief that Poland would side with Germany against Czechoslovakia. "In this case, the task for Russia would be to quickly square things (*régler*) with Poland." Gamelin noted that his visitor rejoiced in the prospect of early military control of Poland, but also learned that Russian diplomacy was somewhat less eager for war than was this particular military agent.[86]

Salvaging the alliance with Poland was for France a military *pis-aller*; Poland could never substitute for Russia on a second, Eastern front against Germany. But much was done as if this were really possible: new staff discussions took place, conventions were signed (too late to be ratified), Polish arms production started (on paper), attachés busied themselves to bring the renewed alliance to life and reality, and France promised that fifteen days from the beginning of her general mobilization she would start an offensive with the main body of her forces. When the attack came, Poland succumbed even faster than her allies had assumed. Her fate was already decided on September 10, when Gamelin wrote the Polish military attaché, who was besieging him for help, that he would start the French offensive even earlier than promised and that he could do no more.[87] It was hardly even a token offensive that he launched.

By the time of the Hitler-Stalin pact relations between the French and Russian armies were almost nonexistent; several months before, Russia had recalled the service attachés from Paris and had never replaced them. In December 1939, at the time of the First Finnish War in which French sympathies and various French observers, including the former military attaché to the Baltic countries, were on the Finnish side, the appointment of new attachés was discussed, but none arrived to witness the fall of France.[88] Thus the Red Army took its stand

---

[86] Gamelin, *Servir*, II, 348.   [87] *Ibid.*, II, 60f.
[88] *Ibid.*, III, 191, 194.

on the "imperialist war" in which, by Russian declaration, the Western powers were the imperialists and aggressors, not Hitler.

The Kremlin did not make it easy to entertain friendly ties with Russia through military channels. The attachés, aside from some sporadic conversations, well calculated by the Russians, were mostly increasingly restricted in movements and contacts, which made observing and judging the Red Army very difficult. They repaid distrust with distrust, even when their countries seemed in need of Russian support. After the Japanese offensive of 1937 had started, and recall of the German advisers from Chiang Kai-shek and cessation of all German arms deliveries threatened, making help from Russia even more imperative, the Chinese military attaché in Moscow let the Germans know that his people still distrusted the Russians.[89]

The shifts in Russia's friend-foe relations proved *durs aux grands*, hard for the great, including the military. Russia's military attaché in London in the first half of the 1930's was General Putna, known in the military world as author of the Russian Manual for the Higher Command of Troops, and later Chief of Staff of Blucher's Far Eastern command. He and his German colleague kept on good terms, though more outwardly than genuinely, according to the German, in order to reflect the intimacies, still surviving at that time, between Reichswehr and Red Army. On the other hand, the new German-Japanese rapprochement had as yet no influence on the relationships of the two countries' attachés. According to the German military attaché from 1933 to 1938: "It was not on the whole usual in London that closer political ties were extended to personal relationships" between the respective service attachés. After the purge in which Putna was killed it was stated in Moscow that he had been guilty of maintaining close personal relations with a German officer during his tour of duty in London. His death was much discussed in military circles: "I would not mind dying," said Colonel Ismay, later Winston Churchill's military adviser, to the Ger-

[89] *Documents on German Foreign Policy*, Ser. D, I, 734.

man attaché, "but it is a terrifying thought to be fusilladed by one's own men.[90]

The distrust of French politicians, unwilling to save the Czechs at the price of Russian control over Poland, nullified any hope of Russian assistance to Czechoslovakia in 1938. With no certainty that France would go to war against the German aggressor, Russia had to limit this assistance to airplanes flown in over intervening Rumania—whose military-and-air attaché in Prague kept the Germans informed on this point as well as on his country's determination to deny permission for the passage of Soviet troops.[91] While the new Czech minister to Moscow retained his belief in Russia's military strength and willingness to help his country, in spite of the recent military purges and the fear of a war on two fronts, his military attaché expressed himself "with much more restraint regarding the possible value of Soviet help."[92] The attaché had been in Moscow for four years.

Through the informal network of the attachés the Germans received information that made the enterprise against the Czechs much less of a military gamble than it appeared to be at the time. On September 9 the German naval attaché in Paris wired the Wilhelmstrasse, "for the Kriegsmarine," that his Italian colleague knew from reliable sources that the French fleet in the Mediterranean had been brought considerably closer to a war footing.[93] But it went beyond the point of information exchange when the Italian told his German colleague a week later that from his very recent conversations with French general staff officers "he had gained the impression that in the General Staff they desired a peaceful solution, and that they could also become reconciled to the peaceful incorporation of the Sudeten German districts, but that on the outbreak of warlike complications between Germany and

[90] Geyr, *Erinnerungen*, pp. 18f.

[91] *Documents on German Foreign Policy*, Ser. D, II, 500.

[92] *Ibid.*, II, 363. Still earlier, up to 1933 at least, Czech soldiers had been suspicious of Russian assistance and had hoped, as two of the Czech military attachés in Berlin had stated, to remain neutral should Germany go to war with Poland and her ally France; the four million Germans in their country made war with Germany quite impossible. Castellan, p. 491.

[93] *Documents on German Foreign Policy*, Ser. D, II, 723.

Czechoslovakia, France would intervene under all circumstances. He had heard General Staff officers from different bureaus express the view that war between France and Germany would have to come some time, and that this would be better under the prevailing circumstances than later on."[94] Detailed information on the call-up of French reservists followed, just in case the Germans did not already possess it.[95] Poland's military attaché in Prague, bent on a share in the Czechoslovak loot, informed the German attaché that in his legation they "were convinced that the question of a European war was no longer acute. Poland would, moreover, put up military resistance to a possible Russian attempt to march through, and would also exercise strong pressure on Rumania to refuse passage to the Russian Army" (September 19).[96]

As the crisis approached, the Little Entente members proceeded to betray their ally, Czechoslovakia, if they had not already done so. Through their service attachés they kept the Germans informed of the mood of the Czech General Staff: on September 22, a week before Munich, the Staff was confident that the alliance with France would come into effect; a query had been sent to Paris, and the reply seemed satisfactory.[97] The Little Entente nations were all eager to avoid their obligations under the existing arrangements,[98] and the service attachés were indispensable in this process of dissolving old alliances and preparing new ones.

Among these Near Eastern military politicos moved the Far Eastern ones, Japan's military attachés.[99] General Oshima in Berlin and his colleague in Warsaw were eager to extend the Anti-Comintern Pact by attracting other states to it, such as Rumania and Poland, both of whom regarded Russia as a military threat. But while the Japanese thought Poland, ruled by colonels, well qualified for inclusion in the anti-communist

[94] *Ibid.*, II, 809. [95] *Ibid.*, II, 809f.

[96] *Ibid.*, II, 838; for reports of the U.S. military attaché in Berlin, Truman Smith, on German-Polish military understanding during the Munich crisis see Charles C. Tansill, *Back Door to War, The Roosevelt Foreign Policy, 1933-1941* (Chicago 1952), p. 431.

[97] *Documents on German Foreign Policy*, Ser. D, II, 881.

[98] *Ibid.*, II, 990.

[99] *Ibid.*, Ser. C, III, 59, 306, 314, 344, 556 (1934) for the beginning of the activities of the Japanese military attachés in diplomacy.

front, the Germans with their ancient grievances against that country found the suggestion hard to take.[100] Oshima, even before he became ambassador in Berlin, dealt by preference through Ribbentrop's *secret du roi* (*Dienststelle Ribbentrop*), and was hardly less important as a negotiator than the ambassador proper. He represented the Army, most eager of all groups in Japan to conclude the Berlin-Tokyo alliance. It was through him that the Wilhelmstrasse tried to influence Tokyo in 1938, when the Japanese Government balked at conceding more to the Germans than a most-favored nation position in occupied North China. Oshima was the person to approach, the man "who promised to contact the General Staff."[101] Much of the field of negotiations which had once been the preserve of diplomats and foreign offices was usurped by service attachés and their home offices on the eve of 1939, and even later. In Japan, as far as Western eyes can see, this mischief started relatively late.[102] Only after their officers had started on the mad career of "government by assassination" had the military become bold enough in Tokyo to launch the service attachés on independent politics from the base of embassies abroad, but the attachés continued such activity longer and later than proved in the best interest of Japan. Her military attaché in Stockholm, one of the few remaining neutral capitals, was a strong adherent of the Tokyo-Berlin axis, like Oshima in Berlin. He believed so strongly and so long in its ultimate victory that he carefully omitted to report to Tokyo or to his superior on the spot a discreet suggestion by King Gustaf, in December 1944, that his Government act as intermediary for Japanese peace offers before it became too late for country and dynasty. Later, when Japan's defeat had become obvious even to the soldiers, the same attaché started peacemaking on his own, without the knowledge of the legation chief, and the Swedes pointed out to the Minister that these

[100] *Ibid.*, Ser. D, I, 750ff.   [101] *Ibid.*, I, 887.

[102] There are occasional indications of the service attaché's fatal penchant for politics. In a cabinet shift of July 1944 General Tojo took in as naval minister an admiral who had formerly been naval attaché in Berlin, a yes-man who like his predecessor declined to see the signs of defeat or point them out to Tojo or other diehards. Toshikazu Kase, *Journey to the "Missouri"* (New Haven 1950), p. 80.

activities were hurting any prospect of peace, rather than helping it. In the indignant words of a Japanese career diplomat
who was working frantically and relatively early for peace:
"such was the mentality of our erratic soldiery that they
showed no scruple in disregarding the Foreign Office. Little
aware of their incompetence, they freely interfered with the
conduct of our foreign policy. In this case the military attaché
was severely reprimanded by the war minister, but the damage
had already been done."[103]

On the Berlin-Rome part of the Axis the Wehrmacht attaché, von Rintelen, tried his diplomatic and military best to
make his superiors understand Italian weaknesses and to make
the Italians accept German advice and support—not always in
time and not always successfully and, according to the resentful Italians, not always tactfully. The two dictators
proved on final military balance more disturbing than helpful as supreme commanders, and so did the two totalitarian
parties when they tried to interfere with the war. After Italy
entered the war Rintelen became "The German General in
the Headquarters of the Italian Armed Forces," largely to
establish and speed up direct communications between the
two supreme commands, avoiding the slow route via embassy
and foreign office which attaché reports had to use; similar
lines were established between the armies, navies and air forces
of the two partners and manned by the service attachés.[104]

In the work of extending the Axis to satellites, the service
attachés played a role hardly less important than that of the
diplomats. Such satellites as Hungary were first informed by
the German military attaché that war against Russia and
possibly Yugoslavia was to be made ready, and that contributions from them were expected.[105] Finland, a late adherent
to the Axis, arranged her reentry into the war through the
German military attaché in Helsinki; as early as September
1940 he brought Marshal Mannerheim's plenipotentiary to
the Führer's HQ to settle details for the attack on Russia.[106]

---

103 *Ibid.*, p. 221; see p. 222 for the peacemaking attempts by the Japanese naval attaché in Berne.
104 Rintelen, *Mussolini als Bundesgenosse*, pp. 53, 96f. and passim.
105 *Trial of the Major War Criminals*, VII, 331ff.
106 *Ibid.*, VII, 327f.

The alliance between Russia and the Western powers, the history of which is far less well documented as yet than are the intra-Axis arrangements, gave the armed forces attachés on each side but little opportunity beyond transmittal of Russian demands for more and more war materials, and even this was largely taken care of by the higher echelons. The American attachés in Moscow could not function as the eyes of Washington because Russia would not allow them to see what use she made of this materiel or how she fought the war, something of high professional interest that heretofore no ally had denied another. The Russians respected the demands of reciprocity at least to the extent that they did not apply for admission of their attachés to the Anglo-American fronts; they endeavored to get at such Western secrets as atomic research by spying behind the front, some of which was directed, as we have seen, by the military attaché in Ottawa.

The British, on the other hand, shared experience and intelligence information with the Americans almost from the beginning of the war. Communication was often through the American attachés in London, one of whom, Captain, later Admiral, Alan G. Kirk, subsequently became Director of Naval Intelligence in Washington,[107] partly on the strength of his London experience. After the pre-Pearl Harbor defense entente between Britain and the United States had changed into a war of coalition, one of the best ever fought as such, attaché liaison was not sufficient, and permanent interallied staffs were created. These survived or reappeared in some postwar organizations such as NATO, and staff members, in the case of some countries like Britain, even came to replace attachés, and took over their remaining work in addition to other duties (1952). How much the earlier bad record of the institution of attachés may have contributed to this suppression has never been stated.

[107] For some details see Watson, pp. 106f., 114, 370f., 505.

CHAPTER 18

SURVIVAL OF THE
SERVICE ATTACHÉ?

"Military attachés have a dubious reputation,"[1] according to one of them. They certainly have a dubious distinction: their abolition has been proposed from time to time for the betterment of mankind or of international relations. Criticism has come from two extremes of peacemindedness, conservative grandseigneurial diplomacy (Count Münster, Vicomte de Noailles and others) and pacifist Socialism. The diplomats spoke from within the Establishment, from specific personal experience with service attachés whose activities and politics had seemed to endanger peace or the smooth functioning of diplomatic business. Outside criticism was usually set off by the occasional public scandals in connection with espionage cases. From time to time pacifists,[2] international lawyers,[3] a newspaper looking for a sensational "cause,"[4] or even a minister of war such as Boulanger, who became utterly irritated by a series of incidents and considered the services rendered by attachés negligible,[5] have joined the outcry against their continued existence.[6] But such agitation cannot be called persistent or prolonged, although on at least three occasions (1899, 1900

[1] Geyr, *Erinnerungen*, p. 9.

[2] Against the pacifist abolitionists it has been argued that service attachés are best suited to supervise the strict performance of engagements to limit armaments.

[3] Pradier-Fodéré, *Cours de droit diplomatique*, 2nd ed. (Paris 1899), II, 185, speaks of these attachés as "soldiers and sailors having strayed into diplomacy," rendering very controversial services. Beauvais, p. 199.

[4] Le Matin in 1896. *Grosse Politik*, XIIII, 3589.

[5] Beauvais, p. 199.

[6] In 1891, the hue and cry of the Paris press against the Germany military attaché became so violent and prolonged, and the protection given him by the French authorities seemed so insufficient that the Germans, the attaché himself included, seriously considered giving up the post and sending the French attaché in Berlin home in retaliation. *Berliner Monatshefte*, XV (1937), 997.

and 1907) the French Socialists demanded in the Chamber that funds for such officers be stricken from the military and naval budgets. Their proposals were voted down every time.

Socialist agitation received its original impetus from the Dreyfus affair, from the spy-and-attaché connections which it had publicly exposed, though the exposure was far from complete. The arguments used are best summarized from a speech by Marcel Sembat in the Chamber of Deputies on March 11, 1899.[7] Count 1 in the indictment: The service attaché is nothing but a spy and the director of his own country's intelligence service. Answer, by the war minister de Freycinet: The suppression of the institution of attachés would not cause the disappearance of espionage. "It was much better to know where to aim one's own counterespionage service than not to know." Count 2: The presence of foreign attachés in one's own country gave traitors an easy opportunity of selling their country's secrets to such foreigners. Answer: A determined traitor will know how to sell his secrets without approaching attachés, who will often be under such strict surveillance that approaching them involves great risks and the danger of detection for the traitor.[8] Count 3: It is dangerous to allow foreign attachés, looking for information, access to military offices such as the war ministry. Who, asked Sembat, would take it upon himself to draw the exact line between the piece of information that is innocuous and can safely be communicated and that which it would be imprudent to hand over? How can one be sure that a document which the foreign atta-

[7] Beauvais, pp. 198ff., where most of the counterarguments will also be found.

[8] "There are various side-roads for the illegal work of an attaché. The 'dirty hens' might be attended to by a helpmate, the assistant military attaché, and he might be disavowed in case of mishap. Also, intelligence work might be based not in the host land but in a third country, in such a way that an attaché accredited to Italy takes over the observation of France. . . . A very good indication of the character of work to be done can be the location of the office. If that of the military attaché is detached from the embassy and located in a disreputable neighborhood, it suggests the idea that visitors of a dubious nature are being received. For this very reason I have opposed, determinedly and successfully, the removal of my offices from the embassy building in spite of the increasing want of space." Geyr, *Erinnerungen*, pp. 10f., on the basis of his experiences as German attaché in London, 1933-1938.

ché wants is without importance? And how can a person, even
if convinced that it is unimportant, decide that it has no importance for the foreigner?

Not only must the entry to the offices of the Ministry of
War, granted to foreign military attachés, be criticized,
there is besides the scandal of promiscuousness among officers and the military strangers who, by virtue of the con-
fraternity of arms, are in continual relationships, with the
result that foreign military attachés receive in broad day-
light and on the basis of international courtesy the information which they want.

Aside from this you have what happens during maneuvers
—this living together after the fatigues of the day, those
meals in company which give the military attaché a chance
to judge the army chiefs as to their physiological and psycho-
logical strength, their ability to remain on horseback, their
tendency towards fatigue, discouragement, and to see
whether they possess sang-froid and lucidity.

Answer: Not all bureaus of the War Ministry are open to such
callers; there is actually only one set apart for their reception
at definite, limited hours. The fear as to observations on maneuvers would apply no less to other foreign observers,
usually admitted to them in far greater numbers. Reciprocity
allows one's own attachés to make the same kind of observations—the better qualified the attaché the better his observations and the resulting information.

Count 4: The French Government ought to set an example by recalling its attachés. Answer: The institution is so
firmly entrenched that as long as there is no general international agreement about abolition, foreign governments
would or could continue sending attachés to Paris; any power
which gave up stationing attachés abroad would thereby
surrender an important position in the international arms
competition.

The French parliament, by voting the funds necessary for
attachés, repeatedly pronounced against these Socialist-
pacifist arguments, doubtless for practical reasons. It was left

to a feudal member, the Marquis de la Ferronnays, to celebrate the chivalrous nature of the mission entrusted to the military attaché, whose "first duty it is to inspire the officers of all the countries with whom he is in daily contact, with a high idea of the honor, the dignity and, if he can, the scientific and the professional worthiness of all his comrades."[9]

The Bolshevists for a time did abolish the service attaché. Realizing, however, the value he might possess in the armaments competition, they reconstituted the office, and used it for all it was worth, including spying among temporary coalition partners, who still remained class enemies in Russian eyes. Only some years after the close of the Second World War did they come to the conclusion that suppression, or near-suppression, might after all be a practical move in the Soviet interest. Hence the systematic hue and cry in Moscow and the satellite capitals against Western military attachés as spies; hence the numerous espionage charges and demands for recall; hence the emphasis on secretiveness as the duty of a Soviet citizen or soldier;[10] and hence the dismissal of legations almost *in toto*, including service attachés, which took place in September 1949 as part of the encirclement of Tito's Yugoslavia. The Russian attitude may portend the end of the exchange of service attachés between East and West, as part of the isolation of the two armed camps. On the other hand, open exponents of arms competition in embassies and legations may be preferable to spies in some sort of camouflage as the only agents in what seems to be an irrepressible race.

Within each camp the exchange of attachés may be carried on as part of increasingly close military ties, but even these ties do not necessarily call for the services of such officers. We saw in the last chapter that in the autumn of 1952 Britain

[9] In Chamber of Deputies, March 2, 1899. Beauvais, p. 92.

[10] In September 1949 the publishing house of the Russian Armed Forces Ministry issued a pamphlet "Guard Military Secrets!" describing in detail the working methods of the intelligence services of the "Imperialists," with the United States in the forefront. The pamphlet listed among their agents "counsellors, second and third secretaries, attachés or simple rank-and-file embassy employees." *The New York Times*, September 23, 1949.

recalled some service attachés stationed in NATO capitals;[11] the reason given was economy, but it may also have meant the dispensability of attachés among friends.

[11] The British Service attachés and their staffs are being withdrawn from Washington, and their duties taken over by the British Joint Services Mission. *Daily Telegraph*, November 8, 1952.

Books

Beauvais, Armand P. *Attachés militaires, attachés navales, et attachés de l'air* (Thèse: Université de Paris), Paris 1937.

Beyens, Eugene Louis, Baron. *Deux années a Berlin, 1912-1914*, 2 vols., Paris 1931.

Bülow, Bernhard, Fürst von. *Denkwürdigkeiten* (ed. F. von Stockhammern), 4 vols., Berlin 1930-1931.

Callwell, Major General Sir Charles Edward. *Field-Marshal Sir Henry Wilson. His Life and Diaries*, 2 vols., New York 1927.

Castellan, Georges. *Le réarmement clandestin du Reich, 1930-1935*, Paris 1954.

Conrad von Hötzendorf, Franz, Graf. *Aus meiner Dienstzeit, 1906-1918*, 5 vols., Vienna 1921-1925.

Dawson, Brigadier General Sir Douglas. *A Soldier Diplomat*, London 1927.

Faramond de Lafayolle, Gontran, vicomte de. *Souvenirs d'un attaché naval en Allemagne et en Autriche, 1910-1914*, Paris 1932.

Fay, Sidney B. *The Origins of the World War*, 2 vols., New York 1928.

Geyr von Schweppenburg, Leo Dietrich, Freiherr. *Erinnerungen eines Militärattachés, London, 1933-1937*, Stuttgart 1949.

————. *The Critical Years*, London 1952.

Giesl von Gieslingen, General Wladimir, Baron. *Zwei Jahrzehnte im Nahen Orient* (ed. General-major Ritter von Steinitz), Berlin 1927.

Glaise-Horstenau, Edmund von. *Franz Josephs Weggefährte: Das Leben des Generalstabschefs Grafen Beck*, Vienna 1930.

Gleichen, Lord Edward. *A Guardsman's Memoires. A Book of Recollections*, Edinburgh and London 1932.

Görlitz, Walter. *Der deutsche Generalstab, 1657-1945*, Frankfurt-am-Main 1950.

Haller, Johannes. *Aus dem Leben des Fürsten Philipp zu Eulenburg-Hertefeld*, Berlin 1924.

Hassell, Ulrich von. *The von Hassell Diaries, 1938-1944: The Story of the Forces against Hitler inside Germany as recorded by Ambassador Ulrich von Hassell*, New York 1947.

Herbette, Jean. *Ein französischer Diplomat über die bolsche-wistische Gefahr*, Berlin 1943.

Hilton, Richard. *Military Attaché in Moscow*, Boston 1951.

Hohenlohe, Chlodwig, Fürst zu. *Denkwürdigkeiten der Reichs-kanzlerzeit* (ed. Karl Alexander von Müller), Stuttgart and Berlin 1931. (Vol. III of *Denkwürdigkeiten des Fürsten Chlodwig zu Hohenlohe-Schillingsfürst.*)

Ignatiev, Lieutenant General A. A. *A Subaltern in Russia* (transl. Ivor Montagu), London 1944.

Knox, Sir Alfred William Fortescue. *With the Russian Army 1914-1917*, London 1921.

Meisner, Heinrich Otto. *Militärattachés und Militärbevoll-mächtigte in Preussen und im Deutschen Reich. Ein Beitrag zur Geschichte der Militärdiplomatie*, East Berlin 1957.

Monts, Anton, Graf. *Erinnerungen und Gedanken des Bots-chafters Anton Graf Monts*, Berlin 1932.

Mott, T. Bentley. *Twenty Years as Military Attaché*, New York 1937.

Oncken, Hermann. *Die Rheinpolitik Kaiser Napoleons III von 1863 bis 1870 und der Ursprung des Krieges von 1870/ 71*, 3 vols., Stuttgart 1926.

Papen, Franz von. *Memoirs*, New York 1952.

Pertinax (pseud.) (André Géraud). *Les Fossoyeurs*, 2 vols., New York 1943.

Potiemkine, Vladimir (ed.). *Histoire de la diplomatie*, 3 vols., Paris 1946-1947.

Rich, Norman, and Fisher, M. H. (eds.). *The Holstein Papers*, 4 vols., Cambridge 1955ff.

Schlözer, Leopold von. *Generalfeldmarschall Freiherr von Loe. Ein militärisches Zeit- und Lebensbild*, Stuttgart 1914.

Schweinitz, Lothar von. *Denkwürdigkeiten*, 2 vols., Berlin 1927.

Stürgkh, Joseph. *Politische und militärische Erinnerungen aus meinem Leben*, Leipzig 1922.

Toutain, Edmond. *Alexandre III et la République française: souvenirs d'un témoin, 1885-1888*, Paris 1929.

Vagts, Alfred. *Deutschland und die Vereinigten Staaten in der Weltpolitik*, 2 vols., New York 1935.

———. *Defense and Diplomacy*, New York 1956.

———. *A History of Militarism*, rev. ed., New York 1959.

———. *Landing Operations*, Harrisburg, Pa. 1946.

Waldersee, Alfred, Graf von. *Aus dem Briefwechsel des Generalfeldmarschalls Grafen von Waldersee* (ed. H. O. Meisner), Berlin 1928.

———. *Denkwürdigkeiten des Generalfeldmarschalls Alfred Grafen von Waldersee* (ed. H. O. Meisner), 2 vols., Stuttgart 1922.

Waters, W.H.H. *Potsdam and Doorn*, London 1930.

———. *"Private and Personal," Further Experiences of a Military Attaché*, London 1928.

———. *"Secret and Confidential," The Experiences of a Military Attaché*, New York 1926.

Watson, Mark S. *Chief of Staff: Prewar Plans and Preparations*, Washington 1950.

Wedel, Erhard, Graf von (ed.). *Zwischen Kaiser und Kanzler*, Leipzig 1943.

Widenmann, Wilhelm. *Marine-Attaché an der kaiserlichdeutschen Botschaft in London, 1907-1912*, Göttingen 1952.

Witzleben, Erich von. *Adolph von Deines*, Berlin 1913.

Documents

AUSTRIA: Ministerium des Aussern. *Oesterreich-Ungarns Aussenpolitik von der Bosnischen Krise 1908 bis zum Kriegsausbruch 1914*. Diplomatische Aktenstucke des österreichischungarischen Ministeriums des Äusserün, 9 vols., Vienna and Leipzig 1930.

FRANCE: Ministère des affaires étrangères. Commission des archives diplomatiques. *Receuil des instructions données aux ambassadeurs et ministres de France depuis les traités de Westphalie jusqu'à la révolution française*, 25 vols. in 27, Paris 1884-1936.

———. Commission de publication des documents relatifs aux origines de la guerre de 1914. *Documents diplomatiques français (1871-1914)*, 3 series, Paris 1929-1950.

GERMANY: *Documents on German Foreign Policy, 1918-1945*, from the Archives of the German Foreign Ministry, Washington 1949.

———. *Die Grosse Politik der europäischen Kabinette, 1871-*

1914, J. Lepsius, A. Mendelssohn Bartholdy, F. Thimme, eds., 40 vols. in 54, Berlin 1922-1927.

———. *Nazi-Soviet Relations, 1939-1941*. Documents from the Archives of the German Foreign Office as released by the Department of State, Washington 1948.

———. Historische Reichskommission. *Die auswärtige Politik Preussens, 1858-1871*, Erich Brandenburg, Otto Hoetzsch, Hermann Oncken, eds. (Reichsinstitut für Geschichte des neuen Deutschlands), 4 vols., Berlin 1932.

GREAT BRITAIN: Foreign Office. *British Documents on the Origins of the War 1898-1914*, G. P. Gooch and Harold Temperley, eds., 11 vols. in 13, London 1926-1938.

———. Foreign Office. *Documents on British Foreign Policy 1919-1939*, E. L. Woodward and Rohan Butler, eds., 3 series, 18 vols., London 1946-1955.

NUREMBERG: *Trial of the Major War Criminals Before the International Military Tribunal, Nuremberg, 14 November 1945—1 October 1946*, 42 vols., Nuremberg 1947-1949.

———. Nuremberg Military Tribunal. *Trials of War Criminals before the Nuremberg Military Tribunals under Control Council Law No. 10, October 1946 to April 1949*, 15 vols., Washington 1949.

UNION OF SOVIET SOCIALIST REPUBLICS: Commission for the Publication of Documents Relating to the Era of Imperialism. *Die internationalen Beziehungen im Zeitalter des Imperialismus: Dokumente aus den Archiven der zarischen und der provisorischen Regierung, hrsg. von der Kommission beim Zentralexekutivkomitee der Sowjetregierung unter dem Vorsitz von M. N. Pokrowski*, hrsg. von Otto Hoetzsch, Berlin 1931-1942.

UNITED STATES: Congress. Joint Committee on Investigation of Pearl Harbor Attack. *Pearl Harbor Attack, Hearings*, 79th Congress, 1st session, 11 parts, Washington 1950.

———. Department of State. *Foreign Relations of the United States. Diplomatic Papers. The Soviet Union 1933-1939*, Washington 1952.